Principles of SECURITY and CRIME PREVENTION

Pamela A. Collins, Ed.D., C.F.E. Eastern Kentucky University

Truett A. Ricks, Ph.D., CPP Eastern Kentucky University

Clifford W. Van Meter, Ph.D. Grand Valley State University and Professor Emeritus, University of Illinois

Fourth Edition

anderson publishing co.
2035 Reading Rd.
Cincinnati, OH 45202
1-800-582-7295

Principles of Security and Crime Prevention, Fourth Edition

Copyright © 1981, 1988, 1994, 2000
Anderson Publishing Co.
2035 Reading Rd.
Cincinnati, OH 45202

Phone 800.582.7295 or 513.421.4142
Web Site www.andersonpublishing.com

Library of Congress Cataloging-in-Publication Data

Collins, Pamela A. (Pamela Ann), 1957-
    Principles of security and crime prevention / Pamela A. Collins, Truett A. Ricks,
Clifford W. Van Meter.--4th ed.
        p.   cm.
    Rev. ed. of: Principles of security / Truett A. Ricks. 3rd ed. 1994.
    Includes bibliographical references and index.
    ISBN 0-87084-305-2 (pbk.)
    1. Private security services--United States. I. Ricks, Truett A. II. Van Meter, Clifford W.
III. Ricks, Truett A. Principles of security. IV. Title.
HV8290 .C658 2000
363.28'9--dc21   99-050278

Cover design: Doug Klocke/Photonics Graphics
Cover illustration: Andrew Judd / Masterfile

EDITOR Gail Eccleston
ASSISTANT EDITOR Sharon L. Boyles
ACQUISITIONS EDITOR Michael C. Braswell

Acknowledgments

Special thanks to my family for their continued support and encouragement. I would also like to thank Mark Bates for his assistance in the area of Locks and Locking Mechanisms, and thanks to Evelyn Mynes and Lee Ann Hume for their assistance on the development of an Instructor's Guide and Power-Point presentation.

Pam Collins

I wish to thank my colleagues in the School of Criminal Justice at Grand Valley State University for their support and assistance. Specifically, thanks to James David Ballard for the assistance in the preparation of the Counterterrorism and Risk Identification material in Appendices E, F, and G. I also wish to thank Robert Hoch, CPP, CFE for his assistance and contribution. In addition, thanks to Clarence H.A. Romig, former associate professor of the Police Training Institute at the University of Illinois, for his contribution to Chapters 5 and 7.

Thanks for the assistance and encouragement from our children, Bill and Tracey, during the first two editions, and to my wife, Judy, who has assisted me with library research and proofreading in all four editions of this book.

And last, but not least, thanks to Gail Eccleston at Anderson Publishing for her persistence and patience in working with the authors.

Cliff Van Meter

Preface

Over the last 25 years, it has become increasingly apparent that public law enforcement agencies can provide neither the resources nor the personnel needed to protect private property. Thus, the role of private security has become more visible and important as the reality of self-protection and loss prevention needs have become recognized and accepted by both public law enforcement and business.

It is the objective of this book to provide the reader with basic principles of security, loss prevention, and crime prevention that are common and fundamental to all areas of business and asset protection. Following a brief review of the history of security, the text provides coverage of the security industry, the threat environment with special emphasis on terrorism, fundamentals of physical security and access control, common security problems, and safety issues. It also focuses on fire prevention and protection, risk analysis and security surveys, legal aspects, and emergency and disaster control. A significant emphasis in this edition is an expansion on the importance of crime prevention. This text also provides extensive coverage of issues related to selection, training, and education of security personnel, cooperative programs, and career orientation. In addition, it addresses the contemporary issues of sexual harassment, Americans With Disabilities Act of 1990 and the Civil Rights Act of 1991.

One of the most interesting aspects of writing this book, from the perspective of the authors, is the constant changes that have occurred, and will continue to occur, in a field of study that continues to undergo rapid change and growth. This book is intended to be a resource for practitioners and students who have a need to understand the complexities of security in the modern era in such diverse endeavors as manufacturing, commerce, finance, healthcare, national defense, government, architecture, law enforcement, etc.—all of which have an inherent requirement for crime prevention, security, and assets protection.

Private security and crime prevention have progressed at a rapid rate since the first edition of this text was published in 1980. The authors have been involved in the research and teaching over these years and are convinced that the quality of information available and used, as well as the quality of personnel involved in security, has improved and will continue to improve into the twenty-first century. Properly educated and trained security personnel, utilizing proven technology and techniques, and crime prevention will ensure that private security, along with improved law enforcement and community involvement, will make the new century a safer environment for all citizens. It is hoped that this text will provide a step in that direction.

Foreword

Principles of Security and Crime Prevention

The ultimate principle of security is to reduce the risks of losses to people, property, and things (assets protection). This security principle, by definition, must have an accepted philosophy that has a foundation which requires security managers through personnel and/or technology to proactively involve all organizational personnel in partnership with clients and outside organizational employees to eliminate or reduce losses through problem solving.

Philosophy   This philosophy of security operates under a dynamic system of fundamental or motivating principles which state that an organization-wide commitment implies change in policies and procedures.

Security Personnel   Under this definition, security personnel would not be the sole provider of attention and detail to any area affiliated with eliminating or reducing losses.

Technology   Technology would be used as a tool to eliminate or reduce risks associated with losses. Technology would be controlled by people and not people controlled by technology.

Proactive/Permanent As part of providing a comprehensive security program, planning, analyzing, and implementation of actions and changes must be done on an ongoing basis. Being offensive minded or making positive changes, as needed, will result in fewer reactive incidents.

Partnership   All organizational personnel will work with security, clients, and outside organizational personnel to assist in eliminating or reducing risks. Eliminating or reducing risks will result in fewer losses.

Location/Place   The goal of a comprehensive security program is to reduce the risks of losses to people, property, and things. This philosophy of reducing losses necessitates that all locations/places involving people, property, and things be involved, not just plants and buildings.

Problem Solving   Under this principle of security, security personnel must redefine their mission by focusing on problem solving. The successes or failures would depend on qualitative outcomes (risks that have been eliminated or reduced) and not always on quantitative results or statistics (number of days without an injury or a 10 percent reduction in losses by motor freight shipping during the last six months).

Table of Contents

SECTION I

HISTORICAL AND PROFESSIONAL PRINCIPLES OF SECURITY AND CRIME PREVENTION

The History
of Security and
Crime Prevention

1

INTRODUCTION

I. ANCIENT TIMES

A. NEOLITHIC PERIOD (7000 – 3000 B.C.)

Historically, security and crime prevention systems have been present in the earliest known forms of prehistoric civilizations. The culture of the prehistoric hunter and food gatherer limited security to the safety and integrity of persons, their social arrangements within the group, and their few possessions which consisted of limited provisions and a few tools of stone and bone. As animal husbandry evolved alongside of agriculture, there was a great need for continuous possession of land. Instead of a nomadic culture that followed their food and water source, small groupings of humans would settle down to build shelters for themselves and their animals. Land, animals, buildings, and crops become central in the lives of these people. As these "communities" continued to grow and stabilize the land, animals, buildings, and crops become a source of wealth and commerce. With this newfound wealth came societal rules and codes to protect life and property in an evolving agricultural society. Around the time of 3000 B.C., people lived in settlements complete with streets, squares, and mud-brick houses centered around a palace-like structure.

These early civilizations found ways of enforcing rules and of maintaining order. The ancient Sumerians had private security forces or bodyguards, as did the Egyptian pharaohs, and the Greek city-states. As communities formed, citizens would band together for mutual protection. Many of these early private guards and civilians evolved into armies and police forces.

B. MYCENAEAN AGE (1500 – 1200 B.C.)

The earliest known forms of civilizations have used both security technology and crime prevention techniques to provide greater safety for their communities. These ancient cities and palaces were often surrounded by walls of great thickness and height. The Mycenaean fortresses normally consisted of a mudbrick rampart, 26 feet high, surrounded by a wall, built of burnt brick and bitumen, and enclosed by a moat, canal, or river. They were characterized by having wide walkways with embattled parapets at their base.

The fortresses described above exemplify a design that would be applicable today. That design establishes four zones of protection: the use of water either as a moat, canal, or river represents the first defense against invaders; the outermost wall represents the second defense against intruders. This perimeter wall, upon excavation, was found to be 23 feet thick and was strengthened by towers about every 140 feet. The third zone is the wall surrounding the Sacred Precincts and Palace. The final zone of defense is the wall of the building used as quarters for the royalty and their valuable possessions. At the weak points (entry gates) in the second zone of defense, the gates are set back from the general face of the wall in such a manner as to form wide spaces in front open to attack from the walls on three sides. There were also guardrooms on either side of the passage through the gateways.

This period also includes the great temples and pyramids of the Egyptians, which represent some of the most noteworthy examples of ancient security and crime prevention techniques. Many of the ancient Egyptian tombs take into consideration Crime Prevention Through Environmental Design (CPTED). Some of this early architecture and security technology is still visible and functional by today's standards. Most notable were the tombs of the great kings of ancient Egypt. One of the more fortified tombs designed to discourage would-be looters over the centuries was that of Tutankhamen. Although robbers had entered the tomb, they had not been able to penetrate the burial chamber (see Figure 1.1). The entrance to the tomb consisted of a flight of stairs leading to a short corridor. At the end of this corridor was the antechamber, which was a room used to store common household items believed to be necessary in the voyage to eternity. Attached to the antechamber was an annex and the burial chamber, which was found intact by archaeologists. Adjacent to the burial chamber is the treasury where all of the kings most valued possessions were stored. Once each of the rooms was filled with the necessary items for the afterlife, stone walls were erected to seal the tomb forever.

The Egyptians are also credited with developing some of the first target-hardening devices such as the lock. Archaeologists discovered Egyptian locks that date back to about 2000 B.C. These intricate locks are considered forerunners to the modern pin tumbler lock. Other ancient Mediterranean cultures produced their own versions of target-hardening devices. The Greeks refined bar

Figure 1.1
Tutankhamen's Tomb

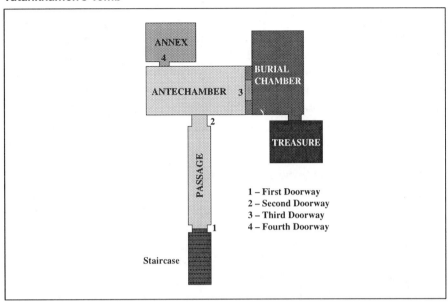

ANNEX
4

BURIAL
CHAMBER

ANTECHAMBER 3

2

TREASURE

PASSAGE

1 – First Doorway
2 – Second Doorway
3 – Third Doorway
4 – Fourth Doorway

1

Staircase

and bolt locks that permitted a door to be unbarred from the outside as well as from the inside. They are also credited with being the first to use keyholes. Roman contributions include the first metal locks, the earliest padlocks, the introduction of small keys, and the development of warded locks (see Figure 1.2).

Figure 1.2
Roman Lock

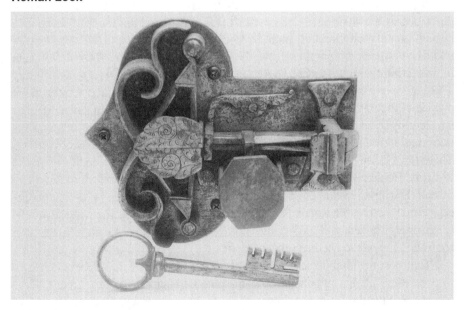

Ancient fortresses can also be found in the western hemisphere, particularly in Central and South America. These early defensive structures consisted of tall boulders set upright and separated at short intervals, with stones and rubble between them. For example, one of the more famous structures, Peru's Machu Pic-chu, is very similar in structure to the Great Wall of China. Excavation of these structures also revealed similarities to the Egyptian Pyramids when a pre-Colombian monument at Palencia, Southern Mexico, revealed a vault. Upon removal of the slab in the floor of the temple, a stairway was discovered which descended down to a second floor, in which another movable slab revealed a burial chamber.

C. GREEK AND ROMAN PERIOD (700 B.C. – 100 A.D.)

The influence of the ancient Greek and Roman cultures can be felt today. The fact that Greece was surrounded by water on the south, east, and west sides and flanked by mountains to the north, contributed significantly to the Greeks' success in maritime commerce. Greek culture spread far beyond its boundaries to as far away as India. The mountains, which served as natural barriers and boundaries, dictated the political character of Greece. This isolation evolved into communities being organized into what the Greeks referred to as *poleis* or city-states. The words police and politics are derived from the term *poleis,* which was used to describe the administration and oversight of communities of people. These early Western civilizations were the first attempts of people to create independent political structures for themselves. The strength of the city-state is similar to our modern-day "neighborhood watch" program; all of the citizens knew each other and served as an active participant in maintaining the integrity of the city. The *poleis* is best described as a small city that was surrounded by a rural, agricultural area. They were self-governing and formed what could be described as a civilian army or guard. It was considered an honor to serve as a "watch" for the city, and all men 18 to 20 years of age would serve as border guards. As these communities grew, the Greeks paid professionals to assist them in protecting their city-states. These "professionals" were referred to as peltasts. These people used small round shields, swords, and javelins and would move outside of the traditional "phalanx" formation used by the civilian guard. A phalanx consisted of eight or more lines of infantry, one behind the other. They served as a kind of special force the Greeks came to rely on in times of conflict. These Greek city-states flourished for nearly three centuries before falling to the Romans. Ironically, Rome began as a Greek city-state in the western Mediterranean. During the years of 264 and 146 B.C., they fought three wars that resulted in final victory for Rome. Rome's history revolves around their unique ability to establish law and order, moving from a city-state to an empire that controlled the whole Mediterranean basin.

The most noted and successful leader of the Romans was Augustus Caesar, who defeated all his opponents and instituted imperial rule at Rome. Caesar reorganized the entire armed forces of Rome beginning with the creation of an elite bodyguard know as the *Praetorian Guard.* Much like that of the modern-day Secret Service, the primary objective of the Praetorian Guard was to protect Caesar from assassination. They were the only troops located in Rome and helped maintain public order. In time, due to the growth of the city, it became more and more difficult for the Praetorian Guard to maintain peace and order. Subsequently, Caesar divided the city into 14 wards in 7 B.C. Then each ward was subdivided into precincts. Initially, it was the responsibility of the magistrate to keep order and provide fire protection for their precincts. When it was evident that the magistrates were unable to effectively direct the efforts of their precincts, Caesar reorganized Rome and assigned ward officials to be responsible for firefighting, but these efforts failed as well. Finally, Caesar formed a night watchmen system, consisting of seven cohorts, each having 1,000 vigils to patrol the streets of Rome. Although their primary responsibility was to watch for fires, they also had the occasion to encounter and deal with burglaries, assaults, and petty crimes. These night watchmen (taken from the word vigil meaning to keep watch) represented one of the earliest known examples of security officers. Not only were they not intended to serve as police, they were also not included in the count of the Roman forces, did not have special barracks, and were recruited from freedmen, a category normally excluded from military service. Moreover, the fact that Caesar created a police force that was responsible for policing the capital strengthens the historical interpretation that the Vigils were in fact more akin to a security force than that of a police force. The police force was made up of Roman citizens and organized like that of the Praetorian Guard. They were also commanded by a battalion commander or captain. Historically, the night watchman system has long been associated with representing what is now referred to as security officers. These Roman Vigils or "watch men" may very well represent one of the first formal security forces in history.

II. THE MIDDLE AGES

A. THE BARBARIANS (300 A.D. – 600 A.D.)

As the Roman empire fell to invasions of barbarians in the fourth and fifth centuries, this marked the beginning of the 1000-year period called the Middle Ages. During this era, armies were almost continually on the march. Muslims, Mongols, and Europeans vied with each other for control of territory, trade routes, and for wealth and power.

Land became scarce on the European continent during this ongoing conflict. Consequently, a group of people referred to as the Anglo-Saxons, a people of German origin, began to migrate to England in large numbers. They took with them a security system of compulsory communal responsibility for protecting and taking care of the security needs of individuals, families, tribes, and villages. Under this system, called the "frankpledge," all of the adult males were responsible for the good behavior of all others. When a crime occurred, a citizen would call together others and pursue the criminal. If there were no witnesses to a crime, the victim was responsible for finding out the criminal's identity.

B. FEUDALISM AND THE NORMAN ERA (700 A.D. – 1700 A.D.)

During the Middle Ages there were no standing armies in Europe. As Genghis Khan was sweeping across Asia and into Europe, Medieval knights were fighting one another in Western Europe for the ownership of land. The system of law and order, or control and protection during this time was referred to as feudalism. The system of feudalism was established gradually, between the eighth and eleventh centuries to the end of the thirteenth century. It is defined as a social system of rights and obligations based on land ownership patterns. Feudalism evolved in a time of disorder, when the central government was helpless to protect the people. Its beginnings can be traced to the breakup of the ancient Roman Empire when small barbarian kingdoms sprang up throughout Europe. The roads and bridges the Romans had built eventually fell into decay along with the Roman monetary system. As common currency disappeared, lords and kings were no longer able to pay their soldiers, thus weakening their systems of protection and exposing them to more barbarian invasions. The villagers or communities relying on the king and his soldiers for protection of their land and possessions now became vulnerable to the invaders. Castles were often the only place of refuge for the villagers, who had to pay for protection.

The villagers were organized into groups of 10 families, or householders, called tithings, and further into groups of 10 tithings called hundreds. Each tithing selected a tithing man to represent the group. Ten tithing men represented a hundred and had a king's reeve to speak for them. Several hundreds made up a shire (a geographical administrative district) and a shire-reeve was the spokesperson for the entire shire (the title sheriff is derived from this office). Several shires constituted an earldom, headed by an earldom-man.

The feudal tithing system stressed social stability and hierarchical control. It was considered the duty of every citizen to be a police officer and members of the group were themselves responsible for whatever offenses were committed within their borders. The tithing man who was elected from the group was given the responsibility for calling the group to action, i.e., raising the "hue and cry" and meting out punishment. This English common law process, wherein every able-bodied man was required to join in the communal pursuit of lawbreakers, was the origin of citizen's arrest.

The basic economic and societal ties of a feudalistic society were kinship and the relationship between an individual and his landlord. The kinship philosophy required kindred to seek vengeance and compensation for an act against a relative. The servant-landlord philosophy was a bilateral (though unequal) agreement: the landlord would protect the servant from outside forces, and in return the servant would till the land to provide the necessary sustenance for life. Because currency was scarce, nobles were very willing to take the land of the villagers in exchange for protection. The landowner was allowed to use the land during his lifetime. At his death it passed into the hands of his protector.

The dual system of the landlord-servant relationship and strength of kindred justice was completely changed in 1066, when William, Duke of Normandy, invaded and conquered England. William dispossessed the old English nobility and initiated a comprehensive political, economic, and social survey of England. A national system that placed emphasis on collective and community security at the expense of individual freedom was initiated. William placed England under martial law, divided the country into 55 military districts, and appointed a tenant-in-chief responsible for the affairs of each district. The Anglo-Saxon system of security through shire-reeves and courts of shires was modified as judicial processes were centralized under the king's judges who traveled throughout the country. These traveling judges were the forerunners of modern-day circuit judges.

Around 1100 A.D. the office of constable was established within the shire system. The word was derived from the Latin *comes stabuli* meaning "an officer of the stable." A constable, who received no pay, was appointed for each 100 citizens to aid the reeve in the conduct of his duties. In 1116 A.D., Henry I, son of William the Conqueror, issued the *Leges Henrici*, in which he gave himself the title of Law Giver. The *Leges Henrici* originated the idea of a separation between those crimes judged to be serious or felonious, and lesser offenses deemed to be misdemeanors. If a felony was committed, officers of both the crown and citizens had equal authority to make an arrest for crimes committed in their presence. In the case of misdemeanors, only officers of the crown had the right to arrest.

The Assize of Clarendon in 1166 revived the Anglo-Saxon system of mutual security or frankpledge. A section of this code established the grand jury and initiated the end of the trial-by-ordeal and trial-by-combat. The creation of the jury system brought about a change in the fundamental concepts of justice by establishing rules of evidence and new protections for the rights of individuals and the security of persons and property.

Between 1300 and 1648 the feudal system of Europe declined. This decline can be linked to the introduction of firearms and cannons in the fourteenth and fifteenth centuries. These new weapons made the more traditional infantry weapons such as the pike, crossbow, longbow, and sword obsolete. The breakdown of the vassal-master relationships forced kings, nobles, and city-state leaders to find other ways of training armies. England used the citizen-solider concept, while the rest of Europe relied upon mercenaries. This practice of hiring foreign mercenaries has been credited with the creation of a document called the Magna Carta or Great Charter.

C. ENGLISH REFORM (1200 A.D. – 1800 A.D.)

King John, an unpopular ruler of England, was forced by the barons to sign the Magna Carta (Great Charter) in 1215. This document, limiting the powers of the monarchy, was imposed on King John by the nobles. It established a clear separation between local and national government and established the principle that the king was subject to the law. The Magna Carta also promulgated due process—the course of legal proceedings designed to protect individual rights and liberties. It served to strengthen the role and importance of local grand juries, circuit judges, coroners, and justices of the peace.

William the Conqueror's innovative national security system had deteriorated by the time the Statute of Winchester (also known as the Statute of Westminster), issued in 1285, re-established a formalized law enforcement system throughout England. The Statute provided that it was a citizen's duty to maintain the peace and any citizen could make an arrest. If offenders were not caught in the act, the citizen or watchman had to call together neighbors to hunt for them. All citizens were required to own weapons and participate in the manhunt. A group of citizens engaged in pursuing criminals was called a *posse comitatus*, a term used by townspeople centuries later in the Western portions of the United States. This Statute required that every area of England implement a security force, which was specified according to time, place, and number of personnel. It established a system of patrolling called watch and ward. Every district was to control crime within its boundaries; the gates of all towns were required to be closed at dusk; all persons not residing in the town were required to check in with local authorities. The night watch and the office of bailiff were initiated by this Statute. Bailiffs checked on strangers and lodgers at inns in the town, and the night watch guarded the city gates from sunset to sunrise to secure the city. Additionally, these watchmen grouped into a marching watch to limit the movement of townspeople during certain hours, establishing the concepts of mobile patrols and curfew as security measures. All citizens were required to own weapons and participate in the chase if needed. Every able male of the community had to serve his turn on the watch.

By the fourteenth century, before the Middle Ages ended, national states were taking the place of feudal governments. A slow but continuous transition in the pattern of the European economy from the fourteenth to the end of the seventeenth century—the Commercial Revolution—brought many changes and trends, including increased trade and exploration and the rise of the merchant class. Advances in transportation expanded commerce throughout the known world. An elaborate system of international markets, trade, and colonization required increased productive capacity and surplus from agriculture, animal husbandry, and the skilled trades.

Large land holdings were essential to the production of economically feasible quantities of agricultural products. The landlords consolidated the small holdings of peasants (who were excluded by enclosure acts from open grazing privileges) into large manor farms. Tenants displaced by the consolidation of lands migrated to the cities. Cultural patterns and family traditions were in upheaval as the constraints of medieval society disintegrated. Mass unemployment, poverty, and health and welfare needs caused social unrest and dynamic changes, as well as increases in security problems. There was no existing civil force that could effectively protect persons and property. For example, the protection of production goods while in storage and transit became such a critical problem for the merchant class that, in order to combat the problem, individual merchants and tradespeople hired guards to protect their buildings, shops, stores of goods, and caravans. It was also during this period that the merchant class began to use the forerunners of private detectives to locate and identify stolen property.

Parochial police also came into existence, as many English cities—arranged in distinct population and geographic districts based on religious or ethnic background—hired their own police to protect them and their property. These private police performed essentially the same function as a public police officer except that their responsibility extended only to the boundary of the district.

Thus, for some 300 years, the cities and countryside of England were policed by a fragmented system of constables and watchmen. The first police officials were the shire-reeve (sheriff) and, later, the parish constable. The parish constables were charged with maintaining law and order and were responsible to the Justice of the Peace. The Justices of the Peace, appointed by the crown, were unpaid and usually selected from the gentry. The appointees frequently used their positions to better their own needs, maintaining the status quo by enforcing the laws in favor of their own social class. Because there was no central authority coordinating this justice system, justice was often fragmented and of inferior quality. Consequently, there was a great deal of corruption within the system.

Prior to eighteenth century, all personnel who received pay for watch duty were paid exclusively by individuals or private groups. For example, on the campuses of fifteenth-century Oxford University, there was a system in place in which servants were appointed to execute the order of the chancellor and the proctor, which included serving writs, exacting fines, and escorting "evildoers" to prison. These individuals were referred to as *Bedels*. The Bedels were charged with keeping order, making lists of offenders, and serving the punishment of fines. The proctors received small payments from the fines collected by the Bedels to cover the costs of the night watch and for the hire and repair of armor (Collins, 1990). However by 1737, George II began to pay watchmen with tax monies collected specifically for security protection.

Thus, the period of the commercial revolution was one of great turmoil and social upheaval. It provided the first real evidence that the English public protective system was unable to cope with the task of providing even a minimal amount of protection for emerging business and commercial enterprises.

III. SECURITY AND CRIME PREVENTION IN THE EARLY AMERICAS

A. PUEBLO IV PERIOD (1300 A.D. – 1600 A.D.)

As the feudal system in Europe was slowly being replaced by the use of mercenaries, warfare or fear of violence was also shaping the history of the early inhabitants of the Americas. The Mogollons were primally hunting and wild-food gathering societies that lived in the mountainous border country between Arizona and New Mexico. The twelfth- to fourteenth-century Mogollon villages were walled and defensively situated and provide examples of early forms of crime prevention through environmental design. The defensive potential of the self-enclosed, large pueblos is obvious, and Spanish accounts of warfare with the Pueblos describe their defensive use. The earlier architecture of the Pueblo dwellings consisted of mud-and-stone storage structures and brush-and-pole ramadas. These early structures over time became more massive, were joined together and, as multi-room structures, were referred to as "unit houses." These houses, made of dry masonry or stone and adobe, replaced pit houses as residencies both in rock shelters and, most especially, at open sites on mesa tops or in valleys. The early pit houses were designed to keep out both predators and the elements. They were dug deep into the ground for warmth. Entry was often made through a tunnel and antechamber built to the east or southeast which provided escape and defense against intruders. Figure 1.3 represents regional variations in Pueblo kiva architectural styles (Ferguson & Rohn, 1987:98).

Figure 1.3
Regional Variations in Pueblo Kiva Architectural Styles

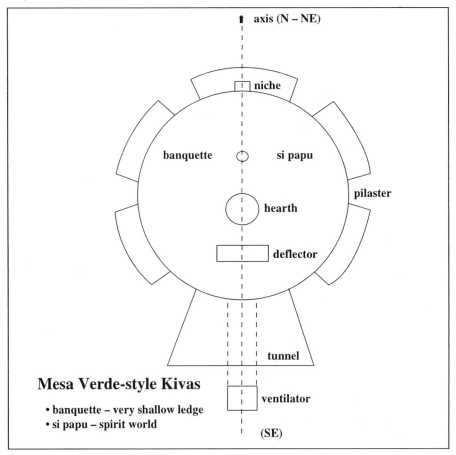

The Mesa Verde was used by Pueblo ancestors to build cliff houses which set under the mesa tops. The Dowa Yolanne, or "Corn Mountain" was often used as a place of refuge and defense. Meanwhile, England was beginning a period of change and reform.

IV. EIGHTEENTH-CENTURY EUROPE

A. THE BOW STREET RUNNERS (1749 – 1829)

The centuries-old system of constables aided by free citizens broke down under the combined effects of industrialization and urbanization. The growth of crime and serious public disorders in cities had become almost intolerable by the late eighteenth century. The noted English author, Patrick Pringle, had the following to say about eighteenth-century England:

> No one thought our policemen wonderful in the eighteenth century. What struck foreigners as remarkable was that we had none. London was the greatest town in the world; it was also the most lawless. This was not because the British were too soft with criminals, although being British they naturally thought they were. In fact, Britain not only had the most criminals; it also had the harshest Criminal Code. Men, women, and children were liable to be hanged for offences that in other countries were considered quite trivial: associating with gypsies or cutting hop-binds, for example, or entering land with intent to kill rabbits; impersonating a Chelsea Pensioner, or chipping bits out of Westminster Bridge. A boy or girl of seven could be sentenced to death for stealing a pocket handkerchief. The law got steadily harsher throughout the century, while in other countries it was getting steadily more humane . . . (Pringle, 1955:11-9)

When England emerged from feudalism she did not need a standing army, for she had no land frontiers; and one result of this geological accident was that England had no men-of-arms to use as police. Her only security legacy from the feudal era was the amateur parish-constable system. This continued to work adequately in country parishes, but it was not suited to larger units, such as towns. By 1700 the population of the metropolis (London), as it was called, was well over one-half million. During the first one-half of the century, the population hardly increased at all, in spite of considerable emigration from the country, for deaths greatly exceeded births. Between 1740 and 1742, for example, there were twice as many burials as baptisms. The main check on the growth of population was the wholesale murder of children by their parents and parish authorities. After a careful investigation, Jonas Hanway estimated that more than 75 percent of all children died before they were five, and that infant mortality among illegitimate children was more than 95 percent. Some illegitimate children were murdered at birth by their mothers or, more commonly, laid out in the streets to die of exposure. Others starved to death in workhouses or in the care of nurses who specialized in taking them off the hands of the parish. Some nurses, however, kept children alive to use them for begging after first blinding or maiming them to increase their value (Pringle, 1955).

Such was the world of Jonathan Wild. In 1743, Henry Fielding, later to become the chief magistrate of the Bow Street area of London, wrote a political satire, *Life of Mr. Jonathan Wild, The Great.* While not a factual biography of the life and times of Jonathan Wild, the events of Fielding's book were drawn from Wild's career as one of England's most notable criminals. Fielding, through the personage of Wild, characterized the aggregate nature of crime and justice in eighteenth-century England. The corruption and ineptness of the English system of justice was evidenced in Wild's criminal ventures as a fence, smuggler, thief-taker, and criminal mastermind.

In 1748, when Henry Fielding became chief magistrate of Bow Street, crime had become rampant. Counterfeit money was more common than good money and there were more than 100 offenses punishable by death. Fielding set himself two tasks: to eliminate existing crime and to prevent fresh outbreaks of crime in the future. To achieve these aims he considered three things necessary: the active cooperation of the public, a stronger police force and the removal of the causes of crime and the conditions in which it flourished. In his five years at Bow Street, Fielding's significant contributions included a foot patrol to make the streets safer, a mounted patrol for the highways, the Bow Street Runners (special investigators) and police courts.

Fielding's scheme was to thwart criminals by actively seeking them out and investigating their activities. Citizens, Fielding realized, might combine togeth-er collectively, go into the streets, trace the perpetrators of crimes in their haunts and meet the instigators of mob gatherings before they had assembled a follow-ing and caused destruction. He saw that it was possible to prevent, instead of repressing crime and disorder . . . (Reith, 1975:135).

This was in complete contrast to the constables and watchmen who could not be found when trouble erupted. Fielding formed a band of volunteers who arrest-ed numerous criminals in the Bow Street area. These early crime fighters (detectives) became known as the Bow Street Runners, and their success was widely known in London. In 1752, Fielding, who was an author prior to becom-ing a magistrate, began publishing *The Covent Garden Journal* in order to circu-late crime news. This literary paper was used as a platform for Fielding's cru-sade against misery, vice, and crime (Phelps, Swanson & Evans, 1979:43).

Even though Fielding's efforts had immense effects in the Bow Street area, his ideas were not applied throughout London. Crime continued to be a major problem, and society's only weapon against crime was the ineffective constable. Fielding's proposal to have salaried magistrates combined with a preventive force of paid constables went unheeded.

In 1796, Patrick Colquhoun published *A Treatise on the Police of the Metrop-olis,* which detailed the crime problem in and around London. Colquhoun esti-mated that the losses from various forms of theft, coining, forgery, and swin-dling amounted to £2,000,000. He called for the formation of a large police force to combat crime in London. In 1785, William Pitt, a member of Parlia-ment, had introduced a bill that resembled Colquhoun's plan, but was met with a storm of protest and was forced to withdraw the proposal. The citizenry was adamantly opposed to the formation of any formal police for fear that such a force would be used by the government, or certain elements of the government, to spy on the people, infringe upon liberty and possibly aid in the formation of a totalitarian government (Reith, 1975:138).

Colquhoun, however, did get a chance to implement some of his ideas. In 1798, a number of West Indian planters and merchants asked him for suggestions on how to alleviate the problem of massive thefts from ships at the London docks. Colquhoun developed an innovative plan for a police organization to control crime on the docks. Merchants, with the approval of the government, would finance the organization. Colquhoun's ideas were put into action and the River Police Office was inaugurated with 80 full-time and 1,120 part-time officers. They not only watched and patrolled the docks, but also participated in the unloading of cargo from ships. The experimental police department was a success. Savings as a result of the reduction of thefts was estimated to be £66,000 in the first eight months. The government assumed control of the department in 1800 and operated it until 1829 when it was incorporated into the Metropolitan Police Department (Reith, 1975:138).

B. THE PEELIAN REFORM (1800 – 1860)

In 1822, when Robert Peel was appointed Home Secretary, he immediately set up a program of social reform that eventually encompassed the police. During Peel's first few years in office, he concerned himself primarily with social and legal reform. First, he consolidated laws dealing with theft and the destruction of property into one volume. He then did the same thing with all laws dealing with offenses against persons. In England at this time there were more than 200 offenses bearing the death penalty. Peel abolished more than 100 of these. Benefit of Clergy, where a clergyman could escape punishment for a first offense in certain felonies, was abolished. He made it easier for victims of sexual offenses to get justice by abolishing prior-required embarrassing evidence (Hewitt, 1965:23-24).

In 1828, Peel appointed a select committee to study the police and on July 27, 1828, they issued their report. The report called for the formation of an Office of Police under the Home Secretary. All magistrates without bench duty would report to the Home Secretary. All police, constables, and watchmen would be incorporated into the Office of Police. The fact that London proper was not placed under the structure aided in its acceptance by Parliament (Hewitt, 1965:24).

The bill passed Parliament without serious argument. The most important of its provisions was placing the responsibility for finances and administration on Parliament, eliminating weak, fragmented local control (Hewitt, 1965:23-24). The bill also addressed a number of other important areas. For example, there was a section on discipline directed to both the police and the citizenry: No policeman on duty could go into a public house except in pursuit of duty. A . . . keeper of any house, shop, room, or other place for the sale of any liquors, whether spirituous or otherwise, who entertained or sold to a policeman could be fined up to five pounds (Lyman, 1975:31).

Peel appointed Sir Charles Rowan and Sir Richard Mayne as the first commissioners for the Metropolitan Police. Rowan was selected for his military background, and Mayne, a former magistrate, was probably selected because of his legal background (Hewitt, 1965:30). One of their first actions was to prepare a book of general instructions delineating the constables' duties and responsibilities.

One of Rowan and Mayne's important contributions was the list of nine principles that guided their department (Reith, 1975:154-166).

1) To prevent crime and disorder, as an alternative to their repression by military force and severity of legal punishment.

2) To recognize always that the power of the police to fulfill their functions and duties is dependent on public approval of their existence, actions and behavior, and on their ability to secure and maintain public respect.

3) To recognize always that to secure and maintain the respect and approval of the public means also the securing of the willing cooperation of the public in the task of securing observance of law.

4) To recognize always that the extent to which cooperation of the public can be secured diminishes proportionately the necessity of the use of physical force and compulsion for achieving police objectives.

5) To seek and preserve public favor, not by pandering to public opinion, but by constantly demonstrating absolutely impartial service to law, in complete independence of policy and without regard to the justice or injustice of individual laws; by ready offering of individual service and friendship to all members of the public without regard to their wealth or social standing; by ready exercise of courtesy and good humor; and by ready offering of individual sacrifice in protecting and preserving life.

6) To use physical force only when the exercise of persuasion, advice and warning is found to be insufficient to obtain public cooperation to an extent necessary to restore order; and to use only the minimum degree of physical force necessary on any particular occasion for achieving a police objective.

7) To maintain at all times a relationship with the public that gives reality to the historic tradition that the police are the public and that the public are the police; the police being only members of the public who are paid to give full-time attention to duties that are incumbent on every citizen, in the interest of community welfare and existence.

8) To recognize always the need for strict adherence to police executive functions, and to refrain from even seeming to usurp the powers of the judiciary or avenging individuals or the state, and of authoritatively judging guilt and punishing the guilty.

9) To recognize always that the test of police efficiency is the absence of crime and disorder, and not the visible evidence of police action in dealing with them.

The principles enumerated by Rowan and Mayne focused on a system of policing in which the police were partners with the public. Rowan and Mayne realized that survival of their new police system was dependent upon the public's acceptance. They emphasized cooperation, justice, equality, and crime prevention. The Metropolitan Police represented the first modern police force in history.

The establishment of the police department was not without opposition. Hostility to the new police ranged from brutal murders of the newly appointed constables to public denunciation by judges, magistrates, cabinet members, the public and—on occasion—by King George IV himself (Reith, 1975:152). Frequently, the constables were referred to as "Peel's bloody gang" and "blue devils." The police were constantly in fear for their lives and it was only through the efforts of Rowan and Mayne that they were able to succeed. The commissioners impressed upon the officers to be polite at all times and to use physical force only as a last resort. This gradually minimized negative interactions with the public.

Eventually, the police were a success. By June of 1830, the force consisted of 3,314 men. Between 1829 and 1831, 8,000 men had been enrolled and more than 3,000 had been discharged for unfitness, incompetence, or drunkenness (Lyman, 1975:37). The new police force brought a reduction of crime, control of riots, and a sense of orderliness to London. The police concept was extended to the boroughs in 1835 and to the counties in stages in 1839 and 1856. Gradually, it spread throughout the British Empire (Reith, 1975:169).

V. EARLY AMERICAN POLICING, SECURITY, AND CRIME PREVENTION

A. AMERICAN POLICING (1600s – 1800s)

When the colonists arrived in America, they promptly instituted a police system similar to the English system. The Massachusetts Bay Colony installed the office of constable, whose duties centered around keeping the peace, raising the hue and cry, controlling drunks, and apprehending criminals. Over time these duties were expanded.

> . . . [B]y 1658 they included informing the magistrator of "new comers," taking charge of the Watch and Ward, raising the hue and cry, tallying votes for deputies to the general court, summoning jurymen for duty, bringing accused before the court, bringing before the court men and women not living with their spouses, collecting taxes, and other sundry duties including the hanging of sheep killing dogs where the owners refused to do so themselves (Phelps et al., 1979:41).

As the small colonial settlements developed into cities, night and day watches appeared. In 1631, Boston established a night watch, and in 1643 a burglar watch was established in New Netherlands (New York) (Bopp & Schultz,

1972:17-18). In 1700, Philadelphia established a night watch in which all citizens were obligated to take their turn. (Fosdick, 1969:59) These early watch systems were not without their problems. As early as 1642, the town government of New Haven proclaimed "It is ordered by the court that, from hence forward, none of the watchmen shall have liberty to sleep during the watch" (Fosdick, 1969:60). Many cities experienced difficulty in inducing citizens to take their turn at the watch, and when on duty, many of the watchmen would drink or sleep.

Fosdick analyzed the evolution of the New York watch force, and found the following conditions:

> Its ranks were made up for the most part of men who pursued regular occupations during the day and who added to their incomes by serving the city at night. "Jaded stevedores, teamsters and mechanics" comprised the New York force. No standards except those of a political nature were applied in selection. One Matthew Young was appointed watchman in Boston "in order that he and his children do not become town charges." An investigating committee of the Board of Aldermen in New York made the finding that the incumbents were selected for political opinions and not for personal merit and that the term of service of the incumbent was uncertain and often very brief, depending on the change of political party. Another investigation in 1838 showed the watchmen dismissed from one ward for neglect or drunkenness found service in another (Fosdick, 1969:61-62).

In 1844 the legislature of New York abolished the watch system and created a police force. The act established a force of 800 men under the direction of a chief of police, who reported to the mayor. Boston, as did other cities, followed New York's example and established a police force in 1854 (National Advisory Committee on Criminal Justice Standards and Goals, 1977:30).

The establishment of the new police forces may have solved some problems, but many new ones were also created. From the beginning most of the major municipal departments were embroiled in politics. The spoils system more or less dominated the administration and operation of many departments for most of the nineteenth century. It essentially caused the departments to deteriorate to nothing more than welfare systems for political cronies. Friends of politicians were appointed as police captains over lieutenants and sergeants with years of experience. In some jurisdictions, neophyte officers could secure employment only through bribery. Also, when a change of political factions occurred, there was generally wholesale firing of police officers, commanders, and administrators as the new mayor appointed new people into the police department to aid the administration in controlling the city.

The last half of the nineteenth century and the first decade of the twentieth century saw the police become puppets in the politicians' hands. Their primary function was to maintain the status quo. America had failed to learn from England's mistakes. A decentralized police system that was corrupt and completely inadequate was allowed to develop. The American police were, to a degree, a part of the criminal element, rather than being a force that controlled criminality.

B. AMERICAN SECURITY (1600S – 1800S)

Colonists settling in America were confronted by a new and alien land. They brought with them the English system of government and its reliance upon mutual protection and collective responsibility. Although there was a degree of Dutch, Spanish, and French influence in the colonies, the preponderance of legal concepts and security practices stemmed from England.

In the New England area, the people depended upon commerce and industry for their livelihood. Thus, many villages and towns were established, most of them utilizing the watch system of their homeland (England) to provide for security and safety. The watchman system remained an important component of the development of security in this country and served as the primary protection system until police departments were established in the latter part of the eighteenth century. In the more rural South, the tendency was to develop the county form of government. As in English counties, the sheriff became the principal law enforcement officer in the southern rural areas of America.

As the Atlantic coastal area became more heavily populated, people began to move westward across the country to settle new land. This westward movement was challenged by Native Americans (Indians) and other nations not aligned with English interests. Many of these early settlers lost their lives and property to hostile forces who saw the newcomers as trespassers on their land.

Most of the frontier areas were without any type of official law enforcement. Thus, the people were mutually dependent upon each other for protection from outlaws and Indians. The wagon train and the fort were two very common examples of how the early settlers attempted to provide for their safety and security through strength in numbers. It was not an uncommon event to find as many as 100 wagons traveling together across the western prairie. The 1800s saw the West at its wildest, with murder, gunfights, fraud, land wars, and political graft as the order of the day.

The rapid growth of the American colonies and the move westward was characterized by increasing needs and pressures for more effective protection. It soon became apparent that the watch system employed by many American cities was neither adequate nor efficient enough to match the escalating needs of society. This realization led to the development of public police forces in the United States. By 1856, police departments had been formed in New York, Boston, Philadelphia, Detroit, Chicago, Cincinnati, Los Angeles, Dallas, and San Francisco. Although often inefficient and corrupt, they represented a vast improvement over the watch system. Their development, however, did not satisfy or alleviate the growing security needs of private citizens. Thus, the mid-nineteenth century saw the birth of the private security industry.

Allan Pinkerton is considered the father of private security in the United States. In 1855, Pinkerton, a former Cook County, Illinois deputy sheriff, started the Pinkerton Detective Agency. For more than 50 years his was the only company providing security and investigative services throughout the United States. During the Civil War, Pinkerton agents acted as an intelligence-gathering unit for the Union Army, but the primary employer throughout the earlier years of the company was the railroad industry. The agency's detectives and investigators concentrated on catching train robbers and providing other security services for the railroads.

The Pinkerton Agency was successful because public law enforcement agencies were unable to provide adequate protection and security to private citizens and private enterprises. In addition, Pinkerton agents were able to engage in interstate activities unhampered by jurisdictional lines that restricted public police agencies.

Within a few years of its inception, the Pinkerton Agency was a successful private security enterprise. The foundation was established so that the provision of security and protective services could be provided by private enterprise in such a way that both the interests of government and private individuals could be served. Today, Pinkerton's Incorporated is international in scope and employs thousands of individuals in a variety of security services and activities.

VI. OTHER NINETEENTH-CENTURY DEVELOPMENTS

Between 1800 and 1840, the dynamic and expansive nature of American life in issues of statehood, politics, justice, and immigration added new problems and hazards for its participants. In this period alone, immigration more than tripled the national population, introducing a new population with varying personal concepts and cross-cultural concerns.

Security Delivery Services

Stagecoach lines during the westward expansion provided passenger, mail, and courier service throughout the country. Wells Fargo and others were the forerunners of the armored car and courier services visible today. By 1900, Brink's Inc. had begun as a freight and package delivery service. As early as 1859, they had a fleet of 85 wagons transporting numerous materials, including payrolls and valuable goods that could not be shipped by other means.

Electronic Alarms

In 1858, Edwin Holmes, a Bostonian, began the first electronic burglar alarm business. The Holmes Protection Company expanded and adapted to technological advances of the day, and by 1880 the company was monitoring business establishments in Boston, New York, and Philadelphia. Perhaps Holmes' most notable contribution to the development of electronic alarm system was his central-station concept of monitoring various alarm sensors installed at numerous locations from a single location. Holmes' electronic burglar alarm predated the electric light and telephone by about 25 years. When the American Telegraph Company was formed in 1874, the use of electronic alarm systems spread to most major United States cities. By the latter part of the century, many companies across the country offered local or district electronic alarm protection.

Railroad Security

As early as 1865, railway police acts were established in many states, granting the railroad industry the right to establish a proprietary security force. In most cases, these forces were given full police powers for the protection of company equipment, rolling stock, and property. By 1860 there were 30,626 miles of railroad in the United States, more than triple the number in existence only 10 years before (Dewhurst, 1955:5). With the westward expansion, railway lines were extended into sparsely settled areas that had little or no public protection. By the very nature of their physical construction, trains and railroad properties became a prime target for attack by Indians and well-organized bands of outlaws who robbed passengers, stole cargo, caused train derailments, destroyed property, and generally disrupted communications and railway traffic. To combat these problems, thousands of watch personnel and detectives were hired by the railroads (Dewhurst, 1955:6).

The early days of railroad police were characterized by confusion, distrust, and inefficiency. There was no central agency for railroad companies within or without to develop and coordinate standards of employment, job requirements, or public relations. The hiring of individuals was done with little or no regard for their overall ability and background, and a number of undesirable characters found their way into the category of railroad police officer (Dewhurst, 1955:7). The measure of a railroad detective or special agent was the ability to handle himself successfully in physical contact with those who preyed upon the railroad. Tact and investigative ability were most often subordinate to expertise in handling a six-gun.

By the early 1900s, some 14,000 railroad police were employed as investigators and patrol officers (Post & Kingsbury, 1970:15). While the railroad police were granted some police powers relative to the protection of railroad operations and properties, they have been—and still are—a proprietary security force with limited law enforcement powers.

VII. THE TWENTIETH CENTURY

By the turn of the century, increases in industrialization, immigration and labor organizations, along with an expanding economy, created many conditions that were conducive to the growth of private security. Because public police forces were organized exclusively on a local basis and their operations were limited by local political boundaries, law enforcement beyond restricted jurisdictions was provided only by private security forces. It was not until 1924 that the Federal Bureau of Investigation (FBI) came into being to provide law enforcement on a nationwide, centralized basis. Until this time, private security agencies such as Pinkerton and Burns were the only agencies within the United States with the capability of providing cross-jurisdictional protection of persons and property.

Prior to and during World War I, the concern for security intensified in American industry, due not only to urbanization and industrial growth but also to the fear of sabotage and espionage by politically active nationalists. The private security industry experienced a short period of rapid growth and expansion as security personnel supplied by private contractors were utilized to guard the nation's factories, utilities, and transportation systems. The end of the war saw a decrease in security concerns, and the status and quality of security services were lowered.

In the 1930s, demand for plant protection and the provision of corporate security services began to appear. Even though the country was suffering the throes of the Depression years, demand for security developed in reaction to labor strikes and unrest in American industry. However, the involvement of security in many cases was controversial, and characterized by overzealous and nefarious acts of violence. Striking workers were beaten and shot by security guards hired to protect company property. Security operatives posing as employees infiltrated workers' groups, relaying information back to the company on strike leaders and employee plans of action. Numerous workers bent on sabotage, work stoppage, etc., were caught in the act due to the information gathered by the "inside" operatives. The Pinkerton Agency alone had informers planted in 93 organizations; many of these operatives held high union offices (Ursic & Pagano, 1974:19). As a result, security services were not held in high esteem by most of the working public.

The beginning of World War II was a tremendous catalyst for the growth of private security services. Almost overnight, thousands of security personnel were employed to protect the nation's industries and working forces. The federal government in many instances required contractors to employ comprehensive security measures to protect materials necessary for the war effort. Wartime concern for the prevention and detection of espionage and sabotage brought a federal decision to bring plant watch and security personnel into the army as an auxiliary unit of the military police. Before the end of the war, more than 200,000 industrial security personnel were sworn in by the Internal Security Division of the War Department after being required to sign an agreement placing them under the Articles of War (Ursic & Pagano, 1974:20). As a result of this heightened emphasis and attention to security by the government, private industry became more aware of the role that plant security could have in the protection of their assets.

Although crime prevention techniques were present in ancient times, the concept as it is used today can be traced back to the early 1960s and the development of public housing. Those credited with being some of the first to voice concerns regarding the design and layout of these housing projects were Elizabeth Wood and her development of a "Social Design Theory." This theory focused attention upon the importance of maintaining a sense of privacy by the occupants, but also a sense of community. Wood's theory suggested that to be effective, public housing facilities should be designed with areas that promoted interaction by residents, such as children playing on a common playground while allowing for maximum observation by the residents. Involvement by local business owners was advocated by Jane Jacobs, a journalist and proponent of Woods. She advocated that in order to establish and maintain a sense of community, local businesses had a duty to contribute to enhancing public safety by involving them in observation and surveillance.

Expanding upon Wood's theory, the phrase Crime Prevention through Environmental Design was coined by Oscar Newman, an architect, who worked with the St. Louis Police Department in the mid-1960s to assist them in the development and design of the Pruit-Ingoe housing project. Based upon Newman's early work with the St. Louis Police Department, he coined the term: *defensible space.* This term was defined as "a model which inhibits crime by creating a physical expression of a social fabric which defends itself" (Newman, 1973), and became associated with Crime Prevention Through Environmental Design (CPTED). Based upon research conducted by Newman, he is credited with linking the design of the environment and crime. The development and expansion of private and public security and crime prevention services has since evolved from the embryonic stage to include some of the most progressive operational and technological techniques of crime prevention, detection, and apprehension in use today. As crime and social problems have outgrown the capacity of public law enforcement agencies to provide an umbrella of public services to varying segments of society, there has been a corresponding increase in the role and function of security and protective services. Contemporary security operations now have the tools and capability to provide an effective and efficient protection program for the total organization.

There are now more private security personnel than public law enforcement officers in the United States. During the past several years, the growth rate of the private security industry has far surpassed that of public law enforcement. A comparison and projected growth of public sector and private sector protective service workers is shown in Figure 1.4.

Figure 1.4
Private Security and Law Enforcement Employment Contrasts

Private vs. Public Enforcement	No. of Full Time Employees: 1984	No. of Full Time Employees: 1990	No. of Full Time Employees: 1996	No. of Full Time Employees: 2006
Security Officers/Guards	733,000	883,000	954,644	1,175,257
Police Patrol Officers	520,000	665,000	412,739	486,080
Difference	213,000	218,000	541,905	689,177
Ration of Security/Police	1.4 to 1	1.3 to 1	2.3 to 1	2.4 to 1

Source: *Occupational Outlook Handbook*, U.S. Department of Labor, Bureau of Labor Statistics, 1986-1996.

Although the response rate is low, according to a recent survey by the American Society of Industrial Security International (ASIS) and JDG Associates, there appears to be an upward trend in the hiring of security professionals. The respondents also indicated that they are increasing their use of the Internet to advertise these positions. A number of security employment Web pages have emerged. "Security Jobs Network" (http://www.securityjobs.net/) describes its web page as "the most comprehensive source of information for the arrest protection professional." They have more than 1,000 professional security positions posted. Some of the position titles include: Security Program Manager, Senior Advisor & Investigator, Risk and Safety Manager (theme park), Cargo Security Manager (High-Tech Electronics Distribution Company). See Appendix A for a Security Programs Manager job description.

FACTORS OF GROWTH

CONTRACT SECURITY SERVICES

Private, contractual guard service firms such as Pinkerton, Burns, Wackenhut, and Guardsmark have achieved enormous growth during the past few years. Proprietary security services (companies providing their own security guards), while not as visible as the contractual services, have experienced some growth, but *The Hallcrest Report II* projected a significant decrease in this area by the year 2000 (Cunningham et al., 1990:185). While the activities and functions of guard service operations are essentially the same, whether contractual or proprietary, the cost of in-house security operations are inherently more expensive. Thus, the contractual component of guard services will experience some growth "at the expense of" their proprietary counterpart. *The Hallcrest Report II* estimated that by the year 2000 there would be 750,000 contract security guards and 280,000 proprietary security guards (the latter down from 393,000 in 1990). However, according to the 1996 Bureau of Labor Statistics (BLS) data, there were approximately 558,563 contract security guards/officers and 396,081 proprietary security guards/officers. It would appear that the contractual component experienced better than expected reductions in proprietary and less than expected increases in contract security forces. The 1996 BLS data reflected a 28 percent increase in contract security officers from 1990 to 1996 and a 25 percent decrease in proprietary security officers from 1990 to 1996. Contrary to *The Hallcrest Report II* estimates that there would be "some growth" in contractual guard service, there was an overall decline of seven percent in the number of security officers in 1996 as compared to 1990. In spite of these differences, both *The Hallcrest Report II* and the Bureau of Labor Statistics predict that employment of security officers is expected to grow *faster than the average (23%)* through the year 2006. By 2006 the BLS estimates that there will be 1,175,257 security guards/officers. This growth is based upon increased concerns about crime, vandalism, and terrorism. These factors are expected to heighten the need for security in and around homes, plants, stores, offices, and recreation areas. The BLS also bases this growth on the demand for private security firms to provide contractual security services at airports, courtrooms, schools, and public buildings. This contract security service expansion includes increasing economic/workplace crime, increasing incidences and cost of civil litigation involving security, decreasing governmental budgetary support of public law enforcement agencies, increasing awareness and fear of crime, improving professional image of security, increasing governmental regulations relative to public and workplace security/safety, and increasing an awareness of security as a cost-effective, money-saving measure.

TECHNOLOGICAL ADVANCES

Technology has played an important role in the growth of the private security industry. Even the lock, one of the oldest security devices, has been subject to drastic changes, e.g., the development of combination locks, time locks, electronic locks, computerized locks with memory capability and access-control systems that incorporate "smart cards," advanced technology of television, minicomputers, and biometrics.

Just as technology developed to improve the quality of television, radio, and communications, other areas of electronics have been adapted and assimilated into various electronic security devices and systems. The progression from vacuum tubes to transistors to integrated circuit technology has played a major role in the growth of the security industry. Today, sophisticated security systems of all types and sizes are monitored and/or managed by computers and operating software, integrating such diverse functions as card access, closed circuit television, life safety, HVAC, audio communications, time and attendance, fuel monitoring, photo identification, and so on. Proper and appropriate utilization of electronics and systems components provides adequate protection of even the largest facility, and at the same time promotes the optimal usage of security personnel (Reed, 1992:38-39).

CRIME AND FRAUD

Without question, the rising crime rate contributed to the growth of security in the United States. Although crime rates have been dropping for a number of years, the fear of crime against persons and property has continued to increase to the point that many live in constant fear of being victimized on the street, at work, and even in their homes. In many parts of the country, the fear of everyday crime exerts a corrosive and dehumanizing effect on how people think, how they act, and how they behave toward one another. Worry about crime, coupled with declining faith in public law enforcement and anxiety about the future, is a primary concern of Americans.

In addition to the traditional crimes of murder, theft, rape, assault, etc., relatively new crime and fraud techniques are being utilized to perpetrate criminal acts. Computer crimes, credit card fraud, counterfeiting, telecommunications fraud, and other forms of white-collar crime continue to become more and more sophisticated and often beyond the scope of a public law enforcement investigation. According to *The Baltimore Business Journal,* "half of the largest companies in the world have been victims of fraud during the past year, with 25 percent of them losing $1 million or more in the past five years." (November, 1997). These types of crime have created a need for a new kind of security professional, capable of developing and employing highly sophisticated security measures to deter, detect, or deny criminal access. The complexity of today's business environment can sometimes be staggering, yet not so complex that an enterprising employee cannot find ways to embezzle, defraud, or otherwise steal from an employer. Studies continue to indicate that employees represent more of a threat to an employer than all the robbers, burglars, and outside thieves combined. Clearly, much of the growth of security has been generated by the threat from within.

Other crimes, while not new, have become more prevalent in recent years. Principal among these is domestic terrorism, such as the Oklahoma City bombing, international terrorism targeted at American corporations and governmental agencies, computer sabotage, computer hacking, Internet fraud, high-tech counterfeiting, telecom fraud, and workplace violence. For example, U.S. embassies have become targets by extreme Arabic terrorist groups in retaliation for American intervention in the Middle East. In 1998, two American embassies in Africa were bombed. American diplomats, vacationers, and business persons have been assassinated, kidnapped, and held for ransom in many parts of the world. These situations, whether politically or criminally motivated, have created a need for security personnel with the knowledge, professional characteristics, and skills necessary to deal with the terrorist threat. While the incidences of terrorist attacks vacillate by time and place, terrorists retain the potential for resuming extensive violence. In many instances, private companies, public institutions, and governments have not only chosen to initiate additional and often elaborate security measures, but also to retain them indefinitely at considerable expense.

GOVERNMENT REGULATION

The Federal Bank Protection Act of 1968 mandated increased security measures and equipment for federal banks. Since January 1973, the Federal Aviation Administration has required screening of air passengers and their carry-on baggage. Many defense contractors must comply with stringent security guidelines regarding the hiring of employees, facility access controls, procedural operations, and security of information. Other laws and regulations, such as the Joint Commission on Accreditation of Healthcare Organization Standards, the Occupational Safety and Health Act (OSHA), Fair Credit Reporting Act of 1971, Economic Espionage Act of 1996, state and local fire codes, Americans with Disabilities Act of 1990 (ADA), Antiterrorism and Effective Death Penalty Act of 1996, Anti-Drug Abuse Act of 1998, Employee Polygraph Protection Act of 1988, the Freedom of Information Law (FOIL), Private Securities Litigation Reform Act of 1995, Private Security Officers Quality Assurance Act of 1995, etc., produce associative and sometimes additional security tasks. Government regulations created to provide for the protection of life and property generate a corresponding demand for related personnel and products to satisfy the new standards. The Barr-Martinez Bill, which has become the Private Security Officers Quality Assurance Act of 1995, could have the greatest impact upon the security profession as we enter the twenty-first century. Historians will look back on this Act as is done with the Industrial Revolution at the turn of the twentieth century. This Act will provide states with FBI criminal background checks of both applicants and recently hired security officers. The training requirements of the original bill were removed because of controversy. As it was originally written, the bill would have required each state to set as a minimum requirement eight hours of classroom training and four hours of on-the-job training for unarmed officers and 15 hours of training for armed officers. Opponents of that original bill argued that each state should regulate employment standards and conditions.

CIVIL LITIGATION

The United States is considered to be one of the most litigious societies. This propensity to use the court systems to resolve disputes or in retaliation to a perceived wrong has profoundly impacted the security profession. In this perceived crime-prone society, the duty owed toward invitees to the premises is greater now than it was a century, or even a generation, ago. The way in which this duty is measured has undergone drastic change. The landlord, the employer, the business, the institution, etc., all have a greater duty to protect those who are invited onto their premises. Owners and/or controllers of property must now be aware not only of actual threats and occurrences that have led to harm or injury, but also of the potential for the same to those who are lawfully on the premises. The property owners and/or controllers of the premises must exercise the same care that a reasonable person knowing all of the circumstances would exercise to protect themselves and others from criminal attack and injury (Moore, 1989).

Legal and social scholars concur that lawsuits by business invitees against commercial and institutional property owners and managers for inadequate security have increased dramatically across the United States in recent years. Most of these lawsuits have been based upon traditional tort principles of negligence, wherein the plaintiff alleges that a business or institution breached its duty to provide reasonable security to protect against foreseeable criminal acts and harmful situations. For example, according to a 1994 study by the Liability Consultants Inc., of Framingham Mass., parking lots were the most likely place for an attack resulting in a premises liability lawsuit (Kangas, 1996). Allegations of negligence range from issues dealing with the proper selection, training, deployment, etc., of security personnel to more traditional questions relative to the selection, installation, maintenance, etc., of doors, windows, and lighting. Allegations have also arisen regarding the selection, utilization and maintenance of security equipment and technology such as closed circuit television (CCTV) and to security issues relative to building design and landscaping features (Spain, 1991).

Reasonable and appropriate security measures designed and utilized to eliminate questions of negligence can be expensive. However, the costs of such equipment, personnel, and procedures may be minimal when measured against the potential of large jury verdicts that assess punitive damages on the basis of the injury or harm sustained, the financial status of the defendant, and whether the enterprise attempted to provide adequate security. Demonstrated concern and appropriate action must be taken if a business or institution is to insulate itself from large punitive damage awards arising from questions of inadequate security. Failure to do so can inflict serious and, in some cases, fatal economic blows to enterprises, even if they are thriving (Anthony & Thornburg, 1989:41-46).

Privatization

Many services traditionally identified with and provided by public law enforcement are candidates for privatization. State and local government spending for a wide variety of private sector security services that were formerly performed by public law enforcement agencies has increased dramatically over the past several years. Tasks such as public building security, parking enforcement, patrolling of public parks, animal control, special event security, funeral escort, court security, prisoner transport, public housing, and security are being contracted out to private security companies in many parts of the country. The value of such arrangements is twofold: (1) it is less costly than employing additional law enforcement personnel to provide such services, and (2) contracting out such support services "frees up" police officers for basic crime fighting (Cunningham, Strauchs & Van Meter, 1991:1-4). Chapter 2 provides a more detailed discussion of the potential impact of privatization.

PROFESSIONAL GROWTH

In 1955, the American Society for Industrial Security (ASIS) was formed. Its membership is made up of security practitioners whose purpose is to advance and enhance the security profession. ASIS, with a 1992 membership in excess of 21,000, serves as a major spokesperson for the security industry and, in recent years, has focused on the need for research in loss prevention, crime reduction, and advanced security education. Additionally, ASIS sponsors a Certified Protection Professional (CPP) program with the major objective of fostering professionalism in the field of security. Candidates must meet experience and educational requirements and pass an in-depth one-day examination before receiving their CPP certification. Since the formation of ASIS, there has been a proliferation of professional associations, such as Association of Certified Fraud Examiners (CFE), International Association for Healthcare Security and Safety, International Association of Professional Security Consultants, International Foundation for Protection Officers, the National Council of Investigation and Security Services, Certified Information Systems Security Professional (CISSP), the Information Systems Security Association (ISSA), the International Computer Security Association, the International Crime Prevention Association, the International Association of College Law Enforcement Association (IACLEA), the National Locksmith Association and the National Burglar and Fire Alarm Association.

Education and training are recognized prerequisites to assuming and acquiring professional competence and recognition. The increasing complexity of the field of security demands that both the pre-service and in-service practitioner develop, refine, and/or acquire the knowledge and skills necessary to achieve measurable success. Numerous states now require that several hours of formal security training be successfully accomplished prior to, or at least immediately following, employment as a contract security officer. Additionally, employers are now cognizant that higher education is an essential attribute of protection management. The critical thinking skills, along with written and oral skills, which are generally enhanced during the course of college study, are inherent to effective security management (Hertig, 1989:87-89).

Security has become a complex and diverse field. The traditional concept of the aging, less-than-active night watchman will no longer suffice. Instead, security has become a professional discipline that requires a college education and an individual with knowledge and experience in business management, security technology systems integration, investigations and interviewing techniques, computer security, risk management and analysis, risk assessment and security surveys, legal issues and civil liability, and most importantly, outstanding oral and written communication skills.

SUMMARY

Security in America finds its historical roots in the scope and range of events that shaped early England. English concepts of law, justice, social structure, and security evolved and were gradually assimilated into early American life. One merely has to look at the societal evolutions of England to discover why and how certain changes occurred in America.

Until 1776, the dominance and influence of England over the American colonies was indisputable, and even in later years many practices and traditions of the colonists were English-born. America's developing law enforcement and justice system was, for the most part, patterned after the English system. As the nation grew, so did its problems. Efforts to begin municipal police departments were fraught with problems of political favoritism and corruption. The westward expansion was characterized by Indian attacks, range wars, outlaw gangs, and sparse law enforcement. At every turn, new problems requiring new solutions were confronted by our forebears.

Security in the private sector began and grew in direct relationship to the needs of American society. The Civil War, the development of an extensive railway system, World Wars I and II, technological advances, a rising crime rate, government regulations, civil liability, and other factors have, in the passage of time, combined to initiate and nurture a significant and growing demand for security products and services. With the coming of the millennium, security and crime prevention will become increasingly important in dealing with such issues as electronic commerce, a global economy, a culturally diverse workforce, technology, protection of intellectual property, downsizing, and an aging population.

DISCUSSION QUESTIONS

1. In what ways did people in ancient times provide security for themselves and their societies?

2. What influence did the Anglo-Saxons have on the development of early England?

3. What changes did William, Duke of Normandy, initiate in eleventh-century England?

4. What modern-day security practices can be traced to the Statute of Winchester?

5. Describe the impact of the Industrial Revolution on eighteenth-century England.

6. What contributions did Henry Fielding, Patrick Colquhoun, and Robert Peel make to the development of security and law enforcement?

7. Who was Allan Pinkerton? What role did he play in the development of private security?

8. What were some of the major problems encountered by law enforcement efforts in nineteenth-century America?

9. Discuss the origin and development of railroad security.

10. Discuss the factors—positive and negative—that have influenced the growth of security in the twentieth century.

11. What is the current and projected relationship between the number of people employed in private security and in public law enforcement now and in the future?

12. Cite some specific reasons and current developments regarding the increased utilization of private security services.

13. Discuss the overall impact of crime on society and its corresponding effect on the private security industry.

14. How and why are the terms litigation and privatization becoming increasingly significant for private security?

15. Provide some examples of how private security services are a product of society and its influences.

REFERENCES

Anthony, A.J. & Thornburg, F.F. (Feb., 1989). "Liability Lessons: Security on Trial." *Security Management.* Arlington, VA.

Bopp, W.J. & Schultz, D.O. (1972). *Principles of American Law Enforcement and Criminal Justice.* Springfield, IL: Charles C Thomas.

Collins, P.A. (1990). *Campus Security: An Historical Analysis of the Campus Infrastructure with Emphasis on Service/Enforcement Orientation and its Relation to Policies and Procedures.* Unpublished doctoral dissertation.

Cunningham, W.C., Strauchs, J.J. & Van Meter, C.W. (1991). *Private Security and Trends.* National Institute of Justice: Research in Brief. Washington, DC: U.S. Department of Justice.

Cunningham, W.C., Strauchs, J.J. & Van Meter, C.W. (1990). *Private Security Trends 1970-2000: The Hallcrest Report II.* Stoneham, MA: Butterworth-Heinemann.

Dewhurst, H.S. (1955). *The Railroad Police.* Springfield, IL: Charles C Thomas.

Ferguson, W.M. & Rohn, A.H. (1987). *Anasazi Ruins of the Southeast in Color.* Albuquerque, NM: University of New Mexico Press.

Fosdick, R.B. (1969). *American Police Systems.* (Reprint Ed.) Montclair, NJ: Patterson Smith.

Hertig, C.A. (Feb., 1989). "A Solid Foundation in Academia." *Security Management.* Arlington, VA: BASIS.

Hewitt, W.H. (1965). *British Police Administration.* Springfield, IL: Charles C Thomas.

Kangas, S.E. (July 1996). "The Fundamentals of Parking Lot Protection." *Security Management.* Arlington, VA.

Lyman, J.L. (1975). "The Metropolitan Police Act of 1829: An Analysis of Certain Events Influencing the Passage and Character of the Metropolitan Police Act in England." In G. Killinger & P. Cromwell (eds.) *Issues in Law Enforcement* (p. 31). Boston, MA: Holbrook Press.

Moore, R.H. (1989, October). *The Need to Protect: Liability for Failure to Provide Adequate Security.* Paper presented at the meeting of the Southern Criminal Justice Association.

National Advisory Committee on Criminal Justice Standards and Goals. Task Force on Private Security (1977). Cincinnati, OH: Anderson Publishing Co.

Newmann, O. (1973). "Architectural Design for Crime Prevention." U.S. Department of Justice, Law Enforcement Assistance Administration. Washington, DC: U.S. Government Printing Office.

Phelps, T.R., Swanson, C.R. & Evans, K.R. (1979). *Introduction to Criminal Justice.* Santa Monica, CA: Goodyear Publishing Company, Inc.

Post, R. & Kingsbury, A.A. (1970). *Security Administration: An Introduction.* Springfield, IL: Charles C Thomas.

Pringle, P. (1955). *Hue and Cry.* Suffolk, England: Richard Clay and Company.

Reed, S.M. (March, 1992). "Customized Security Is No Longer a Luxury." *Access Control, Vol. 35, No. 3,* 38-39.

Reith, C. (1975). *The Blind Eye of History.* (Reprint Edition.) Montclair, NJ: Patterson Smith.

Spain, N.M. (1991). "Inadequate Security Litigation: A Legal Perspective." Unpublished manuscript.

Ursic, H.S. & Pagano, L.E. (1974). *Security Management Systems.* Springfield, IL: Charles C Thomas.

Security Education and Professional Development

2

SECURITY AND CRIME PREVENTION EDUCATION

Past and present efforts to provide quality security education can best be described as limited. However, there are some encouraging signs. The first significant efforts in educating people for private security occurred in the late 1950s at Michigan State University, with the establishment of a Bachelor of Science degree in Industrial Security Administration within the School of Police Administration. The first degrees were awarded during the 1958-59 academic year. It is significant that Michigan State University was already a recognized leader in police education and the degree program was connected with that effort.

Since this initial effort, most private security degree programs have been located within the broader program area of criminal justice. There are, however, significant numbers of private security professionals who feel that this is the wrong approach. They feel that private security education programs should be connected with business programs. A close look at most private security education programs indicates that the developers of the programs are aware of this philosophy because, almost without exception, the curricula include required and/or elective courses in business, as well as broad general education courses, criminal justice courses and specific security courses.

One of the most influential publications relating to the field of private security was distributed in 1972 by the American Society for Industrial Security/ASIS Foundation, Inc.: *Academic Guidelines for Security and Loss Prevention Programs in Community and Junior Colleges*. Most of the certificate and two-year associate degree programs use the curricula guidelines in this publication. Later in this chapter the guidelines are reproduced with further discussion of associate degree programs.

From an employment standpoint, the opportunities are most encouraging. Robert J. Fischer, Department of Law Enforcement Administration, Western Illinois University (WIU), surveyed 1,172 WIU law enforcement graduates in 1979 and found that 15.2 percent were employed in the private security field, even though the school offers only a minor in security administration. On a raw number and percentage basis, only public law enforcement had more persons employed. Other components of the criminal justice system (such as courts and corrections) had less.

Another survey of WIU graduates was conducted in 1985. By the time of the survey, WIU had more than 2,300 graduates. Once again, private security—at either the entry or administrative level—was second only to law enforcement careers. Thirty-eight percent were in law enforcement and 10 percent were in security. Other career fields, such as corrections and probation and parole, had much smaller percentages.

As part of his doctoral dissertation, Clifford W. Van Meter, School of Criminal Justice, Grand Valley State University, also surveyed WIU graduates from 1971 to 1976. This research indicated that approximately 10 percent of the graduates were employed in private security.

Additional research conducted by Fischer (and reported in his doctoral dissertation) provides additional information regarding employment in private security. Most graduates enter employment as management trainees in retail and industrial organizations. This is primarily because the starting salaries are reasonable and opportunities for promotion (especially in the retail field) attract graduates of private security education programs. Similar salaries and opportunities are not prevalent in contract security; this tends to reduce the number of college graduates seeking employment in contract security.

Although there has not been a rapid increase in the percentages of graduates entering private security during the last decade, the entry has been steady and can reasonably be expected to increase as the private security industry continues to grow—especially in relation to public law enforcement employment opportunities.

GUIDELINES FOR SECURITY DEGREE PROGRAMS

In 1977, the Report of the Task Force on Private Security provided an excellent overview of the entire subject of private security education. The Commentary for Standard 8.4 of the report is included because it provides a historical perspective. Most of the observations and recommendations are still pertinent at the present time.

Standard 8.4: Degree Programs for Private Security

The private security industry and the Law Enforcement Assistance Administration (LEAA) should cooperate in the encouragement and development of:

1) Certificate, Associate of Arts or Associate of Science degree programs designed to meet local industry needs;

2) Undergraduate and graduate programs designed to meet private security needs.

Although presently there is no comprehensive involvement by colleges and universities to provide educational opportunities for private security personnel, it should be recognized that there is little evidence that the security industry or government agencies have encouraged their development. This standard is based on the premise that the industry, LEAA, and educational institutions can cooperate with one another for mutual benefit.

Certificate and Associate Degree programs designed to meet the needs of the private security industry are a recent, but potentially significant, resource for improving the delivery of security services. *Academic Guidelines for Security and Loss Prevention Programs in Community and Junior Colleges* identified five certificate programs, two Associate Degree programs, and 58 junior or community colleges offering at least one security course. Research conducted by the Private Security Task Force revealed six certificate programs, 22 Associate Degree programs and 77 junior or community colleges offering at least one security course in 1976. *Private Security Trends 1970-2000: The Hallcrest Report II*, published in 1990, reported a growth to 49 certificate programs and 55 Associate Degree programs. It did not report the number of programs that had "some courses in private security." (Cunningham et al., 1990) Thus, although there has been growth in educational programs, the future offers great challenges to junior and community colleges to offer courses which would help develop the skills, knowledge, and judgment needed by private security personnel (see Figure 2.1 for a summary of the two curriculae).

Certain critics have voiced the opinion that because degree programs in Business Administration, Criminal Justice, Law Enforcement, and other related fields have provided appropriate educational backgrounds in the past for persons in private security, there is no need for specific private security degree programs at this time. Others maintain, however, that private security degree programs will not only enhance the professional movement in private security but also will promote needed research and technological advancements.

Three significant resolutions passed at the First National Conference on Private Security are pertinent to the future development of educational programs. These resolutions are:

1) A multidisciplinary and scholarly approach should be the core concept for the development of degree programs in private security.

2) There is a need to assess both the present and future human resources and training and educational requirements (managerial as well as technical) for the purpose of planning and developing academic programs.

3) There is a body of knowledge about the private security field sufficient to support realistic and meaningful two-year, four-year, and graduate-level college and university programs.

Figure 2.1
Suggested Curriculum for Associate Programs

FIRST YEAR

First Semester	Credits	Second Semester	Credits
English I	3	English II	3
General Psychology	3	Introduction to Sociology	3
Criminal and Civil Law I	3	Criminal and Civil Law II	3
Introduction to Security	3	Security Administration	3
Elective	3	Elective	3
	15		15
Electives:		Electives:	
Accounting I	3	Accounting II	3
Economics I	3	Economics II	3
Science I	3	Science II	3
Administration of Justice	3	Civil Rights & Civil Liberties	3
Principles of Interviewing	3	Report Writing	3
Industrial Relations	3		

SECOND YEAR

First Semester	Credits	Second Semester	Credits
Fundamentals of Speech	3	Criminal Investigation	3
Social Problems	3	Criminology	3
Human Relations	3	Labor & Management Relations	3
Principles of Loss Prevention	3	Current Security Problems	3
Elective	3	Elective	3
	15		15
Electives:		Electives:	
Document & Personnel Security	3	Commercial/Retail Security	3
Business Mathematics	3	Field Practicum	3
Emergency Preparedness	3	Industrial Fire Protection	3
Environmental Security	3	Security Education	3
Physical Security	3	Special Security Problems	3
Safety & Fire Prevention	3		

The following commentary is divided into two sub-areas: (1) Associate Degree programs, and (2) Baccalaureate and Graduate programs. These sub-areas correspond with the differentiation made by most educational institutions.

Associate Degree Programs

A useful starting point in program planning is the "Suggested Curriculum for Associate Programs" contained in *Academic Guidelines for Security and Loss Prevention Programs in Community and Junior Colleges* (see Figure 2.1). A number of educators have indicated that this curriculum could serve as an excellent guide. Detailed course descriptions and other relevant information about designing and implementing programs can be found in the publication.

It would be inappropriate to recommend a set curriculum, however, because any program of private security education should be developed to meet the needs of local industry. Also, before developing and implementing degree programs, a review should be conducted of the assistance that could be provided by colleges and universities through workshops, seminars, and courses (Standard 8.3). Immediate local industry needs can be better met by these forms of education. In any event, educational programs in appropriate forms should be designed with the specific needs of local industry in mind.

When developing degree programs, it may be difficult to identify the target population and to determine appropriate course content. However, it is strongly suggested that certificate, Associate of Arts, and Associate of Science degree programs be developed to include such subject matter as the following:

- Conducting security surveys
- Historical, philosophical, and legal bases of the security field
- Information security
- Interviewing and report writing
- Loss prevention techniques
- Personnel security
- Physical security
- Principles and practices of fire prevention and safety
- Supervision and leadership
- Unique security problems of hotels/motels, banks, manufacturing facilities, and so forth

Baccalaureate Degrees

The lack of viable baccalaureate and graduate degree programs is both a handicap and an advantage. On the negative side, no curriculum model is presently available comparable to that which exists for associate degrees; therefore, each institution would have to develop its own curriculum without a historical frame of reference. However, this handicap, with proper research and planning, can turn into an advantage because no precedents exist that might need to be removed or modified during the developmental process. The following task force viewpoints for development of baccalaureate and graduate programs in private security (not listed in order of importance) are offered for consideration by educators:

Planning Phase

1) Each academic department of law enforcement/criminal justice should determine the number of graduates employed in the private security industry.

2) The academic departments of law enforcement/criminal justice should be the catalyst for development of security administration degree programs, but colleges of business need to be consulted and their courses incorporated into any degree programs. The disciplines of sociology, psychology, and law also should be included in the degree program.

3) New courses should be designed to incorporate the body of knowledge about private security subjects, instead of adapting existing law enforcement/criminal justice courses to meet private security needs. For example, one or two law courses should be developed to relate pertinent legal aspects of the private security industry, rather than requiring security administration students to take a law course designed to prepare students for public law enforcement careers.

4) An advisory board, consisting of private security personnel, should be appointed to assist colleges and universities during the planning phase. This board should remain active after the program is initiated.

5) Boards of higher education in each state should closely monitor all degree proposals in security administration to preclude proliferation of degree programs and to coordinate transfer arrangements between educational institutions.

6) Baccalaureate and Master's degree programs should be designed to prepare students for entrance-level or middle-management positions. Some overlap and duplication of course offerings in certificate and associate degree programs may be necessary, but it should be kept to a minimum.

Implementation Phase

Each institution should determine the most appropriate way to implement private security curriculums, depending on available personnel and physical and financial resources. The following three-step process is recommended:

1) Introduce private security courses; then if needed,

2) Develop a private security minor; then, if needed,

3) Develop Baccalaureate and/or Master's degree program(s).

Between 1977 and 1990, there was an encouraging trend toward more Baccalaureate Degree programs. The 1977 study conducted by the Private Security Task Force reported five programs; *Private Security Trends 1970-2000: The Hallcrest Report II* showed a growth to 46 programs (Figure 2.2). Another significant trend is indicated by the fact that there were no Master's Degree programs in 1977, but by 1990 there were 14 graduate programs. There are presently 51 two- and four-year degree programs in security. It is recognized that many suggestions regarding curriculum design are arbitrary; however, it has been established that a security degree should be interdisciplinary. The contemporary security professional must have a broad and balanced educational background consisting of general education, human relations, business practices, legal issues, loss prevention and control, and security. How else can the security professional function and be successful in accomplishing the tasks of preventing and controlling losses within an organizational environment? There must be an acute awareness and functional understanding of the role of security, how it fits particular and often unique organizational environments, and how it should be perceived and implemented within the context of various activities (e.g., marketing, production, personnel, maintenance, and/or retail, health services, transportation, manufacturing, etc.).

Figure 2.2
Higher Education in Private Security
(Number of Programs Nationwide)

	1977	1990
Some courses in private security	77	Not Reported
Certificate	6	49
Associate Degree	22	55
Baccalaureate Degree	5	46
Master's Degree	0	14

Source: William C. Cunningham, John J. Strauchs, and Clifford W. Van Meter (1990). *Private Security Trends 1970-2000: The Hallcrest Report II,* Table 5.6, p. 150. Stoneham, MA: Butterworth-Heinemann.

An important source on higher education for the security professional is the ongoing work of the Pinkerton Lecture Series, ASIS Foundation, Webster University, and John Jay College of Criminal Justice. Together these three organizations formed the *Annual Academic/Practitioner Symposium.* The purpose of the symposium was to identify a common body of knowledge, essential to all security professionals and to create a survey course in security for business school students. The topics that were identified include: Risk Management, Legal Issues, Investigations, Personnel Integrity and Protection, Technical Management, Information Protection, Intelligence, Current/Topical Security Issues; and Asset Protection and Management. Details regarding the Symposium and the Monograph are available from the American Society of Industrial Security.

Figure 2.3
Security Executives' Rankings of Academically Oriented Training Seminar Topics

SEMINAR TOPICS	PERCENTAGE OF RESPONDENTS			MEAN SCORE*
	No/Minor Need (1)	Some/ Adequate Need (2)	High/Most Need (3)	(4)
1. Total Quality Management Applied in the Security Setting	7.9	38.6	63.5	3.5
2. Marketing Security Within the Corporation	8.2	36.8	54.0	3.5
3. New Technologies for Security in the Industrial Setting	5.9	44.9	49.2	3.4
4. Computer and Telecommunications Security	5.4	45.3	49.4	3.4
5. Finance and Tax Laws Regarding Security Protection for the Non-Financial Manager	21.3	60.4	18.3	2.5
6. Meeting Management Skills	7.2	48.1	44.7	3.3
7. Computer Security Training and Law—Case Studies	10.2	57.5	32.3	3.0
8. Facilitator and Intervention Management Skills	8.0	56.3	35.7	3.0
9. Effective Organizational Design and Management Development	6.5	44.3	49.2	3.4
10. Presentation and Marketing Skill	10.0	49.2	40.8	3.2
11. Crisis Management Studies— Case Studies	5.8	50.6	43.6	3.3
12. International Criminal Justice System Overview	35.4	53.4	11.2	2.1

*Scale 0-5 with 5 being the most important.

Source: *Journal of Security Administration*, 1995 (18)2, p. 27.

Another significant guide to the development or revision of Bachelor's and Master's degree programs can be found in the material provided by Merry Morash, Director, School of Criminal Justice, Michigan State University

(MSU), to participants in "Security Education: Vision 2000" at the end of the forum sponsored by MSU in December, 1992. Following are some highlights from the forum responses.

Undergraduate and Master's Level Curriculum

- Operational, technical, and legal areas of study focused on criminal justice and security are most important at the bachelor's level, specific to security, personnel, information, and physical security are considered to be very important for undergraduates

- Within the criminal justice and security curriculum, research and conceptual and global issues are most important for master's level graduates

- Communication skills and computer security management are ranked as more important than other "traditional" areas considered to be part of a security curriculum, and this is true for both graduate and undergraduate students

- At the bachelor's level, students should have exposure to business courses in the areas of business presentations, discretion and ethics, leadership, strategic planning, and motivation and training of employees

- Employers place some emphasis on graduate students' capacity to deal with issues of privacy and ethics

- Several areas of social science are important for both undergraduates and graduates—most notably group dynamics and behavior, psychology of individuals, employee and labor relations, and industrial psychology

- There was a recognition that the Master's Degree in particular should include course work in foreign policy analysis, cultural diversity, and international relations

Demands for Multidisciplinary Education

- The highest projected need for hiring was of students earning a Bachelor's Degree with a combined background in business and security, or computer science and security

- For master's-level students, there was a projected need to hire more individuals with combined business and security course work, or computer science and security course work, than students with just one area of concentration

Executive Training Needs

- The top executive training needs are in the areas of
  —Total Quality Management
  —Marketing Security within Corporations
  —Computer and Telecommunications Security
  —Presentation and Marketing Skills

The Bachelor of Science program in Assets Protection and Security at Eastern Kentucky University provides an example of an interdisciplinary degree program (see Figure 2.4).

Figure 2.4
Assets Protection and Security Degree Requirements (Core Classes):

Principles of Assets Protection

Security Technology Systems

Assets Protection Law

Assets Protection Management

Assets Protection Ethics and Policy

Government Compliance

Assets Protection Auditing

Applied Assets Protection
plus three hours upper division courses in Assets Protection

Program curricula must be designed to meet the needs of the marketplace, i.e., graduates must possess the prerequisites required for employment in the field of security. Additionally, the curriculum must be dynamic in that it is constantly evaluated and changed to include technological innovations, emerging problems, and critical issues confronting the contemporary security practitioner.

PROFESSIONAL DEVELOPMENT AND TRAINING

SEMINARS, WORKSHOPS, AND NONCREDIT COURSES

Practitioners, many of whom entered private security before private security education was generally available, cannot avail themselves of traditional educational opportunities. Thus, one of the best opportunities for colleges and universities to assist private security is through seminars, workshops, and noncredit courses. In addition, the rapidly changing technology for private security offers an opportunity for colleges and universities to serve as a catalyst to bring information about this technology to practitioners through specific training programs.

Participants at the First National Conference on Private Security resolved that "shared or cooperative training programs utilizing resources of private security, public law enforcement, education and training institutions (should) be pursued to meet the training needs of private security." Training programs need to be developed for both operational and management personnel. Individual programs should be developed in cooperation with local private security employees, associations, and college and university officials. Figure 2.3 provides a reference for developing seminars, workshops, and noncredit courses for private security.

For any list to be meaningful for course development, survey respondents should be requested to set priorities. If need in particular areas is established, several separate courses could become subjects contained in a longer seminar. For example, first aid, firearms training, and patrol methods might be covered in one seminar or workshop for operational personnel.

These abbreviated courses can fill the present short-range need for educational opportunities while academic programs are being developed. Later, they can support the regular academic classes while giving educational institutions a mechanism to provide information to meet continually changing private security situations.

The opportunities for innovative use of seminars and short courses to meet private security needs are apparent. Educational institutions, in cooperation with the private security industry, should take the initiative to provide the physical and personnel resources to implement this standard.

IMPACT OF EDUCATION AND FUTURE DIRECTIONS

A survey conducted for the ASIS Foundation was reported in *Security Management*, February, 1996. The survey involved 227 women. Based on the results, the average woman in security management is 45 years old, is married with children, works for a medium-sized company in the service sector, earns $49,500 per year, has been in the security field for 13 years, has been promoted by her current employer, holds the title of manager, has experienced gender discrimination, and is often under stress on the job.

From an educational standpoint, 8.8 percent have a high school diploma, 28.8 percent have some college, 11.5 percent have associate's degree, 23.9 percent have bachelor's degree, 13.7 percent some graduate work, and 13.3 percent have a graduate degree. Their mean salaries by title are: Supervisor—$42,100, Director—$45,000, Manager—$51,600, and President—$54,500.

Another perspective on the importance of education appeared in the Guardsmark ad in the July, 1998 issue of *Security Management*. It noted that 95 percent of their management have at least four years of college and about 30 percent of their security officers have attended college.

Another source, *Security Management*, August, 1996, reported an analysis of management salaries based on a study conducted by the ASIS.

Level of Education	Average Annual Income
No Degree	$45,843
Some College (no degree)	$65,471
Associate Degree	$61,927
Bachelor's Degree	$66,617
Graduate Degree	$69,073

The most significant research in recent years pertaining to the importance of education in security was conducted by Mahesh K. Nalla and his colleagues at Michigan State University. Their study, reported in *Journal of Security Administration*, 1995 18(2) provides insight into the hiring plans and preferences for undergraduate and graduate degrees. Figure 2.3 summarizes the findings.

One of the continuing problems is the lack of information on the number of degree programs in the United States. During the research for this edition, no comprehensive studies could be found, therefore, the studies conducted by the Private Security Task Force in 1977 and Hallcrest II in 1990 (see Table 16.2) remain the most current. However, a significant effort is being made by ASIS to develop a catalog database for college and university programs in security, private security, and security management. This information will be posted on the ASIS website.

Two graduate programs which have the potential to provide nonresident degree opportunities have recently been initiated. Webster University, St. Louis, MO, has established a graduate degree program at various locations.

The listing of the courses, in the March, 1995 issue of *Security Management,* provides an indication of the focus of the program.

• Security Contracting and Acquisitions Management

• Security Budgeting and Resource Management

• Investigations Management

• Regulatory Aspects of Safety and Environmental Protection

• Logistical Security Management

• Government Security Management

• Terrorism—Tactics, Trends, and Countermeasures

An international effort, through a distance learning program designed for completion over two years, has been initiated by the Scarman Centre at the University of Leicester, in Leicester, England.

Since 1997, the ASIS Foundation has been sponsoring Academic/Practitioner Symposiums in an effort to develop, among other objectives, a body of knowledge for security. Another significant effort is to establish a security course directed primarily toward business students. A draft of the proposed curricula, presented at the 1998 meeting at John Jay College in New York consisted of chapter headings of: risk assessment, legal aspects, investigations, personnel integrity and protection, technical management, information protection, intelligence, issues, and asset protection and management.

SUMMARY

In summary, higher education and training provide the foundation and impetus for improving the professional competence and image of the security industry. There should not be any question as to the value and importance of education and professional training for the security practitioner. The complexities and dynamics of society, the workplace, and the world dictate the need for security professionals who are university educated and prepared to confront a myriad of changing issues and problems.

DISCUSSION QUESTIONS

1. List and discuss the three resolutions passed at the First National Conference on Private Security regarding private security education.

2. How should a college or university go about the development of a security curriculum?

3. Discuss the attributes of an interdisciplinary approach to security education.

4. Discuss the hiring plans in relation to the undergraduate and graduate majors.

REFERENCES

Calder, J., CCP (1975). "Resolutions of the National Conference on Private Security." College Park, MD: University of Maryland, final draft, 1975.

(1985). "College Security Program List Revised." *Journal of Security Administration*, 8:1, 1985.

Collins, P. (1996). "Mastering Sakerhet in Sweden." *Security Management,* October, 1996, 65-70.

(1997). *Columbia College Degree Completion Bulletin, 1997-1999.* Columbia, MO: Columbia College, 1997.

Conrad, J. ed. (1975). Department of Law Enforcement, Western Illinois University, Newsletter #1, Academic Year 1975-1976.

Cunningham, W. Strauchs, J. and Van Meter, C. (1990). *Private Security Trends 1970-2000: The Hallcrest Report II.* Stoneham, MA: Butterworth-Heinemann, 1990.

Cunningham, W. and Taylor, T. (1985). *Private Security and Police in America.* Portland, OR: Chancellor Press, 1985.

Dalton, O. (1997). "Effective Contract Security Management: How to Identify and Select a Qualified Security Provider." Access Control Systems [online].

Fabianic, D. (1998). "The Status of Criminal Justice Ph.D. Programs in Higher Education." *Journal of Criminal Justice*, Vol. 26, No. 5, 1998, 399-408.

Fauth, K., CPP (1975). "The Need for Security Education at the Postsecondary Level." Unpublished doctoral dissertation, 1975.

Fischer, R. (1981). "The Development of Baccalaureate Degree Programs in Private Security 1957-1980." Unpublished doctoral dissertation, Southern Illinois University, 1981.

Flanagan, T. et al. (1998). "Academic Advising in Baccalaureate Criminology and Criminal Justice Programs: A National Assessment." *Journal of Criminal Justice Education*, Vol. 9, No. 2 Fall 1998, 236-239.

(1998). "Foundation Endorses BSA Program." *Security Management*, September, 1995, 179.

Friend, B. (1968). "Profile of the Physical Security Officer: Specialization or Professionalism." Unpublished master's thesis, Michigan State University, 1968.

(1998). *Introduction to Security for Business Students*. Alexandria, VA: American Society for Industrial Security, 1998.

Johnson, B., Van Meter, C., and Walker, R. (1995). "The Effectiveness of Computer-Based Education in Criminal Justice Undergraduate Curricula: An Evaluation." *Police Computer Review*, Vol. 4, No. 3, 1995, 11-18.

Kingsbury, A. (1972). *Academic Guidelines for Security and Loss Prevention Programs in Community and Junior Colleges*. Washington, DC: American Society for Industrial Security, 1972.

Langer, S. (1996). "The Wages of Security." *Security Management*, August, 1996, 76-78.

Larkins, H. (1966). "A Survey of Experiences, Activities, and Views of the Industrial Security Administration Graduates of Michigan State University." Unpublished Master's thesis, Michigan State University, 1966.

(1975). *Law Enforcement and Criminal Justice Education Directory, 1975-1976*, Gaithersburg, MD: International Association of Chiefs of Police, 1977.

Longmore-Etheridge, A. (1996). "Survey Studies Women in Security." *Security Management*, February, 1996, 87-88.

(1970). "Macomb College Looks at Security Education, Industrial Security." *Security Management*, September, 1974.

Moore, M. (1972). "A Study of the Placement and Utilization Patterns and Views of the Criminal Justice Graduates of Michigan State University." Unpublished doctoral dissertation, Michigan State University, 1972.

Nalla, M. et al. (1995). "Hiring Preferences of Security Professionals." *Journal of Security Administration*, 1995, 18(2), 29-40.

Ortmeier, P. (1996). "Adding Class to Security." *Security Management*, July, 1996, 99-101.

(1998). "Second Academic/Practitioner Symposium Held." *Security Management*, December, 1998, 105.

(1998). *Proceedings of the 1997 Educational Symposium*. Alexandria, VA: American Society for Industrial Security, 1998.

(1998). *Security Business Practices Reference*. Alexandria, VA: American Society for Industrial Security, 1998.

(1998)."Survey Says Big-City Chiefs Are Better Educated Outsiders." New York: *Law Enforcement News*, Vol. XXIV, No. 488, April 30, 1998, 7.

(1997). "Symposium on Security to be Held at Webster." *Security Management*, March, 1997, 108.

(1984). "To What Degree?" *Security Management*, 28:4, 1984.

Van Meter, C. (1982). "Perceptions of Selected Criminal Justice Graduates, Faculty, and Police Chiefs on the Impact of Education on Job Performance, Promotion, and Job Satisfaction." Unpublished doctoral dissertation, Southern Illinois University, 1982.

(1995). "Webster College Program Evolves." *Security Management*, March, 1995, 77.

Protective Security and Crime Prevention Services/Resources

3

INTRODUCTION

Increasingly, administrators and managers in many areas of our social, government, and economic systems are recognizing that all problems of disruptions, thefts, vandalism, assaults, etc., cannot be solved through the services and resources of traditional public police agencies. An expanding and variable economy, coupled with increasing crime rates (in most categories), has resulted in the police being unable to protect business and industry, hospitals, transportation centers, and the like. Public law enforcement cannot be expected to provide protection against computer crimes, employee theft and fraud, and other complex economic crimes, most of which occur behind the doors of the workplace. The police cannot patrol corporate plants, office buildings, or computer facilities; they must await requests for police assistance or legal cause to be involved. Additionally, technological advances and innovations have created new and valuable kinds of assets and processes that are often beyond the protective and investigative capabilities of public law enforcement involvement. For these reasons and others, traditional and emerging users of the private security industry are demanding significant increases in guard services, protective alarm services, armored car services, private investigative services, locksmith services, and security consultant services.

The costs and inconveniences associated with numerous acts of unlawful conduct and unethical practices have influenced owners and managers in such areas as transportation, commerce, healthcare, retailing, industry, government, and schools to look beyond their own resources and those of public law enforcement to alternative means of protection, i.e., private security. Without question, the primary impetus for the services and resources that can be provided by private security is economic crime. *Private Security Trends 1970-2000: The Hallcrest Report II* estimated that American businesses lose $114 billion or more per year to economic crime.

Economic crime is illicit behavior having as its object the unjust enrichment of the perpetrator at the expense of the economic system as a whole and its individual components. The consequences of economic crime are increased costs that are passed on to consumers and taxpayers and that place a financial burden upon business, the government, and, ultimately, the public. It encompasses the terms of white-collar crime, crimes against business, management fraud, ordinary workplace crimes, and fraud against the government, business, and consumers (Cunningham et al., 1990:19-20).

Thus, the impact of economic crime on American citizens is pervasive and inescapable. Businesses and citizens spend $52 billion annually for security products and services to combat crime and prevent losses (Cunningham et al., 1990:19). Until economic crime and other significant influences (e.g., drug abuse, terrorism, etc.) can be diminished, the demand for private security services will continue to increase.

SECURITY SERVICES/RESOURCES

Currently there are approximately 92,270 private security companies involved in the provision of security services and products. Some of these companies may offer a wide variety of security services and products while others provide a singular service or product. Security services are estimated to generate approximately $62 billion annually, growing at a rate of 7.9 percent per year, with security services and products to exceed 100,000 by the year 2006 (Security Business, 1996). Correspondingly, the employees of these businesses may perform limited security duties, as do some receptionists and nightwatch guards assigned to often perfunctory positions of responsibility and authority; or some may work in highly specialized fields, such as the investigation of computer crimes and alarm services. Regardless of the company's size or range of services and products or the level of employee responsibility and expertise, these businesses are involved in the overall protective services of our communities and nation. As such, they have a direct and important bearing on crime prevention and crime reduction. Figure 3.1 depicts the composition of private security employment for the top 10 major segments of the security industry from 1996 to the year 2006 (Bureau of Labor Statistics). Revenues from these security services were projected to be $25 billion by the year 2000, growing at an annual rate of 7.9 percent. The security equipment industry revenues were estimated at $13 billion by the year 2000 and growing at a rate of 8 percent annually. By the year 2006, security services are projected to generate as much as $112 billion (Security Business, 1996).

Figure 3.1
Growth of Private Security 1996-2006

Industry	1996 Employment		Projected 2006 employment		Change, 1996-2006	
	Number	Percent distribution	Number	Percent distribution	Number	Percent
Total, all industries	954,644	100.00	1,175,257	100.00	220,613	23.1
Miscellaneous business services	558,563	58.51	759,752	64.65	201,189	36.0
Education, public and private	41,249	4.32	43,758	3.72	2,510	6.1
Real estate operators and lessors	39,124	4.10	39,860	3.39	736	1.9
Hospitals, public and private	35,517	3.72	34,322	2.92	-1,196	-3.4
Hotels and other lodging places	26,961	2.82	31,396	2.67	4,435	16.5
Real estate agents and managers	21,090	2.21	24,016	2.04	2,925	13.9
Local government, except education and hospitals	18,305	1.92	18,016	1.53	-289	-1.6
Department stores	17,919	1.88	15,859	1.35	-2,060	-11.5
All other amusement and recreation facilities	12,068	1.26	14,611	1.24	2,544	21.1
Museums and botanical and zoological gardens	6,618	0.69	7,992	0.68	1,374	20.8

GUARD AND PATROL SERVICES

There are approximately 10,000 security companies in the United States, employing 1.8 million guards (Security Letter, 1997). Guard and patrol services include personnel who work in such places as industrial plants, financial institutions, educational institutions, office buildings, retail establishments, commercial complexes (including hotels and motels), healthcare facilities, recreation facilities, libraries and museums, residence and housing developments, charitable institutions, transportation vehicles and facilities (public and common carriers), and warehouses and goods distribution depots. They perform the following functions either contractually or internally:

- Prevention and/or detection of intrusion, unauthorized entry or activity, vandalism or trespass on private property;

- Prevention and/or detection of theft, loss, embezzlement, misappropriation, or concealment of merchandise, money, bonds, stocks, notes, or other valuable documents or papers;

- Control, regulation, or direction of the flow or movements of the public, whether by vehicle or otherwise, to assure the protection of property;

- Protection of individuals from bodily harm; and

- Enforcement of rules, regulations, and policies related to crime reduction.

These functions may be provided at one location or several. Guard functions are generally provided at one central location for one client or employer. Patrol functions, however, are performed at several locations, often for several clients.

To the general public, the uniformed security guard seen at retail stores, industrial plants, office complexes, banks, hospitals, sports complexes, and governmental facilities is the most visible part of the private security industry. Some wear the distinctive insignia of the organization being protected, while others wear the insignia of a private, contractual guard firm. Security officers held about 955,000 jobs in 1996. Industrial security firms and guard agencies employed 59 percent of all guards. Employment opportunities in this area are expected to be favorable through the year 2006. Compared to unarmed security guards, armed guards and special police enjoy higher earnings and benefits, greater job security, more advancement potential, and are usually given more training and responsibility. Demand for security officers will grow as private security firms increasingly perform duties such as monitoring crowds at airports and providing security in courts—duties formerly handled by government police officers and marshals. In either case, individual officers may be armed or unarmed (current estimates are that only 10 percent of all security personnel are armed). There are, then, two distinct types of guard services: (1) contract guard services and (2) proprietary guard services.

1. CONTRACT GUARD SERVICES

This type of guard service is purchased from a firm outside the organization, generally for a rate per guard hour. The rate per guard hour that the contract security firm receives covers the cost of the guard's salary, fringe benefits, worker's compensation, liability insurance, office expenses, telephone services, travel expenses, and supervisory salaries. The guard personnel are employees of the contracting firm. Their duties and responsibilities, whether highly technical or mundane, are defined by the contract and administered by the contracting agency. Management and/or supervisory personnel of the contracting firm are usually consulted for advice and assistance before any new security program is implemented. Most new security programs are carried out by the personnel from the contracting firm. Such contracting agencies may be very large international organizations, such as Pinkerton or Burns, or they might be very small and operate in a limited geographical area.

In recent years, contract guard services have grown and changed in response to economic and technological developments, reductions in the funding of public services, and changing client demands. Developments have led to an industry-wide focus on several important issues: (1) the trade-off between cost and quality of service, (2) liability and insurance, (3) the delivery of quality service, (4) client expectations of quality and protection, (5) training, (6) guard turnover, and (7) government regulations.

Once wages, benefits, and fees are agreed upon and the contract is signed, contract guard firms must take steps to ensure that the quality service they advertised will actually be delivered. Adequate funding to allow good pay and benefits is only the first step. Good hiring practices, training programs, close supervision, and a sensible management structure are also important.

The issue of liability and insurance is generally recognized as a serious problem for the security field. Liability issues are closely aligned to employee turnover, training, and quality of employees. As more security personnel are involved in questionable practices, more suits are filed. When the courts award plaintiffs large settlements, contract security firms find their insurance rates rapidly escalating. Most insurance companies are becoming increasingly reluctant to insure high-risk contract security firms.

Government regulations, especially state statutes, will provide the needed impetus to establish standards for employment and training. Such standards should dictate a balance between contract and proprietary guard services and armed versus unarmed personnel.

The majority of contract security companies have less than 8,000 employees. The five largest contract security companies are the (1) Borg-Warner Security Corporation: Loomis Wells Fargo Armored Car Service – employs more than 88,000 security personnel and has revenues of $1.2 billion; (2) Pinkerton Corporation: Contract Security Officers and Investigators – employs 45,000 security personnel and has revenues of $747 million; (3) The Wackenhut Corporation: Contract Security Officers and Investigators – employs 22,000 security personnel and has revenues of $580 million; (4) American Protective Services: Contract Security Officers and Investigators – employs 16,500 and has revenues of $354 million; (5) Guardsmark Corporation: Contract Security Officers and Investigators – employs 11,500 and has revenues of $212 million (Security Letter, 1997:1).

> The median annual earnings of guards who worked full time in 1996 were about $17,300. Depending on the guards experience, newly hired guards in the Federal Government earned $15,500 or $17,500 a year in 1997. Guards employed by the Federal Government averaged about $22,900 a year in 1997. (Bureau of Labor Statistics, 1999)

2. PROPRIETARY GUARD SERVICES

Proprietary guard services are often referred to as "in-house security" because the security personnel are employees of the organization being protected. Salaries and other benefits are paid directly to the employee in contrast to the way contracting firm personnel are paid. Duties and responsibilities are defined and controlled by the organization, not by an outside agency. Managers and supervisors of proprietary security personnel, as part of management, are often involved in the corporate decision-making processes of planning and implementing security and safety programs. Many such in-house security forces are referred to as plant protection units, because their duties include accident prevention and investigation, complicated control of traffic and pedestrian movement, clearance and escort of non-employees, fire prevention and protection, as well as basic law enforcement within the facility.

INVESTIGATIVE SERVICES

Investigations represent a service that either internal security professionals or external investigators are uniquely equipped to perform for an organization. Investigations are often necessary to gather information on specific situations or events such as embezzlement, pre-employment screening, workers compensation fraud, theft, litigation investigations, accident reconstruction, kickbacks, and a long list of specific investigative activities. Investigative techniques vary depending upon the type of investigation. For example, if the case involves a retail environment, investigations techniques could involve covert surveillance to detect employees stealing merchandise or cash, or the use of a shopping service which uses persons to come into the store and make a series of purchases to test the honesty of the employee. For example they may make a purchase for the correct amount and leave without taking their receipt. A dishonest employee could void the receipt and keep the cash. Investigations in a retail environment may involve dishonest customers who steal merchandise. In these instances, closed-circuit cameras (CCTV) are used to videotape the thieves. Although security professionals may be called upon to conduct various types of incidents, there are generally seven types of investigations that require specific skills: (1) legal investigations, (2) corporate investigations, (3) financial investigations, (4) loss prevention investigations, (5) insurance fraud investigations, (6) computer fraud investigations, and (7) core investigations.

Legal investigations require the investigator to specialize in cases involving the courts. Legal investigators assist in preparing both criminal defenses and civil litigation, both of which require specific investigative techniques. For example, in criminal defense cases, the investigator often locates witnesses, interviews the police, gathers and reviews evidence, takes photographs, and testifies in court. In civil litigation cases, they interview prospective witnesses, collect information on the parties to the litigation, and search out testimonial, documentary, or physical evidence.

Corporate investigators normally conduct internal and external investigations. An external investigation may consist of undercover operations aimed at preventing criminal schemes, thefts of company assets, or fraudulent deliveries of products by suppliers. In internal investigations, they may investigate drug use in the workplace, ensure that expense accounts are not abused, and determine if employees are stealing merchandise or information.

Financial investigators are skilled in accounting and finance and tend to focus on developing a case against an employee or client who is suspected of embezzlement or fraud schemes. They begin by developing confidential financial profiles of individuals or companies who may be parties to large financial transactions and often work with investment bankers and accountants to determine how a theft is occurring and who would have the opportunity, desire, and motive to perpetrate the fraud. Often individuals specializing in financial investigations will have the Certified Fraud Investigator certification. A recent case of Internet investment fraud was uncovered by Federal securities investigators. There were four separate schemes which deceived investors worldwide by fraudulently promoting stocks in Internet junk mail and message boards, online newsletters, and Web sites. The perpetrators collected nearly one-half million dollars from the "pump and dump" scheme. They raised the value of junk stocks by making false claims about the company and then sold their stock shares for artificially high prices. This is just one case uncovered by a nationwide crackdown against cyberspace investment fraud (*USA Today*, Friday, Feb. 2, 1999). This type of fraud has created an entirely new financial fraud niche for investigators with both financial and computer skills.

Loss prevention investigators often work for retail organizations and are responsible for investigating both internal and external theft of assets. They are responsible for safeguarding the assets of retail stores by apprehending employees and customers who steal merchandise, cash, or destroy property. They also conduct periodic inspections or audits of stock areas, dressing rooms, and often assist in the opening and closing of the store.

Insurance fraud investigators are becoming more and more prevalent as insurance companies have come to recognize the tremendous amount of losses associated with insurance fraud, which is estimated in excess of $120 billion annually. These investigators have either academic or professional experience in the insurance profession and work on many different types of cases in which individuals or groups are attempting to fraud the insurance carrier. Insurance fraud occurs in all types of insurance, including automobile, workers compensation, disability, healthcare, life, and homeowners. An insurance holding company, Twentieth Century Industries, filed an $8 million lawsuit against a Glendale, California chiropractor. The insurance company claimed that the doctor submitted fraudulent bills to patients and the insurance company. More specifically, the fraud scheme was called "upcoding." This is a technique by which physicians and other medical staff bill patients and insurance companies for more expensive medical procedures than what was actually performed (Twentieth Century Press, 1999).

A rapidly growing area of insurance fraud investigations is the healthcare industry. A growing number of insurance commissions throughout the United States have mandated that health insurance assume responsibility for unnecessary losses that result from fraud. In order to comply with these mandates, healthcare organizations must:

1) Report all fraudulent activities to appropriate state and federal agencies;

2) Develop a written anti-fraud plan for insurance commissions;

3) Provide training in fraud and abuse sensitivity and corrective actions; and

4) Establish anti-fraud and abuse units.

An excellent source for insurance fraud investigations is the National Insurance Crime Bureau. The Bureau is a not-for-profit organization that provides investigative services for insurers and law enforcement agencies in the investigation and prosecution of organized rings and persons or companies perpetrating insurance fraud. Their Web site is http://www.nicb.org.

Computer fraud investigators represent a rapidly growing discipline for the millennium. According to a study reported in *The Baltimore Business Journal* in 1997, "half of the largest companies in the world have been victims of fraud during the past year, with 25 percent of them losing one million or more in the past five years." These types of investigations rely upon a technique referred to as computer forensics. This computer investigative technique refers to the art and science of building evidence to prove computer or cyber-criminal activities exist. Computer security investigators turn to such organizations as Information Systems Security Association (ISSA), the Computer Security Institute (CSI) and the System Administration Networking and Security Groups (SANS). Computer security professionals are strongly encouraged to obtain the certification designation of Certified Information Systems Security Professional (CISSP). For more information, visit the Web site at http://www.isc2.org/.

The core investigative services provided by either the investigative component of private security may be provided contractually or internally at places and facilities such as industrial plants, financial institutions, educational institutions, retail establishments, commercial complexes, hotels and motels, and healthcare facilities. The services are provided for a variety of clients, including insurance companies, law firms, retailers, and individuals. Investigative personnel are primarily concerned with obtaining information with reference to any of the following matters:

1) Crimes or wrongs committed or threatened;

2) The identity, habits, conduct, movements, whereabouts, affiliations, associations, transactions, reputation, or character of any person, group of persons, association, organization, society, other group of persons, or partnership or corporation;

3) Pre-employment background checks of personnel applicants;

4) The conduct, honesty, efficiency, loyalty, or activities of employees, agents, contractors, and subcontractors;

5) Incidents and illicit or illegal activities by persons against the employer or employer's property;

6)   Retail shoplifting;

7)   Internal theft by employees or other employee crime;

8)   The truth or falsity of any statement or representation;

9)   The whereabouts of missing persons;

10) The location or recovery of lost or stolen property;

11) The causes, origin of or responsibility for fires, libel or slander, losses, accidents, injuries or damages to property;

12) The credibility of informants, witnesses, or other persons; and

13) The securing of evidence to be used before investigating committees, boards of award or arbitration, or in the trial of civil or criminal cases and the preparation thereof.

Detective or investigative activity is distinguished from the guard or watch function in that the investigator obtains information, whereas guard or watch personnel usually act on information (or events). Employment of private detectives and investigators is expected to grow through the year 2006. Increased demand for private detectives and investigators is expected to be generated by fear of crime, increased litigation, and the need to protect confidential information and property of all kinds. Additionally, private investigators will be needed by law firms to meet the needs for criminal defense and civil litigation among companies and individuals. Greater corporate financial activity worldwide will increase the demand for investigators to control internal and external financial losses as well as to discover what competitors are doing to prevent industrial spying.

Earnings of private detectives and investigators vary greatly depending on their employer, speciality, and the geographic area in which they work. According to a study by Abbott, Langer & Associates, security/loss prevention directors and vice presidents earned an average $67,700 a year in 1996, investigators about $37,800 a year, and store detectives about $19,100.

ALARM SERVICES

Alarm services include selling, installing, servicing, and emergency response to alarm signal devices. Alarm devices are employed in one of four basic modes: local alarm, proprietary alarm, central station alarm, or police-connected alarm. Alarm signal devices include a variety of equipment, ranging from simple magnetic switches to complex ultrasonic Doppler and sound systems. Various electronic, electromechanical and photoelectrical devices, and microwave Dopplers are also utilized.

Alarm personnel include three categories of employees: alarm sales personnel, alarm systems installers/servicers, and alarm respondents. Persons in alarm sales engage in customer/client contact, pre-sale security surveys, and post-sale customer relations. Alarm installers and servicers are trained technicians who install and wire alarm systems, perform scheduled maintenance, and provide emergency servicing as well as regular repair of alarm systems. (Alarm installers and servicers may be the same, depending on the employer.) Alarm respondents respond to an alarm condition at the protected site of a client. The alarm respondent inspects the protected site to determine the nature of the alarm, protects or secures the client's facility for the client until alarm system integrity can be restored, and assists law enforcement agencies according to local arrangements. The alarm respondent may be armed and also may be a servicer.

ARMORED CAR AND ARMED COURIER SERVICES

Armored car services include the provision of protection, safekeeping, and secured transportation of currency, coins, bullion, securities, bonds, jewelry, or other items of value. This secured transportation, from one place or point to another place or point, is accomplished by specially constructed bullet-resistant armored vehicles and vaults under armed guard. Armed courier services also include the armed protection and transportation (from one place or point to another place or point) of currency, coins, bullion, securities, bonds, jewelry, or other articles of unusual value. Armed courier services are distinguished from armored car services in that the transportation is provided by means other than specially constructed bullet-resistant armored vehicles. There are also courier service companies that employ non-armed persons to transport documents, business papers, checks, and other time-sensitive items that require expeditious delivery.

The major distinction between the services provided by armored cars and armed couriers and those furnished by guards and watch personnel is liability. Armored car guards and armed couriers are engaged exclusively in the safe transportation and custody of valuables, and the firms providing these services are liable for the face, declared, or contractual value of the client's property. These service companies are bailees of the valuable property and the guards and couriers are protecting the property of their employer. This liability extends from the time the valuables are received until the time a receipt is executed by the consignee at delivery. Except for war risks, the armored car company is absolutely liable for the valuable property during protective custody. Conversely, guards, watch personnel and their employers do not assume comparable liability for the property being protected.

CRIME PREVENTION SERVICES

Many commercial enterprises, industrial operations, institutional facilities, and private homes utilize a wide variety of protective security equipment and related services. Access control systems, intrusion detection alarms, robbery alert alarms, safes and security storage containers, security lighting equipment, security fencing and barriers, locking hardware, bomb detection and X-ray equipment, computer security equipment, fire detection systems, and so on, are manufactured, sold, installed, maintained and/or monitored by many companies throughout the country. Currently, alarm companies and manufacturers/distributors of protective security equipment products and services account for approximately 32 percent of all companies involved in the private security industry. By the year 2000, more than 92,000 companies will be in the business of providing security products and services. The industrial and manufacturing sector is the largest purchaser of security equipment and related services (Cunningham et al., 1990:198). A variety of arrangements exists between the consumers/users and the providers of security products and services by which purchasing, installation, maintenance, and even monitoring are accomplished.

1. ARMORED CAR SERVICES

Some security agencies specialize in guarding and transporting cash, securities, gold, jewelry, or other valuables. These security operations provide a distinct service to financial institutions, commercial operations, and others who must transport valuables from one location to another. One of the oldest of such agencies is Brink's, Inc., established in 1889. In 1980, there were about 120 armored car companies. By 1990, due to acquisitions and mergers, the number decreased to 70. According to *The Hallcrest Report II,* the number will decrease further to about 60 companies over the next several years.

2. PRIVATE INVESTIGATIVE SERVICES

Private investigative agencies, ranging from one-person local operations to multi-employee international operations, offer their services to private citizens, attorneys, and commercial and industrial enterprises. Private persons who desire discreet investigation of members of their family, potential family members—or perhaps even criminal situations or unsolved crimes in which the client has a personal interest—will often hire private investigators. Attorneys who desire information relating to clients, witnesses, jurors, suspects, or opposing parties also often utilize the services of a private investigator. Industrial and commercial concerns that desire credit information, background checks on potential and current employees, or information on competitors employ private investigative services quite extensively.

3. LOCKSMITH SERVICES

Locksmiths provide a distinct and often very critical function in the security industry. Choosing locking devices and keying systems to fit a particular situation can be best accomplished by the trained locksmith. While locksmiths often can provide a needed security service, their skills are often underutilized. Most locks are manufactured by large, national companies and distributed by various types of retailers and suppliers. They are usually purchased through retailers and installed by general contractors or in-house maintenance personnel. Such persons very often do not have the expertise and knowledge of security possessed by the professional locksmith.

4. SECURITY CONSULTANT SERVICES

Private security consultants are a somewhat new addition to the security industry. These individuals usually have several years of experience and can provide valuable assistance to industrial, commercial, or institutional clients who desire outside assistance on security-related problems. Two areas that have generated significant demands for specialized security consultant services are terrorism (particularly international terrorism) and computer-related crimes.

SPECIALIZED AREAS OF SECURITY

There are other private security services, usually highly specialized, not encompassed by the breakdown above. The "other" security personnel and companies include such services as executive protection, expert witness, forensic analysis, guard dogs, shopping (honesty) services, eavesdropping detection, etc. A single private security agency may offer a variety of such specialized security services to clients.

To place the security function or activity in proper perspective, one must recognize that it can be either a service provided by a private agency on a contractual basis, or an integral, operating component of the organization itself. In either case, security operations cannot function independently of the organization they serve.

In order to obtain a comprehensive and distinct profile of the application of security services, one must look to the whole range of businesses, industries, and organizations in which security fulfills a vital function. The type of security service and the degree of its application depend on the specific needs and problems of the entity being served.

1. TRANSPORTATION

Every year, millions of passengers and billions of tons of cargo are processed by various modes of transportation. Each of the component parts of the transportation system have both common and unique security problems. Most governmental or quasi-governmental facilities operate from a different legal position than facilities owned and operated by private enterprise. For example, security employees of airport authorities, port authorities, and some mass transit agencies generally have the same powers of arrest as a regular police officer of that jurisdiction. Proprietary security officers and employees of a contract security firm doing business as a private enterprise venture do not have that same power of arrest.

Generally, unless deputized, commissioned, or provided for by an ordinance or state statute, private security personnel possess no greater legal powers than any other private citizen. However, due to the positions they occupy, security officers in transportation settings must perform their duties within the framework of numerous statutes and regulations. In many situations, they will have a much greater opportunity to use their citizens' powers than will the ordinary citizen. Correspondingly, considerable attention must be given to the training needs of security personnel employed in the transportation industry.

2. AIRPORTS AND AIRLINES

During the 1960s, the crime of skyjacking became a critical and threatening challenge to the safety and security of airlines. The number of skyjackings reached its zenith in 1968 and 1969, with most commandeered flights forced to land in Cuba. Monetary gain and political reasons were the predominant motives for skyjacking. One of the most famous cases (assumed to be for monetary gain) involved Dan Cooper who, on November 24, 1971, hijacked a plane after boarding in Portland, Oregon, for a flight to Seattle, Washington. Money and parachutes were demanded and given to him. Then he bailed out of the plane somewhere over isolated, mountainous terrain between Seattle, Washington and Reno, Nevada, never to be heard from again.

Responding to the hue and cry from the public, the Federal Aviation Administration assisted in developing a psychological profile of a skyjacker. Subsequently, metal detectors were put into use at airports to screen selected persons based on the established profile. The profile system was only partially effective, and as a result, the sky marshal program (a short-lived effort that attempted to deter skyjackings by placing federal agents on high-risk flights) went into effect in 1970. Like the profile system, it was only partially effective and skyjackings still occurred.

With the concept of concentration of security on the ground for airline safety, new rules for airlines and airports were developed: Part 107 of the Federal Aviation Regulations (FAR) for airports, and Section 538 of FAR, Part 121 for scheduled carriers. Airports would be responsible for controlling air operational areas and carriers would be responsible for preventing sabotage devices and weapons from being carried aboard airliners. Furthermore, it was intended that passengers' baggage be checked. Because airports and carriers were required to design their own security plans, there were many different approaches and arguments about the degree of responsibility placed upon airports and that required of carriers. Many of these problems appeared to be solved in 1976 when the Security Committee of the Air Transportation Association developed a Standard Security Program.

The Anti-Hijacking Act of 1974 and the Air Transportation Security Act of 1974 implemented an international attitude toward skyjacking as expressed by The Hague Convention for the suppression of unlawful seizure of aircraft. Within the scope of international affairs, the President of the United States has the right to suspend summarily, without notice or hearing, for an indeterminate period of time, the right of any carrier to engage in air transportation between the United States and any nation that permits its lands to be used by terrorist organizations or that promotes or engages in air piracy. Moreover, a secondary boycott could be imposed by the President that would suspend air commerce between the United States and any foreign nation that maintains air service between itself and an offending country. The Secretary of Transportation was given the power, subject to approval by the Secretary of State, to bring sanctions against any airline that fails to maintain minimum standards set by the Convention on International Civil Aviation.

In 1975, FAR 129 (Foreign Air Corridor Security Program) required all foreign air carriers landing in and departing from the United States to screen all passengers and carry-on luggage. It also provided for the search of planes threatened by terrorists and prohibited the carrying of weapons in cabins.

Among other provisions of public law, "in flight" was defined to be from the moment all external doors were closed following embarkation until the moment all external doors are opened for disembarking. This definition was necessary to clarify jurisdiction over suspects apprehended during several stages of travel by air. It also was made an offense to attempt in any way to carry a weapon aboard a plane. Under these provisions, the Federal Aviation Administration (FAA) would have exclusive responsibility for the direction of law enforcement activities affecting the safety of persons in flight. Another deterrent was provided when the death penalty was authorized for conviction of a skyjacking that caused a death.

More recently, Section 905(d)(4) of the Federal Aviation Act of 1958 (49 U.S.C. App. 147(d)(4)) was amended on August 15, 1990. The amendments were incorporated into sections 107 and 108 of 14 CFR (Code of Federal Regulations), which govern the FAA. Changes involving Section 107.3 of the code were directed to various terms, definitions, responsibilities, etc., of airports and carriers (domestic and foreign) regarding security operations and procedures. While some distinctions were made in airports according to regularly scheduled passenger operations—normal carrier operations having a passenger seating capacity of more than 60 seats and smaller airports normally servicing carriers having more than 30 but less than 61 seating capacity—the basic requirements of the new standards for either situation had the same impact. The following is an overview of the directives of the 1990 amendment as it applies to airport operators who must comply with the new law. They must have a security program that:

1) Provides for the safety of persons and property traveling in air transportation and intrastate air transportation against acts of criminal violence and aircraft piracy;

2) Is in writing and signed by the airport operator;

3) Has been approved by the Director of Civil Aviation Security;

4) Includes a description of each air operations area, including its dimensions, boundaries, and pertinent features;

5) Includes a description of each area on or adjacent to the airport that affects the security of any air operations area;

6) Includes a detailed description of each exclusive area;

7) Includes a description of the procedures, facilities, and equipment used to perform the security control functions required of the airport operator and of each air carrier having security responsibility over an exclusive area;

8) Includes the procedures each air carrier having security responsibility will use to notify the airport operator when current security procedures, facilities, and equipment are not adequate to perform respective security control functions;

9) Includes a description of alternate security procedures that the airport operator intends to use in emergency and contingency situations;

10) Includes a description of the law enforcement support necessary to comply with the regulations;

11) Includes a description of the training program for law enforcement officers necessary to comply with regulations;

12) Includes a description of the system for maintaining records necessary to comply with regulations;

13) Maintains at least one complete copy of its approved security program and makes it available for review upon request by any Civil Aviation Security Special Agent; and

14) Restricts the distribution, disclosure, and availability of information contained in the security program.

The 1990 amendment of the Federal Aviation Act served to further clarify and establish a format of uniformity and standards for security programs required of airports and airlines. The FAA Civil Penalty Administrative Assessment Act of July 1992 made permanent the authority of the Federal Aviation Administration to impose civil penalties for violations of aviation laws and regulations. Prior to this time, the authority of the FAA to impose penalties went through several periods of limited authority, administrative and judicial backlogs, and severe criticism by the aviation community.

Air cargo thefts, passenger checks, skyjacking, and terrorist acts are the major security problems faced by airports and airlines. Most airport authorities have proprietary security/law enforcement forces to perform security functions associated with airport properties. Passenger checks, however, are generally performed by employees of contract security firms. Large international airports may have a permanent contingent of various governmental enforcement/regulatory agencies, each concerned with a specific aspect of the factors and problems associated with international air travel.

3. RAILROADS

The railroad police are perhaps the oldest and best organized segment of the private security industry. Because the railroads pay their security personnel salaries and fringe benefits comparable to those paid to railroad employees, they are able to attract and maintain an excellent security force. Investigators and physical security specialists are confronted with cargo thefts, vandalism, and thefts of railroad maintenance and construction materials. According to *USA Today*, there is a growing trend of increasing utilization of train travel by tourists and business people. Amtrak, the primary provider of commercial railway passenger service in the United States, is currently adding more routes, improving passenger amenities, and offering competitive rates (compared to air travel costs) to entice travelers (Richards, 1990:11E). Security measures corresponding to servicing increasing numbers of passengers and providing for their safety will generate a need for additional personnel.

4. MARITIME

Many large cities have a maritime authority that operates under governmental or quasi-governmental authority. Proprietary security forces dominate the maritime field, though the individual companies that lease facilities from the maritime authority may use a combination of proprietary and contract security services. Cargo theft is the major ongoing security problem associated with the maritime industry. Procedural security involving inventory and cargo controls and access control measures are key elements in accomplishing effective maritime security programs.

Like the aviation industry, leisure cruise lines face the threat of terrorism. With large numbers of travelers on a single vessel, terrorists have begun to view cruise lines as another means of gaining the public spotlight and satisfying their objectives. This was exemplified by four Palestine Liberation Front terrorists hijacking the *Achille Lauro*, an Italian cruise ship, while it was in port at Alexandria, Egypt on October 7, 1985. In another example, in July 1988, three terrorists boarded the cruise ferry, *City of Poros*, in the Mediterranean Sea, opened fire with automatic weapons and tossed hand grenades around the ship, killing nine passengers and injuring 100. Following these incidents, the International Maritime Organization (IMO) drafted and approved comprehensive guidelines titled, "Measures to Prevent Unlawful Acts Against Passengers and Crews on Board Ships." Included in the guidelines were recommendations relative to security surveys, establishing specific responsibilities for security, passenger screening, designation of restricted areas, and use of barriers, security lighting, security alarms, communication systems, and access control measures. However, unlike the statutes and regulations governing airlines and airports, the IMO recommendations do not carry the weight of law. Port authorities, terminal managers and vessel operators may use some, all, or none of the recommended measures.

5. TRUCKING

The majority of the transportation of materials and goods in the United States is accomplished by the trucking industry. Common carriers—trucking companies that contract with others to transport their goods and materials—move more than company-owned transportation fleets. Trucking firms generally rely on a small proprietary security force to deal with major thefts and utilize the services of contract security firms at fixed locations such as terminals or distribution centers. Cargo theft, in the form of employee theft or hijacking, is the trucking industry's major security problem. Currently, there are several variations of electronic computerized tracking and communication systems being developed and utilized by the trucking industry. Such systems allow for almost instant communication with the driver and/or pinpoint the exact location of the vehicle on a computerized map. Traditional procedural controls involving timed and specified routes, driver call-ins to dispatch, and similar techniques are still being used but will, in time, be replaced by more sophisticated methods.

6. TRANSIT AUTHORITIES

Transit authorities (e.g., the Chicago Transit Authority) are generally quasi-governmental agencies, financially supported by both public funds and revenues from passenger services. One of the primary financial concerns of mass transit systems is the loss of revenues as a result of fear of crime. In the past, mass transit authorities have relied almost exclusively on proprietary security forces to deal with the problems of assaults, robberies, and vandalism. Currently, however, there is a growing trend toward utilizing the services of contract security agencies. Faced with an emerging economy that demands operational cost-effectiveness, transit system planners and managers must weigh the advantages of contract security in their efforts to improve profit margins and patron perceptions of safety. Generally, the utilization of contract security has the distinct advantage of being less costly than proprietary security. Thus, the bottom line for the consumer of contract services is a better profit margin. However, because many mass transit authority proprietary security personnel have special police powers of arrest, they would, in all likelihood, not be replaced in total. Contract security personnel would be particularly adaptable to:

1) Station patrols;

2) Revenue pickups;

3) Parking areas;

4) Property yards and buildings;

5) Monitoring security hardware; and

6) Other miscellaneous security areas. (Arko, 1992:26-31)

Improvements in the utilization of security officers, operational and security hardware, and facilities design, have been undertaken with some degree of success, to increase visibility in passenger waiting areas, to reduce patron waiting time, and to provide quick detection and response to criminal incidents.

7. COMMERCE

Commercial facilities have security problems that are not easily solved by current police practices. Public law enforcement agencies have neither the workforce nor the capability to provide security for the vast number of banks, gasoline stations, minute markets, jewelry stores, hotels/motels, and other commercial enterprises in the United States. These businesses, whether isolated or part of a commercial complex, cater to the general public and must encourage a feeling of openness and availability if they are to remain competitive. Yet at the same time, commercial enterprises must project an image of solidarity and security. Commercial facilities need to provide protection against an array of criminal activities ranging from the simple theft of items from a motel room to computer embezzlement resulting in the loss of millions of dollars.

8. HOTEL/MOTEL FACILITIES

Hotel and motel managers must provide their customers with a safe and secure environment. The security problems associated with the hotel/motel industry are for the most part related to crime in the surrounding area. Major security problems associated with the hotel/motel industry are thefts from guests' automobiles parked in a parking lot, thefts from rooms, and vandalism to the property of both the facility and guests. Primary contributing factors include the density of population, the traffic patterns of vehicular and pedestrian traffic, the crime rate and the type of crime that prevails in the area, as well as any other features of the location that may make the hotel more vulnerable to adverse incidents. Other features include the kinds of businesses in the area, the security protection maintained by those businesses and the availability of nearby public services that lessen the probability for undesirable incidents. Of particular importance is the presence or proximity of police, i.e., are streets patrolled by walking patrols, motorized patrols, or both? What is the response time of the public police?

The relative size of a hotel/motel can be considered in terms of length, width, and height. It can also be measured by the number of guest rooms, ancillary facilities, parking lots, swimming pools, bars, restaurants, theaters, conference rooms, offices, and shops. Generally, the larger the building, the more numerous the guest rooms and other facilities that can complicate the security mission. Yet the design of the building(s) and utilization of the grounds can offset some of the disadvantages of size and complexity relative to configuration and featured activities. If the building is a high-rise with the proper number of entrances and exits that can be controlled for safety, security personnel can be used with economy and efficiency. If the personnel who staff the desks, render personal services, and operate shops and entertainment activities are used as eyes and ears to enhance safety and security, size can become a relative matter. Correspondingly, some of the service and activity areas requiring constant attention include:

1) Employee exits and entrance;

2) Luggage storage and holdover points;

3) Access points (day and night);

4) Guest check-in and registration areas;

5) Public areas and access thereto;

6) Delivery procedures and receiving areas; and

7) Guest parking areas, floors, and rooms. (Walpole, 1991:83-85)

Proper choice and use of hardware and anti-intrusion devices can further reduce the threat attributed to size. Scheduling of security personnel during shifts when they are most needed is important in reducing vulnerability. Most problems (such as trespassing, vandalism, theft from vehicles, etc.) are committed during the evening hours. During late hours or early morning hours, there is less activity in the establishment and correspondingly fewer people to observe intruders. This situation may affect the deployment of security personnel and the assignments and locations of other members of the staff.

Not only should security and management consider the obvious hazards that have been pointed out by experience and documentation, they also must look for potential hazards that have not yet manifested themselves. A lesson was learned from a near-fatal event that occurred in Atlantic City, New Jersey, when a security officer was shot in the eye during an attempted robbery at the Merv Griffin's Resorts Casino & Hotel. The robbery took place when a security guard supervisor was transferring approximately $1 million in cash to an armored car and the perpetrator grabbed one of the money bags containing $400,000. The officer struggled with the robber, who shot her in the eye at point-blank range (Hotel/Motel Security And Safety Management, 1997:13). Security management must plan for a shift of street crime from outside the hotel premises to its grounds and buildings as well as for crimes generated within the facility itself. Because the potential for litigation is always present, it is axiomatic that any act or situation—regardless of its origin or nature—that threatens the well-being of guests and/or employees be considered and dealt with appropriately.

Security services are generally provided by a proprietary staff supplemented by employees of a contract security firm. The security manager is the decisionmaker and the contract employee performs the assigned security tasks and responsibilities. Appendix C includes a hotel/motel security survey or audit instrument.

9. OFFICE BUILDINGS

Large commercial office buildings typically have elevator banks in the lobby area. In this situation, security personnel can monitor most of the pedestrian traffic from one central location; usually with closed-circuit television (CCTV) systems which are now commonplace in office buildings. Security is generally provided by contract security personnel, whose duties include access control, monitoring the CCTV system and making regular security checks throughout the building. Building occupants and activities can range from a single tenant, such as a corporate entity, to multiple tenants involved in a wide variety of business interests and pursuits. The major security problems for commercial office buildings are after-hours burglaries and thefts, and incidents of internal theft.

10. FINANCIAL INSTITUTIONS

Financial institutions are faced with security problems that are quite different from those of other commercial enterprises. In contrast to the many indirect losses sustained by other businesses, most losses to financial institutions are direct financial losses. During the 1960s, financial institutions grew at a rapid rate. Significant increases in robberies, larcenies, and burglaries during that period led Congress to pass the Bank Protection Act of 1968. This Act provided that federally insured banks and savings and loan associations and (later) federally insured credit unions: (1) designate someone to be a security officer; (2) cooperate with and seek security advice from various law enforcement agencies; and (3) develop comprehensive security programs and implement protection measures.

The FBI has estimated that more money is stolen by bank officials and other insiders each year than is lost due to bank robbers and burglars. Criminal misconduct by financial institution insiders was a major factor in about 50 percent of all bank failures in recent years. Moreover, the situation is not helped by the punishment meted out: the small number of insiders prosecuted and convicted spend minimal time in prison. For example, during the first 10 months of the 1992 federal government fiscal year, 28,539 bank fraud cases were referred by the FBI to the Justice Department for prosecution. However, the Justice Department declined to prosecute 52.6 percent of the cases. (Associated Press, 1992)

Even though the incidence of bank robberies has declined in recent years, it is still important that financial institutions have adequate photographic or video-taping equipment available and in place in case of a robbery. Without a usable photograph or videotape to aid in identification, it is extremely difficult for the FBI to conduct a speedy investigation.

Fraudulent use of bank credit cards and computer crimes are, for the most part, the responsibility of the FBI. Major losses from both credit card schemes and computer crimes caused Congress to enact federal legislation mandating that such crimes be under the FBI's investigative authority. Counterfeiting of bank notes is under the investigative authority of the United States Secret Service, an agency of the Department of the Treasury. Even though many crimes committed against banks are handled by local law enforcement and the FBI, most financial institutions have a security director and small cadre of investigators for recovery of "bad" checks, credit card fraud, property recovery, etc. Contract security services are also used to provide courier services, alarm monitoring, and physical security.

Since automatic teller machines (ATMs) first appeared in the early 1970s, there have been numerous incidents of assaults, robberies, rapes, abductions, and even killings of bank patrons at or near the more than 83,000 units now located at banks, grocery stores, malls, bowling alleys, college campuses, and other locations. In New York City, problems became so serious at ATM sites that a new law was enacted in July 1992 requiring surveillance cameras at all ATM locations. Besides making cash withdrawals or deposits, it is now possible to purchase postage stamps, bus passes, renew driver's licenses, and even obtain welfare benefits via automated teller machines. It is quite clear that the banking public likes having 24-hour-a-day, seven-day-a-week access to their money (Hannah, 1992:E-1).

It has become very obvious, particularly in the past few years, that criminals view ATM sites as prime places to carry out criminal acts. Financial institutions are now "under the gun" to develop and implement objectives and strategies toward reducing the crime opportunity and the desire to commit crimes at or against ATM facilities. Regardless of what banks and financial institutions attempt or decide to do, the traditional goals of psychological target hardening and physical target hardening will be preeminent, i.e., criminals are discouraged from committing crimes when the ATM's environment suggests that the crime would be very difficult or impossible to commit successfully. Methods undertaken to secure an ATM site should necessarily be inclusive of securing the ATM unit itself from manipulation and direct attack, operational and procedural safeguards for machine maintenance and servicing, and providing for the maximal level of customer safety and convenience.

Some very basic ATM site security measures include:

1) Persons inside ATM enclosure areas should have an unobstructed view of the surrounding area;

2) Shrubbery and vegetation should be limited so that no means of cover or concealment are apparent;

3) Nighttime lighting should equate to natural daylight;

4) Lighting should be sufficient to illuminate the total facility and the ATM unit in particular;

5) Lighting should be continuous and constant during the hours of darkness;

6) Site should be equipped with emergency lighting;

7) There should be visible and appropriate CCTV coverage of the ATM area;

8) There should be some measure or means for customers to signal that a transaction is being made under duress or that they are in danger; and

9) Customers should be given orientation and education information regarding the proper procedures of safe ATM usage.

11. HEALTHCARE FACILITIES

Many security problems are unique to the healthcare industry. A hospital, for example, must remain open to admit the sick and injured, allow patients to have visitors, and carry on the normal activities required in caring for those who are unable to care for themselves. Because of this openness, adequate physical security—especially access control—is difficult to attain.

a. Hospital Security

Healthcare security has grown many times over in the last three decades. Socioeconomic changes and environmental transitions in this period have had a tremendous impact on security at various kinds of healthcare institutions, particularly those located in inner-city areas. The decline of the inner city in many metropolitan areas has forced healthcare administrators to deal with mounting problems of security. In the past, healthcare administrators were not skilled in the area of security, nor did they want to become skilled. In most healthcare facilities, the security duties were given to an assistant administrator, who also was not skilled in security matters. Recognizing the need for a professional organization to study the problems of healthcare security, particularly hospital security, the International Association of Hospital Security (IAHS) was founded in 1968. Since the inception of IAHS, more emphasis has been placed on having a full-time person who is directly responsible for security services.

IAHS has a certification program for individual members of hospital security forces. Certification is available for security officers, security supervisors, and security directors. IAHS also offers a nationwide certification program for trainers on a yearly basis. Most directors of security at hospitals believe that IAHS plays a greater role than the Joint Commission on Accreditation of Healthcare Organizations (JCAHO) in providing professional security personnel and services. They attribute this to the emphasis on training. Just as in other areas that need security, training (or the lack of it) is one of the major problems in hospital and healthcare security.

The Joint Commission on Accreditation of Healthcare Organizations (JCAHO), based in Chicago, also applies pressure on healthcare management to meet certain security standards. It is composed of persons appointed from the American College of Physicians, American College of Surgeons, the American Hospital Association, and the American Medical Association. Healthcare facilities can voluntarily seek accreditation, and those that do must agree to a security survey or audit that includes prescribed standards of performance and operation. A prescriptive accreditation manual is published and updated annually. In January 1992, new Joint Commission on Accreditation of Healthcare Organizations standards, "Standards for Plant, Technology, and Safety Management" (PTSM), became effective. The thrust of the new regulations was to establish measurable standards of performance and processes designed to assure that desirable outcomes are achieved and undesirable outcomes avoided in the application of technology to the care of patients within the healthcare environment. Inclusive of security, the new standards combined five elements—(1) general safety, (2) safety education, (3) emergency preparedness, (4) hazardous materials and wastes, and (5) safety devices and operational practices—into a single management process. Item PL.1.2.2 of the new standards was particularly applicable to the hospital security program. It reads: "The safety management program is based on monitoring and evaluation of organizational experience, applicable law and regulation, and accepted practice and includes a risk assessment program that evaluates the impact on patient care and safety of the buildings, grounds, equipment, occupants, and internal physical systems." Thus, a facility that is a member of JCAHO must have a security program that addresses all security-related concerns regarding patients, visitors, personnel, and property if it is to retain its accreditation. This may create a dilemma for many facilities because security falls under the responsibility of the "risk manager." Particularly in many private hospitals, this individual may not have the background or expertise to evaluate and determine the effectiveness level of the security program (Robinson, 1991:45).

One of the major problems facing healthcare security is fraud and internal employee theft. According to the Health Care Financing Administration, healthcare fraud is estimated to be between 7 percent and 10 percent of all healthcare billings. Healthcare spending in the United States exceeded $1 trillion in 1997. Healthcare fraud is defined as any activity involving the healthcare industry that is designed for illegal financial gain. Examples include billing for services not rendered, inflating the cost of the service provided, the deliberate performance of medically unnecessary services, and the payment of "kickbacks." The governmental agency responsible for investigating fraud has traditionally been the FBI. The Health Insurance Portability and Accountability Act of 1996 enhanced criminal statutes and penalties as well as civil penalties targeting fraud within the healthcare industry. Security has the additional responsibility for serving the public and minimizing the chance that any person coming on the premises will suffer serious injury. There are certain standards that must be met to comply with laws, regulations and codes, particularly in the realm of fire protection and safety.

Other vulnerable areas are receiving locations, cash registers (business office, cafeteria, shops, etc.), food services, package and parcel inspection, removal of bodies, laundry/linen, lost and found, utilities, building accesses, employer locker areas, and parking and traffic control. Of particular concern are procedural controls for storage and dispensing of drugs. Other areas of vulnerability that need special attention—overlapping several of those already mentioned—include maternity wards, emergency rooms, and visitor control.

a. *Maternity Wards*—Footprinting of infants at birth is essential to establishing subsequent identification of newborns. Infant kidnapping and switching of babies by design or accident is of foremost concern in this area. Although infant abductions have been on the decline over the last decade, there are still incidents of abductions that emphasize the importance of neonatal security techniques.

The Grady Memorial Hospital in Atlanta, Georgia, has had its fair share of abductions, most of which have ended with the child either being returned to the hospital or otherwise recovered. In nearly all of the cases, the infants were taken from a pediatric recovery room either before or immediately following a surgical procedure.

The hospital uses an infant protection system from Sensormatic Electronic Corporation. The system includes an infant-tagging security system, access to control alarms, and CCTV activation. As a result of the latest infant abduction in 1996 in which a two-day-old baby was kidnapped, the hospital has increased security measures. That hospital now posts security at the entrance to the nursery whenever the system is down, the number of rounds by security have been increased, color CCTVs are more prevalent, they expect stricter compliance with nursery procedures, nurses escort infants to and from medical procedures, and an in-service crime and infant protection program has been implemented.

An example of the effectiveness of the infant protection program is illustrated by events that occurred at the Maine Medical Center in November of 1996:

> A 26-year-old woman whom police and hospital officials believe donned pink scrubs and carried a clipboard while visiting both hospitals to look at newborn babies has been charged with kidnapping . . .

> The woman was spotted in the lobby area of Maine Medical Center with the eight-hour-old child by Lt. Michael Woodman, a private security officer employed by First Security Services Corp., Boston, MA, who is the hospital's safety officer. He had just come from a meeting of the hospital's "Code Pink" response team which had been reviewing incidents from the previous day, including still photographs from Waterville police that were produced from hospital surveillance cameras. The photos allegedly showed the suspect, who was reported seen by a nurse acting suspiciously in the maternity ward of the hospital the day prior to the incident. During their meeting, the response team received a page that a baby had been abducted from Eastern Maine Medical Center.

> Immediately after leaving the meeting, Woodman saw and recognized the suspect who was holding a baby from the photos . . . According to published reports, the woman, a divorced mother of two, admitted abducting the newborn and that she had suffered a series of miscarriages. Police believe she was going to call her mother from the Waterville hospital, tell her that she had a baby (she allegedly had tried to make herself look pregnant in the weeks prior to the incident), and to come and pick her up (Infant Kidnapping Update, 1997:5-10).

Nurseries must be maintained as a secure area. The maternity ward itself should be strictly guarded with hardware and/or people. Infants should be in the nursery during visiting hours and nursery personnel should wear distinct uniforms. Correspondingly, the storage and distribution of uniforms and identification badges and name tags should be tightly controlled. A parent must know that persons wearing a distinct uniform are responsible hospital personnel. When mother and infant are discharged, a staff member should accompany them to the point of discharge and stay with them until they depart.

b. *Emergency Rooms*—In this area, the security officer or hospital staff is likely to encounter belligerent patients and visitors. Arguments between family members and other parties often continue into the emergency room and, frequently, people are intoxicated, emotionally upset, or severely incapacitated. These people cannot be allowed to roam the area unsupervised. Facilities such as vending machines, washrooms, and telephones should be available in the waiting room. The corridors and other areas of the hospital should be separated from the emergency area so that they can be controlled with a minimum number of supervisory personnel. Sometimes it is advisable to station a security officer in the area. Furthermore, it is in the emergency room that a security officer is most likely to interact with law enforcement personnel. Provision should be made for law enforcement officers to have an isolated room in which to conduct interviews.

c. *Visitors and Visitor Control*—There are several kinds of visitors to whom the hospital owes varying degrees of care. While these visitors may fall into categories of invitees, licensees, or trespassers, they also can be placed in categories as employees, administrative personnel, purchasers of supplies, other hospital functionaries, and visitors to patients.

There is firm consensus that patients need visitors for their well-being. With this in mind, visitors should be controlled so that the number and kind of visitors are balanced with the treatment and care required for the patient. Visitors should not be allowed to become a nuisance. There are six areas of special consideration for control of visitors: (1) psychiatric units, (2) surgical units, (3) intensive care units, (4) pediatric units, (5) obstetrical units, and (6) isolation units.

The most favored visiting schedule is twice daily with a two-hour limit for each period and two visitors at a time per patient. The times of visits are normally in the afternoon and evening.

There is general acceptance among healthcare security personnel of card, pass, or badge control systems for visitors. If any of these systems is used, it must be assured that the authorization to visit (whether pass, badge, or card) is not lost or duplicated. It stands to reason that if the visitor is expected to wear a badge on the outside of his or her clothing, all personnel of the hospital must wear a comparable kind of identification. If this is not done, a visitor has only to remove the badge in order to pass as a hospital employee. One innovative system is the use of a 5" x 6" card, which is difficult for the visitor to hide or lose. It should be laminated with the patient's name and room number on it. There are many variations that can be utilized in such a system. For example, a different colored card can be used for each day of the week. Cards can be imprinted with instructions indicating that the card must be carried visibly in the hand and returned when the visitor leaves the hospital. In addition, visitor rules and regulations can be printed on the back of the card.

Hospital personnel and volunteers should be utilized to observe and perhaps even control the movement and circulation of visitors as much as possible. It is not recommended that security be assigned this task as a primary mission. Above all, it should not be the security officer who announces that visiting hours are over. Unit personnel should assume that responsibility. Facility policy must be clearly stated with regard to visitors remaining in or entering the hospital during nonvisiting hours. Those people who attempt to enter the hospital during the evening hours should be challenged at the point of entry. All perimeter doors should be secured or otherwise monitored. The night entrance, which is usually the emergency room, should be under continuous surveillance and control by security personnel. If the hospital has an attached physicians' office building, the connecting corridor may be used as an effective control point. There always will be exceptional cases, so security officers must be kept informed as to the non-hospital personnel who might stay in or have a need to enter the facility during non-visiting hours. A relative or spouse of a patient might be allowed to visit at any time; a visitor from out of town may be an exception; a change in the condition of the patient might be a cause to allow visits at unusual hours; or a person who needs medical care might need to seek admittance.

The relationship between a patient and a healthcare facility is contractual. The facility assumes a special duty toward the patient and his or her well-being. The negligence of any of its agents or employees can involve the facility in embarrassing legal action and impose serious liability upon it. If a third party suffers injury or damage to property because of the negligence of an employee who is acting within the scope of employment, the facility can become liable under the doctrine of respondeat superior.

In some states, a peculiar arrangement occurs in healthcare facilities where attending physicians and private nurses are considered to be independent contractors and are not employees or agents of the facility. In these states, residents and interns are likely to be considered as falling within the doctrine of respondeat superior. Nevertheless, the facility as a corporate entity may be negligent and subject to suits for damages if it maintains its buildings and grounds negligently, furnishes defective supplies, employs incompetent people, or fails to meet accepted standards of safety. Security will be in the forefront when lawsuits are mentioned.

Healthcare facilities utilize both proprietary and contract security services. Arrangements vary from an all-proprietary force to total reliance upon a contract security agency. Despite the increased attention given to security, there are still many situations in which security is prevented, intentionally or unintentionally, from contributing its full potential to the field. This may be attributable to institutional leadership, security directors, or both.

b. *Nursing Homes*

Nursing homes generally are healthcare units for the elderly. A limited number of nursing facilities exist in metropolitan areas that allow a patient to have restricted medical services that amount to less than the full-service plan provided by most major hospitals. Cost and the need for the restricted service are the determining factors for patients utilizing this type of facility. Just like other types of healthcare facilities, the nursing home is faced with security problems of visitor control and internal theft. Thefts are quite common, with the elderly occupants of the nursing home most often being the victims. Most Americans are very protective of their elderly relatives and any criminal or negligent act by which an occupant is victimized or harmed must be taken seriously by administrators of nursing homes. Additionally, nursing homes must be vigilant for patient "walkaways," because many of their elderly charges may become easily confused and disoriented. Electronic asset protection tagging systems are sometimes used for protection of the elderly, particularly for those that might stray from the facility. Visitor controls, restricted access and egress doors, fire detection and suppression systems, drug storage and procedural controls, and CCTV are widely employed by nursing homes. Nursing homes that have uniformed security services usually employ a contract security firm.

12. RETAIL

The retail industry is a part of society with which the average citizen has direct contact on a regular basis. As in any commercial area, the more persons who come into contact with a particular facility, the more security problems that facility is likely to experience. Loss of merchandise is the greatest security problem associated with the retail industry. In most cases, how and when the merchandise was taken is unknown. Retailing in most areas is a very competitive business; a few losses of valuable merchandise could make the difference between remaining in business and closing. The option of raising prices to cover losses may not be a viable alternative, particularly if competing businesses are not forced to do the same. Generally speaking, however, the consumer will pay more for all items purchased because of losses due to theft suffered by the business(es).

a. Shopping Centers and Malls

Shopping centers and malls are constructed to accommodate numerous retail stores in one large complex. Generally, at least one large department store will dominate, with several small specialty shops in close proximity. Parking garages or open parking lots allow thousands of automobiles to park near the facilities. This congregation of people and automobiles in a relatively small geographical area creates a security problem. In fact, one of the greatest problem areas for malls and shopping centers involves customer vehicles, i.e., vehicle thefts, break-ins, and vandalism. While property crimes usually do not generate civil suits, incidents in which a mall/shopping center customer is assaulted, robbed, or otherwise harmed (physically or psychologically, in fact or perceived), a lawsuit alleging damages is likely to follow. Because many customers will not shop at stores where thefts and robberies are known to occur on a regular basis, malls and shopping centers have an inherent interest in projecting and assuring an ambience of safety and security. The flow of pedestrian traffic is monitored in many shopping centers and malls by CCTV. This is not done so much as a security measure as it is to monitor the area for any obstructions to access by customers. Shoplifting and thefts from a particular store are usually handled by that store. However, cooperation is closely maintained between the security personnel of the shopping center/mall and the security personnel of a store. In addition, close contact is maintained with local law enforcement agencies.

After closing hours, fire watch, prevention of burglaries, and order maintenance in parking areas are the primary functions of shopping center security personnel. Both daytime and nighttime services are generally provided by a contract security firm.

b. Individual Retail Establishments

The loss of merchandise by retail stores is one of the three major problems facing retail businesses (along with a lack of expertise in the particular field and a lack of capital). The crime loss experienced by retail establishments is almost twice that of industries such as manufacturing, wholesaling, services, and transportation. Shoplifting and employee theft are the principal security problems associated with most retail establishments. Modern merchandising techniques create a significant security problem by emphasizing accessibility to merchandise. Even though major improvements have been made in electronic detection systems, shoplifting has continued to plague most retail establishments. Internal thefts by employees also account for a significant percentage of losses to most retail establishments. In many cases, losses due to shoplifting and employee thefts are equal to or greater than the net profit of the business.

Most large retail establishments operating on regional and national levels employ a proprietary security force. These employees have major responsibilities for planning, training, and implementing all phases of various security operations. Because security services are closely related to safety services, many companies assign responsibilities in all areas of loss prevention to their security forces.

13. INDUSTRIAL

Some industrial companies must provide for the security of thousands of acres of land and a variety of seemingly unrelated activities. On the other hand, some industrial operations are very small, with just a few employees engaged in one basic activity. Regardless of the size of the operation, however, industrial facilities have common security problems related to the protection of their property, personnel, and information. In fact, some of the most progressive security practices are to be found in the area of industrial security, which in many cases also encompasses such activities as fire protection, traffic control, investigation, and other aspects of protecting life and property within an industrial enterprise.

14. MANUFACTURERS

Manufacturing facilities are as varied in size as they are in the products they make. Security for a small, localized manufacturing plant with just a few employees may be relatively simple, while security for a huge multinational corporation may encompass a variety of potential contingencies, often having implications that affect the entire United States. Security in the manufacturing industry must be concerned with theft of both raw materials and finished products, the physical security of installations, personnel security, and the security of classified information.

The traditional "night watchman," while still apparent in many manufacturing facilities, is rapidly being replaced by security departments responsible for a wide range of loss prevention activities. This has encouraged the development of the security manager position, which has duties that include rules and regulations enforcement, fire prevention and protection, accident investigation, public relations, and other areas of security and safety. Traditionally, the manufacturing industry—particularly larger companies and facilities—relied heavily upon proprietary security, but, as noted in Chapter 1, the usage of contract services is becoming more common.

15.   PUBLIC AND PRIVATE UTILITIES

The energy problem in America during the last few years has focused attention on utility companies. In several foreign countries, terrorist organizations have been able to immobilize major parts of cities, and the same potential exists in this country. Sabotage of an electric power plant or a major substation may cause a blackout that could last for hours or days. A damaged natural gas or water facility could cause problems for a large segment of a city, especially during severe winter months. Most public and private utilities have a proprietary security staff supplemented by employees of a contract security firm.

Nuclear facilities were brought to the forefront of public attention with the nuclear accident at Three Mile Island, near Middletown, Pennsylvania. Not only are potential accidents a major security problem, but the attention given to nuclear plants is creating a security problem that did not exist a few years ago. Environmental groups and ordinary citizens have demonstrated in large numbers at nuclear facilities in operation and under construction. The general public maintains a basic suspicion of nuclear energy and its capacity for destruction. Thus, security at a nuclear facility is a complex, integrated program designed to: (1) protect the facility from radiological sabotage, (2) ensure the health and safety of employees, and (3) preserve the facility's integrity and generating capacity (Higgins, 1988:71-74). Security at nuclear facilities is required and defined by Title 10 of the Code of Federal Regulations.

16.   ENERGY COMPANIES

For years, energy in America has been synonymous with oil companies. The oil and gasoline crises of 1974 and 1979, and more recently, the Persian Gulf War, have focused national attention on oil companies and the supply of oil to world markets. The Federal Department of Energy requires minimum levels of security for manufacturing and storage areas. Such facilities have the potential for large-scale disaster. Whether humanly generated or natural, fires and/or explosions occurring at oil facilities have tremendous destructive capabilities. Additionally, oil spills constitute a crisis situation, a fact that was exemplified by the Exxon *Valdez* spill in Alaskan waters in 1989. Energy facilities tend to be regionalized and the resultant need for security personnel is likewise regionalized. Coal is the major fossil fuel in America and more attention will likely be devoted to this resource in the future. And because it too is located only in a few states, it will also become a regional security problem.

Most oil companies are multinational corporations, subject to worldwide security problems. Kidnapping of executives, which has been a problem for several years in foreign countries, is potentially a major security problem for American firms. Both oil and coal companies generally have proprietary security personnel augmented by contract officers.

17. ENTERTAINMENT

In most major cities, private security plays a significant role in order maintenance and traffic control at special events such as football games, fairs, concerts, and amusement centers. Such events can last from a few hours to several days. Local law enforcement agencies generally do not have the budget or personnel required to service such special events. On a national basis, a few contract security firms specialize in providing security services for all types of special events.

a. Civic Centers

Civic centers are multi-purpose facilities usually owned or controlled by local government. Their primary security problems are order maintenance and traffic control. The major difference between one large crowd and another is the emotional excitement caused by the entertainment. Rock concerts arouse a different type of emotion than does a professional sporting event, and so on. A contract security firm generally provides security for all events.

b. Amusement Parks

The traveling, seasonal carnival is almost a thing of the past. It has been replaced, or at least it seems, by huge amusement parks located throughout the United States. These facilities cover hundreds of acres and include many separate structures. Depending on their geographical location, some of these facilities are open throughout the year. They include such well known parks as Walt Disney World, Kings Island, Six Flags, Universal Studios, and the Centennial Olympic Park. On October 14, 1998, Eric Robert Rudolph, age 32, was charged with the fatal bombing at Atlanta's Centennial Olympic Park, as well as the double bombings at the Sandy Springs Professional Building in north Atlanta on January 16, 1997, and the double bombings at The Otherside Lounge in Atlanta on February 21, 1997. Rudolph was charged in February of 1998, with the bombing at the New Woman/All Women Health Care Clinic in Birmingham, Alabama, on January 29, 1998. That bomb killed Birmingham police officer Robert Sanderson, and severely injured the clinic's head nurse, Emily Lyons.

Order maintenance, parking, and safety are the primary concerns of amusement center security. The need for a safe and orderly flow of thousands of visitors per day necessitates a security force designed to react to any contingency affecting the security of visitors or employees. Almost all amusement centers utilize a proprietary security force.

c. Fairs and Exhibits

Public facilities and properties for fairs and exhibits are often used throughout the year. The quantity and quality of security needed for each event depends upon the type of function and the number of people attending.

At most events, security problems include crowd control, parking, and order maintenance. However, at certain events such as art exhibits or antique shows, physical security and the prevention of thefts are of primary concern. During idle times, vandalism and theft are problems. In some facilities this necessitates a full-time security force. Many large fair and exhibition centers utilize a proprietary security force throughout the year, while others employ a contract agency when an activity requires such coverage.

d. Museums

Museums and art galleries bring people and valuable objects close together. Many of these objects are of priceless historical significance and, if lost or damaged, could not be replaced. Other objects are valuable from a monetary standpoint and must be protected as an asset of the museum and, in a general sense, protected for the greater benefit of society as a whole. According to the Museum Security Network, there have been more than $1 million in museum and cultural property thefts. The most expensive theft took place in 1990 at the Gardner Museum in Boston, Massachusetts. In this case, the thieves, posing as Boston policemen, told security officers that they were responding to a disturbance call. Contrary to museum regulations, the officers let the would-be robbers into the museum. They then took 12 paintings, which included works by Rembrandt, Degas, and Monet, valued at $200 million. This case still remains unsolved and is listed on the FBI's web site with a $5 million reward (Museum Security Network, 1999:4).

Figure 3.2
Categories of Theft by Victim 1991 - 1998

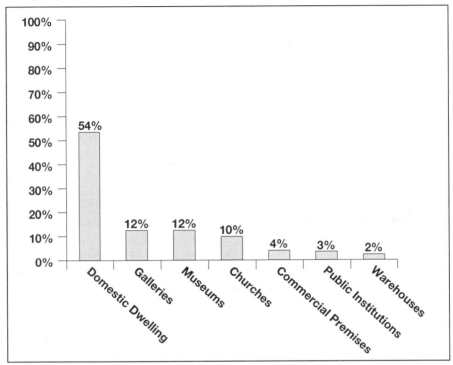

Another source on museum security is The Art Loss Register (ALR), the largest private database of stolen and missing works of art, antiques, and valuables in the world. They have offices in London, New York, Dusseldorf, and Dublin. According to the ALR, the following represents categories of theft by victims from 1991 to 1998. Museum loss prevention programs must be multi-faceted because art and historical objects are subject not only to theft and vandalism but are also very susceptible to wear, breakage, fire, water, sunlight, humidity, temperature, pollution, and other factors that can diminish their appeal, value, and/or longevity. Most museums utilize a proprietary central alarm station to monitor security, fire, environmental, and critical facility systems. Coupled with the usage and application of a wide variety of physical security hardware and sensory devices, an appropriate emergency power system, a communications network and a trained security force, museum security programs should equate to a well-secured environment. Museums use various arrangements of proprietary and contract security forces, ranging from an all-proprietary force to an all-contract force to various combinations of the two.

18. GOVERNMENT

The security of government buildings and related real and personal property is an immense task. It requires that protection be provided for thousands of acres of land and buildings located throughout the United States. The vast number of government buildings and holdings makes it impossible for regular law enforcement units to provide service sufficient to satisfy all the demands for security. Some governmental agencies, such as the Tennessee Valley Authority and the General Services Administration, maintain large proprietary security forces. On the other hand, smaller governmental units at the state and local levels utilize either small proprietary security staffs or employ a contract agency. Even some military facilities employ contract security personnel to handle certain security tasks.

Security problems for government lands and buildings range from vandalism and theft to the threat of terrorism. Security has come of age as a full and equal partner with the other services required to operate government buildings and facilities.

a. Tennessee Valley Authority

The Tennessee Valley Authority (TVA), headquartered in Knoxville, Tennessee, is the largest government-owned utility conglomerate in the United States. TVA operates all types of electric utility plants—hydroelectric, coal, and nuclear. In addition, TVA operates picnic areas and recreational facilities on most of its property. A huge recreational area is operated at the Land Between the Lakes facility in western Kentucky, where there are provisions for hunting, fishing, camping, and boating. TVA has a proprietary security force that operates like a regular police force. Since TVA property is federal property, most of the citations and arrests are handled in federal court.

b. Government Buildings

The General Services Administration (GSA) is charged with managing, operating, maintaining, and protecting federal buildings and related real and personal property. It operates the Federal Protection Service Division and has approximately 5,000 personnel. The regular force of Federal Protective Officers is augmented by private guards on contract to GSA at locations and buildings that need more protection. Location also dictates whether GSA utilizes the services of a private contracting agency or the regular GSA force. Many federal buildings are located in isolated areas, making it impractical and uneconomical to utilize federal employees.

Federal Protective Officers are required to attend a service training academy and regular in-service training courses. Federal Protective Officers have the same powers of arrest as regular police officers while on federal property under GSA control. The contract guards have only the powers and authority of private citizens.

Most states have similar security forces that have jurisdiction over the security of buildings and property owned, leased, and occupied by the state. The authority of such personnel is generally limited to the property being protected.

c. Public Housing

In large metropolitan areas, housing authorities have been established to provide housing for low-income persons. With the advent of multi-unit apartments in relatively small geographical areas, security quickly became a problem. Housing authorities are generally governmental or quasi-governmental and have a proprietary security force. The power of arrest may be the same held by the regular police force for the jurisdiction. Private housing projects have been constructed under the auspices of the Department of Housing and Urban Development. Contract firms handle the security services in such projects. However, the federal government currently has grant monies available to municipal police departments for establishing community-based police programs in federally supported housing centers, e.g., dedicated police patrol operations, youth programs and centers, education/training projects, etc. Protection of life and property, and often order maintenance, are the primary security problems associated with public housing projects. Thefts, assaults, and vandalism are the specific crimes that police and security officers handle on a regular basis.

19. CARGO SECURITY

According to the National Cargo Security Council (NCSC), the United States industry lost approximately $10 billion in 1998 to theft. This represents a sizable loss to a $400 billion industry. The Council indicates that cargo theft has been on the increase. They attribute these losses to insufficient personnel and antiquated inventory and controlling systems.

20. SCHOOL SECURITY

a. College Campus Security

Colleges and universities have long recognized the need for their own security force. Many have well-organized forces comprised of personnel that have increased in both quality and quantity during the past several years. It is quite common to find two distinct types of security personnel on university campuses, i.e., the security officer responsible for physical security of buildings and grounds, and the security/police officer with powers of arrest. Elementary and secondary schools outside of large cities do not have a long history of having or requiring security services. It has only been during the last few years that elementary and secondary school security programs have become common across the country.

b. Elementary and Secondary Schools

In numerous school districts across the country, elementary and secondary schools are experiencing seemingly uncontrollable security problems. School violence has received national attention as a result of school shootings. According to the survey on school crime, produced by the National Center for Education and Statistics, there are 11,000 physical attacks or fights in which a weapon was used; 7,000 robberies, and 4,000 rapes or other kinds of sexual assault. A growing area of expertise for the millennium will be school security professionals and school officers.

Vandalism has become so extensive that administrators have assigned teachers regular duties to patrol hallways and restrooms. Recognizing that teachers are employed to teach rather than handle security (especially discipline matters occurring outside the classroom), most school administrators have accepted a proprietary security department. Even though safety of individuals is the primary concern of school safety/security officers, order maintenance and vandalism are the problems that occupy most of their time (See Appendix D: School Safety Resources).

21. INFORMATION AND COMPUTER SECURITY (INFO SECURITY)

Certain records and information in many organizations are absolutely vital to effective continued operation. The physical destruction of such information, or the loss of its confidentiality, could result in one or more of the following:

1) Decreased or terminated production capability;

2) Loss of competitive edge in marketplace;

3) Inability to provide services or products;

4) Inability to satisfy certain legal requirements;

5) Complication of dealings with suppliers and customers;

6) Financial detriment to employees and stockholders.

Some of the more common records or information kept by organizations include:

Accounts Receivable	Trade Secrets
Accounts Payable	Engineering Data
Financial Reports	Process Formulas
Bank Records	Sales Records
Contracts	Tax Records
Inventory Records	General Ledgers
Legal Documents	Negotiable Instruments
Production Records	Stockholder Records
Payroll and Personnel Records	Research Data

There is no universal method applicable to the security and protection of every kind of organizational record. Information comes in a variety of forms, and its relative importance can vary from organization to organization. Thus, the first stage in providing security and protection of information is to develop a procedure for evaluation and control. Generally, the following four steps must be taken:

1) a complete inventory of all organizational records and information;

2) an appraisal of the organizational value of each type of information;

3) development of an information classification system; and

4) application of appropriate levels of security as determined by the information classification system.

Once all the sources and types of information have been determined, a classification system must be established to differentiate between the records that are vital and those that are merely helpful. There are a number of different terms that can be used to separate and identify the various categories of information according to organizational value. The most common terms used to establish categories of business records and information include:

1) Vital Records—Records that are basically irreplaceable and are of the greatest value to continued operation of the organization.

2) Important Records—Records that can be replaced only at great expense of time and money.

3) Useful Records—Records that, when lost, would create inconveniences but could be replaced rather quickly.

4) Nonessential Records—Records that are not essential to effective organizational operation.

Other terms that could be used to categorize records are "top secret," "secret," "confidential," etc., with the same result: a system that implies the importance and composition of organizational information.

Methods of Protection

The protection of information can be accomplished by one or more of three methods: procedural controls, duplication, and storage. In each case, consideration must be given to the relative vulnerability of the information and the nature of the threat from which the information must be protected. See Chapter 8 for a discussion of industrial espionage and telecommunications fraud, which can occur and be perpetrated from both within and without the organization. Generally, the procedural and technological techniques used to accomplish information integrity and security must stay one step ahead of those who would misuse, steal, or otherwise damage organizational information. The potential risks and threats to valuable information must be determined and appropriate proactive countermeasures implemented.

Procedural controls are critical to all areas of security—especially information security. The initial step of the process of information classification is establishing control of the flow of information through the organization. Procedural controls must be established to ensure that availability, responsibility, and accountability of information to personnel is restricted and based only on "the need to know." Such measures would preclude the likelihood of access to protected information by employees who do not need to know and those outside the organization who may attempt to gain the information for various reasons, e.g., fraud, espionage, manipulation, or simply the challenge of defeating the information security program. Organizational records should be secured and protected in descending order of importance—that is, the more vital the record and the information contained therein, the greater the degree of control and security.

Duplication of records is both a security risk and a security asset. It provides for needed dissemination of information throughout the organization, but it also provides a means by which information can be copied surreptitiously and made available to others outside the organization. Thus, procedural controls must be adopted to ensure that unwarranted duplication does not occur. However, duplication of records can be used to provide an essential element of additional security. Any record that is vital or important to the organization can be duplicated and dispersed to one or more secure remote locations away from the primary storage. In the event that the primary source of this information is lost, the organization can continue without interruption.

The manner in which information storage is accomplished is a determining factor in the effective level of security. Information stored in desks and ordinary file cabinets has minimal protection against forcible entry, whereas information kept in a safe or vault is much more secure. Correspondingly, information stored in the computer or stored on disk or tape must be appropriately secured. Information declared to be important or vital should be protected by an appropriate security storage container. A careful analysis of risk factors must be done in order to decide the type of protection needed. The kinds of threats that must be considered include fire, espionage, and theft.

COMPUTER SECURITY

When information security is the primary topic of concern, the significance of computer security becomes readily apparent. Computer storage of information has become commonplace in business, industry, and government. Computers have greatly increased the ability to store, retrieve, manipulate, and transmit vital information, yet the misuse, damage, or loss of a computer can render helpless or destroy an entire company. Given this destructive potential, electronic data processing systems must be afforded an appropriately high level of security. Access to and operation of the computer unit must be controlled, and any attempt to enter, manipulate, or otherwise obtain information must be preventable and detectable.

Storage of data and programs on magnetic tapes, cards, disks, or drums is a vital part of any computer operation. The capacity to store such a large amount of data on such small physical devices is both a liability and an asset. Steps must be taken to provide security for their physical storage. Special storage units for the various forms of data provide not only security but also a controlled environment, because the temperature and humidity of some storage units or tape libraries must be within acceptable limits. Risks involving computers include fire, espionage, sabotage, accidental losses, data manipulation, theft, fraud, embezzlement, and natural disasters.

Securing the computer and its information from harm at one time meant surrounding the computer facility with locks, access control devices, and security personnel. Today, however, computers are not confined to a single room. They can be found almost anywhere in the business environment. Thus, physical security of computers is expanded to a variety of workstations and operational environments. The following are basic measures of physical and information security controls.

Physical Security Controls for Computers

1) Prevent intentional damage, unauthorized use, and theft. Consider computer locations and corresponding accessibility to unauthorized persons and susceptibility to hazards. Apply a level of security appropriate to information sensitivity and criticality—security controls must exceed identified risks and threats. Secure telephone and computer transmission lines from outside influence.

2) Take appropriate measures to prevent, detect, and minimize the effects of hazards such as water, fire, heat, humidity, and electrical power problems.

3) Protect and secure usage, storage, and disposal of computer storage media (documents, tapes, disks, printouts, etc.).

4) Contingency plans for continuous operations must be written, tested, and regularly communicated.

5) The integrity of computer personnel is essential to an effective computer security and information security program. All involved must have a supportive and working knowledge of computer and information security procedures and practices. Personnel selection and training are key components of any program designed to protect computer equipment and provide information security.

Computer Information Security Controls

1) Control access to both computer information and computer applications. Ensure that only authorized users have access to user identification, authentication, and password codes. Monitor and change authorized user codes periodically and randomly.

2) Provide procedures for the protection and integrity of all input and output information. Provide for checks on input accuracy and transactions.

3) Protect systems software. Developmental controls and policies should include security procedures for changing, accepting, and testing software prior to implementation. Controls should be incorporated that prevent unauthorized persons from obtaining, altering, or adding programs via remote terminals.

4) Enhance the adequacy of security controls by incorporating various auditing techniques for deterrence and detection of misuse and abuse. For example, audit trail printouts should be reviewed regularly and frequently.

5) Consider and apply appropriate measures for protection against any form of eavesdropping.

Decisions regarding the protection of information necessarily include the protection of computers and their usage from inside misuse and outside penetration. It is imperative that security managers provide sequential levels of security for computers and related information resources:

1) Prevention—Procedures and measures must be taken to restrict access to information and equipment to authorized personnel who perform only authorized functions.

2) Detection—Provide mechanisms and procedures for early discovery of abuses and crimes if prevention measures are circumvented.

3) Limitation—Provide for measures that will restrict losses if misuse or crime occurs despite prevention and detection controls.

4) Recovery—Provide measures for efficient information recovery through appropriate contingency plans.

The security requirements of each facility must be individually analyzed in light of physical factors, type and extent of risk exposure, and business experience. Whether the center of concern is a safe or a vault, it is security that decreases the chances for criminal success.

Information is a primary asset and must be protected as such. Only after an in-depth evaluation of all records can an effective and appropriate level of security be accomplished for the control of the flow and storage of information. Appropriate and adequate security measures must be taken to ensure the integrity of computers and their operations. Employees with access to computer equipment and automated information are increasing throughout the organizational hierarchy.

New sources of information regarding the protection of information and computer security become available on approximately a weekly basis. An excellent source for staying current on the issues is the Security Wire Daily which is a news service available free to the public at *www.infosecuritymag.com/securitywire.*

Security Wire features articles focusing on the news, events, and people closely involved with the infosecurity industry. They also feature a column called *CryptoRhythm* that focuses on cryptography. The same group that processes Security Wire also has available the *Information Society Magazine* that is distributed monthly to more than 41,000 Information Security professionals. The magazine is published by ICSA, Inc. and can be reached by visiting their Web site at *www.icsa.net.*

SUMMARY: SECURITY TODAY

Although crime rates have declined for the sixth consecutive year, the fear of crime continues to rise. Americans are reaching out for protection beyond that which can be provided by the nation's overcommitted and understaffed public law enforcement agencies. As a result, the number of private security personnel now exceeds that of public law enforcement, and the number of companies doing business in security products and services has and is projected to increase dramatically. There is little doubt that there is a growing need for the resources and talents of private security in society.

This significant growth has resulted from the recognition of private security's potential for contribution to national crime prevention and reduction. It is here that the distinction between the roles of private security and public law enforcement is clearest. Public law enforcement forces are apprehension-oriented. That is, they usually act after the crime has already occurred. On the other hand, private security is prevention-oriented and emphasizes the prevention of crime. While their orientations are different, the goal is the same: the elimination of crime. Serving a common goal emphasizes the common interests of private security and the public law enforcement system. The private security sector cannot and was never intended to replace public law enforcement. Instead, each complements the other in the effort to control crime. The scope and range of the nation's crime problem dictate that the two components work closely together without competition or disharmony. The current trend toward increased professionalism in private security will serve to upgrade existing practices and procedures. Higher standards of employment, training, and licensing requirements will increase the effectiveness of private security services and provide for a more mutually productive relationship between private security and public law enforcement.

DISCUSSION QUESTIONS

1. Why can't public law enforcement agencies provide adequate protection for business and industry against crime?

2. What is economic crime? Who suffers the impact?

3. Outline the major differences between contract guard services and proprietary guard services.

4. What factors have generated an increasing demand for contract guard services?

5. Why are airlines and airports principal targets of terrorist acts?

6. What are some of the key security areas in hotels and motels?

7. List three aspects of the Bank Protection Act of 1968.

8. Describe some of the features of a secure ATM site.

9. Why is security such a critical concern for healthcare facilities?

10. What is the role of the General Services Administration?

11. Why is there a need for security in public schools?

12. What changes were initiated for campus security programs with the passage of the Crime Awareness and Campus Security Act of 1990?

13. Discuss the differences in orientation between public law enforcement and private security? Is there a common goal?

14. Discuss the future of private security—areas of growth, decline, change, etc.

REFERENCES

Twentieth Century Press Release (Jan. 7, 1999). "Yahoo!" *Finance*.

Arko, R.L. (July 1992). "Contract Security Rolls Into the Transit Industry." *Security Management*. Arlington, VA.

Associated Press (1992, October 19). "GAO Says U.S. Isn't Prosecuting Many of FBI's Bank Fraud Cases." *Lexington Herald-Leader*, p. A5.

Bureau of Labor Statistics (April 1999). [online]

Cunningham, W.C., Strauchs, J.J. & Van Meter, C.W. (1990). *Private Security Trends 1970-2000: The Hallcrest Report II.* Stoneham, MA: Butterworth-Heinemann.

Hannah, J. (May 1992). "Need Quick $20.00 Stamps? New License? Just Slip the Right Card into a Machine." *Louisville Courier Journal, 31.*

Higgins, C.E. (May 1988). "Energize! Nuclear Security." *Security Management.* Arlington, VA.

Infant Kidnapping Update (Feb., 1997). "Infant Kidnapping Update: Electronic Security, Officer Training, Parent Alertness Help Foil Abductors in 1996." *Hospital Security and Safety Management.*

Museum Security Network (May 2, 1999). [online] http://museum-security.org

Richards, R. (1990, October 22). "Amtrak Makes Tracks in the West." *USA Today,* p. 11E.

Robinson, C.H. (May, 1991). "The Hospital Dilemma." *Security Management.* Arlington, VA.

Security Business (Sept., 1996). "Global Market for Security Services Projected to Increase 7.9% Annually thru Year 2000." *Security Business,* Vol. XXVI, No. 16, Part III.

Security Letter (April, 1997). "Largest US Security Guard, Patrol and Investigative Companies." *Security Letter, Part III.*

Walpole, J.J. (February 1991). "The Brave New World of Hotel Security." *Security Management.* Arlington, VA.

USA Today (Feb. 2, 1999). "Feds Charge 13 in Net Investment Fraud." p. 6B.

(May, 1997). *Hotel/Motel Security and Safety Management,* Vol. 15, No. 6.

Security Personnel

4

INTRODUCTION

The U.S. Department of Labor estimates that approximately 70 percent of all companies rely extensively on contract security forces. Outsourcing became popular in the mid to late 1980s and is now common practice. This reliance on outside service, now referred to as strategic partnering or outsourcing, has become commonplace in organizations. Private security personnel continue to outnumber public law enforcement officers in the United States. According to the Bureau of Labor Statistics, there were 420,750 Police Patrol Officers in 1997 as compared to 954,644 Security Officers. There are a number of reasons for this: the general economic growth of the post-war period; the movement of population from the central cities to the suburbs, which has led to the development of shopping centers and malls; tax restraints, such as Proposition 13 in California and the Gramm-Rudman-Hollings Act, which often reduce the funds available for public law enforcement; and an increasing fear of crime that has caused Americans to demand more security.

Because of the importance of private security, there is a need for a thorough understanding of the processes that must be utilized to maximize the efficiency and effectiveness of private security personnel. At this point, there is no need to differentiate between contract and proprietary security services because both must deal with the same problems of recruitment, selection, training, and licensing. The issue of contract vs. proprietary personnel is a real and controversial issue. For example, in some states legislation provides one set of selection and training standards for contract security and another for proprietary security. Strangely enough, this is often accomplished through "non-legislation" as it relates to proprietary security personnel. The legislatures simply do not make the legislation binding on proprietary services. Contract security companies have argued (with little success to date) that this discriminates against them by reducing their opportunity to compete in the marketplace with companies that have proprietary forces. Obviously, although most security personnel will publicly deny it, the real issue seems to be "turf protection" for proprietary security. As long as the contract companies have legislation that costs them money, they will be less capable of taking over security services at companies that presently have proprietary forces. To the new person in the field of private security, this issue of separate legislation may seem minor, but to those who have experience in private security, the issue is real and important.

CURRENT INDUSTRY CRITICISM

The use of contract security by organizations continues to be seen as nothing more than the hiring of a guard for the purpose of controlling some predefined perimeter. Neither they, nor the contract security company as a "preferred vendor," are seen as providing an important service to the organization. An explanation for this type of relationship, or lack thereof, between organizations and contract security companies has been described by management author Dennis Dalton as follows: "A recent study conducted for California State University at Hayward found that companies typically do not begin to think about security in a formal way until their annual sales and/or assets exceed $400 million." (Dalton, 1997). Most private security personnel will readily admit that the industry is criticized because of the lack of employment criteria such as specific educational requirements and the absence of uniform training requirements. Unfortunately, much of that criticism is warranted. However, criticism is also leveled at public law enforcement, courts, corrections, and almost all other organizations and services that deal with the public. Certainly the professions of teaching, law, and medicine have increasingly been criticized recently. Thus, private security personnel should not be overly defensive in their response to criticism. Level of competency comparisons are often made between security officers and police officers. This is an unfair comparison because the roles and responsibilities between security and law enforcement are very different. Moreover, salaries and compensation are also very different between the two. For example, in 1997 the mean hourly wage for security officers was $8.34, the mean annual wage was $17,350 as compared to police officers who had a mean hourly wage of $18.17 and a mean annual wage of $37,800. Law enforcement has made considerable strides in obtaining improved salaries, comprehensive and mandatory training, and annual in-service training. Although there have been numerous attempts over the years to mandate security officer training, every bill that has been introduced has been struck down. The opposing argument is that it needs to be a state-by-state requirement. Unfortunately, very few states have set forth hiring and training requirements for security officers. Until there is federal legislation setting forth minimum requirements, it is unlikely that states will make any changes to their current requirements for the hiring and training of security personnel. This remains the greatest stumbling block for the advancement and professionalism of the security officer profession.

Most recent studies conducted of the age, race, education, demographics, general physical characteristics, etc., of private security personnel have found that differences between private and public law enforcement with regard to these factors are minimal. The only exception was a study conducted in the early 1970s by the RAND Corporation. However, it should be noted that the RAND study was done with a small sample and in one geographic location (southern California), and it is generally agreed that their sample was not typical of the industry as a whole. (It is interesting to note, however, that the RAND study is more often cited in the literature than the other research that has been conducted.)

Anthony Potter, at the First Annual Conference on Private Security, conducted at the University of Maryland in December, 1975, provided valuable insight into the subject of ineffective security personnel with the "Private Security Vicious Circle, depicted in Figure 4.1. Most persons involved in the private security industry see few positive steps being taken to help people "break out" of that circle.

Figure 4.1
Private Security Vicious Circle

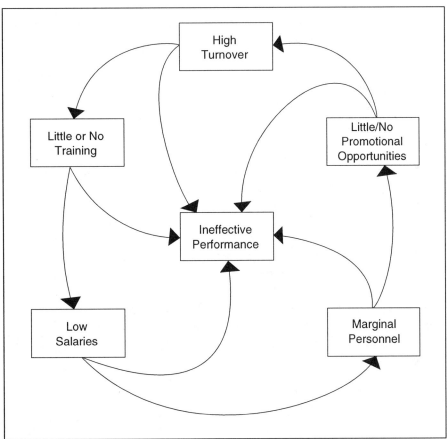

If we accept the statement that differences are minimal as outlined above, the problem lies in the factors that cannot be quantified. These factors include motivation, dedication, common sense, and many other psychological factors. For example, it is fairly well-accepted that persons sometimes enter the field of private security because of what is called the "John Wayne Syndrome," i.e., the opportunity to carry a gun and be recognized as a powerful person has motivated some people to enter the field. It is also known that the same motivation has caused some individuals to apply for public law enforcement positions. The difference is that, for the most part, public law enforcement uses testing and referrals to psychologists and psychiatrists to try to determine the applicants' thoughts and perceptions about these matters. Private security firms, on the other hand, almost never take the time, effort, and money to review applicants' feelings about this issue.

OBSERVATIONS ON SELECTION AND TERMINATION PROCESSES

One study of applicants, reported in *Security* (March, 1997), provided data which supports the need for screening.

WHY SCREEN?

7.3% – Had a criminal record in the last seven years
10% – Had four or more moving violations, two or more accidents, a DUI or DWI, or had a suspended license
17% – Have credit records showing a judgment, lien, or bankruptcy
21% – Had a previous workers' compensation claim
30% – Misrepresented employment records
47% – Had one or more accidents or moving violations on driving record

While many of these factors would not, in and of themselves, be justification for not hiring they do indicate that there is a need for a good selection process for private security employees.

CHC Forecast Inc. in *Security* (April, 1996) provided the following information related to the need for proper screening. The information was based on 10,000 randomly selected tests given to retail job applicants. Of the 10,000 25 percent were rated "high-risk."

STATEMENTS MADE BY "HIGH-RISK" APPLICANTS ON AN HONESTY TEST

Percent

32.8	Could be tempted to steal from their employer
17.6	Might help friends steal from their company
21.3	Had frequently associated with fellow employees who admitted they were stealing merchandise from the company
12.4	Stated they are not an honest person and might cheat or steal
17.6	Had stolen money within the past three years
15.4	Had stolen merchandise within the past three years
21.3	Said they would possibly use marijuana or other illegal drug in the future
3.6	Admitted to previously selling marijuana or other illegal drugs

Another study, reported in *Security Senior's Digest*, August 13, 1997, found that in a 1995 survey of 1,331 personnel department workers by the Society for Human Resources Management, revealed that 63 percent of the respondents said that fear of a lawsuit kept them from providing information about a former employee. Seventeen percent said disgruntled former employees had challenged them over allegedly inaccurate references. The problem has become so widespread that 26 states have passed laws giving employers limited immunity when they give a reference.

John W. Jones and Joseph A. Orban in *Security* (September, 1990) outlined some of the dangers in hiring "any warm body" and some of the specific problems that can occur such as:

* Increased theft and shrinkage

* Exposure to negligent hiring claims

* Increased accidents and insurance losses

* Lower quality service

* Unskilled workers require more supervision

* Higher turnover

* Charges of unfair hiring practices

Most predictions by the U.S. Department of Labor and others show that the potential workforce is growing at a rate of less than two percent annually. As we move into the twenty-first century, this will require that private security employers use realistic and viable selection processes.

Equally disturbing for employers are the statistics related to wrongful terminations which, unfortunately, is often related to poor selection processes.

USA Today (April 2, 1998) presented a series of statistics and observations worth noting.

- More than 24,000 wrongful termination suits were filed in federal court in 1997. This is up 77 percent from the number filed in 1993.

- Costs to companies for wrongful termination coverage will increase from $130 million in premiums now to $1 billion in five years.

- Judges still throw out many wrongful termination lawsuits, but juries are finding for workers more than half the time.

- The Civil Rights Restoration Act of 1991 greatly strengthened the 1964 law by letting plaintiffs recover not just back wages but legal fees and punitive damages up to $300,000. The result is that lawyers accept more cases.

- The Family and Medical Leave Act of 1993 allows workers to sue if they are fired for taking up to 12 weeks of unpaid time off to care for a sick family member.

- Many companies hire workers from temporary services or outsource work to avoid the potential liability.

- In 1997 13 percent of lawsuits against companies were for wrongful termination compared to 5 percent for discrimination and 3 percent for harassment.

- Juries awarded a median of $205,794 for wrongful termination in 1996. This is an increase of 38 percent from $149,385 in 1995.

- In cases settled out of court the median award jumped to $81,250 in 1996 from $38,000 in 1995 and $25,000 in 1994.

- In 1997 the average compensatory award for wrongful termination was $532,000 compared to $501,000 for sex discrimination or $158,000 for disability discrimination.

SELECTION

There are no selection standards that apply to the entire private security industry. Extensive research has been conducted on this subject and the conclusions are always the same—no uniformity exists.

RECRUITMENT

At present, newspaper advertisements and listings of contract security companies in the Yellow Pages provide the potential employee with the best leads to employment opportunities. Almost every day, in newspapers throughout the

United States, there are advertisements placed by companies seeking applicants. Because of the low salaries in most private security jobs, the advertisements are seldom large. Furthermore, careful reading will show clearly that the qualifications are, at best, minimal. Traditional qualifications for employment, such as education and experience, are seldom listed. About the only general qualification is a "clean police record," which certainly should be expected. Unfortunately, there is often little agreement among employees about what is considered a "clean record," and what is acceptable to one employer might not be acceptable to another. Most security firms in major cities maintain full-time employment offices. However, opportunities are somewhat limited for potential employees from other areas. The larger contract companies and larger corporations do, from time to time, send recruiters to the nonmetropolitan areas, but this is usually as a last resort when they cannot find applicants locally. Thus, for the most part, private security employees come from areas close to where they live. From a recruitment standpoint this is not a disadvantage, because most employers are happy to find any type of person and are not overly concerned with their qualifications.

The recruitment of management personnel follows a somewhat different process. Companies fill these positions by promoting present employees or recruiting persons from the outside. Two major sources of recruitment are heavily utilized. First, the companies actively maintain contacts with public law enforcement agencies through personal contacts and local public law enforcement associations. For example, it is not uncommon for a representative of private security to make an announcement of a position opening at a law enforcement association meeting, and to promote the position informally before and after the meeting.

The second source used is campus recruitment. In some cases the recruitment is done by the security department, usually in coordination with the criminal justice faculty. In many cases, however, the companies simply utilize the college recruitment processes of the company and do not make any special effort to recruit security personnel independently.

The recruitment of security personnel is not a complex or sophisticated process. Job opportunities for persons seeking work as guards are expected to be favorable through the year 2006. High turnover and this occupation's large size rank it among those providing the greatest number of job openings in the economy. Many opportunities are expected for persons seeking full-time employment, as well as for those seeking part-time or second jobs at night or on weekends. However, some competition is expected for higher-paying, high security positions. Compared to unarmed security guards, armed guards and special police enjoy higher earnings and benefits, greater job security, more advancement potential, and are usually given more training and responsibility.

In summary, the high turnover rate (more than 100 percent in one year) is one of the main problems faced by security firms; this is reflected in the constant advertising done by the employers. Management positions are filled by a somewhat different procedure. Obtaining management positions will take more initiative on the part of applicants because the recruitment of retiring police officers and college recruiting are the main methods now being used. Individuals who do not have the experience or opportunity to learn of openings through these processes will have to send résumés, visit employment offices, and follow other traditional job-hunting methods if they want to obtain management positions.

Application

Companies must be careful to insure that the questions asked do not violate any provisions of the Americans with Disabilities Act, Civil Rights Acts, and other applicable guidelines. It should accomplish at least three things. First, it should permit the candidate to demonstrate the ability to read and comprehend instructions. Second, it should allow the employer to determine if the writing skills are commensurate with the job. Third, it should form the frame of reference for the background investigation.

Screening Interview

The screening interview is a two-way communication—employer to applicant and applicant to employer. Although somewhat subjective, it allows both parties to assess the job situation. Employer questions should include: (1) "Why do you want the job?"; (2) "What are your career objectives?"; (3) "What interests you about the job?"; and (4) other job-related questions.

The employer should clearly indicate to the applicant: the requirements, any positive and negative aspects, salary, fringe benefits, and other pertinent factors about the job. The screening interview also allows the employer to assess the applicant's character. Although such an assessment is admittedly highly subjective, the applicant's demeanor and attitude during the interview may indicate the need for more careful background investigation or even psychological testing.

Testing

Skills tests – in developing these tests, the key issue is to insure that the skills are job-related. For example, it would probably not be correct to require a candidate to type, unless there was no provision for them to write or print reports.

Personality/Psychological Tests – These tests have resulted in a number of lawsuits and/or complaints to the Equal Employment Opportunity Commission. However, they can be valuable in determining the probability of an employee remaining on the job for a reasonable length of time and can also help to detect undesirable traits such as dishonesty. These tests also can be beneficial in determining whether a person should be placed in a position that has high levels of interaction with other employees or would be better placed in a position that has limited contact with others.

An important EEOC guideline regarding this matter is that psychological screening exams are not considered medical exams and can be administered before an offer of employment has been made.

The key issue in regard to these, and other, tests is test validation. Three key points are: (1) If it measures personal characteristics that are related to job performance; (2) If it tests skill to be used while performing the job; and (3) If it can be connected to predicted performance.

Honesty Test

For the purpose of this standard, honesty tests refer only to written tests that allow employers to gain insights into a prospective employee's honesty without extensive costs. In general terms, honesty tests are designed to measure trustworthiness, attitude toward honesty, and the need to steal.

Several paper-and-pencil honesty tests were reviewed. This independent evaluation determined that the tests appear to have high face validity. Several validity and reliability studies supporting such tests have been published in scholarly journals. However, it should be noted that much of the supporting evidence is based on subsequent detection-of-deception examinations of persons who had taken the written honesty tests. Nevertheless, honesty tests used with background investigations should furnish a reliable method of determining honesty.

BACKGROUND INVESTIGATIONS

Many companies rely on the state licensing board to conduct background investigation, which normally consists of a fingerprint check for criminal activities. While this practice is widespread, there is general agreement that it is not effective unless used in conjunction with a thorough background check. Whenever practical, both phone and in person contacts should be made in an effort to obtain necessary information, verify statements on application, and obtain a perspective as to how others view the applicant based on their contacts with the potential employee. It is important to constantly remember that the purpose of the background investigation, like the other steps, is to access the ability and potential to perform job-related duties.

Since many employers are reluctant to provide information on former employees because of possible litigation, it is very important that the potential employee sign letters of authorization to schools, references, and previous employers. In many cases, unless this step is accomplished the previous employers will provide no response or a response that is so vague that it is really not useful in making an employment decision.

Background investigations should be conducted prior to employment and/or assignment. Too often, employers either do not conduct any background investigations, or their investigations are sketchy. Many employers use only the telephone and/or form letters for background information. Such methods do not provide sufficient data for effective verification and evaluation. Although costly, field investigations provide valuable information about an individual's character and ability that cannot be gained by other means and should be encouraged.

FINAL INTERVIEW

This provides an opportunity for the applicant to respond to any questions or concerns that might have evolved during the selection process. With careful consideration to the confidential nature of the information obtained from others, it is a reasonable practice to allow the applicant to check the records to make sure that they are accurate. For example, a credit check could reveal information that has changed since the time it was obtained. After the final interview, the potential new employer should be sent an offering letter outlining the specific duties of the job, assignments, and salary and benefits.

DRUG AND MEDICAL EXAMINATIONS

An important consideration in regard to those tests is at what point they should be given. There are two perspectives that must be examined. First, in many cases these are the most expensive tests and from a financial standpoint should only be given to candidates that appear to be qualified based on the other tests. Second, and in many ways more important, are the legal restrictions placed on the timing primarily as required by government regulations and guidelines. ADA plays a significant role in regard to these tests. Except in very specific instances the medical test cannot be given until after a job offer has been made and accepted. However, the drug test is not considered a "medical test" and can be given at any time during the selection process. Most experts agree that, if a drug test is to be used, it should be administered to all applicants who are being seriously considered for employment.

EEOC and ADA provide guidelines as to the definitions of a medical exam. They can be summarized as:

- A medical exam is a procedure that is administered by a health professional, including a psychologist.

- Medical exam results are interpreted by a healthcare professional.

- A medical exam is invasive – it requires the drawing of blood, urine, or breath – or it would normally take place in a medical setting and be administered using medical equipment.

- A medical exam measures physiological or psychological responses of a test taker, as opposed to simply measuring performance on a task.

ADDITIONAL CONCERNS AND ISSUES PERTAINING
TO THE SELECTION PROCESS

Because of the critical importance of the selection process it is the subject of many articles in professional journals. While it would be impractical to try to include all concerns and issues these seem to be especially important.

One concern is the issue of negligent hiring and the lawsuits that can and are filed as a result of this situation. *Security Director's Digest* (July 2, 1997) gave an example of a 27-year-old department store executive who was sexually assaulted by a security guard where she worked. She sued her employer for hiring him.

Employers appear to be making greater use of public law enforcement records. Of course, except in unusual cases, the records are not public and require that the employer obtain written authorization to make the checks. *Security Director's Digest* (March 5, 1997) reported that the Hamilton County Sheriff's office in northern Kentucky processed approximately 53,000 background checks in 1996 and a neighboring department, Cincinnati, Ohio, processed about 50,000. Most law enforcement agencies charge a nominal fee for each check.

David L. Johnston, CPP, CFE in an article in *Security Director's Digest* (July 18, 1995) cautioned about the possibility of imposters taking tests. He reports that more than 3,000 organizations in North America have developed paper and pencil tests or computerized testing programs to measure a candidate's level of professional knowledge. Several suggestions are to develop a positive identification program based on photographs, thumbprint, or signatures and make sure that the tests are stored in a secure area and counted on a regular basis to make sure none are missing.

The use of consumer reporting agencies appears to be increasing. *Security Management* (April 1995) outlined one program that is used by security companies. The company that collects the data is a qualified reporting agency under the Fair Credit Reporting Act which tends to reduce the exposure to liability. The information collected and disseminated on security guards includes such items as: names, social security numbers, periods of employment, guard registration numbers (if appropriate), rehire status, reasons for leaving, positions held, and work records. Companies that belong to the service pay an initial fee, which can be avoided or reduced if they provide relevant data on their officers. The consumer reporting agency requires that the employer obtain a signed statement from the applicant allowing access to their records.

A practice that has been common in the private security industry for many years has resulted in a court decision that could alter the situation. Contract companies often obtain new contracts and in some cases it is to their advantage to try to hire employees away from the company that has lost the contract. *Security Management* (February, 1997) provided an analysis of the court decision and made several important points. First, noncompete agreements between employers and entry-level security employees do not violate U.S. antitrust laws. Second, the noncompete agreement was for only one site and for one year it did not place an undue hardship on the employee. Third, the court recognized the investment in screening and training of the employees. The case is: *Borg-Warner Protective Services, Corp. et al. v. Guardsmark, Inc.*, U.S. District Court for the Eastern District of Kentucky, No. 94-169, 1996.

QUALIFICATIONS AND SELECTION CRITERIA

The following is from the work of the International Association of Chiefs of Police Private Security Liaison Committee and was published in 1998.

All private security officers must meet the applicable statutory requirements and the established criteria of the employer, which may exceed minimum mandated requirements. Federal law mandates that candidates for employment must be citizens or possess legal alien status prior to employment. All applicants who are hired or certified as a private security officer should meet the following minimum criteria:

A. Be at least 18 years of age—"unarmed" private security officer.

B. Be at least 21 years of age—"armed" private security officer and comply with U.S. Public Law 104-208 Section 658 (The Omnibus Consolidated Appropriations Act of 1997).

C. Possess a valid state driver's license (if applicable).

D. Have not been:

   1. Convicted of or pled guilty or nolo contendere to a felony in any jurisdiction;

   2. Convicted of or pled guilty or nolo contendere to a misdemeanor involving moral turpitude, acts of dishonesty, or acts against governmental authority, including the use and/or possession of a controlled substance within a seven-year period;

   3. Convicted or pled guilty or nolo contendere to any crime in any jurisdiction involving the sale, delivery, or manufacture of a controlled substance; or

   4, Declared by any court to be incompetent by reason of mental disease or defect that has not been removed or expunged.

E. Submit two sets of classifiable fingerprints and two passport-sized photographs, along with applicant's name, address, date of birth, social security number, citizenship status, and a statement of conviction of crimes in order to conduct a state criminal record check, and, where possible, a FBI criminal history check, prior to permanent employment as a private security officer. In all instances, these actions must be taken prior to private security officer's being armed;

F. Furnish information about all prior employment through the employer making a reasonable effort to verify the last seven years of employment history, and checking three personal references; and

G. Successfully pass a recognized pre-employment drug screen.

Suggested non-regulated pre-employment applicant criteria include the following:

A. High school education or equivalent;

B. Military discharge records (DD 214);

C. Mental and physical capacity to perform duties for which being employed;

D. Armed applicants shall successfully complete a relevant psychological evaluation to verify that the applicant is suited for duties for which being employed.

Commentary

There is genuine potential for security employees and police officers or sheriffs' deputies to be simultaneously involved in an active crime scene. It is for this reason, as well as the need to ensure that private-security personnel are capable of making good decisions in the field, that great care must be exercised in their recruitment and selection. A second and equally important consideration is that these private-security officers possess high-quality ethical standards since they will be entrusted to safeguard the persons, homes, and businesses of their communities.

OTHER SCREENING CONSIDERATIONS

It is shocking to realize that many armed guards are not screened to determine whether they have major psychological problems that would render them unacceptable for employment involving carrying a deadly weapon. Obviously, extreme care should be taken to ensure that all screening measures are job-related and are not an invasion of the applicant's individual rights. It is also important that screening methods be administered and evaluated by competent personnel and the results carefully protected from illegal release. Properly conducted pre-employment screening will aid employers in selecting capable and trustworthy employees. By eliminating those unsuited for private security work, such screening processes will lead to increased productivity and lower turnover rates.

Another issue is the exchange of information between employers. At first glance this would seem to be quite simple, but it is not. For example, Company A might have a "bad" employee who is either fired or has resigned. Shortly thereafter, Company B calls Company A to verify employment. Company A is aware that Company B has a contract with the XYZ Company and would like to have that contract for themselves. There is now a strong incentive or Company A to give a good recommendation for the employee, in hopes that he or she will be hired, perform poorly, and thus cause the XYZ Company to become dissatisfied with Company B. This could cause Company A to obtain the bid themselves. Despite this type of situation, it is in the best interests of private security, generally, for the employers to exchange information on at least the following items: dependability, honesty, initiative, judgment, and loyalty.

Another issue encompasses affirmative action and equal employment opportunity practices. Most government contracts require this in the selection process, but many smaller firms have no government contracts and are difficult to monitor with regard to these issues. Studies by the Private Security Task Force in New Orleans, Louisiana, and St. Louis, Missouri, in 1975 indicate that, in comparison to race ratios in those cities, private security has a proportionate ratio of minority employees. In 1990 a follow-up study in St. Louis verified that the ratio of minority employees to city race ratios is the same.

A comprehensive study on this issue was conducted by Hallcrest Systems, Inc. of McLean, Virginia and reported in *Private Security and Police in America: The Hallcrest Report I*. This book is based on a 30-month descriptive research project under a grant from the National Institute of Justice, U.S. Department of Justice. One interesting aspect of this information is that it provides data on both proprietary and contract security personnel. While many people continue to believe that older persons are the main source for private security employment, this is not true. The median age for both groups in this study was 31-35 years of age. Also, 95 percent of the proprietary personnel and 90 percent of the contractual personnel had at least a high school degree or GED.

A factor that has become very apparent, especially in the last decade, is that private security is making greater use of women than public law enforcement. Separate studies conducted by Jack Molden and Michael Hoefling of the University of Illinois Police Training Institute reveal that 5 percent of police personnel in Illinois are female. A study reported in the Hallcrest Report indicated that 6 percent of public law enforcement officers were female. Other studies in the Hallcrest Report revealed that 24 percent of the employees in proprietary companies and 12 percent in contractual companies were female. This is especially significant because, in 1990, there were approximately 900,000 more employees in private security than in public law enforcement.

Another problem was that various states had developed rules and regulations regarding access to their Criminal Justice Information Systems and, for the most part, private security employers were denied access. This put a serious restraint on the ability of private security employers to assess the applicant's qualifications. Many employers used an informal system, through cooperation with various public agencies, to sidestep this restriction. Moreover, this process, in addition to being illegal, did not meet the needs of the employers. One security executive indicated his total frustration with the situation with this example. His company did some government contracting that required security clearances for certain employees and was responsible for conducting the screening and selection of these persons. Because this individual did not have official access to the necessary information, he had to, in effect, violate one law in order to comply with another.

Recently, there have been some encouraging changes with regard to these situations. The Freedom of Information Act has required states to review—and in most cases revise—their policies and procedures regarding allowing access to their criminal conviction records. For example, in Illinois, private security companies can obtain the criminal conviction records for current and prospective employees for a nominal service charge. Other states have adopted or are in the process of adopting similar policies and procedures for access to their records. Private security executives have urged these changes for many decades and now must use the new opportunity.

AMERICANS WITH DISABILITIES ACT OF 1990 AND CIVIL RIGHTS ACT OF 1991

Two federal acts—the Americans with Disabilities Act of 1990 (ADA) and the Civil Rights Act of 1991—have the potential to greatly influence all employment decisions in the future for both public and private employers. Most experts agree that these acts will be subjected to wide interpretations and that the real impact will be determined through additional clarifying legislation and/or court decisions. However, a basic understanding of these acts is important in relation to the employment of private security personnel.

Because both acts focus on employee rights, it is appropriate to combine the key elements of both in an attempt to understand their potential impact on all aspects of employment. The following information is provided in the form of a checklist and is not presented in any particular order of priority. It is not intended to include all aspects of the new laws. Persons who will be making employment decisions are encouraged to closely monitor the many legislative changes and/or court decisions that occur in relation to these laws. The key issues for employees and employers are:

1) Review affirmative action plans to make sure they do not have differential treatment for written exams, oral exams, or physical agility tests.

2) Ensure that all job descriptions are current and written before the hiring process has been initiated. Special emphasis must be given to the essential job tasks and requirements for these tasks.

3) Under ADA, a disabled person is:

    —a person with a mental or physical impairment that substantially limits one or more major life activities

    —a person with a record of such impairment

    —a person regarded as having such impairment

4) Prior mental disorders and alcohol or drug use cannot be used in making employment decisions.

5) Current mental disorders and alcohol or drug use may be used in making employment decisions if these factors can be clearly established to be job-related.

6) Medical examinations cannot be given until after an offer of employment or promotion has been made, and then can be used to deny employment or promotion only if the results can be clearly defended as job-related.

7) Drug tests can be administered before an employment decision is made, provided that the test is job-related.

8) A key term in the ADA is "reasonable accommodation." This means that employers may have to change work schedules, restructure jobs and/or make accommodations in office arrangements, or purchase new equipment to accommodate disabled workers.

9) ADA makes it unlawful to discriminate in all employment decisions such as recruitment, hiring, job assignments, pay, layoffs, firing, training, promotions, benefits, and leave.

This checklist is not intended to be all-inclusive. Private security employees and employers must constantly monitor legislative and/or court orders to ensure that they understand and comply with these acts.

AFFIRMATIVE ACTION

For more than three decades, affirmative action has been a factor in the selection, retention, and promotion of private security personnel. Only two studies could be found that provide any opportunity to determine whether private security has supported this effort. One, a longitudinal analysis that covered a 30-year period (1959-1989) in St. Louis, provides some information on this subject. Trends over this 30-year period indicate:

• The number of women doubled every 15 years.

• 10 percent of security employees in 1959 were black.

• Percentages for Black and Caucasian security employees remained constant at about 50 percent between from 1975-1989.

A comparison with public law enforcement can be seen by referring to Figure 4.3. While generalizations based on this limited analysis can be misleading it does tend to support a position that private security employers have been supporting affirmative action efforts.

Figure 4.2
Characteristics of Private Security Personnel
St. Louis Missouri (1959-1989)

Total Licensed Security Personnel	1959 n = 819	1975 n = 2,977	1989 n = 4,322
Profile Data	%	%	%
Sex			
Male	100	93	86
Female	0	7	14
Race			
Caucasian	90	50	49
Black	10	50	51
Other	0	0	0
Age			
Average (in yrs.)	52	42	N/A
24 and under		13	14
25-34		21	38
35-44		22	22
45-54		22	11
55-64		16	10
65-74		5	4
75 and over		0.2	1
Height (average)	N/A	5'8"	N/A
Weight (average)	N/A	181	N/A
Education (average)	9	11	See Note
Marital Status (%)			
Married	74	50	50
Single	19	43	50
Divorced	7	7	
Totals may not add to 100% due to rounding.			
Note: Averages not available, but data are greater than 12 years; 1,535 equal to 12 years: 2,201; less than 12 years: 586			

Source: William C. Cunningham, John J. Strauchs, and Clifford W. Van Meter (1990). *Private Security Trends 1970-2000: The Hallcrest Report II*, Table 5.1, p. 138. Stoneham, MA: Butterworth-Heinemann.

Figure 4.3
Police Recruit Profile

		1986	**1987**	**1988**	**Average**
Age		26.2 yrs.	26.4 yrs.	26.4 yrs.	26.4 yrs.
Sex					
	Male	94.2%	92.8%	88.8%	92.05%
	Female	5.8%	7.2%	11.2%	8.0%
Race					
	White	94.7%	89.7%	96.3%	93.3%
	Black	5.3%	10.3%	3.75%	6.7%
Education		13.8 yrs.	13.5 yrs.	13.6 yrs.	13.6 yrs.

Source: William C. Cunningham, John J. Strauchs, and Clifford W. Van Meter (1990). *Private Security Trends 1970-2000: The Hallcrest Report II*, Table 5.3, p. 140. Stoneham, MA: Butterworth-Heinemann.

From a hiring standpoint, it is not imperative that the security employee or employer know the positions for and against affirmative action. However, a basic understanding of the positions can be important in understanding the impact on the selection, retention, and promotion policies in private security.

Parade Magazine (May 31, 1998) presented several points on this matter.

FOR	AGAINST
• It's a form of reparation for past discrimination.	• It's a form of reverse discrimination.
• It fosters opportunity for women shut out by the "old-boys' network."	• Preferences are minorities and based on color and gender.

In considering the importance of affirmative action it is important, as it is for other reasons, to have a well-researched and written job description. It is the job description that determines if a candidate has the right qualifications, knowledge, skills, and abilities to get the job done. Of no importance is race, color, sex, religion, age, national origin, citizenship status, veteran status, or disability unless there is a clear relationship between the criteria and the job to be performed.

During the interview process certain questions should not be asked or considered when making the hiring decision. The following questions were selected from the Grand Valley State University Recruitment & Affirmative Action Policies and Procedures for Faculty, Executive, Administrative & Professional Staff and Clerical, Office & Technical Staff 1997-1998.

Questions NOT to Ask

- medical or mental history;

- national origin and citizenship status;

- height, weight, or physical characteristics;

- membership in professional or civic organizations that would reveal national origin, race, gender, religion, or any of the protected classes under fair employment practice laws;

- military service history;

- marital status;

- sexual orientation;

- previous address;

- names of relatives;

- receipt of unemployment insurance, workers' compensation, or disability benefits;

- foreign languages;

- child care, family planning, or number of children;

- religion or religious beliefs;

- past rejection for bonding; and

- salary history

Questions That CAN Be Asked if Related to Job

- completing incomplete information on application form;

- gaps in work experience or education;

- if applicable, geographic preferences and feelings about relocation;

- working hours;

- if applicable, overnight travel;

- reasons for leaving previous jobs;

- personal attributes that could contribute to job performance;

- job-related achievements;

- signs of initiative and self-direction;

- indications of work habits;

- specialized knowledge or expertise;

- lack of details concerning experience; and

- meaning of former job titles.

While this list of questions is not intended to cover every employment situation, it does provide a framework for potential employees and employers to consider.

ADA IN THE FUTURE

When the legislation was passed in the early 1990s most experts agreed that the full impact of ADA would be determined by court actions which would clarify some of the wording that many felt was ambiguous and thus subject to many interpretations.

The American Red Cross in an April, 1998 memo to Easter Seal Donors noted that 66 percent of disabled adult Americans 16-64 do not have jobs. While it can be assumed that not all of these people would be working because of ADA it stands to reason that many have had difficulties finding employment prior to the implementation of ADA and did not obtain the proper training and education because of the lack of opportunities. The Red Cross memo notes that with the passing of ADA the opportunities are improving.

One impact of ADA that is very apparent and has had a major impact on private security is in relation to doorways, stairways, elevators, and fire and emergency alarms. Almost every building has a handicapped entrance and specially designed controls to enable disabled people to operate elevators. In addition, emergency alarms have been changed to include different visual and audio signals.

Security Management has been diligent in keeping track of interpretations from the Equal Employment Opportunity Commission (EEOC) and various State and Federal court cases regarding ADA. Following is a summary of some of the information reported in the magazine.

- In 1995 a report from EEOC broadened the definition of "disability" to include perceived or future illnesses. The original Act provided for two conditions that could cause a person to be disabled. First, a physical or mental impairment that affects the person's daily life. Second, was a history of the disability. The report added a third conditions: individuals who are regarded by their employer as having an impairment even if they do not. This added provision can best be explained by an example. A person is offered a position and a medical examination is given. The medical report indicates that the potential employee might develop colon cancer in the future. The employer cannot deny the employment based on this future possibility. (*Security Management*, June, 1995)

- In 1995 the U.S. District Court for the Northern District of Texas (*Robert Burch v. Coca-Cola* 3:94-CV-1894-G, 1995) found an employer guilty for firing an employee who was being treated for alcoholism. This case focuses on the provision that the treatment of alcoholism is a disability under the Act. (*Security Management*, September, 1995)

- The issue of obtaining workers' compensation records is covered by ADA. ADA guidelines prohibit the obtaining of these records until a conditional offer of employment is made. The difficulty for the employer is to determine if the potential employee has suffered a legitimate on-the-job injury or is an unscrupulous worker who uses it to obtain money for not working. ADA is designed to protect the employee who has incurred a legitimate injury. (*Security Management*, November, 1995)

- Research conducted by the American Bar Association revealed that a substantial portion of cases filed, in 1996, for damages or accommodations under ADA are being decided in favor of employers. This reference did not provide any specific numbers, but did indicate that employees must convince courts that the disability substantially limits major life activities or that they are otherwise able to perform the essential functions of their job. (*Security Management*, September, 1997)

- In 1997 the United States Court of Appeals for the Seventh Circuit (*Christian v. St. Anthony Medical Center*, No. 96-3986, 1977) ruled that medical treatment can be considered disabling even if the underlying condition is not covered by the ADA. In this case the court ruled that the treatment of a condition that is not itself disabling can count as a disability. For example, aggressive chemotherapy for the treatment of cancer can be considered a disability though the cancer itself is not a disability. (*Security Management*, October, 1997)

- In 1997 another case by the United States Court of Appeals for the Seventh Circuit (*Monte K. Sieberns v. Wal-Mart Stores, Inc.*, No. 96-4199, 1997) ruled that employers are not required to make accommodations for potential employees who are unable to perform the essential functions of the position. The attorney for the defense, Edward Hollis, indicates that the ruling only applies to prospective employees and should an employee become unqualified through an accident, for example, the employer must try to reassign or make reasonable accommodations for the employee.

- Another 1997 case from the United States Court of Appeals for the Second Circuit (*Buckley v. Consolidated Edison*, No. 96-9039, 1997) provides clarification regarding the employers use of drug testing of employees. In this case the requirement of a urine test was deemed to be reasonable and does not violate the ADA.

- In an article, John Parry, of the American Bar Association, provides guidance regarding security implications in regard to mental disabilities and the direct threat to the health and safety of others. Mr. Parry indicates that "the key to determining whether a person poses a direct threat is an individualized and objective assessment of risk of harm that considers four (4) factors: the duration of the risk; the nature and severity of the potential harm; the likelihood that the harm will occur; and the imminence of the harm. (*Security Management*, March, 1998)

As indicated earlier these examples and cases are not intended to be a complete and thorough examination of the implications of ADA on private security. However, security administrators must constantly monitor the trends and respond with reasonable and realistic solutions for the disabled workers covered under the Act.

SEXUAL HARASSMENT

In 1986 the United States Supreme Court ruled that employees could sue for sexual harassment. In 1998, in a series of three cases the court changed some of the rules. In general, experts have always agreed that touching a person in a sexual manner is clearly off limits, and avoiding sex jokes was highly recommended. *U.S. News & World Report* (July 6, 1998) and *Security Management* (August, 1998) reported the cases and the resulting changes in the way sexual harassment cases should be handled.

The changes were based on three cases: (1) *Gebser et al. v. Lago Vista Independent School District*, U.S. Supreme Court, No. 96-1866, 1998; (2) *Burlington Industries, Inc. v. Ellerth*, U.S. Supreme Court, No. 97-569, 1998; and (3) *Faragher v. City of Boca Raton*, U.S. Supreme Court, No. 97-282, 1998.

From a security standpoint the facts are less important than the rules that result from the cases. The following, from *U.S. News & World Report* focuses on the key issues resolved by the Supreme Court.

What Is Harassment?

Old Rule: To prove harassment, a worker has to show that because she resisted sexual advances she was punished in terms of salary, assignments, or promotions.

New Rule: It can count as harassment even if an employee is otherwise treated well.

Justice Anthony Kennedy may have given a clue when he noted in the *Ellerth* case "involves numerous alleged threats, and we express no opinion as to whether a single unfulfilled threat is sufficient to constitute discrimination."

Is Ignorance a Defense?

Old Rule: If a manager isn't informed that one of his employers is harassing other workers, the supervisor probably isn't responsible for the harasser's actions.

New Rule: The manager can be held responsible for a harasser's actions – unless a company has a strong system of dealing with problems.

The key issue here is that it is not enough to have a sexual harassment policy; it must be disseminated and enforced effectively.

Whom Do You Inform?

Old Rule: Tell someone if you have been harassed.

New Rule: Tell a person with decision-making power if you have been harassed.

The Supreme Court indicated that in addition to reporting the harassment the employee has a corresponding obligation of reasonable care to avoid harm. In the *Ellerth* case, the Supreme Court noted that an employer may be spared liability if it can prove that it "exercised reasonable care to prevent and correct any sexual harassment behavior" and that the "employee failed to take advantage of any preventive or corrective opportunities provided by the employer."

INVESTIGATION OF SEXUAL HARASSMENT ALLEGATIONS

Security Management, in an article by Eddy L. McClain, "Sex, Lies, and Liability" (March, 1997) outlined some guidelines for security in terms of investigation of allegations involving sexual harassment. The article also provided some statistics to show the importance of this matter. In 1995, 15,549 sexual harassment claims were filed with the EEOC. The agency obtained $24.3 million for claimants – and that covered only cases settled without going to court.

Security personnel should be actively involved in the development of the sexual harassment policy specifically as it relates to when and how investigations should be conducted. As a general guideline the investigation should commence soon after the allegations are reported. Security investigators should never pre-judge the situation and conduct an objective effort to seek the truth.

It is important to remember that most sexual harassment cases do not involve physical evidence, so the interview is extremely important. Investigators must be careful in the types of questions they ask and how they ask them. For example, the question should not be "Did you see X touch Y?" but rather, "Have you seen anyone touch X in a way that would make X uncomfortable?"

Select a place for the interview that has privacy, but is not intimidating. In addition, avoid having a desk between the investigator and the person being interviewed. Desks create a mental barrier and prohibit viewing of the body language of the interviewee. Whenever an investigator is interviewing a person of the opposite sex, there should also be a witness present who is of the sex of the person being interviewed.

It is important that the complainant provide as much of the who, what, where, when, why, and how as possible to assist the investigator in interviews with possible witnesses.

The last person to be interviewed should be the accused. They should be allowed the opportunity to admit, deny, or explain the actions that led to the complaint.

Finally, as in all investigations, the report must be complete, concise, and present the evidence obtained during the investigative process.

Management will then have the information to take whatever action is appropriate based on the circumstances of the case. An important aspect of the entire process is to have a well-prepared position description for the job. See Appendix B for an example used for a security officer at a national shopping center.

TRAINING OF SECURITY PERSONNEL

There is probably no more important issue in private security today than the training (or lack of it) received by private security personnel. All who have studied this issue have concluded that there is a lack of realistic and viable training for operational level personnel. However, there have been improvements in the training of supervisory and management personnel in recent years. This issue is discussed more thoroughly in Chapter 2. There are a number of major differences between private and public law enforcement operations, but the differences are most glaring on the issue of training. Today, almost all states have adopted comprehensive training programs for those employed in the public sector, especially for new officers. Most of these programs require a minimum of 400 hours of entry-level training; many states exceed that amount. Improvements have also occurred in regard to private security training. Studies conducted by the Private Security Task Force in 1975 revealed that seven states had training requirements. Another study, reported in the *Private Security and Police in America: The Hallcrest Report I* in 1985, indicated that 16 states had training requirements. Even more important is the perception of training by security employees. Seventy percent of the proprietary and 65 percent of the contractual employees expressed the opinion that their training was adequate when responding to a survey sent as part of the research conducted by Hallcrest Systems (Cunningham & Taylor, 1990).

The most recent study, published in 1990, in *Private Security Trends 1970-2000: The Hallcrest Report II*, noted that 23 states require some form of security training. However, only 14 states require any training for unarmed guards. The amount of training varies between 4 and 40 hours, depending on whether the guard is armed or unarmed. Figure 4.4 provides information on a state-by-state basis.

In a press release, one organization, the International Foundation for Protection Officers (IFPO), reported that as of September 9, 1998 they had certified more than 6,200 officers and another 2,700 plus were currently enrolled and were expected to receive their certificates before the year 2000.

The Certified Protection Officer process involves the submission of an application, studying course materials, and a proctored examination graded by IFPO. A minimum score of 70 percent is required.

Figure 4.4
State-Imposed Training Requirements

Alabama	N	Illinois	Y	Montana	Y	Rhode Island	**
Alaska	Y	Indiana	N	Nebraska	N	South Carolina	Y
Arizona	Y	Iowa	*	Nevada	*	South Dakota	N
Arkansas	Y	Kansas	*	New Hampshire	*	Tennessee	N
California	Y	Kentucky	N	New Jersey	N	Texas	Y
Colorado	N	Louisiana	Y	New Mexico	N	Utah	Y
Connecticut	*	Maine	N	New York	N	Vermont	*
Delaware	N	Maryland	N	North Carolina	*	Virginia	Y
D.C.	N	Massachusetts	N	North Dakota	N	Washington	N
Florida	*	Michigan	Y	Ohio	N	West Virginia	**
Georgia	Y	Minnesota	N	Oklahoma	N	Wisconsin	Y
Hawaii	N	Mississippi	N	Oregon	N	Wyoming	N
Idaho	N	Missouri	N	Pennsylvania	*		

Y= Yes   N= No   *If firearms are carried   **Not in private security statute

Source: Richter Moore and Norman Spain, *Security,* July 1989. From William C. Cunningham, John J. Strauchs, and Clifford W. Van Meter (1990). *Private Security Trends 1970-2000: The Hallcrest Report II,* Table 5.5, p. 147. Stoneham, MA: Butterworth-Heinemann.

The future of private security training seems to be closely aligned to technology. Two innovative programs were presented in an article by Cristopher A. Chung (*Security Management*, October, 1998). The University of Houston, funded by a grant from the National Institute of Justice (NIJ), has developed a computer program for bomb threat training. Cameron University, in Lawton, Oklahoma, is using CD-ROM technology to provide training for public and private security employees. The lessons, such as search and seizure, guard touring, and vehicle stops are set up on an individual basis so that some or all of the lessons can be used by a student. This allows the trainer to select the topics most pertinent to the security setting.

The Professional Security Television Network in Carrollton, Texas continues to provide comprehensive basic and supervisor training modules.

PSTN
12-Part Basic Security Officer Training Series

Module #1 – Introduction to Security
Overview of the BSOTS Course Purposes of patrol
The history and role of private security
The importance of private security and its objectives

Module #2 – The Importance of the Security Officer
Overview of the major conditions that create workplace crime
The importance of criticality and vulnerability
The three major security functions

The roles of the security officer
The qualities essential to a security officer
Code of Ethics for security officers

Module #3 – Legal Issues – Part I
The eight sources of legal authority
Definition of law
Definition of criminal law
Definition of a crime
Definition of civil law
The five typical crimes encountered by a security officer

Module #4 – Legal Issues – Part 2
Definition and explanation of citizen's arrest
Detention
False imprisonment
Search and seizure
Requirements for investigations and interrogations
Use of force
Defamation
Sprinkler systems

Module #5 – Human and Public Relations
Understanding the "human side" of security
A look at "bad Public Relations"
Explanation of the various "publics" with whom the security officer comes in contact
The basic needs of all people
Techniques for improving relations with others

Module #6 – Communications
The definition of communications
Three components of the communications process
Two levels of communication
Obstacles to communications
Four principles of effective communications
10 ways to improve communication skills
Telephone etiquette

Module #7 – Patrol
Purposes of patrol
Types of patrol and techniques
Equipment needed for patrol
Using the five senses on patrol
Importance of the first patrol of the shift
Hazards of patrol

Module #8 – General Duties
Rules, policies and regulations
Security barriers
Alarms
Access control systems
Key/Card systems

Functions on post
Preliminary investigations

Module #9 – Report Writing
The importance of and need for reports
Seven essentials of report writing
Five requirements of a report
Style
Field note-taking
Common problems in report preparation

Module #10 – Fire Prevention and Control
Fire prevention and fire hazards
Classes of fire
Classes of fire extinguishers
Sprinkler systems
Emergency procedures
Controlling fires
Fire fighting equipment

Module #11 – Emergency Situations
Medical emergencies
Bomb threats and explosions
Natural disasters
Civil disturbance
Criminal act
Dealing with the media

Module #12 – Safety
The officer's responsibility for safety
General hazards and unsafe acts
Unsafe conditions and hazardous materials
Basic components of an accident report

PSTN Supervisor Training Series

Module #1
Principles of Leadership I
Role of Private Security
Leadership and the Security Mission
Leadership and Supervisory Skills

Module #2
Principles of Leadership II
The Key Principles of Leadership
The Ethics of Professional Leadership
The Management of Conflict

Module #3
Effective Communications
The Communications Process
Methods of Communication

Barriers to Effective Communication
Types of Communication Systems

Module #4
Employee Performance Evaluations
Performing a Job Analysis
Writing Job Descriptions
The Standards of Performance
The Methods of Evaluating Employees
Counseling Employees after the Evaluation

Module #5
Time Management
Prioritizing Activities
Effective Planning
Time-Robbers
Time Management Tools

Module #6
Behavior & Motivation
Understanding People's Motives
Preventing Job Dissatisfaction
Motivating Superior Performance

Module #7
Counseling & Sexual Harassment
Four Areas of Employee Counseling
Purpose of Performance Counseling
Guidelines for Counseling
Forms of Sexual Harassment
Dealing with Specific Cases of Harassment

Module #8
Substance Abuse
Symptoms of Substance Abuse
Documentation Guidelines
The Leader's Role in Substance Abuse
Written Substance Abuse Policy
Drug Awareness Training
Employee Assistance Programs
Discipline & Termination

Module #9
Discrimination & Affirmative Action
The Changing Face of the Work Force
Understanding the Civil Rights Legislation
Implementing Affirmative Action Plans

Module #10
Career Opportunities
Career Development Skills
Being Proactive and Choosing Your Course
Beginning with the End in Mind

Developing the Attitude of "Win-Win"
Understanding Attributes Others Bring to the Job
Learning to Learn All the Time

More than 200 individual lessons are also available on a wide range of topics such as:

- Security management

- Supervision

- Motivation and personal development

- Compliance

- Healthcare security

- Bank and financial security

- Contract security

- Industrial fire protection

- Retail security

The use of technology in training is relatively new compared to the traditional lecture centered approach, but some research, conducted at Grand Valley State University in Allendale, Michigan supports the use of technology. While most of the students surveyed were not employed in public or private law enforcement it is estimated that, based on general data of the students, that 10-20 percent were employed in criminal justice and private security agencies. Seven hundred thirty-eight (738) students enrolled in the various courses from Fall 1992 through Fall 1998 completed the survey.

The survey instruments were distributed by the author and other faculty members and completed by the students after they had completed the lessons and taken a traditional paper and pencil test based on the lessons. They were machine scored by the Academic Computing Center at Grand Valley State University. The survey instrument was developed by Dr. Clifford W. Van Meter with the advice and counsel of Dr. Roy Walker and Dr. Allen Avner of the University of Illinois.

1. Computer-based learning was effective in terms of my ability to understand the material:

STRONGLY AGREE	AGREE	DISAGREE	STRONGLY DISAGREE
(277) 38%	(404) 55%	(48) 7%	(9) 1%

2. Compared to learning the same amount of material from lecture, the computer-based method was easier:

STRONGLY AGREE	AGREE	DISAGREE	STRONGLY DISAGREE
(228) 31%	(377) 51%	(112) 15%	(21) 3%

3. Compared to learning the same amount of material from a textbook, the computer-based method was easier:

STRONGLY AGREE   AGREE   DISAGREE   STRONGLY DISAGREE
   (356) 48%   (305) 41%   (70) 9%   (7) 1%

4. As a part of this course, computer-based learning was:

VERY HELPFUL   HELPFUL   UNHELPFUL   VERY UNHELPFUL
   (201) 27%   (455) 62%   (73) 10%   (9) 1%

5. The information provided through computer-based learning was:

VERY CLEAR   CLEAR   UNCLEAR   VERY UNCLEAR
   (279) 38%   (422) 57%   (31) 4%   (6) 1%

Notes:
1. Parenthesis (   ) indicate raw numbers.
2. Some percentages do not equal 100 percent because of rounding.

Brian Johnson conducted research based on 53 students enrolled in two sections of CJ 410 (Police and Society) during Fall 1994. The complete results, including methodology, are reported in *Police Computer Review*, Volume 4, Number 3, 1995. The summary of the results were:

(1) Based on pre- and post-test scores ". . . the computer exercise was an effective learning tool as 77% of the students achieved mastery level on the exercise."

(2) After using the computer lessons the students were given a paper and pencil test later in the semester. There was not a statistically significant difference between the post test scores taken on the computer and the pen and pencil test taken in the classroom. ". . . this finding suggests that students retained the information obtained through the computer lesson."

Another opportunity is available through computer-based training provided by the Police Law Institute, Inc. in Iowa City, Iowa. This company provides monthly legal updates for thousands of police officers in Florida, Illinois, and Missouri. In a study done in Missouri and reported in the "Law Enforcement Manager's Legal Notes" in May, 1992, police liability for cities that participate has declined. From fiscal years 1989 to 1991, the costs of losses, on a per officer basis, had declined 66 percent. The cost of losses for 1989 were three times those of 1991.

Private security trainers should begin to explore the possibilities for training by greater use of video and the introduction of computer technology. There may be an immediate payback of the investment in terms of reduced liability.

The key distinction that must be made in discussing private security training is between armed and unarmed personnel. At least on the philosophical level, there is agreement—even among private security executives—regarding the need for training of armed personnel. Although the firearm may never have to be used, its misuse can cause difficult legal consequences, injury, and/or death.

The material in Appendix H from the Task Force Report was prepared after, and as a result of, extensive dialogue between the Private Security Task Force and the private security industry. Probably no other portion of the report was debated more intensely or with more emotion. Originally, the staff of the task force recommended a 40-hour pre-assignment training course, but through the public hearing process this was reduced to eight hours of formal preassignment training and 32 additional hours of training within three months of assignment. It should also be noted that 16 of the 32 hours can consist of supervised on-the-job training. Because Standard 2.5 is the most thorough and detailed curriculum and discussion of the issue that is available, it is reproduced in Appendix H.

As noted earlier, there is some agreement on the issue of training for armed personnel. Though there was disagreement while the Private Security Task Force was conducting public hearings as to the amount of training, the result of that process was accepted by the task force and private security industry representatives with little debate or change. It closely follows the 24-hour training program designed by the Illinois Local Governmental Law Enforcement Officers Training Board in 1976 for the training of full-time and part-time public law enforcement officers in Illinois. It involves both training prior to a job that requires a firearm and requalification training at least once every 12 months. This requalification requirement exceeds that of many public law enforcement regulations or statutes. Even the Illinois requirements do not have a requalification provision. In 1985 the State of Illinois increased the firearms training program to 40 hours, but did not add a requalification program.

The amount of time devoted to firearms training of private security personnel continues to be a problem. An analysis of state statutes regulating the private security industry and the requirements for hiring and training of security officers for all 50 states was undertaken. Based on the results of that analysis, training for armed security guards ranged from four hours to 40 hours. The type of training varies as well from state to state. Some states require classroom training on the legal and moral issues of firearms use and firearm safety. Other states mandate that firearm maintenance be included. Of the 22 states requiring firearms training, only one state requires the use of deadly force to be included in the training curriculum (Maacks et al., 1998).

From these figures it is apparent that adequate time for firearms training in private security has not been attained. While there appears to be some improvement in the last decade, such as the 30-hour training requirement in Texas, there is still a long way to go before most of the firearms training in private security will be realistic in terms of the safety of the trainees and the citizens they may contact while performing their security functions.

Although there is limited in-depth research available, it is the opinion of most people involved in private security that there is a definite trend away from armed personnel. In an article by Peter Olhausen in a 1988 issue of *Security Management*, Thomas Wathen, a respected leader in the field, responded to the pros and cons of arming. Wathen, who is the current president of Pinkerton's, responded with "I didn't know there were any pros at all!"

With regard to armed personnel, the "Findings, Recommendations, and Forecasts" section of *Private Security Trends 1970-2000: The Hallcrest Report II* states:

> A dramatic decrease in the carrying of firearms by security person-nel has occurred in the past 20 years. An estimated 50 percent of security guards carried firearms in 1970, dropping to about 10 per-cent by the mid-1980s. By the year 2000, perhaps only five percent of security personnel will be armed. This substantial reduction in armed personnel came about for three reasons: high insurance pre-miums for armed workers, higher liability and greater risk for employers, and stricter state and local government regulation of armed security personnel (Cunningham et al., 1990).

Several studies conducted after *Hallcrest II* tend to indicate that the number of armed security officers may be higher than estimated. Sherry Harowitz, in an arti-cle in *Security Management* (October, 1995), reported that, based on a survey of 12 states, the number of armed guards averages 10-20 percent. Florida, which has data on proprietary and contract employees, indicated that 15 percent were armed.

Another study reported in *Security* (September, 1997) also indicates that the projections reported in *Hallcrest II* may be conservative. This study, based on responses from almost 500 private security executives, indicated that 9 percent field armed personnel while another 18 percent have armed and unarmed per-sonnel. Still, the largest number, 73 percent, reported using only unarmed per-sonnel. The shift to armed officers appears to be focused primarily on retail, education, urbanized healthcare, and industrial businesses.

The research reported in *Private Security and Police in America: The Hall-crest Report I* and presented in Figure 4.5 tends to indicate that the model train-ing courses developed by the Private Security Task Force have been used as a guide for private security training. Increased training is a positive step toward attacking the private security "vicious circle" described earlier in this chapter.

Figure 4.5
Training Subjects Reported By Security Employees

TRAINING SUBJECT	CONTRACT PROPRIETARY	ALARM GUARDS	RUNNERS
Fire Protection & Prevention	76%	81%	82%
First Aid	69%	48%	55%
Legal Powers: Arrest, Search, Seizure	83%	74%	55%
Investigation & Detention Procedures	75%	62%	64%
Firearms (classroom)	13%	10%	64%
Firearms (firing range)	21%	7%	64%
Building Safety	61%	69%	64%
Crisis Handling	51%	55%	27%
Crowd Control	45%	41%	18%
Equipment Use	64%	48%	82%
Report Writing	82%	79%	73%

(Hallcrest Systems, Inc., 1982)

Another consideration in trends in armed training is reflected in a report, in 1998, published by the Private Sector Liaison Committee (PSLC) of the International Association of the Chiefs of Police. This report, Private Security Officer Selection, Training, and Licensing Guidelines, does not set out any specific training requirements, but does recommend "All private security officer training should be reviewed and approved for certification by a state regulator agency."

Training Considerations

The following are recommended:

A. Minimum basic training requirements and relevant, continuous in-service training for private security officers should be required. A formal mechanism to establish curriculum requirements and hours of training should be established.

B. All private security officer training should be reviewed and approved for certification by a state regulatory agency.

C. Private security officer basic or in-service training should include the following elements based upon needs analysis related to job function:

1. Security officers fall into one or more of these categories based upon their job function:

a) Unarmed security officers

b) Armed security officers

c) Unarmed non-sworn alarm responder

d) Armed non-sworn alarm responder

e) Armed car guard

2. Security officers' training needs will be addressed in large part under these topic areas as appropriate:

a) Legal

b) Operational

c) Firearms

d) Administrative

e) Electronic

f) Armored transport

g) Use of force

D. Due to the varied nature of security tasks and duties along with the proper training for each, the demands for each specific setting should be for the level of training certification to build public trust and confidence.

Commentary

If there has been any one element of policing that has produced the recognized quality of personal performance by today's officers and deputies, it has been the advent of recognized professional selection/training standards beginning in the early 1970s. This was the cornerstone that has brought policing to being a genuine profession. The same approach can apply to the security officer position. There is every reason to believe that with proper employment screening, coupled with meaningful training and responsible supervision, security officers can earn the respect of communities and law enforcement. If there is anything that will calm those who would be critical, it is the careful administration of statutorily required employment/training standards for all licensed or certified private security officers.

It has been with the welfare of security officers, their employers, and the general public in mind that the above guidelines were developed. The use of these guidelines by all interests having responsibility for or a financial interest in the provision of security officer services can be a foundation from which to draft state legislation or improve existing practices/statutes. An approach that has been helpful in policing in its professional growth has been the use of advisory boards, committees, councils, or commissions. Use of such advisory bodies should be applied in the development/maintenance of security officer standards. Active participation by a wide range of stakeholders also produces the best chances for compliance as well as measurable results. The inclusive spirit of the Commission on Accreditation of Law Enforcement Agencies is a proven model for the security industry.

LICENSING AND REGISTRATION

Thus far in this chapter, we have discussed the recruitment, selection, and training of private security personnel. These activities are important steps toward improving private security services. However, there is another step in the process: registration of individual employees with a state regulatory agency or board.

Even though businesses generally oppose any type of additional government control, those in private security recognize the need for some type of government regulation to ensure uniformity of requirements. Though the concept of regulation is accepted, there is no unanimity on the issue of who should be the "regulator." There is, however, general agreement that it should not be the same agency or board that regulates public law enforcement. It is also agreed that private security representatives (along with some public law enforcement officials, other government officials and citizens) should be involved in the establishment and enforcement of the registration issues. For readers interested in a detailed study of this matter, the "Report of the Task Force on Private Security" (1977) provides an in-depth review of the issue and offers detailed recommendations.

LICENSING

A survey conducted in 1997 by Craig Hemmens and Jeffrey R. Maahs and summarized in the December, 1997 issue of *Security Management* revealed some significant changes in the regulation of private security officers since 1981. Their analysis indicated that 66 percent of the states regulated private security in 1981, but by 1997 82 percent of the states had regulations pertaining to private security. The authors of the study correctly indicate an important aspect of their study which is that it is related only to the statutes in the states, not the rules and regulations promulgated by the regulator boards established in the states. This accounts, in part, for the differences between their study and, for example, the study conducted by Moore and Spain (1989). An example of the types of differences that can and do occur is in relation to training standards. Hemmens and Maahs report only 11 states requiring training, but Moore and Spain report 23 states. An example of how this difference can occur is in Illinois. The state law does not require training, but the regulatory agency does require training.

Following is a brief analysis of some of the major provisions of the regulations based on the study by Hemmens and Maahs.

Hiring Prerequisites – the most common minimum age is 18, but some states require an older age for persons who will be armed. An interesting point is that only 14 states require the employees to be either citizens or legal residents of the United States.

Criminal History – fingerprinting and criminal history checks are the most commonly used by the states. Some states require an "employee statement" which normally includes basic employment information and a statement that he or she meets the requirements for the position. Most states disqualify felons; however, five states disqualify felons only if the offenses occurred recently, and four states prohibit security employers from "knowingly" hiring a felon. Many states also exclude persons convicted of nonfelony offenses. Crimes that commonly appear on the list include misdemeanors, acts of violence, sex offenses, drug offenses, weapon offenses, and theft.

Psychological – Only one state (Oklahoma) requires psychological testing and only seven states use "a judicial finding of incompetence" to disqualify applicants.

Other studies have been conducted, but once again, their is no uniformity of the findings. Sandra Davies in the September, 1997 issue of *Security Management* reported that 22 states have minimum training and licensing requirements and eleven other states have some form of state regulated training for armed officers.

George Bruce and Mark Button reported in *Security Management* in March 1995 that only Great Britain, Iceland, Ireland, Switzerland, and the United States did not have national licensing or registration for private security.

What is obvious to everyone who looks into licensing and registration is that their is a serious deficiency in the uniformity of the research. This problem has been identified by the three major studies of private security since 1975. First, the Private Security Task Force conducted the most extensive survey ever conducted and even with that effort realized that their data was not completely accurate. *Hallcrest I* and *Hallcrest II* also recognized the lack of data about these issues.

For a better understanding of the issue of licensing and registration in this chapter, several terms must be defined.

> Licensing—The act of requiring permission from a *competent authority* to carry on the business of providing security services on a contractual basis.

> Registration—The act of requiring permission from a *state authority* before being employed in the private security industry.

The italicized portions of the above definitions highlight the differences. Licensing does not (and in the opinion of many should not) apply to proprietary security services since, in most cases, the companies that operate them are already licensed by some government authority to produce a product or sell a service. Specific licensing of proprietary security personnel, in their opinion, would be unnecessary. On the other hand, the individual employees in both proprietary and contract services should be registered to ensure uniformity.

As noted earlier in this chapter, there have been significant changes in the number of females as well as increased training for private security personnel during the last 10 years. This is not true with regard to licensing and registration. There have been relatively few attempts to establish licensing and registration in additional states, though there have been modifications made in some states. Thirty-five states license guard and patrol companies, but only 22 states and the District of Columbia require the registration of guards.

Once again a distinction can and should be made between armed and unarmed personnel. Further, it is generally conceded that there should be both temporary and permanent permits. The temporary permit should apply for a limited duration (e.g., 30 days) and require at least a check with local law enforcement agencies and other available sources with regard to the background of the applicant. The primary responsibility for this action rests with the employing agency. The permanent registration permit should be issued by the state agency. The Private Security Task Force established two Standards (11.2 and 11.3) that provide guidance on this issue (see Appendix H). It should be noted that these standards generally agree with the recommendations in this chapter regarding selection and training of private security personnel.

NATIONAL OVERVIEW

There is no uniform or cohesive system of governmental licensing and registration. Charles Buikema and Frank Horvath, in an article titled "Security Regulation: A State-by-State Update" published in a 1984 issue of *Security Manage-*

ment, provided information that reflects the lack of uniform or cohesive government licensing and registration. They reported their research on three services (or duties performed): security guard services, both contract and proprietary; alarm system contractors; and private detective services. Some of the summaries that can be made from their study are:

- Thirty-seven of the 47 states that responded to the survey (Oklahoma, South Dakota, and Tennessee did not respond) regulate at least one of the services.

- Thirty-three states regulate contract security and guard services, but only three regulate proprietary guard services.

- Thirty-three states regulate private investigators.

- Eight states regulate alarm system contractors.

- Nineteen states regulate minimum age of 18 for employment, seven a minimum age of 21 for employment, one a minimum age of 22 for employment, and seven a minimum age of 25 for employment.

- Sixteen states require a minimal level of training for armed personnel.

- Four states require training of unarmed personnel.

- Ten states require a fingerprint check, but only five states require a national FBI check.

These summaries reflect the lack of uniformity and cohesiveness in regulating the private security industry. The situation is compounded for security operations that are located in bi-state areas such as Chicago, Illinois/Gary, Indiana or St. Louis, Missouri/East St. Louis, Illinois.

Nearly 15 years later, there were still as many as seven states that had no statutes regulating security guards. Moreover, only 16 states require employers to train their security guards. An alarming statistic is that only 44 percent of states require training for armed security guards (Maacks et al., 1998).

There has been very little discussion (and no serious proposals) for any form of national licensing or registration for the private security industry, with the possible exception of a Senate Bill, introduced in 1991 by then-Senator Al Gore, Jr., which would require minimum levels of screening and training for all guards hired by the federal government. There was also the Private Security Officers Quality Assurance Act of 1995, which is still awaiting passage.

The pace of change is slow and perhaps will increase in tempo as the threat of civil liability becomes more menacing.

As they did for screening and training, the Private Sector Liaison Committee of the International Association of Chiefs of Police provided some recommendations regarding licensing and registration.

LICENSES AND CERTIFICATION

Types of Licenses or Certifications for Private Security Officers—These guidelines establish the following types of license or certification classifications:

Temporary Security Officer Permit

Class I Security Officer/Unarmed Alarm Responder
Class II Armed Security Officer/Armed Alarm Responder
Class III Armored Car Security Officer

Qualifications for a Temporary Security Officer Permit

1. An employer may issue a temporary security officer permit to a person, providing the employer has submitted to the state licensing and certification agency the application required for a registration permit, including the statement from a certified trainer verifying completion of the pre-assignment training requirements.

2. Under no circumstances may the holder of a temporary permit carry a firearm.

Additional Requirements for Class II and Class III Licenses or Certification

In addition to meeting the minimum requirements for a Class I License, an applicant for a Class II and Class III License or Certification shall:

1. be at least 21 years of age;

2. submit a statement by a state-recognized firearms instructor verifying that the firearms training and range qualification requirements of these guidelines have been completed.

License Renewal

It is recognized that security officers who have been licensed or issued a permit can commit crimes without their employer or state regulators' knowing of these events. Accordingly, there should exist a procedure that requires regulators to conduct appropriate state and/or national records checks of security personnel at the time of license/permit renewal. If the person involved has continued to work and reside in the same state, a state records check may well be sufficient. This will reduce the risk that a licensee could commit crimes without the employer or regulatory authority's knowing of them at the time of renewal.

Commentary

One of the more vexing problems associated with licensing, certifying, or registering security officers is the amount of time required. In an industry that has historically experienced high turnover, each processing step needs to be handled with accuracy and timeliness. Failure to streamline each aspect of the selection and approval process has led to instances of abuse of the temporary permit concept. It will be critical for all involved parties from both sectors to cooperate in the shared use of technological advancements that are being implemented at the federal and state levels. This cooperation and coordination are critical to quality assurance being associated with the fielding of security officers in our private facilities and public areas.

DUTIES PERFORMED

So far in this chapter we have addressed the issue of private security personnel from initial contact to hiring. At this point we will discuss what the job duties are after the employee has been hired. This is a rather complex problem, because of the wide variety of duties and functions performed by employees in the broad category of "private security personnel." A reasonable starting point is the approach taken by the Private Security Task Force in emphasizing the need for job descriptions for private security personnel. This process, which unfortunately is not common in private security, is an important step in clarifying the duties to be performed. Standard 2.3 of the Private Security Task Force Report provides a concise analysis of the issue. Also, earlier in this chapter, there is a position description presented for a security officer at a national shopping center.

As a general guide, the data recorded in job descriptions should relate to two essential features of each position: (1) the nature of the work involved, and (2) the employee type who appears best suited for the position. With respect to the nature of the job, the following data should be included:

1) The job title;

2) Classification title and number, if any;

3) Number of employees holding the job;

4) A job summary, outlining major functions in one to three paragraphs;

5) A job breakdown, listing the sequence of operations that constitutes the job and noting the difficulty levels;

6) A description of equipment used;

7) A statement of the relationship of the job to other closely related jobs;

8) A notation of the jobs from which workers are promoted and those to which workers may be promoted from this job;

9) Training required and usual methods of providing such training;

10) Amounts and types of compensation;

11) Usual working hours; and

12) Peculiar conditions of employment, including unusual circumstances of heat or cold, humidity, light, and ventilation.

With respect to the employee, the data generally available should include:

1) Necessary and special physical characteristics;

2) Necessary physical dexterities;

3) Emotional characteristics, such as disposition, mood, and introversion or extroversion;

4) Special mental abilities required; and

5) Experience and skill requirements.

All job descriptions should be carefully checked to ensure that they comply with the ADA of 1990 and CRA of 1991. Appendix B provides information on a job description that considers the impact of these Acts. This outline is not intended to be all-inclusive. It is presented to highlight the depth to which job descriptions should be prepared if they are to be effective. It was noted, however, that some job descriptions reviewed included nonsecurity functions, such as running errands. This practice should be discouraged, because it detracts from the overall effectiveness and morale of private security personnel.

In summary, the preparation of high-quality job descriptions is a critical step in the personnel selection, assignment, and training processes. Without job descriptions, the employer, employee, and person responsible for developing training programs are at a tremendous disadvantage. Further, the need to relate training to the job is vital if training is to carry more significance than mere time spent sitting in a classroom.

One of the major difficulties in discussing the issue of duties performed by private security is the complexity of the issue. For example, the General Services Administration employs its own guards and at the same time contracts for similar services. While the duties performed may be very similar, there is wide misunderstanding as to the classification of the employees. In some cases they are federal employees, and in some cases they are federal contract employees. Some people try to make a thin-line distinction and classify the latter category as "quasi-government employees."

Another example is transit authority operations. In some cities (e.g., Chicago), the personnel in these operations are defined by the legislature as public officers, while in other cities they perform the same duties but are identified as private security personnel. Probably the best way to resolve this issue is not to be concerned with the duties they perform, but rather to classify them by the source of their funds. If they are paid directly by public funds, they are "public," and if they are paid with government funds through a contract, they are "private." Regardless of the source of funds, the duties performed can be classified broadly into four areas.

GUARD AND PATROL SERVICES

Guard and patrol services include the provision of personnel who perform the following functions, either contractually or internally at such places and facilities as industrial plants, financial institutions, educational institutions, office buildings, retail establishments, commercial complexes (including hotels and motels), healthcare facilities, recreation facilities, libraries and museums, residence and housing developments, charitable institutions, transportation vehicles and facilities (public and common carriers), and warehouses and good distribution depots:

- Prevention and/or detection of intrusion, unauthorized entry or activity, vandalism or trespass on private property;

- Prevention and/or detection of theft, loss, embezzlement, misappropriation or concealment of merchandise, money, bonds, stocks, notes or other valuable documents or papers;

- Control, regulation, or direction of the flow or movements of the public, whether by vehicle or otherwise, to assure the protection of property;

- Protection of individuals from bodily harm; and

- Enforcement of rules, regulations, and policies related to crime reduction.

These functions may be provided at one location or several. Guard functions are generally provided at one central location for one client or employer. Patrol functions, however, are performed at several locations, often for several clients.

INVESTIGATIVE SERVICES

The major services provided by the investigative component of private security may be provided contractually or internally at places and facilities such as industrial plants, financial institutions, educational institutions, retail establishments, commercial complexes, hotels and motels, and healthcare facilities. The services are provided for a variety of clients, including insurance companies, law firms, retailers, and individuals. Investigative personnel are primarily concerned with obtaining information with reference to any of the following matters:

1) Crimes or wrongs committed or threatened;

2) The identity, habits, conduct, movements, whereabouts, affiliations, associations, transactions, reputation, or character of any person, group of persons, association, organization, society, other group of persons, or partnership or corporation;

3) Pre-employment background checks of personnel applicants;

4) The conduct, honesty, efficiency, loyalty, or activities of employees, agents, contractors, and subcontractors;

5) Incidents and illicit or illegal activities by persons against the employer or employer's property;

6) Retail shoplifting;

7) Internal theft by employees or other employee crime;

8) The truth or falsity of any statement or representation;

9) The whereabouts of missing persons;

10) The location or recovery of lost or stolen property;

11) The causes, origin of or responsibility for fires, libels or slanders, losses, accidents, damage, or injuries to property;

12) The credibility of informants, witnesses, or other persons; and

13) The securing of evidence to be used before investigating committees, boards of award or arbitration, or in the trial of civil or criminal cases and the preparation thereof.

Detective or investigative activity is distinguished from the guard or watch function in that the investigator obtains information, whereas guard or watch personnel usually act on information (or events).

Alarm Services

Alarm services include selling, installing, servicing, and emergency response to alarm signal devices. Alarm devices are employed in one of four basic modes: local alarm, proprietary alarm, central station alarm, or police-connected alarm. Alarm signal devices include a variety of equipment, ranging from simple magnetic switches to complex ultrasonic Doppler and sound systems. Various electronic, electromechanical, and photoelectrical devices and microwave Dopplers are also utilized.

Alarm personnel include three categories of employees: alarm sales personnel, alarm systems installers/servicers, and alarm respondents. Persons in alarm sales engage in customer/client contact, pre-sale security surveys, and post-sale customer relations. Alarm installers and servicers are trained technicians who install and wire alarm systems, perform scheduled maintenance and provide emergency servicing as well as regular repair of alarm systems. (Alarm installers and servicers may be the same depending on the employer.) Alarm respondents respond to an alarm condition at the protected site of the client. The alarm respondent inspects the protected site to determine the nature of the alarm, protects or secures the client's facility for the client until the alarm system integrity can be restored, and assists law enforcement agencies according to local arrangements. The alarm respondent may be armed and also may be a servicer.

ARMORED CAR AND ARMED COURIER SERVICES

Armored car services include the provision of protection, safekeeping, and secured transportation of currency, coins, bullion, securities, bonds, jewelry, or other items of value. This secured transportation, from one place or point to another place or point, is accomplished by specially constructed bullet-resistant armored vehicles and vaults under armed guard. Armed courier services also include the armed protection and transportation (from one place or point to another place or point) of currency, coins, bullion, securities, bonds, jewelry, or other articles of unusual value. Armed courier services are distinguished from armored car services in that the transportation is provided by means other than specially constructed bullet-resistant armored vehicles. There are also courier service companies that employ non-armed persons to transport documents, business papers, checks, and other time-sensitive items that require expeditious delivery.

The major distinction between the services provided by armored cars and armed couriers and those furnished by guards and watch personnel is liability. Armored car guards and armed couriers are engaged exclusively in the safe transportation and custody of valuables, and the firms providing these services are liable for the face, declared, or contractual value of the client's property. These service companies are bailees of the valuable property, and the guards and couriers are protecting the property of their employer. This liability extends from the time the valuables are received until the time a receipt is executed by the consignee at delivery. Except for war risks, the armored car company is absolutely liable for the valuable property during protective custody. Conversely, guards, watch personnel, and their employers do not assume comparable liability for the property being protected.

SUMMARY

As stated at the beginning of this chapter, the number of persons employed in private security outnumber the persons employed in public law enforcement. Thus, the greatest improvements in the services provided by private security will be realized by proper recruitment, selection, training, licensing and registration, and performance by the personnel employed. This chapter has identified the issues and provided plans for the improvement of security personnel. Of significant importance is the enactment of the Americans with Disabilities Act of 1990 and the Civil Rights Act of 1991, which will have to be closely monitored because of their potential impact on employment in the private security industry.

DISCUSSION QUESTIONS

1. Discuss the "Private Security Vicious Circle."

2. What are the key issues in the Americans with Disabilities Act of 1990 and the Civil Rights Act of 1991?

3. Do you agree/disagree with the questions to be asked or not asked during the interview process?

4. What changes could or should be made in the steps in the selection process?

5. Discuss the issues involved in private security training.

6. Define and discuss the issues related to licensing and/or registration of private security personnel.

7. List the four major categories of duties performed by private security personnel, and give two examples of types of duties performed for each category.

REFERENCES

Abernathy, W.B. (1998). "War Against Wages." *Security Management*, September, 1998, 35-39.

Anderson, T. (1995). "Fool Me Once." *Security Management*, April, 1995, 15-16.

Anderson, T. (1995). "Judicial Decisions: Preemployment Screening." *Security Management*, May, 1995, 102.

Anderson, T. (1995). "Security Officer Training." *Security Management*, May, 1995, 105.

Anderson, T. (1995). "Regulatory Activity: Disability." *Security Management*, June, 1995, 71-72.

Anderson, T. (1995). "Judicial Decisions: ADA Discrimination." *Security Management*, September, 1995, 170.

Anderson, T. (1995). "Judicial Decisions: Sexual Harassment." *Security Management*, November, 1995, 86-87.

Anderson, T. (1995). "Judicial Decisions: Employee Screening." *Security Management*, December, 1995, 76-77.

Anderson, T. (1996). "Judicial Decisions: Negligent Misrepresentation." *Security Management*, April, 1996, 82-83.

Anderson, T. (1996). "Legislative Update: Security Officer Training." *Security Management*, April, 1996, 85.

Anderson, T. (1996). "Judicial Decisions: Negligent Hiring." *Security Management*, September, 1996, 171.

Anderson, T. (1996). "Judicial Decisions: Discrimination." *Security Management*, October, 1996, 77.

Anderson, T. (1997). "Judicial Decisions. Noncompete Agreements." *Security Management*, February, 1997, 85.

Anderson, T. (1997). "Judicial Decisions: ADA." *Security Management*, April, 1997, 83-84.

Anderson, T. (1997). "Judicial Decisions: ADA." *Security Management*, September, 1997, 183-184.

Anderson, T. (1997). "Judicial Decisions: ADA." *Security Management*, October, 1997, 87-88.

Anderson, T. (1997). "Judicial Decisions: Sexual Harassment." *Security Management*, October, 1997, 87.

Anderson, T. (1997). "Judicial Decisions: ADA." *Security Management*, December, 1997, 127-128.

Anderson, T. (1997). "Judicial Decisions: ADA." *Security Management*, January, 1998, 78.

Anderson, T. (1998). "Judicial Decisions: ADA/EEOC." *Security Management*, April, 1998, 80-81.

Anderson, T. (1998). "Judicial Decisions: Negligent Hiring/Sexual Harassment." *Security Management*, June, 1998, 89-90.

Anderson, T. (1998). "Supreme Court Clarifies Sexual Harassment Claims." *Security Management*, August, 1998, 81-84.

Anderson, T. (1998). "Judicial Decisions: ADA." *Security Management*, August, 1998, 86.

Anderson, T. (1998). "Judicial Decisions: Discrimination." *Security Management*, October, 1998, 77.

Aratha, M.J. (1995). "Where Access Control Meets ADA." *Security Management*, September, 1995, 69-72.

Brown, D.A. (1996). "On Target with Firearms Training." *Security Management*, September, 1996, 69-73.

Brown, H. (1998). "Background Investigations Are Worth the Money and Effort." *Security*, August, 1998, 81.

(1997). "3 Black Teens Awarded $1 Million from Eddie Bauer in Security Guard Case." *Security Director's Digest*, October 15, 1997, 1-2.

Buikema, C. and Horvath, F. (1984). "Security Regulation: A State-by-Sate Update." *Security Management*, Month Unknown, 1984.

(1997). "Federal Law Enforcement Officers, 1996." *Bureau of Justice Statistics Bulletin*, December, 1997.

Burley-Allen, M. (1995). "Conducting Reasonable Reprimands." *Security Management*, November, 1995, 21-22.

Canton, L. Jr. (1997). "Building a Talented Team." *Security Management*, October, 1997, 25-27.

(Date unknown). *Career Opportunities in Security*. Alexandria, VA: American Society of Industrial Security.

Chiaramonte, J. (1995). "Background Checks: Past as Prologue." *Security Management*, May, 1995, 72-77.

Chuda, T.T. CPP (1995). "Taking Training Beyond the Basics." *Security Management*, February, 1995, 57-59.

Chung, C. (1998). "High-Tech Training Tools." *Security Management*, October, 1998, 56-60.

Clark, B. CPP (1995). "A Call to Arms." *Security Management*, October, 1995, 48, 50.

Collins, P. (1996). "Mastering Sakerhet in Sweden." *Security Management*, June, 1996, 65-70.

Collins, P. (1997). "Companies Striving to Weed Out Potentially Violent Employees." *Security Directors' Digest*, April 2, 1997, 4.

Cottringer, W. (1995). "Selecting the Best of the Bunch." *Security Management*, October 1995, 21-22.

Cunningham, W.C. and Taylor, T.H. (1990). *Private Security and Police in America: The Hallcrest Report I*. Stoneham, MA: Butterworth-Heinemann.

Cunningham, W.C., Strauchs, J.J. and Van Meter, C.W. (1990). *Private Security Trends 1970-2000: The Hallcrest Report II*. Stoneham, MA: Butterworth-Heinemann.

Davies, S. (1998). "Over 6,200 Security Officers Certified." http://www.ifpo.com/programs.html, October 10, 1998.

Davies, S.J. (1997). "Teach them Well." *Security Management*, September, 1997, 83-85.

(1995). "Deciphering Discrimination." *Security Management*, January, 1995, 12-13.

DeGeneste, H.I. (1995). "A Disarming Question." *Security Management*, October, 1995, 49, 51.

Durham, N.C. (1995). "Rules for Rulemaking." *Security Management*, August, 1995, 79-83.

(1997). "Executive Briefing." *Security*, November, 1997, 115.

(1997). "Firms Outsourcing More Screening Tools in Hiring." *Security Management*, February, 1997, 85.

Fisher, C.E. CPP (1996). "Making a List Checking it Twice." *Security Management*, May, 1996, 69-70.

(1995). "Five Guidelines on Integrity Tests." *Security*, April, 1995, 65.

George, B. MP and Button, M. (1995). "Should Great Britain Regulate Private Security?" Security Management, March, 1995, 89-90.

Gips, M. (1995). "Security Spotlight: Hiring Headaches." *Security Management*, November, 1995, 9.

Gips, M. (1996). "Security Spotlight: Seeding Security's Future." *Security Management*, February, 1996, 8.

Goodboe, M.E. (1995). "Practice Andragogy." *Security Management*, April, 1995, 65-67.

(1995). Grand Valley State University: Recruitment & Affirmative Action Policies and Procedures for Faculty, Executive, Administrative & Professional Staff and Clerical, Office, & Technical Staff 1997-1998, 47-51 (also Fair Employment Practice Manual – 315:7201).

(1995). "Guard Employment Standards Clash in Proposed Bill." *Security*, September, 1995, 77.

Hacker, C. (1997). "Profiling Job Applicants." *Security Management*, May, 1997, 25-27.

Hall, J.L. (1998). "Letter Regarding 1998 Easter Seal Campaign." April, 1998.

Harowitz, S. (1995). "A Shot in the Dark." *Security Management*, October, 1995, 47.

(1997). "Help Yourself to Background Checks." *Security*, March, 1997.

Hemmens, C. and Maahs, J. (1997). "Security Officer Regulation: A Statutory Analysis." http://www.securitymanagement.com/library00453.html October 13, 1998.

Hertig, C. (1997). "Officer Training Regulation Laws Deserve Support." *Security*, July, 1997, 85-86.

Hertig, C. (1997). "The Rising Tide of Security Officer Regulation." *Security*, June, 1997, 99-100.

Higginbotham, J. (1991). "The Americans with Disability Act." *FBI Law Enforcement Bulletin*, 60:8.

(1995). "Hiring Headaches." *Security Management*, November, 1995, 9.

Hodgson, K. (1994). "How Effective Are Drug Tests?" *Security*, February, 1994, 32-34.

Hodgson, K. (1996). "The Truth About Honesty Test." *Security*, April, 1996, 83-84.

Horn, M. (1998). "Sex and the CEO." *U.S. News & World Report*, July 6, 1998, 32-40.

Hunt, W. (1995). "Getting the Word on Deception." *Security Management*, June, 1995, 26-27.

(1997). "Integrity Tests Reduce Risk of Dishonest Behavior." *Security*, September, 1997, 79-81.

Jackson, F. and Locklear, J. (1997). "A Few Good Men." *Security Management*, September, 1997, 87-91.

Jacobs, R. and Jones, M. (1997). "Teaching Tools: When to Use on-the-Job-Training." *Security Management*, September, 1997, 35-39.

Johnston, D. (1995). "Flunk Those Test Cheats." *Security*, July, 1995, 55.

Jones, D. (1998). "Laws, Juries Shift Protection to Terminated Employees." *USA Today*, April 2, 1998, 1-2.

Jones, J. and Orbon, J. (1990). "Preemployment Testing and Labor Market Trends—The Squeeze Is Coming." *Security*, September, 1990, 15-16.

Kohout, F. and Arnold, D. (1997). "EEOC Guidelines Clarify Psychiatric Disabilities." *Security Management*, November, 1997, 91.

Langer, S. (1996). "The Wages of Security." *Security Management*, August, 1996, 76-78.

Lavelle, M. (1998). "The New Rules of Sexual Harassment." *U.S. News & World Report*, July 6, 1998, 30-31.

(1992). *Law Enforcement Manager's Legal Notes*. Iowa City, IA: The Police Law Institute.

(1997). "Lawsuit Fear Keeps Business from Giving References." *Security Directors' Digest*, August 13, 1997, 9-10.

Leeds, J.P. and Burroughs, W. (1997). "Finding the Right Staff." *Security Management*, March, 1997, 33-43.

Longmore-Etheridge, A. (1998). "ASIS Aids IACP in Formulating Guidelines." *Security Management*, June, 1998, 103-104.

McClain, E. (1997). "Sex, Lies and Liability." *Security Management*, March, 1997, 44-50.

Metscher, R. (1997). "Finding the Path of Reason." *Security Management*, December, 1997, 25-26.

Micucci, A.J. (1995). "The Changing of the Guard: The Transformation of Private Security." *Journal of Security Administration*, 18(1), 21-45.

Moore, R. and Spain, N. (July 1989). "No Joke: Training Cuts Liability." *Security*.

Nalla, M. et al. (1995). "Executive Training Needs: A National Survey of Security Professionals." *Journal of Security Administration*, 18(2), 18-28.

Neeley, D. (1998). "Judicial Decisions: Employee Termination." *Security Management*, August, 1998, 86.

Neeley, D. (1998). "Judicial Decisions: Sexual Harassment/ADA." *Security Management*, September, 1998, 178-182.

(1997). "Negligent Hiring Lawsuits are Preventable, Experts Say." *Security Directors' Digest*, July 2, 1997, 8.

(1997). "New Oregon Law Requires All Security Employees to Be Certified by State." *Security Directors' Digest*, January 15, 1997, 1-2.

(1997). "N.Y. Company Accused of Providing Fake Training for Armed Security Guards." *Security Directors' Digest,* May 14, 1997, 4-5.

Nichter, D.A. CPP (1995). "Training on Trial." *Security Management*, September, 1996, 75-78.

Odom, R.C. (1995). "Candid Candidates: What's Behind the Résumé?" *Security Management*, May 1995, 66-70.

Ortmeier, P.J. (1996). "Adding Class to Security." *Security Management*, July, 1996, 99-101.

Parry, J. (1998). "Mental Disabilities and the ADA." *Security Management*, March, 1998, 118-119.

(1998). "Pinkerton Women: 150 Years of Success." Encino, CA: *Pinkerton Solutions*, Fall, 1998, 18-21.

Pitarres, J.R. (1995). "Examining Discrimination Claims." *Security Management*, August, 1995, 86.

(1997). "Police Computers Checks Used to Screen Job Applicants." *Security Directors' Digest*, March 5, 1997, 9-10.

(1998). "Private Security Officer Selection, Training and Licensing Guidelines." Alexandria, VA: International Association of Chiefs of Police, 1998.

(Date unknown). *The PSTN Catalog, Volume II.* Carrollton, TX: PSTN.

St. Clair, M. and Arnold, D. (1995). "Preemployment Screening: No More Test Stress." *Security Management*, February, 1995, 73.

(1995). "The Science of Honesty Testing." *Security*, March, 1995, 11.

(1996). "Security/Loss Prevention Pays from $10,000 to $250,000." *Security Directors' Digest*, March 27, 1996, 7-8.

Shapiro, J.P. (1998). "The Americans with Minor Disabilities Act." U.S. News & World Report, July 6, 1998, 41-42.

Sundberg, E.A. (1995). "Car Managers Screen Good Employees In?" *Security Management*, June, 1995, 92.

Tatum, C. and Whittle, T. (1995). "Defensive Weapons Do's and Don'ts." *Security Management*, March, 1995, 26-31.

Terry, W. (1998). "Racial Preferences are Outdated." *Parade Magazine*, May 31, 1998, 4-5.

Thiel, M. (1996). "Using Preemployment Screening Information." *Security Management*, February, 1996, 80-81.

(1996). "To Arm or Not to Arm Security Officers, A Complex Issue." *Security*, May, 1998, 77-78.

U.S. Equal Employment Opportunity Commission (1991). "The Americans with Disabilities Act: Questions and Answers." Washington, DC: U.S. Government Printing Office, 1991.

U.S. Equal Employment Opportunity Commission (1991). "The Americans with Disabilities Act: Your Responsibilities as an Employer." Washington, DC: U.S. Government Printing Office, 1991.

Westerfield, D.L. (1997). "The Dilemma of Educating and Training Professionals in Security." Paper presented to ASIS Educational Symposium, St. Louis, MO, June, 1997.

Zalud, B. (1997). "More Contract Officers, More Are Armed: Survey." *Security*, September, 1997, 112-115.

SECTION II

RISK MANAGEMENT AND LOSS CONTROL PRINCIPLES

Risk Management: Risk Analysis and Security Surveys

5

INTRODUCTION

Every business endeavor, whether run by an individual entrepreneur or a conglomerate, faces daily risks to its well-being and survival. Top management is ultimately responsible for organizational security. It must thoroughly investigate the policies and procedures of the organization, the conditions of the physical facility, the backgrounds and attitudes of the employees, and the relationships of the organization with the rest of the world before any worthwhile efforts can be undertaken to make the organization more secure from the threat of losses due to injury, death, damage, or destruction. In this respect, the risks discussed here are actual hazards or threats by natural or other forces and do not include the risks inherent in competitive business ventures conducted within legal bounds. It should also be understood that, although top management is responsible for security, the authority is usually delegated to another individual, i.e., the security director or manager within the organization.

Physical security can be provided for any size organization as long as it has something—personnel, real property, a service, or a product—to protect. An organization can be a one-chair barbershop, a municipal school, or a corporation with personnel employed nationwide and internationally. Differences in physical structure, product or service, number of employees, or local environmental factors mean that each organization must protect itself from different kinds of threats, but the basic principles of security are applicable to organizations of any size or type.

This chapter will outline the processes undertaken to conduct a risk assessment, establish loss probability, and design surveys appropriate for various types of organizations. The section concerning cost-benefit analysis will explain why the employment of the most sophisticated and complex security equipment and security personnel may not be financially appropriate or strategically necessary

145

to safeguard every facility or activity. Finally, there will be some suggestions for the development and maintenance of support for the security plans and programs by the operational and management personnel.

RISK ASSESSMENTS

Many activities occurring in the day-to-day business setting form the basis for the need to have viable risk analysis completed and the importance of security surveys. Some of these activities and their risk factors need to be discussed as a prelude to the procedures used to attack the problems.

Computers—The rapid expansion in the use of computers in almost every business activity has resulted in increased risks associated with computers. In the April 17, 1996 issue of *Security Director's Digest*, the unique spectrum of legal risks was listed as:

- Absent or inadequate computer security to prevent wrongful access to systems and networks or secure electronic transactions;

- Confidentiality and privacy abuses;

- Using language or images on e-mail systems that can defame or create an abusive workplace;

- Infringement of intellectual property rights;

- Failure to properly archive data; or

- To have an ineffective disaster recovery program.

Fraud—Unlike the specific risks associated with computers as a new risk, fraud has a long history as a source of risks. In the April, 1998 issue of *Security*, the "problems" and "vulnerability assessment" were presented as follows:

Salient Signs of Possible Fraud Problems

- Infighting among top management;

- Low morale and motivation among employees;

- Employee lives a lavish life style;

- High level of complaints from customers, suppliers or regulatory agencies;

- Supplies and inconsistent cash flow deficiencies; and

- Understaffed accounting department.

Fraud Vulnerability Assessment

- Internal controls weak or not monitored;

- Company or department dominated by a few managers;

- Management compensation linked to short term financial results;

- Employees poorly managed and underpaid;

- Company line of credit used to the limit for long periods of time; and

- Increasing number of year end adjusting journal entries.

Workplace Violence—As reported in the *Bureau of Justice Statistics Special Report on Workplace Violence* from the National Crime Victimization Surveys (NCVS) for 1992-1996, statistics indicate that, during each year, U.S. residents experienced more than 2 million violent victimizations while they were working or on duty. Clearly the most common type of workplace violent crime was simple assault, with a total of 1.5 million. However, 396,000 suffered aggravated assaults, 51,000 rapes and sexual assaults, 84,000 robberies, and 1,000 homicides.

A comprehensive 1998 Survey of Fortune 1000 Companies conducted by Pinkerton and reported in their publication *Top Security Threats Facing Corporate America,* resulted in a broad listing of potential security threats. The methodology which resulted in the following table was based on a question that asked respondents to list the "top three issues" overall.

Table 5.1

1997	**Potential Security Threats** Rank listed as a "Top 3 issue"	**# of times**
1	Workplace Violence	48
2	Employee Theft	33
3	Crisis Management & Executive Protection	28
4	Employee Selection	23
5	Computer Crime: Hardware & Software Theft	21
6	Fraud & White Collar Crime	20
7	Intellectual Property Protection	20
8	Computer Crime: Internet Security	19
9	Product Diversion & Transshipment	12
10	Negligent Security Litigation: Inadequate Security	9

While the data presented here is not intended to cover all aspects of risk, it does indicate that there is a need for risk analysis and security surveys as presented in this chapter.

THE PURPOSE OF RISK ASSESSMENTS

There are different purposes for risk assessments of various types of organizations, activities, or facilities. Basically, risk assessments are made to determine the degree of exposure to hazards or dangers to personnel or property. A risk assessment conducted to establish the security of a facility from a natural disaster would not satisfy the requirements of a physical security or crime prevention survey. The differences between these types of assessments or surveys will be explained throughout this chapter.

TYPES OF SECURITY SURVEYS

It is important to understand the terminology used by the security industry. In the previous paragraph, one can see the synonymous use of the words assessment, analysis, and survey. Although they are not precisely synonymous, those words, as well as audit, evaluation, inspection, investigation, measurement, and study, are all used to describe an activity that identifies exposures to risk.

1. COMPANY POLICY

Prior to developing and completing the security survey, the organization's policies and procedures should be studied for the existence of any rules, regulations, goals, standard operating procedures or instructions related to security that previously have been or are presently in force. It is necessary to review all of this data in order to know what has already been done and to understand the reasons for current security procedures. It is possible that earlier recommendations had been tested extensively and were found to have little or no effect, meaning that a revision of the policy would be of no benefit. This review should determine what current security-related policies do exist, or if new policies must be developed. The review may also provide guidelines against which to measure the existing security policies and give reasons for updating or creating additional policies.

2. IN-HOUSE SURVEYORS

Risk assessments can be made by security specialists presently employed by an organization or by outside consultants hired for that purpose. There are advantages and disadvantages to both methods. A present employee has the advantage of knowing the physical and organizational structure of the organization, its goals, and its own method of operation. On the other hand, security employees are too often overwhelmed by current crises or interdepartmental rivalries, and may have limited authority or status.

Large organizations with full-time security directors tend to be reluctant to admit the need for outside assistance, regardless of how limited the experience of their own personnel. Most smaller organizations assume they cannot afford to hire outside consultants and many feel they can acquire adequate security advice from their insurance agents or local police departments. Other organizations feel that an outside consultant would be primarily interested in the sale of security hardware, regardless of the need for it. For these reasons and others, risk assessments are usually performed internally, utilizing standard form checklists.

3. CONTRACTED SURVEYORS

One of the advantages of employing an outside consultant to conduct risk assessments is that the consultant has no organizational loyalties to contend with, which helps reduce competitiveness and internal rivalries. An outsider may observe threatening factors that have been accepted by a regular security employee as a normal condition or something that cannot be changed. Yet, the outsider suffers the disadvantage of limited exposure to the organization and its environs, the diverse personalities and attitudes of the employees and management, and the subtle interplay of the formal and informal power structures within the organization. The outsider may attain only a superficial understanding of the situation if the survey is constrained by inadequate time and support factors.

4. SUPPORT FOR THE SURVEY

Finally, an effective risk assessment can be attained only when there is wholehearted support by both management and operational personnel. Management must provide the authority and financial support necessary for the survey. Still, there often will be some resistance to the intrusion of security personnel into areas previously thought to be private domain by certain employees. This problem will be discussed.

RISK ASSESSMENT AND LOSS PROBABILITY

The purpose of a risk assessment is the determination of the vulnerability of a specific organization, facility, or activity to hazards or dangers caused by natural or other forces. The person selected to conduct the assessment frequently receives no further directions or instructions. He or she will have to develop a survey plan based on the fact that the total security of an establishment is possible, but that total security may not be cost-effective or supported by top management. Therefore, priorities must be developed so that both high- and low-value items receive security commensurate with their value.

1. ESTABLISH CRITICALITY

The first criterion in a security survey is to determine the value, impact, or cost of any asset, should it be lost as the result of natural or other forces. The person conducting the survey will need to ascertain from the operational personnel the identification and relative value of the buildings, equipment, and activities in the area to be surveyed, and how important they are to continued productivity for the entire organization. For example, in a factory complex, one of the buildings may house manufacturing processes that require unique, sophisticated equipment. If the operations of the entire factory depend completely upon the product of that special equipment, which is either irreplaceable or would take so long to replace that the company could not survive, its protection should be afforded a high priority over operations that could be performed in other spaces. Examples of losses of assets are not confined to property, equipment, or product alone, but can include the loss of employee time as well.

2. PRIORITIES OF CRITICALITY

Priorities for protection should be assigned so that the areas most critical to the survival of the organization receive the best security, while non-critical areas are assigned a lesser priority for protection. In a situation in which two facilities have equal production processes, output capability, numbers of personnel and structural size, yet one is self-sufficient in its supply of necessary water or power, and the second is supported from external sources, the more self-sufficient facility may be given a higher priority because it would provide the most cost-effective product during and after an emergency.

The same principles for assigning priorities for security apply to all types of facilities. For example, one can assign priorities for security in a small retail store. The location of the items of the highest value should be ascertained. One problem may be that during the business day the area with the highest value items might be the jewelry or camera department, while at night all cash is collected from throughout the store and placed into a safe in the office. In such a situation, the high-priority area for security changes from day to night.

3. ESTABLISH ACTUAL VERSUS DESIRED ACTIVITIES

As noted earlier, the person conducting the survey will need to gain the cooperation of the operating personnel in order to discover the actual processes followed in a normal period of operation. When surveying small businesses, it is not unusual for top management personnel to outline the procedures for the handling of cash or high-value items, and then to learn from the operational personnel that the cash is hidden in the building overnight to avoid a trip to the bank's night depository. As the surveyor verifies each of the actual procedures undertaken by the operating personnel, a decision must be made whether to assign each one a high-priority or low-priority rating.

After a facility has been inspected by the surveyor and the ratings of priority have been given to the various physical areas or operational phases of the unit, the ratings can be displayed on a chart that will graphically identify the priorities assigned. Figure 5.1 is an example of the results of the priority ratings assigned to the major units in a small production facility.

Figure 5.1
Priority Assignments

	Very high Priority (A)	High Priority (B)	Some Priority (C)	No Priority (D)
Entrance			X	
Visitor's lounge				X
Cafeteria			X	
Employee lounge				X
Personnel office			X	
Executive office		X		
Management office			X	
Auditor's office		X		
Finance office	X			
Shipping and receiving	X			
Production rooms			X	
Warehouse		X		
Inflammable storage		X		
Vehicle maintenance			X	
Security gate and office			X	

Frequently, situations arise in which certain management or operational personnel strongly oppose the priority ratings arrived at by the surveyor. One way to forestall such opposition is to form a three-person committee with representation by interested and knowledgeable management and employee personnel, as well as the surveyor. Each committee member can assign individual priority ratings and then discuss with the other two members the reasons for the rating if all do not agree. Surprisingly, fair ratings often can be attained by averaging the ratings by the three committee members.

One way to make the priority ratings more objective is to determine actual replacement figure costs. Once the costs of replacement, downtime, lost customers, and employee diversion or unemployment are tabulated for the various units of a facility, the rating of priorities becomes a simple and objective matter.

4. DETERMINE VULNERABILITY

The second criterion of a risk assessment is determining the degree of vulnerability the facility or activity has with regard to damage or attack by natural or other forces. Empirical data has shown that buildings with larger numbers of openings to the outside (doors, windows, skylights, etc.) are the objects of more attacks by persons than buildings with fewer openings. Similarly, buildings with fences, lights, and guards are victimized less frequently than buildings without such security. The vulnerability to attacks of lesser-protected buildings is higher than better-protected buildings. The amount of criminal activity in the surrounding area also should be taken into account.

The vulnerability risk is also heightened by the value and size of items maintained in the facility. Large amounts of cash and small but valuable items such as jewelry, cameras, or drugs are more frequently the target of theft than are items such as pre-cast concrete sewer pipes, structural steel or crude oil in large storage tanks.

The vulnerability of an organization, facility, or activity to natural forces must be analyzed somewhat differently. Again, local records should be reviewed to determine the frequency and severity of earthquakes, floods, or other natural disasters. Still, recent records may not be sufficient to predict the possibility of threats of natural disasters, so state or federal level sources should be queried concerning the actual vulnerability of the local area to such natural phenomena. Further, certain types of physical structures are more susceptible to damage or destruction than others, so assistance should be solicited from engineers to inspect the soundness of buildings included in the survey. Finally, it must be taken into account that the vulnerability to theft or looting is increased after natural disasters.

a. The Vulnerability Inspection

There are several ways to determine the vulnerability of a facility or activity to damage or attack. The first is for the experienced surveyor to personally inspect the facility for physical or operational weaknesses. Such an inspection entails more than one visit. The facility should be observed during peak operational periods as well as during closed or slack times. Nighttime visits are important, even if the facility is non-operational. It is not unusual to find employees washing or polishing cars, playing cards, or using company equipment and supplies at times that management believes the facility is vacated. The surveyor should inspect the facilities to ascertain the degree of security and discover weak points. The absence or inoperability of security hardware may be a source of vulnerability to the assets of an organization.

b. A History of Losses

Another method to ascertain the vulnerability of a facility is to look at its records of losses and to determine whether all losses have been properly reported and recorded. A high or obviously increasing rate of losses should alert the surveyor to a vulnerability problem. One must note here that many losses are not reported to higher management because the operational personnel are afraid that they will be held responsible. Many firms are self-insured and simply absorb losses without any further action. Some businesses fail to report losses because they have been advised that additional claims for losses will cause an increase in their insurance premiums. In cases such as these, there will be few formal records of losses. The surveyor will have to get such information from the employees by routine interview methods.

c. Internal Threat Considerations

Determining whether high-value property or items are properly safeguarded from theft by insiders is a third way to determine the vulnerability of a facility. Frequently, the location for high-risk items is chosen without the possibility of internal theft in mind, and may be near exits, lavatories, or trash bins. Such locations should be analyzed, and if there is no real need for high-risk items to be located there, they should be relocated to a less traveled or more private area. For example, retail stores most frequently locate the cashier's office, camera department and other high-risk areas some distance away from outside doors. The knowledge that a long route must be traversed in order to escape has an effect upon the number of transgressions occurring deep within the store by employees as well as by outsiders.

d. Graphic Display of Vulnerability

As the survey is conducted, a chart can be prepared that illustrates the degree of vulnerability of the various areas. Figure 5.2 is an example of the combination of a listing of high-value items located in various units and a listing of the losses that have taken place during the past year. Based on Figure 5.2, it can be seen that, if no increased security measures have been taken since the previous losses, property in the warehouse and shipping and receiving areas are most vulnerable to loss.

Figure 5.2
Graphic Display of Vulnerability to Loss, and Loss in Previous Year

	Cash on hand	Pilferable supplies	High-value items	Loss past year
Entrance	—	—	—	—
Visitors' lounge	—	—	—	—
Cafeteria	yes	yes		$300 cash
Employee lounge	—	—	—	—
Personnel office	—	yes	yes	$125 adding machine
Executive office	—	—	—	—
Auditor's office	—	—	yes	—
Finance office	yes	yes	yes	$30 pocket calculator
Shipping/Receiving	—	yes	yes	$2,000 inventory shortage
Production rooms	—	yes	—	—
Warehouse	—	yes	yes	$3,500 inventory shortage
Inflammable storage	—	yes	—	$5 paint
Vehicle maintenance	—	yes	—	$80 carburetor
Security gate and office	—	—	—	—

PROBABILITY OF OCCURRENCE

The third criterion applicable to a risk assessment is the degree of probability that natural or other forces will strike any given organization, facility, or activity. There is a high probability that disastrous storms will take place along the hurricane belt. Blizzards are commonplace in the northern and midwestern states. Low-lying valleys with rivers or valleys below dams stand a high chance of flash floods during rainy seasons. Earthquakes occur with regularity in the west, and sometimes volcanoes erupt. The degree of probability of such occurrences can be estimated with fair success when based upon past experiences. Attacks by humans can likewise be predicted after all the high-priority and vulnerability factors have been considered.

1. RATE OF NATURAL OCCURRENCES

Generally, one can observe the rate of past experiences and determine whether there is an increase, decrease, or relatively constant number of hazardous events occurring over a period of time. When coupled with such factors as high priority for security, a high vulnerability risk, and frequent devastating storms, the probability of loss is high. The lack or infrequency of natural disasters, the absence of physical losses and low impact in event of loss would predict a lower or insignificant loss probability.

2. RATE OF OCCURRENCES CAUSED BY HUMANS

The loss probability can likewise be estimated for attacks by humans. A chart can be prepared to show the number of known depredations committed during various periods in the past. There is some value to reviewing the loss records for as long ago as 10 or more years. Such a review might disclose a favorable or unfavorable record of security but, more importantly, the record allows a comparison with the rate of criminal activity during the past year. Increasing or decreasing trends in crime can be determined and may provide top management with the data that will support a request for a stronger security policy or additional funding.

The information collected in Figure 5.3 tends to show that in the past year a slightly higher-than-average number of criminal acts had been recorded in one production facility. This predicts an increasing probability of loss and indicates a need to upgrade security policies and provide more (or better) security measures. There does not appear to be an increase in destructive natural events. However, because there had been an earthquake in the area in the past 100 years, the probability exists that another earthquake might occur. Otherwise the prediction for the probability for loss by means of natural forces is minimal.

Figure 5.3
Probability Assessment Scale: Frequency of Occurrences in the Past

	100 years	50 years	10 years	1 year
Earthquake	11	—	—	—
Tornado or windstorm	unknown	75	15	2
Flood	unknown	30	17	1
Blizzard	unknown	unknown	13	1
Other	—	—	—	—
Burglary	—	—	20	4
Robbery	—	—	11	—
Vandalism	—	—	29	5
Internal theft	—	—	14	3
Fraud	—	—	13	2

One major source of risk not indicated in the figure above is the risk of terrorism. While the number of terrorist incidents in the United States is relatively small, the potential severity is overwhelming. Two obvious examples are the bombings of the World Trade Center and the Federal Building in Oklahoma City. However, at this point, a brief overview through the use of a "Counterrorism Security Checklist" is presented in Appendix C. Also, a detailed survey for use in terrorism prevention is presented in Appendix D.

RELATIONSHIP OF SECURITY TO LIABILITY

A phenomenal outgrowth of a better-educated citizenry, the high-technology age and an expanded business and industrial climate has been a backdrop for a veritable tidal wave of lawsuits. Every business, profession, and industry has been affected. Some accounts report that payments in security-related lawsuits have been increasing at a rate of 300 percent annually since 1967. Litigation against businesses in which security services had no direct involvement have increased at a similar rate. A brief look at some of the issues of the lawsuits will provide additional guidelines and impetus for the conduct of security surveys.

1.   THE THREAT OF CIVIL LITIGATION

Security-related lawsuits have affected virtually every type of organization that employs security personnel, including stores, hotels, hospitals, and schools. The largest number of payments were for "inadequate security" or a failure to prevent crimes in motel or hotel rooms, hallways, or parking lots. The next largest group involved crimes committed by employees, improper security actions against invitees and libel over employee crime. Non-security-related lawsuits that could have been prevented were for physical injuries due to faulty or poorly maintained equipment, sidewalks, stairwells, or lighting.

There are several factors that seem to be involved in this exceptional growth of litigation. One profession recently claimed that the contingency fee basis and the excessive number of practicing attorneys coupled with the "deep pockets" of the profession or their insurance companies, made a tempting target. The security field has also seen a large growth in personnel and equipment, which is a very visible target when any improper action is taken or equipment malfunctions. Businesses that will not or cannot afford to provide the same level of security found in similar businesses can be faulted for not providing a standard level of protection. The courts have become so active in their interpretations of standards of security that it is difficult to find two definitions of "adequate security" that agree.

Some of the cue phrases in the holdings cited by the courts are that security forces and their employers have a "duty to protect" not only employees, but invitees as well; that injurious acts—especially crimes—are "foreseeable"; and that "adequate security" was not provided. This latter aspect includes complaints of inadequate selection, training, or supervision of security personnel. Perhaps greater care should have been paid to these factors in earlier years. Now security forces and their employers have no choice but to improve their services.

2.   MANDATED ACCESSIBILITY

In a similar vein, there lies the threat of large fines and additional civil liability for the violation of federally mandated rules and regulations concerning employee and visitor access and safety within occupational, transportation, and public facilities. These problems of civil and criminal employee liability are a challenge for the physical security survey. The surveyor must approach each facility with the goal of identifying situations or activities that could potentially lead to lawsuits, as well as identifying the usual risks to lives and property. The inclusion in the survey report of obvious safety hazards and violations of federal regulations can be an immeasurable cost-saving device to the employing firm. These prevention tactics cost much less than the expense of lengthy litigation.

SECURITY SURVEYS

The type of security survey to be conducted is dictated by the purpose of the survey and the kind of organization, facility, or activity to be surveyed. As stated earlier, surveys can be conducted to determine the relative risks of losses from natural or other forces; but not all the information gathered by one type of survey will be of help in recommending protective services for the other. Therefore, most surveys will have to be carefully designed to incorporate the specific goals and the unique physical and personnel structure of each organization.

Surveys generally specify one or more of the following listed objectives:

1. Determine the existent vulnerabilities to injury, death, damage, or destruction by natural causes.

2. Determine the existent vulnerabilities of corporate assets due to criminal activity from outside the organization.

3. Determine the existent vulnerabilities of corporate assets due to criminal activity from within the organization.

4. Determine the existent conditions of physical security of corporate property.

5. Identify physical hazards, operational procedures, or personnel activities that could lead to legal liability for damages or injuries to employees, patrons, or the general public.

6. Measure the effectiveness of the current protection policies and standards.

7. Measure the conformity of the employees to the published security standards.

8. Audit the accounts and procedures of the firm to detect policy violations, fraud, and use of improper procedures.

9. Inspect the conditions and procedures that cause the problems of inventory shortages, cash or property losses, vandalism, or other unexplained crime within the plant.

10. Investigate the economic, sociological, and political conditions in the community to predict outside activities that could be adverse to the well-being or survival of the company.

A cursory glance at these objectives will reveal that the requested surveys may be instigated as a reaction to recurring problems within the organization, or simply as a result of a regularly scheduled program to assess conditions before they become risks or losses.

1. DISTINCTION BETWEEN TYPES OF SURVEYS

In practice, there are some security agencies that make a distinction between physical security surveys and crime prevention surveys. The rationale given is that although physical security measures do prevent crime, they are oriented more toward the security of property and facilities; whereas, crime prevention measures encompass the deterrence of criminal activity regardless of the extent or availability of physical safeguards.

a. Physical Security Surveys

One operative definition of physical security is: "that part of security concerned with the physical measures designed to safeguard personnel, to prevent unauthorized access to equipment, facilities, material and documents, and to safeguard them against espionage, sabotage, damage and theft." In other words, a physical security survey is directed toward a detailed examination and specific recommendations for the application of physical measures to prevent the opportunity to commit a crime.

b. Crime Prevention Surveys

The foregoing definition does not conflict with a currently popular definition for crime prevention, adapted from the British Home Office Crime Prevention Program: "The anticipation, recognition, and appraisal of a crime risk and the initiation of action to remove or reduce it." The definition's omission of physical measures has perhaps influenced some practitioners into believing that this definition is incompatible with physical security.

c. Survey Checklists

Despite the proliferation of survey checklists throughout the security industry, few are totally compatible with all of the survey objectives or are applicable to all facilities; yet they do provide a guideline to the surveyor so that the most obvious conditions are not overlooked.

There are advantages and disadvantages to the use of checklists. They serve as a reminder that specific subjects or areas should be inspected and can be devised to be used as an outlined draft of the final report. They can direct the examination of the facility from the exterior to the interior, or from the general to the specific features that must be observed and reported. The use of a checklist also can help other surveyors continue a survey should the initial surveyor have to leave an assignment.

On the other hand, many surveyors do no more than what is prescribed by the checklist, thereby limiting their own contribution. A checklist adapted from another facility or agency may not be totally applicable to the surveyed facility. Surveyors can become accustomed to checking off items rather than describing the situation by their own (probably more precise) terminology. Finally, checklists tend to allow the surveyors to make only a cursory inspection, whereas narrative reports require a more detailed examination to properly describe the item reported.

It has become somewhat common for security personnel to give checklists to facility owners or managers so they can perform a self-study of their security measures. Even after they have observed surveyors performing the same tasks, most owners and managers overlook details that identify security risks to the trained surveyor. Worse yet is the fact that many of the owners who get the checklists continue to do their own surveys thereafter to save re-employing the contracted surveyor. Handing out checklists is a good public relations gimmick, but can foster a false sense of independence and security. Samples of various survey checklists are included in Appendix C of this text.

d. A Sample of Survey Activities

There are no hard and fast rules on how to conduct a survey. Some are performed as hasty "walk-throughs" with a single-page checklist, while others involve lengthy preparation and visits for several weeks. The more experienced surveyor may be able to complete a survey in a fraction of the time it would take a novice. In any case, the following design of survey activities is offered as a guide to follow if there are no further instructions available from the requesting office.

Preliminary Activities

1) Written authority to conduct the survey should be obtained. This authority should clearly outline the goals and objectives of the survey and establish time, support, and availability of administrative facilities for the use of the surveyor.

2) The historical, geographical, and other background data of the facility and its environs should be reviewed. The local media and public records should be checked to establish the relationships and attitudes

of the facility and the local community. Local crime rates should be compared with the rate of crime occurring in the facility.

3) A review should be made of the written policies, rules, regulations, standard operating procedures, or other instructions relating to security.

4) Maps, floor plans, or architectural drawings should be obtained to determine main characteristics, especially the locations of doors and windows.

5) A review should be made of any previous surveys that have been reported.

6) A checklist should be assembled that contains questions that must be answered to satisfy the initial purpose of the survey.

e. Performing the Survey

1) The surveyor should review, with the management personnel and supervisors of the organization, the facilities or activities to be surveyed and the purposes of the survey. This review should engender their cooperation and solicit their continued contributions to the survey.

2) An orientation tour should be made to establish the limits of the facility. The area supervisors should be solicited for their concept of the corporate security policy and standards. They also should demonstrate all security procedures applicable to their area of supervision.

3) Arrangements should be made to review these procedures with supervisors on all shifts.

4) The facility should be visited during peak and low operating periods to observe the personnel, procedures, and physical measures, including the perimeter barriers, lighting, locking devices, intrusion detection systems, storage containers, and security personnel.

5) The survey checklist should be expanded wherever there is a need to do so. Narrative descriptions of any features of the security program should be recorded if necessary. Photographs should be taken of objects or situations that are difficult to describe.

f. Review of Survey Results

There should be a review with the local supervisors of all the deficiencies noted so that immediate corrective action can be taken. In some security programs, the local supervisors must prepare a written list of corrective actions taken shortly after this review.

On occasion, local supervisors will disagree with the survey findings. For this reason and for the sake of fairness, the surveyor must be careful to point out only genuine deficiencies in security, and not exaggerate or employ harassment tactics.

g. The Survey Report

Survey reports must follow the requirements of the requestor. The extent of the details of the survey report should be prescribed by the original request. It may be true that the requestor need not be provided with details beyond a brief list of deficiencies and recommendations. Some reports are merely cover letters attached to the checklists. Some survey reports spell out a complete narrative description of the physical plant and prescribed security policies or standards so that direct comparisons can be made with the facility surveyed.

When there is a notation in the report that there is a deficiency because an existent security measure does not meet the organizational standard, it would be redundant to add that the deficiency should be removed. However, reasonable recommendations should not be avoided.

h. The Follow-Up Survey

A follow-up survey is performed to establish whether deficiencies have been corrected or are actively and consistently under repair. It should be scheduled after a sufficient period of time has passed—30, 60, or 90 days—in which corrective action can be taken to eliminate the deficiencies. Any period longer than that may leave security risks uncorrected for too long a time. The follow-up survey reviews only those areas with deficiencies listed in the original report.

Any evidence that the deficiencies and recommendations have been ignored must be taken to the top management level of the organization. There may have been a communication problem or other valid reason why corrective action was not taken. Once top management is advised of the situation, it is their decision to take whatever action they deem necessary.

i. Frequency of Surveys

There are no strict rules that prescribe how often surveys should be conducted in a specific facility. Corporate-level security policy should provide some flexible guidelines for the security surveyor to follow. The following listed conditions may help to determine the appropriate frequency of surveys.

In the case of a new organization, facility, or activity, a thorough survey should be made to ensure that there is a complete record of the security measures and any security deficiencies. The frequency of subsequent surveys should consider the extent of the risks of vulnerability, priority (criticality), and probability. If the facility is in a high-risk category and depredations against corporate property are constant, surveys should be scheduled at greater frequencies—perhaps as often as quarterly or semiannually. When the facility appears to have a low-risk rating, annual surveys should be considered.

j. Surveys of Sub-Units

One method to provide the impression that security has a high priority is to conduct inspections of sub-units of the larger organization throughout the year after the initial survey. In this manner, smaller inspections or audits of physical security measures or operating procedures, alternated throughout the organization, may provide a habit of security consciousness among employees. Organization-wide surveys would not need to be conducted more frequently than annually. The smaller units inspected may be selected on a rotational or random basis, or they may be selected based upon the number of security problems that surface after the initial survey.

k. Problems Dictate Need for Survey

Frequency of security surveys also may be increased after serious or repeated depredations against the firm. However, the actual point of attack may not be the weak link in security, so any investigation of the security problem should extend beyond the obvious scene. In the case of repeated attacks, the survey frequency should be increased until a way has been found to solve or reduce the problem.

New surveys should be considered every time the facility reorganizes its physical structures or personnel, or after the acquisition of a new building or expensive equipment. The risk probability, vulnerability factors, and security priorities will no doubt change under those conditions. Extensive changes of property or equipment indicate a need for all-inclusive surveys; minor changes or additions of new equipment in already high-security areas may need only a less-inclusive update survey.

These suggestions do not include every reason why a new or additional survey should be made. It is the responsibility of the security supervisors and top management to promptly evaluate any change that may increase risk to the organization's well-being or survival.

COST-BENEFIT ANALYSIS

Not all commercial or industrial firms or institutions have regularly organized security plans, programs, or personnel. About 58 percent of the 10 million businesses in this country gross less than $100,000 annually. Taken together, these smaller firms suffer larger losses from criminal action and employ a disproportionately smaller number of security measures to protect their assets. Additionally, the smaller firms suffer a higher rate of bankruptcies, and more than a few of the bankruptcies are caused by shoplifting and employee theft. Small business owners may complain that they cannot afford security, but in reality they cannot afford not to have security.

At first glance, an outsider might conjecture that security personnel are only "window dressing," and do not contribute productively to business firms. That line of reasoning is fallacious. Even in the "old days" when every factory had its own guard to watch the buildings for security purposes, guards were additionally productive by oiling machinery, emptying trash cans, and providing other non-security services. They may have earned more of their pay by their other services, unless they were lucky enough to prevent a fire, thwart a burglary, or perform some lifesaving act for an employee. Those kinds of events were rare, however, and are still relatively rare today.

The most difficult task of the modern security manager is to justify the expense of security. The security program is still largely seen as a group of little old men making certain that the coffee pots are unplugged and that some worker has not thrown a smoldering cigarette butt into a paper-filled trash can.

The security manager can change that image of the security department by preparing a cost-benefit analysis for any given unit within the security survey. A cost-benefit analysis is a direct comparison of the costs of the operation of the security unit and all security measures with the amount of corporate property saved or recovered and the elimination or reduction of losses caused by injuries and lost production time. Despite the claim that it is impossible to compute the savings incurred through the crime prevented by the security officer's presence, there are methods for computing the relative value of security measures.

The first rule of a cost-benefit accounting system is to refrain from recommending a security measure that is not cost-effective. One should never spend $10,000 to protect a $5.00 item. Nor should one erect a $10,000 fence to secure industrial salvage worth $100. But a $10,000 fence would be cost-effective if it were built to protect property several times more expensive than the fence or to eliminate a guard position that is more costly.

Extending that idea, the security manager should be able to show over a period of time that the services of the department, at a cost of X dollars, have effectively decreased losses from X dollars in one year to Y dollars in another year. In other instances, the security manager may be able to show that, although the remainder of the community had a crime rate increase, the jurisdiction under security management had a decrease.

Although a direct dollar loss or gain cannot always be seen in such a direct comparison, some evaluations may be estimated for illustration purposes. Every structure and its contents has a dollar value assigned by the organization. Estimates of the cost of fire, vandalism, or theft can be made and projected showing the probable rate of occurrence if security is not effective. Estimates of lost time due to theft of equipment or materials would likewise present a good argu-

Do not spend more on something that it is worth

ment that security is cost-effective in its preventive measures. There are often reductions in insurance premium rates if alarm systems, fire sprinklers or guards are employed, which also contributes to a cost saving.

If the security personnel actually improve their apprehension and recovery rate, the total value of the property saved and recovered, along with decreased expenses, may show a surprisingly satisfactory cost-benefit relationship.

Ultimately, the security manager may investigate the possibility of replacing some of the security personnel with electronic devices that would cost a fraction of the guards' annual salary. Not only would the operating budget be lowered by such mechanisms, but management may become so appreciative of the cost-benefit results that the money saved might be returned to the security unit's budget as an increase the following year.

SELLING THE SECURITY SURVEY RESULTS

There is no single method for selling security survey results to management. The best way to sell any security plan is to apply logical principles to the preparation of the security plan so that management will readily recognize that the proper work has been done.

1. STEPS OF THE PROPOSAL

The traditional steps in planning should be followed when a security measure is proposed: (1) recognize a need, (2) state the objectives, (3) gather the relevant data, (4) develop alternatives, (5) prepare a course of action, (6) analyze the capabilities, (7) review the plan, and (8) present the plan to management.

The starting point of any plan is the recognition that a security problem exists. A problem may be indicated by a series of losses or cases of vandalism. It should be ascertained that the losses are not coincidental, and that a problem is truly there to be solved. The second step is to state the objective of the plan. The objective may be simply to investigate the causes of the recent losses and devise measures to decrease future losses.

In order to determine how the property was lost, all records and people must be checked to verify actual possession and subsequent loss. These sources of information might not lead one to identify the perpetrator but, at the very least, they will provide data for the next step: developing alternatives. Various methods of securing the property in the future should be listed, such as (a) securing in a locked shed, (b) placing it in a locked, fenced area, (c) posting a guard, and (d) employing electronic security devices.

2. SELECTING THE MOST FAVORABLE ALTERNATIVE

After analyzing the alternative courses of action (and keeping in mind their costs and benefits), the proposition most favorable to the firm should be selected for presentation to management. If presently there are insufficient guards to post one at the storage area and the budget precludes additional hiring, another alternative should be selected. This final arrangement should be reviewed as to its feasibility and prepared for presentation to the person responsible for the final decision.

3. CONSIDER THE FIRM'S FINANCIAL SITUATION

Any presentation must be made with consideration of the organization's financial situation at the time of the proposal. If the firm is cutting back its budget, any savings suggested by the plan should be highlighted. If the organization is in an expansion phase, the presentation should emphasize how the proposal fits into such a plan. The security manager should be able to dovetail any proposal into the firm's present plans, otherwise there may be a summary rejection because the plan is out of step with organizational goals.

4. PRESENTATION TIPS

Most proposals for changes or additions to programs must be presented to management in a fashion that will attract favorable attention. Clean, well-prepared reports, audiovisual aids, large charts, etc., will serve to get across the message that effort was expended to present this case. Nothing should be left to chance. The more that is known about the plan to be sold to management, the greater the presenter's confidence will be. And the greater the confidence, the easier it will be to convince management that the plan will work. There is no guarantee that all proposals will be accepted by management, but completion of these steps will provide for a better presentation.

5. MAINTAINING CORPORATE SUPPORT

After the new security plan has been sold to management, the security manager will have the responsibility of implementing the plan and maintaining management's continued support for the plan. Without both moral and financial support, most programs seldom last very long.

One of the most effective ways for the security director to maintain the interest and support of management is to become a more involved member of management. Several ways to become more active and accepted by management include ready acceptance of added responsibilities, participation in less popular programs, and the exhibition of an attitude and demeanor that sets an example of honesty, seriousness, and dependability.

The security director must be the leader, not only in the security specialty, but among other activities of the organization. Volunteering to assist in fund drives, setting the example by quickly responding to those in need and consistently serving selflessly will engender admiration and support from all levels of personnel. In that respect, management would be hard-pressed not to support their most proficient manager.

SUMMARY

A risk analysis provides the opportunity to establish whether there is a need to implement security measures to protect the lives and property that make up an organization. The degree of protection afforded personnel or property must be determined by their relative value to the organization's productivity and continuity of operation. The extent to which the organization is vulnerable to loss must be reasonably predicted by a review of the records of past losses. Isolated losses suffered by the neighboring community may have as much impact on the organization's well-being as internal theft, or natural or accidental disasters.

A risk analysis survey entails the interview of operational personnel, as well as the direct observation of the physical plant and personnel during and after normal operating hours. The survey results must be presented to the requesting agency in such a manner that recommendations for changes or improvements engender support from all levels of management. Surveys should not recommend security that costs more than the property to be protected. Surveys should be conducted of the entire organization or by sub-units. The frequency of surveys is determined either by unexpected recurring losses or by time periods mandated by top management. A sample survey is located in Appendix I.

DISCUSSION QUESTIONS

1. List the steps necessary before action can be undertaken to minimize losses by injury, death, or damage within an organization.

2. Why is it necessary for a surveyor to become familiar with company policies, regulations, goals, and standard operating procedures before a risk assessment is initiated?

3. List some advantages and disadvantages in having risk assessments conducted by persons from outside the organization.

4. Not all personnel, activities, or facilities have equal needs for protection. Identify the criteria for establishing priorities for security.

5. List the methods used to assess the vulnerability of a facility.

6. Identify several purposes of surveys of organizations.

7. List several advantages and disadvantages of survey checklists.

8. Outline the major steps of a risk assessment survey.

9. List the traditional steps of planning that can be utilized to propose security measures to management.

REFERENCES

Anderson, T. (November, 1998). "Judicial Decisions: OSHA." *Security Management*, 87.

Cizmadia, R. (June, 1998). "Workplace Violence: A Continuum from Threat to Death." *Security Management,* 109.

(1996). *Combating Workplace Violence: Guidelines for Employers and Law Enforcement.* Alexandria, VA: International Association of Chiefs of Police, 1996.

Ferreira, W. CPP (May, 1995). "Protecting Safe Security." *Security Management*, 52-54.

Hodgson, K. (January, 1994). "Positive Steps for Screening out Workplace Violence." *Security,* 67-68.

Irvine, M. (November 1, 1998). "Hired to Fire: Ex-Cop a Pro a Pink-Slipping." *Grand Rapids Press,* A9.

(April 17, 1996). "Lack of Computer Protection can be Legal Liability Trap." *Security Director's Digest*, 7-8.

Lesce, T. (Sept./Oct., 1998). "New Mexico Chapter Probes Workplace Violence." Alexandria, VA: *ASIS Dynamics*, 16-17.

(June, 1997). "OSHA Update." *Security Management,* 15.

(April, 1998). "Real Mountie Travels 'Due South' to Fight Crime." *Security*, 83-84.

Roughton, J. (Feb., 1995). "The OSHA Man Cometh." *Security Management,* 41-47.

Waller, J.M. (1998). "These Spies Steal American Jobs." *Reader's Digest Large Print Edition, February, 1998*, 151-158.

Warchol, G. (1998). *Workplace Violence 1992-96.* Washington, DC: Bureau of Justice Statistics, July, 1998.

(1997). *World Class Advantage.* Encino, CA: Pinkerton World Support Center.

Fire Prevention and Safety

6

INTRODUCTION

The managers of an organization have a responsibility to develop and implement programs in security, safety, and fire prevention. While the duties and responsibilities of these three areas are different, the goal is the same: to prevent, reduce, and control the losses of company assets. The functions of these areas may be combined into one major department or may operate as individual, cooperative units within the company. Major corporations frequently staff separate security, fire, and safety departments all under a corporate director of loss prevention. Regardless of the administrative arrangement, the role of security within an organization requires that security personnel be familiar with the principles and techniques of fire prevention and control and employee safety.

CHARACTERISTICS OF FIRE

Fire is one of the major threats to life and property in any business, and all security employees should therefore be aware of the fundamentals of fire and fire protection.

1. THE TRIANGLE CONCEPT OF FIRE

Fire is defined as rapid oxidation, accompanied by heat and light. *Oxidation* is the chemical union of oxygen with another substance. For example, the rusting of iron is oxidation, but it is not fire because no light is generated, and only a little heat is generated.

Fire can occur only when three elements are present in sufficient quantity: (1) oxygen, (2) fuel to combine with the oxygen, and (3) sufficient heat to maintain combustion. The removal or sufficient depletion of any one of these three elements will result in extinguishment of the fire. The classic "fire triangle" illustrates this by showing each of the three elements occupying one of the sides of the triangle (see Figure 6.1).

The fire triangle is a simplified illustration of the elements necessary to initiate and sustain a fire. A more scientific and thorough explanation is a concept called the "tetrahedron of fire." This explanation of fire adds a fourth element: "uninhibited chain reactions." This is an expansion of the "heat" side of the fire triangle and is used to show that there are a limited number of sources of activation energy other than heat that, given the right conditions, can initiate the chain reaction necessary to cause a fire (Bryan, 1974). The following discussion illustrates both the fire triangle and tetrahedron concepts of fire.

Figure 6.1
The Fire Triangle

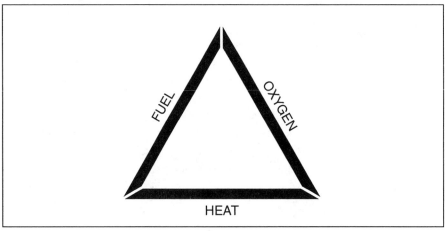

A. Oxygen

Most fires draw needed oxygen from the air. If a fire burns in an enclosed area, the oxygen is gradually used up and the fire diminishes, often to the point of extinguishment. If a limited but continuous supply of oxygen is present, the fire may enter a smoldering stage. Because oxygen is readily available from the air, eliminating it as a factor of combustion is usually impractical. However, in efforts to suppress an ongoing fire, various extinguishing agents can be used to "smother" the fire.

B. Heat

Heat for ignition can come from many sources: the sun, lightning, open flames, friction, electrical sparks, and so on. In most circumstances, a fire occurs when a source of sufficient external heat comes in contact with a combustible material. In some cases, the material itself creates enough internal heat to trigger combustion (spontaneous ignition). The degree of heat necessary to start combustion varies depending on the type of fuel present. For combustion to occur, most materials must be heated rather rapidly and, once ignition temperature has been reached, burning will continue as long as the fuel remains above this temperature. Heat of combustion varies with each type of fuel and is usually expressed in British Thermal Units (BTUs). A BTU is the quantity of heat required to raise the temperature of one pound of water one degree Fahrenheit at a specified temperature (as 39°F).

The heat side of the fire triangle offers many ways to prevent and extinguish fires. One way is to keep all sources of ignition away from material to be protected. If heat is required nearby, one may apply safeguards to the heating devices or insulate the materials. Extinguishment of a fire involves lowering the temperature of the fire to a point below the fuel's ignition temperature. The most common extinguishing agent used to accomplish this cooling effect is water.

C. Fuel

Fuels may be in a gaseous, liquid, or solid form, but combustion normally occurs when a fuel is in the gaseous or vapor state. Solids and liquids, therefore, must vaporize before oxygen can react with the fuel in combustion. There are exceptions, but they are unique and limited. Most ordinary combustible solids are compounds of carbon, hydrogen, nitrogen, and oxygen along with other, smaller portions of other minerals. When free burning in air occurs, oxygen reacts with carbon to form carbon dioxide and with hydrogen to form water vapor. The minerals and nitrogen compounds usually remain in a solid state as ash.

When a material in liquid form is heated, it reaches a temperature above which it cannot go and still remain a liquid. This temperature is called the boiling point. It is at this stage that the liquids undergo rapid vaporization and mix with the air. The chance of a fire starting in a given flammable liquid and the speed of its combustion depend upon the liquid's particular characteristics and surrounding environmental conditions.

Fuels in the gaseous state are divided into two broad groups: flammable and inflammable. Flammable gases are perhaps the most difficult fuels to deal with because many are colorless and odorless. For safety and fire prevention, all gases should be stored in airtight containers or pipes.

The triangular concept of fire and fire prevention rests upon the following principles:

1) An oxidizing agent (oxygen), a combustible material (fuel), and an ignition source (heat) are essential for combustion.

2) The combustible material must be heated to its ignition temperature before it will burn.

3) Combustion will continue until:

(a) combustible material is removed or consumed,

(b) oxidizing agent concentration is lowered to below the concentration needed to support combustion, or

(c) combustible material is cooled to below its ignition temperature.

As a fire condition develops and starts, four distinct stages of the combustion process are involved, progressing from one stage or level to the next. Each stage may develop and progress to the next level over a period of time or the entire process can occur in an instant.

1) Incipient stage—At this initial stage, invisible products of combustion are given off; the oxidation process has begun. There is very little heat and neither flame nor smoke is visible.

2) Smoldering stage—Smoke is visible at this stage, but there is still little appreciable heat or flame.

3) Flame stage—Flame and smoke are both visible, but excessive heat is still not apparent.

4) Heat stage—Almost simultaneous with the flame stage is the generation of excessive heat and rapid expansion of air.

Each of these successive stages of fire is unique and can be detected by fire protection-sensing devices that are activated by the characteristics of a specific stage.

2. THE TETRAHEDRON CONCEPT OF FIRE

The chemical reaction involved in fire is not as simple as the classic fire triangle indicates. A fourth factor, "reaction chain," is of equal importance to the other three elements: heat, fuel, and oxidizing agent. Thus, the fire triangle is converted to a three-dimensional pyramid, known as the "tetrahedron of fire" (see Figure 6.2).

Giving support to this concept was the discovery of various extinguishing agents that are more effective than those that simply manage to disrupt the triangle. Neutralization of the fire tetrahedron is accomplished by a breaking of the chain reactions by chemical and/or physical means. An example of the process is described by Bush and McLaughlin:

> This reaction chain is caused by the breakdown and recombination of the molecules that make up a combustible material with the oxygen of the atmosphere. A piece of paper, made up of cellulose molecules, is a good example of a combustible material. Those molecules that are close to the heat source begin to vibrate at an enormously increased

rate, and, almost instantaneously, begin to break apart. In a series of chemical reactions, these fragments continue to break up, producing free carbon and hydrogen that combine with the oxygen in the air. This combination releases additional energy. Some of the released energy breaks up still more cellulose molecules, releasing more free carbon and hydrogen, which, in turn, combine with more oxygen, releasing more energy, and so on. The flames will continue until fuel is exhausted, oxygen is excluded in some way, heat is dissipated, or the flame reaction-chain is disrupted (Bush & McLaughlin, 1979:31).

Figure 6.2
Fire Tetrahedron

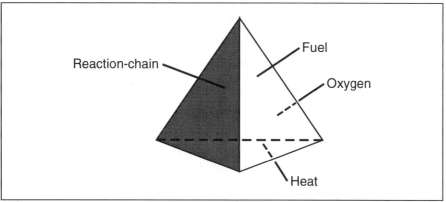

Reprinted with the permission of Macmillan Publishing Company from *Introduction to Fire Science* by Loren S. Bush and James H. McLaughlin. Copyright ©1979 by Macmillan Publishing Company.

3. PRODUCTS OF COMBUSTION

The importance of fire prevention and protection can be demonstrated by looking at the products of the combustion process and their effects on life and property. The products of combustion are divided into four categories: (1) fire gases, (2) flame, (3) heat, and (4) smoke. Each of the products can have an injurious, damaging, or fatal effect on property and human life.

Fire gases refer to the gaseous products given off during combustion. The chemical composition of these gases depends on many variables—the principal ones being the chemical composition of the material being burned, the amount of available oxygen and the temperature or heat present. Many of the gases are dangerous and, in sufficient quantity, can be fatal. Carbon monoxide, a common fire gas formed when the air supply is very low, poisons by asphyxiation. The hazardous properties of fire gases are particularly apparent in looking at the actual causes of fire deaths. Statistics indicate that fire fatalities from the inhalation of hot fire gases and hot air are far more common than fire deaths from all other causes combined.

Burns can be caused by direct contact with flame or heat radiated from flames. When flame is visible, it can be assumed that it is probably not separated by an appreciable distance from the burning materials. Flame is a distinct indicator that materials are burning in the presence of an oxygen-rich atmosphere.

Heat is the final stage of the combustion process. Exposure to heated air can cause dehydration, heat exhaustion, blockage of the respiratory tract by fluids, and burns. Burns are commonly classified into three categories: first-degree, second-degree, and third-degree.

A first-degree burn is characterized by heat, pain, and reddening of the burned skin surface, but does not exhibit blistering or chapping of skin tissues. A second-degree burn is marked by pain, blistering, and superficial destruction of the dermis, with fluid accumulation and possible swelling of the tissues beneath the burn. The most serious type, the third-degree burn, is characterized by destruction of the skin through the depth of the dermis and possibly into underlying tissues, accompanied by loss of body fluids and sometimes shock.

Smoke (the solid and liquid particles in suspension in the gases) can also have harmful effects. Smoke particles can be irritating when inhaled, and extended exposure to them can cause damage to the respiratory tract. Smoke, with its ability to obscure visibility and inhibit breathing, is a principal life hazard in a fire. Smoke can provide an early warning of fire, but at the same time it may generate or contribute to panic on the part of observers.

The best protection against fire is prevention. Participants in any situation must be able to protect lives and property, understand the characteristics and nature of fire, and be able to take the steps necessary to prevent the creation of a fire hazard. No environment can be absolutely free of a potential fire. Buildings are never fireproof; however, many do have fire-resistant properties. Participants in any situation are not always safety conscious. Mistakes can be made or unforeseen conditions can develop that make it imperative to have an effective, working program of fire prevention and control.

SECURITY'S ROLE

Though the organizational placement and role of security may vary from company to company, security will generally have either a direct or indirect responsibility for the development, operation, and enforcement of any fire prevention program. Security operations to protect property against fire usually fall into three categories: (1) to facilitate and control the movement of persons within the premises, (2) to ensure orderly conduct on the property, and (3) to protect life and property at all times. These security operations can include the following duties:

1) Prevent entry of unauthorized persons who might set a fire intentionally or unintentionally.

2) Control the activities of people authorized to be on the property who may not be aware of procedures established for the prevention of fire.

3) Control pedestrian and vehicular traffic during exit drills, and control evacuation of the property or parts of it during emergencies.

4) Control gates and vehicular traffic to facilitate access to the property by the public fire department, members of any private fire brigade, and off-duty emergency personnel in case of fire and emergencies.

5) Check permits for heat-related work (including cutting and welding). Where necessary, stand by to operate fire extinguishing equipment.

6) Detect conditions likely to cause a fire, such as leaks, spills, and faulty equipment.

7) Detect conditions likely to reduce the effectiveness with which a fire may be controlled, such as out-of-place portable fire extinguishers, closed sprinkler valves, and impaired water supplies.

8) Perform operations to ensure that fire equipment will function effectively. Operations may include testing automatic sprinklers or other fixed fire protection systems, fire pumps, and equipment related to these systems. It also means assisting in maintenance of the equipment; checking portable fire extinguishers and fire hoses, and assisting in pressure tests and maintenance service on these items; testing fire alarm equipment by actuating transmitting devices; and checking equipment provided on any motorized fire apparatus and conducting periodic tests and maintenance operations required for it.

9) Promptly discover a fire and call the public fire department (and the fire brigade of the property, if there is one).

10) Operate fire control equipment after giving the alarm and before the response of other persons to the alarm.

11) Monitor signals of protective signaling systems, such as alarms from manual fire alarm boxes on a system private to the property, signals for water flow in sprinkler systems, signals from systems for detecting fires and abnormal conditions, and signals indicating equipment malfunctions.

12) Make patrols over routes chosen to ensure surveillance of all the property at appropriate intervals.

13) Start up and shut down certain equipment when there are no other personnel provided for the purpose. (National Fire Protection Association [NFPA], 1971)

Every time security personnel go on routine patrol or inspection, their instructions should include taking immediate and/or appropriate action on the following types of situations:

1) Outside doors and gates should be closed and locked; windows, skylights, fire doors, and fire shutters should be closed.

2) All oily waste, rags, paint residue, rubbish, and similar items should be removed from buildings or placed in approved containers.

3) All fire apparatus should be in place and not obstructed.

4) Aisles should be clear.

5) Motors or machines carelessly left running should be shut off and reported.

6) All offices, conference rooms, and smoking areas should be checked for carelessly discarded smoking materials.

7) All gas and electric heaters, coal and oil stoves, and other heating devices on the premises should be checked.

8) All hazardous manufacturing processes should be left in a safe condition. The temperature of dryers, annealing furnaces, and other equipment that continue to operate during the night, on holidays and weekends should be noted on all rounds.

9) Hazardous materials, such as gasoline, should be kept in proper containers or removed from buildings.

10) All sprinkler valves should be open, with gauges indicating proper pressures. If they are closed, immediate action should be taken.

11) All rooms should be checked during cold weather to determine whether they are heated properly.

12) All water lines, air valves, steam lines, etc., found to be leaking should be closed and/or reported.

13) Particular attention should be given to new construction and maintenance projects. (NFPA, 1971)

TRAINING FOR FIRE PREVENTION AND PROTECTION

Security personnel must be thoroughly acquainted with the property being protected. They must be familiar with the physical features of the property; the materials utilized and stored on the premises; the fire characteristics of buildings, equipment, and materials; the location and operation of fire fighting equipment; and the location of critical control valves and switches. Areas of basic training for security personnel should include fire, first aid, extinguishing agents, extinguishing equipment, and support services.

1. HAZARDOUS MATERIALS

Central to any training for fire prevention and control is an understanding of fire hazards. A grouping of materials referred to as fire hazards includes:

1) Light combustible materials: wood shavings, cotton, paper, etc.;

2) Combustible dusts;

3) Flammable and combustible liquids;

4) Flammable gases;

5) Materials subject to spontaneous heating and ignition; and

6) Explosive materials, acids, and oxidizing agents.

All materials identified as hazardous should be visibly marked and rated in one or more of the following categories: (1) hazardousness to health, (2) flammability, and/or (3) reactivity. The following system of identifying, rating, and categorizing fire hazards has been devised by the National Fire Protection Association.

Colors are used to designate the type of hazard; numbers denote the level of severity. Figure 6.3 shows a sample sign. In the form of an adhesive label or tag, it can be attached to containers holding materials having hazardous properties, or in the case of a hazardous area, can be placed on doors, walls, partitions, etc.

Figure 6.3
Hazardous Materials Marking System Devised by the National Fire Protection Association

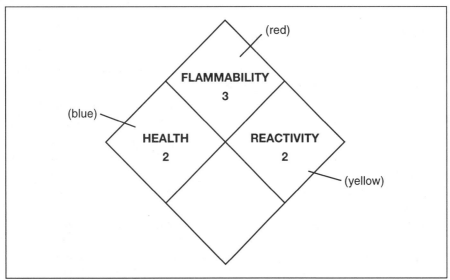

The color red denotes flammability hazards; blue denotes health hazards; and yellow denotes reactivity hazards. Numbers indicate the order of severity, ranging from "4," indicating a severe hazard, to "0," indicating no special hazard. The fourth and open space can be used to denote any unusual characteristic of a hazardous material, such as radioactivity or reactivity with water. Security should be instrumental in evaluating, inspecting, and enforcing any program designed to identify and control the usage and availability of hazardous materials.

2. Classes of Fire

There are four classes of fire with which security personnel should be familiar.

Class A—Fires involving common combustible material, such as wood, paper, cloth, rubber, and some plastics.

Class B—Fires involving flammable liquids, such as petroleum-based gas and oil products.

Class C—Fires involving electrical equipment.

Class D—Fires involving combustible metals such as sodium, magnesium, and potassium.

Each of the above classes of fire involve specific materials (fuels)—all of which may be present at a given facility. It is essential for security personnel to be aware of and able to classify all the materials used and stored at their facility. A basic knowledge of the combustibles involved in each class of fire is essential for the selection of the proper extinguishing agent.

3. Classes of Extinguishers

Portable fire extinguishers are designed to discharge a contained amount of fire extinguishing agent which can be carried or moved to the scene of a fire. Effectiveness depends on the use of the proper extinguisher and extinguishing agent for the fire encountered, the proper method of use, the adequacy of the amount of extinguishing agent and the proper functioning of the unit. Some portable extinguishers are effective on only one type of fire, while others are suitable for two or more classes of fire. Extinguishers are classified as A, B, C, or D according to the class of fire they are designed to extinguish.

Class A—Class A extinguishers are used to extinguish fires involving common combustibles that require a heat-absorbing extinguishing agent. Class A extinguishers accomplish this cooling effect with water, water solutions, or the coating effects of certain dry chemicals.

Class B—Class B extinguishers are used on fires involving flammable liquids. Class B extinguishers smother fires by cutting off the oxygen supply. A number of powdered chemicals, foam compounds, heavy non-combustible gases, and other agents will accomplish this.

Class C—A fire involving electrical equipment should be extinguished by an agent that does not conduct electricity. Carbon dioxide (CO_2) is a common Class C fire extinguisher.

Class D—A fire involving combustible metals requires a heat-absorbing extinguishing agent. Class D extinguishers may contain various dry powders that will not react with the burning metal.

Most manufacturers of extinguishing equipment utilize distinctive markings for extinguishers in order to indicate the class of fire on which they should be used (see Figure 6.4).

Figure 6.4
Classes of Fire Extinguishers

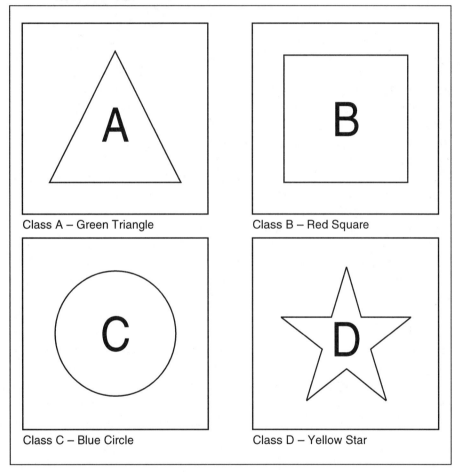

Class A – Green Triangle

Class B – Red Square

Class C – Blue Circle

Class D – Yellow Star

Some portable fire extinguishers are rated as multi-purpose extinguishers. For example, some dry chemical extinguishers are rated as ABC extinguishers. However, an extinguisher thus rated may not be as effective on one class of fire as it is on another. The size of the extinguisher, the type of extinguishing agent, and the type of fire determine the rating (i.e., the relative extinguishing effectiveness of the unit). The relative effectiveness of a portable extinguisher is denoted by a number that precedes the class letter on the identifying label. For example, an extinguisher may be rated 4-A, 16-B, and C. This indicates that the extinguisher should:

1) Extinguish approximately twice as large a Class A fire as a 2-A extinguisher (2½ gallon water extinguisher is rated 2-A).

2) Extinguish about 16 times as large a Class B fire as a 1-B extinguisher (tested to extinguish a 16-square-foot flammable liquid pan fire).

3) Be suitable for use on live electrical equipment (rating of 1-C is the same as a C rating).

Selecting the proper extinguisher depends primarily on the hazards present at a particular facility. Before deciding which extinguishers to purchase, an in-depth survey of the facility must be made. The survey should give an accurate picture of the potential hazards of operation confronting each specific area and the facility as a whole. Selection of extinguishers must also consider the work force (e.g., some people may not be able to handle and operate heavy extinguishers, so lighter-weight units should be chosen). In the choice of extinguishers and extinguishing agents, the safety of the operator must also be considered, because some extinguishing agents may react with hot metal or other substances to produce toxic vapors when used in closed or confined spaces.

After a portable extinguisher is properly selected, security personnel and other employees must be trained as to its most efficient and effective operation. Many companies require that all employees be trained in the use of extinguishers during their initial employment and also receive periodic refresher training. If a proprietary fire department or permanent fire brigade is not present, the responsibility for such training is often given to security.

Another necessary and important aspect of the proper utilization of portable extinguishers is that they must be correctly installed and maintained. This means that extinguishers must be located and installed to conform with OSHA standards and other fire regulations. They must be mounted at the proper height and/or placed in approved containers. Regular inspections (at least monthly) should be made to make certain that extinguishers are where they should be, have not been activated, damaged or tampered with, and are not blocked by materials or equipment.

4. EXTINGUISHING AGENTS

The suppression and extinguishment of fire involves two essential elements: (1) an extinguishing agent, and (2) a means or system for applying the extinguishing agent. The utilization of an extinguishing agent and its method of delivery must be related to the particular space and property to be protected. The effectiveness of fire suppression efforts depends on the proper selection and application of extinguishing agents if the fire cycle is to be disrupted.

a. Water

For most common combustibles (Class A), such as wood, paper, and cloth, the simplest and most effective means of removing the heat of a fire is through the application of water. The application of water will depend on the properties of the fire. Applying water to a burning fuel, whether by a stationary sprinkler system, portable extinguisher, or fire waterhose, cools the fuel to the point at which insufficient heat is present to support continued combustion.

b. Foam

Foam-extinguishing systems have been used extensively for many years, especially in the petrochemical industry and crash-rescue units at airports. Foam-extinguishing agents, produced by chemical or mechanical means, are air/water emulsions that serve to exclude oxygen from the surface of the burning material. Both mechanical and chemical types of foam are effective on Class A and Class C fires.

c. Carbon Dioxide

Carbon dioxide is a colorless, odorless, inert, and electrically nonconductive agent that is approximately 50 percent heavier than air. It serves to extinguish a fire by displacing the normal atmosphere, that is, it reduces the oxygen content below the level required for continued combustion. Because carbon dioxide is discharged in a gaseous form by internal storage pressure, and the vapors are heavier than air, carbon dioxide extinguishing systems are usually found in interior locations, protecting areas containing electrical hazards, gaseous and liquid flammable materials, and food preparation operations. Portable carbon dioxide units are particularly applicable to electrical substations, motors, computer equipment, office equipment, and vaults.

d. Halogenated Agents

Halogenated extinguishing agents, commonly referred to as Halons, are either vaporizing liquids or liquefied gases capable of extinguishing and suppressing fires in various materials when applied at proper rates and in proper concentrations. Halons can be used for portable extinguishing units or stationary systems.

A Halon is a hydrocarbon in which some of the hydrogen atoms have been replaced by such elements as bromine, chlorine, fluorine, iodine, etc., or by combinations of these, in order to create a fire-extinguishing gas or liquid. In vapor form, these halogenated hydrocarbons change to other chemical compounds that inhibit or prevent oxidation; however, a number of halons are toxic—thus, hazardous to humans. Halon systems must be designed to provide for controlled concentrations when activated, so that occupant evacuations can be accomplished before a hazardous concentration level is reached.

Both Halon 1211 and Halon 1301 were being used for various protection applications, including electrical equipment, airplane engines, and computer centers until 1995. These extinguishing agents are no longer produced. Systems incorporating Halon and other chlorofluorocarbons were required to be replaced with alternative extinguishing agents.

e. Dry Chemical

Dry chemical extinguishing agents consist of finely divided powders that effectively snuff out a fire when applied by portable extinguishers, hose lines, or stationary systems. Dry chemicals are particularly effective for fires in flammable liquids and in certain types of ordinary combustibles and electrical equipment, depending on the type of chemical agent used. The basic chemical agents used include: (1) sodium bicarbonate, (2) potassium bicarbonate, (3) potassium chloride, (4) ureapotassium bicarbonate, and (5) monoammonium phosphate. Dry chemical agents are non-toxic, stable at temperature extremes and nonconductive.

f. Dry Powder

The increased use of combustible metals such as magnesium, sodium, lithium, etc., created a need for a special agent to extinguish fires involving these materials. Extinguishing agents developed for combustible metals are designated as dry powders. Delivery systems include portable extinguishers, wheel units, and stationary units. Class D fires create unique problems, and successful control and extinguishment of such fires depend on adequate knowledge and training of the firefighter.

g. Sprinkler Protection

Portable fire extinguishers are designed to be taken to the fire location, whereas fixed or stationary fire extinguishing equipment is designed to control and extinguish a fire in a given area. Fixed fire extinguishing systems can utilize a variety of extinguishing agents. They are automatic in operation and are designed to discharge the extinguishing agent upon activation. While various extinguishing agents are available for use in fixed extinguishing systems, the most common type is the automatic water sprinkler system. Standard sprinkler installations usually consist of a combination of water discharge devices (sprinklers); one or more sources of water under pressure; water-flow controlling devices (valves); distribution piping to supply the water to the discharge devices; and auxiliary equipment such as alarms and supervisory devices. Outdoor fire hydrants, indoor hose standpipes, and hand hose connections are also common components of these systems. The fundamentals of water sprinkler protection revolve around the principle of the automatic discharge of water in sufficient density to control or extinguish a fire in its initial stages.

There are two major types of automatic water sprinkler systems: the dry pipe system and the wet pipe system. The type of sprinkler system most appropriate in a given location usually depends on whether the piping would be subject to freezing temperatures and on the type of materials being protected.

h. Wet Pipe Sprinkler Systems

A wet pipe sprinkler system consists of automatic sprinklers attached to a system of piping that holds water and is connected to a water supply. Usually the sprinkler head contains a fusible element that will melt at a predetermined temperature and discharge the water, extinguishing fire in the area of the activated unit. Wet pipe sprinkler systems are found in areas not subject to freezing and where hazardous conditions are minimal. The principal advantage of the wet pipe system is that, when activated, it will discharge water only in the immediate area of the fire. Its primary disadvantage is that the fusible element contained in the sprinkler head must be melted before water is discharged; thus, there is a time lag during which the temperature must build up to the predetermined level of heat necessary to melt the fusible element. A fire developing on the outer fringes or in the area of overlap between two sprinkler heads has an opportunity to grow before the sprinkler head(s) are activated.

i. Dry Pipe Sprinkler Systems

The dry pipe sprinkler system is used in areas that cannot be heated properly or where conditions of occupancy or special hazards require immediate application of water over a given area. Dry pipe sprinkler systems consist of sprinkler units attached to piping that contains air under pressure. When air is released by activation of a sensing/detection device, this opens a dry pipe valve that allows water to flow into the piping system and to be discharged through the open sprinklers. Thus, until a sensing device is activated, there is no water in the piping. A variation of the dry pipe system is the deluge system, which consists of open sprinkler units attached to larger piping to allow a large quantity of water flow. When activated, a deluge system can release huge quantities of water very quickly.

A routine program of inspection and maintenance of sprinkler systems should be developed. Security personnel often are given the responsibility of inspecting and ensuring that all components of the fire protection system are functional and in good working condition. Therefore, adequate training in the operation and care of sprinkler equipment should be given to security personnel.

j. Fire Protection Signals

Protective signaling devices play a major role in fire detection and protection. The signaling device may be as simple as a hand-operated gong or as complex as an extensive electrical system that covers an entire facility. The device may be a local alarm operated manually or automatically, or one that generates a local alarm and also transmits a warning signal to a remote location. Protective signaling devices can be used for many purposes:

1) to notify people of a fire;

2) to call or alert the fire department, private fire brigade, security department, or other receiving locations;

3) to monitor extinguishing systems and warn of activation or nonfunctioning conditions;

4) to monitor industrial processes and warn of hazardous conditions;

5) to supervise people electronically; and

6) to activate control equipment. (National Fire Protection Association, 1968)

Fire protection signaling devices are an integral part of any fire protection system. Because the first few seconds of a fire are so critical in fire protection and suppression, the presence and proper functioning of a protective signaling system may make the difference between life or death. Various types of detection and monitoring devices can be utilized in a protective signaling system. Some are used to monitor water and/or air pressure of the system; they activate when a sprinkler system, fire pump, or other fire protection device is activated or malfunctions. Others detect and react to fire or combustible conditions with or without the activation of fire-extinguishing equipment. Some of these include fixed or rate-of-rise heat-sensitive devices, ionization detectors sensitive to smoke and gaseous products of combustion, photoelectric detectors sensitive to smoke, pneumatic tube detectors sensitive to air pressure variation, and so on.

SAFETY MANAGEMENT

Federal, state, and local laws and the standards set by insurance carriers require that almost every employer provide a safe and healthful work environment for employees. The Occupational Safety and Health Act (OSHA) passed by Congress in 1970 spells out in great detail what the employer must do to ensure safe working conditions for employees. It specifies requirements for general housekeeping, equipment and equipment operation, environmental health controls, production operations, hazardous material handling and storage, fire protection equipment, materials handling and storage, and so on.

In addition to OSHA, most employers must satisfy state and local regulations relating to safety and fire protection. In fact, some states have safe work laws and environmental protection laws that go beyond those set by OSHA and the federal government. Other restrictions and standards may be set by the insurance companies for their commercial and industrial clients. Frequently, insurance carriers refuse to provide coverage for potential clients (or drop existing clients) because of unsafe conditions at a facility. Some facilities, such as many healthcare institutions, belong to a professional organization similar to the Joint Commission on Accreditation of Healthcare Organizations, which imposes strict safety standards upon its members.

Every organization is dependent for its success on preserving the efficiency and effectiveness of its productive capability. Whether its product is a manufactured item or a service, an organization is dependent on its primary asset, i.e., the people that make its existence possible. To expose this asset to a hazardous or unsafe environment is to invite disruption and even destruction. Safety and loss prevention are prime responsibilities of operating management. An unsafe environment or accident is a sign that something is wrong in the management system. Companies are thus motivated to have a safe work environment by moral, legal, and self-interest considerations. The degree of concern for the safety of employees can range from a disinterested attitude to one of strict and fair regulation. If company leadership projects a strong positive attitude toward safety, it is likely that such an attitude will filter down and throughout the company hierarchy, resulting in high morale and efficient, maximal production.

1. THE OCCUPATIONAL SAFETY AND HEALTH ACT (OSHA)

The Occupational Safety and Health Act was signed into law on December 29, 1970. Its purpose was to ensure, so far as possible, safe and healthful working conditions for every working man and woman in the nation. As defined by the Act, a covered employer is any "person engaged in a business affecting commerce who has employees, but does not include the United States or any State or political subdivision of a State." The following employers/situations are not covered under the Act:

1) self-employed persons;

2) family-owned and-operated farms; and

3) workplaces already protected under other federal statutes.

Because federal agencies are not subject to OSHA regulations and enforcement provisions, each agency is required to establish and maintain an effective and comprehensive job safety and health program of its own. State and local governments, while exempt from OSHA in their role as employers, can apply to OSHA for approval of their respective programs.

Under the Act, each covered employer

1) has the general duty to furnish each employee employment and places of employment that are free from recognized hazards that are causing or likely to cause death or serious physical harm, and

2) has the specific duty of complying with safety and health standards promulgated under the act. (National Safety Council [NSC], 1974)

Each employee, in turn, has the obligation to comply with the safety and health standards, and all rules, regulations, and orders applicable to his or her own actions and conduct on the job. Employers generally are required to post OSHA-required information materials in a conspicuous manner, to keep records and report certain occurrences relative to safety and accidents, to report variances from standards, to cooperate with OSHA compliance officers, and to comply with recommended or mandated changes under the Act. Today, almost all organizations accept the idea of moral, legal, and financial responsibility for work-related injuries.

2. WORKER RIGHT-TO-KNOW LAWS AND OSHA HAZARD COMMUNICATION STANDARD

Prior to enactment of the OSHA Hazard Communication Standard in 1985, several states had already legislated Worker Right-to-Know Laws. With the standard's passage, however, the state laws had to equal or supersede the federal statute. The idea behind both the federal and state laws was that employees had a right to know about proven and suspected health hazards that may result from working with toxic substances. The OSHA Hazard Communication Standard affected the same employers and employees covered under OSHA. The OSHA Hazard Communication Standard is designed to inform workers about the hazards with which they work. The covered employer is required to:

1) carry out defined hazard evaluation procedures of the workplace;

2) provide for appropriate labeling of all containers with identified hazardous materials;

3) complete, and make available to workers, material safety data sheets (MSDS) on all identified hazardous materials found in the workplace;

4) establish a written hazard communication program for employees; and

5) establish an employee education and training program regarding workplace hazardous materials.

The concept of the above laws was taken further in 1986 when a Federal "Community Right-to-Know Law" was passed. It requires companies and organizations to report certain information regarding hazardous materials (as identified by OSHA) to local governing bodies and agencies.

3. WORKERS' COMPENSATION

Workers' compensation statutes are intended to provide compensation benefits for personal injury caused by accident or conditions arising out of and in the course of employment. Workers' compensation programs generally have the following common objectives:

1) income replacement;

2) restoration of earning capacity and return to productive employment;

3) industrial accident prevention and reduction;

4) proper allocation of costs; and

5) achievement of all workers' compensation objectives in the most efficient manner possible. (NSC, 1974)

Workers' compensation acts and programs in the United States provide incentives to employers to introduce measures that will decrease the frequency and severity of accidents. That is, the costs of workers' compensation insurance, which the employer must pay, are tied to safety practices: the safer the workplace, the lower the costs.

4. ACCIDENT PREVENTION

An effective accident prevention and occupational safety program in the workplace must be related to proper job performance. When people are trained to function properly in their work environment they will perform more safely.

Safety is a term encompassing the areas of fire safety, personal security, and accident prevention. All employees must be initially trained—and periodically retrained—in general safety practices and specific job-related responsibilities. Safety awareness, from the top of the management hierarchy to the lowest job classification, is imperative if safety hazards and violations are to be found, understood, and eliminated.

A security department has a natural role to play in safety awareness and accident prevention. Security personnel who are knowledgeable about required safety standards and practices can be instrumental in correcting or bringing about the correction of safety hazards and violations. The performance of such security duties as patrols, inspections, access control, etc., expose security personnel to most, if not all, of the work environment, employees, and operations.

It would be unfortunate if their observations, contacts, and suggestions were not utilized.

Given their functional responsibilities and operational procedures, security personnel can play a significant role in responding to calls for assistance. Personnel trained to respond to accidents and personal illnesses and to render emergency medical treatment should be available to any facility having an appreciable number of employees and/or people. Security personnel can either assist other, more highly trained personnel or deliver basic medical treatment themselves.

SUMMARY

Fire is one of the most destructive forces known to humankind. It can occur as an act of nature, as an accident, or as an act of sabotage. Regardless of its source, the potential for its occurrence can be reduced with an adequate fire prevention and protection program. This can be accomplished only if the people involved in the program recognize the problems, understand the possible alternatives, and arrive at the best solutions. A knowledge of the chemistry and nature of fire, an awareness of the hazardous properties of the facility to be protected, proper selection of the appropriate fire protection equipment, and effective utilization and coordination of equipment, procedures, and personnel must all be present before an environment can be safe and secure.

Under ideal circumstances, the security department would provide support services to specialized fire protection personnel. However, the situation often demands that security personnel also have the duty of being firefighters. Where this is the case, security personnel must be trained to be better members of a loss prevention team.

Safety is an important aspect of any environment. Legislation such as OSHA and Workers' Compensation laws mandate that most work environments be safe and healthful places to work. Various responsibilities regarding safety and accident prevention in the workplace can be assigned to security. In most cases, such duties are a natural addition to the existing security functions and tasks.

DISCUSSION QUESTIONS

1. What are the elements necessary for combustion?
2. Outline the stages through which a fire usually progresses.
3. What roles can security play in protecting a facility against fire loss?
4. Distinguish between wet pipe sprinklers and dry pipe sprinklers.
5. List and briefly explain the significance of the various groups of materials referred to as fire hazards.
6. What are the products of the combustion process?

7. List the classes of fire and their respective fuel types.

8. Why should users of Halon begin to look for a different extinguishing agent?

9. What is OSHA? Who is covered by OSHA? What are employers covered by OSHA required to do?

10. Explain why it is in the best interests of the employer to reduce accidents, particularly those that fall under Workers' Compensation laws.

REFERENCES

Bryan, J.L. (1974). *Fire Suppression and Detection Systems.* Encino, CA: Glencoe Press.

Bush, L.S. & McLaughlin, J.H. (1979). *Introduction to Fire Science.* New York, NY: Macmillan Publishing Company.

National Fire Protection Association (1971). *Fire Protection Handbook.* Boston, MA: National Fire Protection Association.

National Fire Protection Association (1968). *Industrial Fire Brigades.* Boston, MA: National Fire Protection Association.

National Safety Council (1974). *Accident Prevention Manual for Industrial Operations.* Chicago, IL.

Emergency and Disaster Preparedness

7

INTRODUCTION

Businesses, industries, and institutions fare with various degrees of success during emergency or disaster conditions. Some organizations are well-prepared to safeguard the lives of their employees, protect their physical facilities, and even arrange to continue production during a crisis. Other organizations may not be as prepared, but are able to resume functioning due to their unique product or service, or continue functioning due to their escaping the worst consequences of a disastrous situation. However, the majority of American businesses, industries and institutions suffer catastrophic losses every time a disaster strikes their facilities. These different results are not due to differences in wealth, physical size, or number of employees, but rather to different degrees of emergency and disaster planning and preparation.

THE NEED FOR EMERGENCY PLANNING

The traditional way of looking at the need for emergency planning is that the disasters will be natural or caused by humans. To put the need for emergency planning and disaster control into proper perspective, some facts and figures seem appropriate.

NATURAL

- Worldwide from January, 1997 to August, 1998, 16,000 people killed by weather and $50 billion in damages.

- In the United States, during the same period, 456 dead and $13 billion in damages.

- 800 tornadoes a year in the United States, of which 24 percent cause extensive damage.

- October, 1995 hurricane Opal lashed Florida, North Carolina, and Georgia causing $50 million in damages to boats and at least $1.8 billion in property damage and claimed the lives of at least 19 persons.

- The Mississippi River flood of 1993 caused extensive damage along the 2,000 miles from Minnesota to the Gulf of Mexico. The greatest damage occurred from Minnesota to Missouri. Some areas received 30 inches of rain—nearly 200 percent of normal (Miller, 1998).

Obviously, these are not all of the natural disasters that have occurred in the United States over the past decade; however, they do emphasize the need for security operations to be ready when needed.

HUMAN

Humans can cause damage in many ways such as setting fires, bombings, facility attacks (for example, banks), hijacking, kidnapping, and maiming. Today, the most talked and written about factor is terrorism. Again, some statistics put the need for proper emergency planning and disaster control into perspective. However, an important consideration is that, unlike natural disasters, security personnel can take actions to prevent terrorist incidents and do not have to deal solely with the aftermath. Included in the appendices at the end of this book are some guidelines that can be used to plan for terrorist incidents, and in Appendices F and G, there are terrorist surveys that should be reviewed.

- The 1995 bombing of the Alfred P. Murrah Federal Building in Oklahoma City was caused by a 4,800-pound bomb which killed 168 people and wounded many more.

- From 1985-1995, more than 1,000 passengers and crew died because someone smuggled a bomb on civilian airlines.

- One person, Osama Bin Laden, has been linked to a half-dozen terrorist incidents and was secretly indicted by a United Stated Federal Grand Jury.

- The 1996 Al-Khobar Towers Military Complex bombing in Saudi Arabia resulted in the death of 19 Americans and injury to 109 (Barber, 1997).

Pinkerton Global Intelligence Services (PGIS) has been tracking and reporting incidents of terrorism and other political violence and compiling the data in an annual report. Following are some key points from their 1996 and 1997 reports entitled Pinkerton Risk Assessment Services: Annual Risk Assessment Worldwide (Including United States).

- 1992   5,404 incidents
- 1993   4,954 incidents
- 1994   3,830 incidents
- 1995   4,063 incidents
- 1996   3,638 incidents
- 1997   3,588 incidents

Another way to look at these statistics is in terms of the number of incidents that, while occurring outside the United States, involve United States interests. In 1995 – 93 incidents, in 1996 – 75 incidents, and in 1997 – 88 incidents met this criteria.

NORTH AMERICA AND THE UNITED STATES

- North America accounts for less than one percent of the terrorist and other political violence in the world.

However, almost all of the incidents occur in the United States.

- Since 1988 there has been an average of 18 incidents per year in the United States.

Thus, looking at the statistics it appears that the United States should not be overly concerned about terrorism. However, the bombing at the World Trade Center in New York, the Murrah Federal Building in Oklahoma City, Pan American Flight 103, Olympic Park in Atlanta, and the Unabomber are vivid examples of why there remains a need for effective countermeasures as well as emergency planning and disaster control procedures.

The Grand Rapids Press, November 22, 1998, provided information on the Federal Bureau of Investigation's high-tech center that can handle up to five crises simultaneously. Built at a cost of $20 million, it is nearly the size of a football field with 35 separate rooms that can seat 450 people. The new Strategic Information and Operations Center is located on the fifth floor of the FBI Building in Washington DC.

A PERIOD OF DISASTER

During the three-year period between Hurricane Hugo and Hurricane Andrew, forest fires devastated hundreds of thousands of acres of timber, thousands of homes and several entire villages in the western states. Earthquakes demolished bridges, highways, buildings, and public utilities. Floods ravaged cities and towns in all parts of the country. Hurricanes swept over land areas on the east coast, the gulf states, Guam, and Hawaii. Civil disorders resulted in burned out, looted, and destroyed businesses and small factories in more than one major city. In one report, the American Red Cross stated that it had responded to more than 5,000 disasters in those three years, ranging from explosions in separate buildings to Hurricane Andrew, the most destructive natural disaster in modern times.

The technological advances in news reporting via radio and television brought scenes of most of those disasters into American living rooms. Especially heartrending were interviews of individual victims of burned, destroyed, or severely damaged homes. Unfortunately, many of the victims did not have the foresight to build or buy more sturdy dwellings, avoid building in flood plains, or even insure their property. Many small businesses and institutions suffered similarly.

The media relayed urgent pleas for help throughout and vividly displayed a lack of preparation or self-sufficiency on behalf of the general public. Although relief agencies appeared slow to respond, a few authorities tried to explain that despite a national network of emergency services, large-scale assistance would take time to mobilize. The public was impatient. Many businesses, industries, and institutions did not wait for help. Some were so organized or prepared for emergencies that they were able to provide some assistance to the local community. The following are examples of how three organizations coped with emergencies that affected their personnel and property.

THREE CASE STUDIES

The following are brief descriptions of three actual disasters and how different organizations coped with them. Attention should be given to the fact that in the two cases in which regular security personnel were available to the organizations, the security forces were not given overall control of the response to the emergency, nor did the security forces provide the total emergency response.

1. POWER SHUT-DOWN: AN EXAMPLE OF POOR PLANNING

In a 24-hour period one winter, a severe snowstorm blanketed a Midwest region the size of Indiana with 12 inches of snow. Electrical power was disrupted in more than one-half of the area, with outages ranging from three to 30 hours. Roads and highways were impassable because the snow removal equipment could not keep up with the drifting snow. Thousands of persons were stranded away from home or from work, and five people were later found frozen to death in their vehicles. One of the dead victims had left his job in a medium-sized manufacturing plant when the electrical power was interrupted. The plant did not have an emergency source of power. All employees were dismissed from work; most stayed in the plant, while several took rooms at a nearby motel. A few of the line supervisors stayed in the plant, but none of the executives remained behind.

The power interruption caused irreparable damage to some of the equipment and the mixture of chemical products. After drinking alcohol they had brought into the plant, three employees became involved in an altercation in which one employee was seriously injured. The small cafeteria did not contain enough food to feed all the stranded employees beyond the first day. The marooned workers were restless and worried about their families elsewhere, and became generally unruly. The production line was not restarted until two days after the storm.

This plant had no security force or emergency plans. With proper planning and preparation, the facility could have prevented one death and one incarceration, and saved one day's worth of chemical mixture, the damaged equipment, two work days on the production line and possibly most of the more than $300,000 in direct losses sustained as a result of this snowstorm.

2.   RADIOACTIVE LEAK: AN EXAMPLE OF PROPER RESPONSE

In this example, planning and preparation preceded an emergency situation and thereby contributed inestimably to both good public relations and community safety during the week-long emergency. It began with a radio announcement that a local nuclear power plant had an uncontrolled radiation leak, upon which local residents were injudiciously advised by radio personnel to evacuate the area.

The security directors of several large nearby firms and the local telephone company set their emergency operations into action. They checked various sources for the urgency of the problem and then continued business as usual with their normal operating personnel. Their employees were apprised of the situation and continued working during their regular shifts. Arrangements were made to have additional contract guards stand by, in anticipation of looting should there be a further evacuation of residents. Packages were prepared with medication and other supplies needed by individual patients in the event that the local hospital would have to be evacuated. The local police were fully mobilized and the state national guard was placed on alert—ready to move within hours. By the end of the first week, most of the residents who had fled the area earlier returned, while others decided to leave at that late date. It seems that the residents in the community that did not have connection to the larger industrial firms simply were not made aware of the true situation and were frightened by baseless rumors.

No injuries or deaths occurred in this near-disaster. The industrial firms with emergency preparations continued business as usual, with few absentee workers. The emergency was treated as real, and lessons were learned that were incorporated later into the emergency response plan. Panic, injuries, and deaths were avoided by intelligent emergency procedures employed by trained personnel.

3. HURRICANE: AN EXAMPLE OF PROPER POST-DISASTER PROCEDURE

The third example illustrates procedures employed in the aftermath of a disaster. After a hurricane caused more than $700 million in losses and destroyed electrical transmission to more than 300,000 customers in one metropolitan area alone, emergency crews of repair technicians were assembled from power companies in adjacent states. The repair process lasted three weeks and was compounded by thousands of downed poles, transformers, and power lines that were susceptible to theft due to the high value of scrap aluminum and copper.

Additional contract security guards were hired from outside the affected area because all local guards were employed to protect other damaged businesses. Fuel, food, and other supplies were imported and made available to the power company personnel and guards. The security department had a threefold objective during this repair phase. One was to patrol the areas with the largest amounts of power company property lying on the ground. Another was to coordinate the deployment of guards to protect repair equipment, supplies, and vehicles. The third objective was to protect damaged power company buildings and their contents. This last objective was made easier by the fact that the power company had previously removed some valuable equipment to a more secure area in anticipation of damage to the buildings and subsequent looting. Again, prior planning and preparation for emergencies paid generous dividends by keeping further losses of property to a minimum after the disaster.

ANALYSIS

In the first example, the manufacturing plant was not prepared for emergency situations. When an emergency did occur, the costs were unnecessarily high in the loss of personnel, equipment, products, and productivity. Another important loss was the loss of faith in the organization by the employees and the community.

The latter two examples demonstrate the successes of organizations in reducing risks to their employees, protecting property and continuing work operations. By providing emergency leadership, ensuring the safety and welfare of their employees, and continuing to serve their communities, these organizations gained not only the esteem of their communities, but also the respect and future support of their employees.

The difference between the successful and unsuccessful responses to the disasters can be directly attributed to careful planning and appropriate preparedness. Undoubtedly, such planning and preparation would make employees more aware of the need to extend their knowledge to the protection of their own families and private property.

PLANNING FOR DISASTERS

The only thing certain about planning to protect lives or property from natural or person-caused emergencies or disasters is that there is no location in the world that is absolutely free from danger in one form or another. The varieties of potential dangers can be identified, and measures can be taken to reduce the risk of exposure to those dangers. Planning will not prevent a flood, explosion, or strike; however, thorough planning and preparation may prevent the escalation of a dangerous situation into a catastrophe.

Unless the organization is very small, all official planning for emergencies or disasters should be done by high-ranking representatives from all branches, departments or divisions, working together in a committee. The disaster committee should be large enough to ensure representation from all segments of the organization, but not so large that agreements cannot be reached. Someone with knowledge of the security field, whether a staff member with responsibility for security or an outside security consultant, should be on the committee. A security manager who is not in a high position of authority in the company should not head the committee. The following factors should be included in the planning process for an emergency and disaster control plan.

1. AUTHORITY

The owner, manager, or governing body of an organization should prepare a simple, written order to authorize the committee to develop an emergency control plan. The order should provide the committee with the necessary authority to develop a written plan, and then organize, train, and assign responsibilities to an emergency force within the organization. This statement should be brief and flexible so the committee can adjust its deliberations as necessary.

Existing organizational rules and regulations will have to be researched to ensure that there is not already an emergency plan that has been overlooked or forgotten. A previous plan may or may not be adequate for the present situation, so it should be carefully reviewed and updated, or declared void. Provisions for the new or revised emergency plan should follow the organization's established policies, rules, and regulations, so that there is a formal, legal foundation for the emergency control program. Especially important at this stage is the need to consider how the emergency plan might be affected by the firm's compliance with federal and state legislation, i.e., Occupational Safety and Health Administration (OSHA), Equal Employment Opportunity Commission (EEOC) and Americans with Disabilities Act (ADA) laws and regulations. The emergency plan should be compatible with the organization's overall goals and policies.

An emergency response leadership team, developed from existing high-level supervisors or managers, should coordinate the response decisions and activities for the organization during the emergency. These people should be selected from the regular company leadership so they have the necessary sense of loyalty and responsibility to protect the interests of the organization.

Written authority should exist to organize certain personnel into a special force during declared emergencies. There may be personnel occupying certain responsible positions who would object to such an extra assignment, or who might be physically or emotionally unsuited for assignment to an emergency force. For this reason, an effort should be made to attract willing and able volunteers from the organization to serve in the emergency force. Consideration for assignment to the force should be given to persons with unusual abilities and special interests that would be beneficial, such as those with emergency medical training, former police or military members, and people with extraordinary mechanical abilities.

The personnel selected for the emergency force should undergo training in primary and alternate emergency duties. Cross-training the emergency force allows for a greater range of assignments and the assumption of responsibilities in the event that member is absent or becomes incapacitated.

Within larger organizations there may be authority for personnel to be assigned as emergency coordinators for shifts, floors, buildings, or satellite facilities. This will ensure that there are trained personnel available throughout the organization to provide a continuity of calm leadership in an emergency.

The order of authority also should provide a chain of command that specifies the individuals who have the authority to order certain activities or changes or assume leadership roles in the event that higher-ranking personnel are unavailable during an emergency. The emergency response team should have the authority to take immediate action, absent the normal organizational leadership hierarchy, when it is necessary to safeguard lives or property.

2. VULNERABILITY ASSESSMENT

Organizations that want to develop an emergency and disaster control plan must be aware of their existing vulnerabilities so that effective safeguards can be planned. A vulnerability assessment is performed in several phases. These phases include consideration of the frequency of threats, organizational property and facilities, present guard services, and the extent of dependence upon outside water, drainage, electrical power, and communications.

A small committee should be appointed to conduct vulnerability assessments. The first assessment merely identifies the types and frequencies of all natural and person-caused emergencies and disasters recorded in the past in the area of the organization. If certain types of emergencies recur with regularity, predictions can be made as to the periods of the threats. Natural disasters seem to occur more regularly than other disasters.

The second phase of the vulnerability assessment requires an estimation of the structural strength of the buildings of the organization. An engineer should assist the committee in determining which of the buildings are sufficiently strong for use as personnel shelters and which are adequate for use as storage facilities for sensitive or valuable equipment.

The third phase of the assessment should be an analysis of the organization's present security measures. If proprietary or contract guards are used, their terms of employment may cause them to be unavailable during periods of emergency. The employment of off-duty police officers or national guard personnel could be a problem, as they could be mobilized by the police department or national guard during a general emergency and thus be unavailable to the private employer.

Another vulnerability assessment that should be made is the extent to which the organization would be affected by a disruption in electrical, water, sewage and communication services, and the degree of isolation the facility would experience in the event of flooded roadways, collapsed bridges, or other obstructions to normal transportation. The assessment should determine what alternate outside sources would be readily available under disaster conditions, and assess similar services and equipment available from within the organization itself.

In organizations that operate using mostly outside cartage, supply, or labor, the capability of the vendors of those services should be assessed to determine their ability to perform under certain emergency conditions. During major emergencies or disasters, outside sources of assistance are often commandeered by governmental agencies or firms that have first call on their goods or services by virtue of contractual agreements.

Supplies and services within an organization can be counted on only if they are accessible during the emergency. Emergency supplies that are inaccessible (e.g., stored across town) are useless; supplies that have deteriorated over time in storage are also useless; emergency services such as electrical generators, cellular telephones, and other standby equipment that may be on a wish list in a file drawer are equally useless. A thorough inventory will establish what supplies and services can be put to use at a moment's notice from within the organization.

3. DETERMINING THE REQUIRED SECURITY NEEDS

Vulnerability assessments should result in lists of unprotected points in the physical structures and surrounding areas, the maintenance of power, communications and supplies, and sustained personnel support. Ultimately, the safeguarding of lives is of primary importance. Therefore, the disaster plan development committee should recommend to the facility administrator an order of the priority of emergency responses to make under various threatening conditions. Questions such as when to order the evacuation of employees to in-house shelters or other safe locations, whether any personnel should be exposed to danger by remaining in outlying buildings during the disaster, or when to order a shutdown of the production line must be resolved. Commensurate instructions must be included in the disaster plan.

There must be a preestablished set of conditions and instructions prepared to cover any emergency. Limited personal discretion should be allowed for personnel involved in emergency operations, but the emergency response team must have the authority to take the necessary action to safeguard lives and property when the situation so requires.

4. APPOINTING THE EMERGENCY AND DISASTER CONTROL COORDINATOR

Large organizations may have the resources to appoint a full-time emergency or disaster control coordinator to manage the development or implementation of the plan. In smaller organizations, someone may have to assume that role on a part-time basis. In any event, the coordinator should be of sufficient stature and authority in the organization to be able to deal effectively with others at all levels in the organizational hierarchy. Not only must a coordinator understand the value of preparedness, he or she must engender support for the program in periods when emergencies seem distant. In all cases, a coordinator is responsible for ensuring that every facet of the plan be cost-effective.

The appointment of the coordinator does not terminate the original committee's responsibilities in developing the disaster plan. Rather, the appointment is a sign from top management that there will be support for this project. The continued active use of this committee will also help in maintaining support from the separate departments represented on committee.

5. ESTABLISHING THE EMERGENCY OPERATIONS CENTER

The vulnerability assessment should have identified a secure room, area, or building within which the emergency leadership team could operate during emergency conditions. The operating center need not be used for that purpose only. A conference room, lounge, or other facility that could be rapidly converted or jointly used should suffice. However, there should be emergency equipment installed so that, in time of need, there would be no scurrying around to collect the needed supplies. Alternate sites should be identified in case the first selected site becomes unsuitable as an emergency operating center.

6. GAINING MANAGEMENT SUPPORT

The next step in the planning process is to acquaint all management levels with the vulnerabilities of the organization to emergencies or disasters, and to solicit their advice and cooperation for the development of a disaster control program. The support of management is necessary because there will need to be financial expenditures, personnel use, and the possible acquisition or sharing of equipment.

7. USING IN-HOUSE PERSONNEL

Regardless of the size of the organization, the presently employed personnel should perform the majority, if not all, of the necessary emergency duties. The nucleus of the emergency organization can be those personnel already trained and utilized to perform routine and emergency services, such as supervisors and other key administrative personnel, as well as the existing medical, fire, and safety/security staff. Other emergency response personnel can be selected from the regular employees who have demonstrated special talents or interests that could be useful, such as CB or ham radio operators, volunteer or auxiliary police or firefighters, first aid instructors, or operators of recreational vehicles (e.g., boats, snowmobiles, aircraft).

The regular maintenance or engineering employees could help to survey, establish, and maintain emergency facilities and make damage assessments. Personnel administrators could be responsible for the shelter and welfare services in the facility. Research personnel or scientifically oriented personnel could be used to monitor radiological sensors or other essential equipment or communications. As the emergency preparedness plan develops, other employees may be found to have special skills (or an interest in training to acquire additional skills) that would contribute to the response effort.

There are several ways to increase personnel strengths from within the organization. One way is to eliminate or decrease non-critical activities and temporarily reassign the affected personnel. Another way is to reduce administrative staffs by deferring or postponing non-essential duties until after the emergency subsides. A third way is to solicit spouses, relatives of present employees, and recent retirees from the organization to either contribute their services or accept temporary employment. The employment of additional personnel from among people with an interest in the organization may be more productive and involve less risk than hiring outsiders who have no knowledge of or loyalty to the organization.

8. SEEKING OTHER SOURCES OF ASSISTANCE

The previous section outlined the way to utilize in-house personnel as staff for an emergency or disaster situation. Planning must incorporate as much self-help as possible during emergencies to minimize the cost to the organization.

9. SELF-HELP

An important aspect of the vulnerability assessment is to identify the activities and materials presently located within the surveyed facility. Not only must the regular employees be selected and trained for their responsive roles, but any material or supplies (such as food, water, tools, portable equipment, lumber, or other property) that could be used to protect or repair the facility or to recover from interrupted services must be inventoried and kept in usable condition. The vulnerability assessment also should estimate the amount of emergency supplies (sandbags, plywood, nails, etc.) that would be necessary in the event that a certain building or facility had to be protected or occupied throughout an emergency. Many organizations will have within their facilities supplies that could be utilized as makeshift material to block doors and windows, provide a limited water supply, or serve as emergency rations.

In the case of large organizations that are widely dispersed geographically, the assessment might identify necessary items that would be available within the organization, and estimate the effort that would be required to shift those items to wherever they would be most needed. Such organizational self-help is usually less expensive and less objectionable to organizational managers than a request to purchase extra material and equipment that would be of use only during an emergency.

10. MUTUAL AID AGREEMENTS

It is well known that people tend to help each other during emergencies. To benefit the most from this, one should plan ahead for the emergencies that are most likely to occur and thereby maximize the chances that help will be available from (and to) others as needed.

A mutual aid agreement could involve distant facilities of the main organization, similar organizations, businesses within the neighborhood, or governmental agencies. There are advantages and disadvantages of using mutual aid agreements, so the committee doing the planning will have to explore all possible assistance sources, select the most advantageous of them and maintain open communications for changing to more appropriate sources if necessary.

As mentioned in the section concerning the use of in-house personnel during emergencies or disasters, whenever there is an emergency, certain personnel (e.g., National Guard personnel, firefighters, police officers) may have a legal obligation to report elsewhere, and so will be unavailable for emergency or disaster assignments within the organization. When in-house personnel are unavailable and human resources are needed, another organization might have a list of volunteers who would agree to assist the requesting firm. Electrical power companies do this frequently. There should be no expectations that temporary personnel can be hired through normal employment agencies during emergencies. During an area-wide emergency or disaster, people on a temporary hire waiting list might be tending to their own personal property and have little motivation to work for someone else. Naturally, supplies, equipment, special clothing, food, and financial remuneration must be made available to any outside personnel, just as would be done for in-house employees working beyond normal periods. The legal liabilities for damages, injuries, and deaths caused by both in-house and mutual aid agreement personnel must be established during this planning stage.

When some supplies, material, or equipment are not available within the organization, a mutual agreement with the nearest facility that has such items may be warranted. However, it must always be considered that whenever one facility is in need of such items, the same items may also be needed by the facility that possesses them. Another factor to be considered is that when there is a dire need for certain property in scarce supply, the price may become very high, if not exorbitant. For these reasons, alternate sources should be identified locally as well as at some distance from the affected area.

Mutual aid agreements can be entered into by private firms and governmental agencies (such as fire or police departments). In such agreements, private fire fighting equipment and personnel are pledged to stand by whenever the public firefighters are called out. Private security personnel are also afforded limited police powers when they are deputized or are provided such limited powers by local ordinance for special occurrences. In such cases, the mutual aid agreements are limited because the police and fire departments may have mutual aid pacts with other governmental agencies that take precedence over agreements with private entities.

11. GOVERNMENT AND PUBLIC SERVICES

It may be surprising, but even organizations that prepare emergency plans often do not take advantage of available government information on the subject. For example, the federal government provides guidelines to follow in response to hazardous material spills, environmental pollution and other areas circumscribed by compliance laws. The emergency planning committee should contact the various government agencies that can provide this assistance.

1) The Federal Emergency Management Agency (2400 M Street N.W., Washington, DC, 20472) provides published information and recommendations on how to counteract and minimize losses caused by enemy action and natural or human-caused disasters. That office should be contacted for an up-to-date bibliography of related U.S. Government Printing Office publications.

2) Regional emergency and disaster agencies can provide additional information that may have a more local orientation concerning the emergencies most likely to occur. As the local coordinating agency for emergency and disaster situations, they can also provide recommendations for local responses to ensure the fullest cooperation and protective measures appropriate to the area.

3) State and local governments provide police, fire, and other services, including environmental protection, health and welfare, and many more services, during normal periods as well as during emergency conditions.

4) Public and private utility companies may provide water, electricity, telephone communications, sanitation and other services. These agencies should be contacted to learn how they plan to continue their services during an emergency.

Not every police department, fire department or other public agency will be able to provide the same level of services. For that reason, it is the planning committee's responsibility to establish exactly what services would be available during various emergency situations, and acquire information on how alternative services can be obtained.

12. CONSIDERING HEALTH AND COMFORT CONCERNS

One problem seldom considered in emergency planning is the identification of employees with unusual health or disability impairments. There are many people in the general population who can function only with constant medical attention, medication, and clinical services. Those persons afflicted with severe color blindness, night blindness, diabetes or epilepsy, for instance, may not only be unable to contribute to emergency functions, but may require special help and attention themselves during an emergency. Therefore, such people should provide instructions as to how they might be helped (name and phone number of physician, medication source, etc.) in the event their health conditions are aggravated during an emergency. Additionally, those employees should be encouraged to keep an adequate supply of medication readily available.

Along these same lines, many people have special dietary needs that an organization would be unable to predict when stocking emergency provisions for use by employees remaining in the facility for the duration of the emergency. Ignoring those special needs might result in illnesses or severe discomfort of personnel to the degree that they may be unable to effectively contribute or become an additional burden.

Cold or inclement weather seasons present additional problems, especially when electrical power or heating equipment are temporarily out of service. Foul weather gear or industrial-grade, insulated coveralls might be a worthwhile investment, as well as commercial weight blankets provided to personnel temporarily marooned in a cold building. For the facility that might suffer a power failure that shuts down the water and sewage pumping systems, portable toilet facilities should be considered.

In recent years the federal government has enacted a plethora of civil rights acts that mandate equal employment opportunities, accommodations for disabled workers or visitors, and occupational safety and health measures that affect most employers or facilities. The personnel or human resources office should provide guidelines for the implementation of the federal regulations that are pertinent to the emergency and disaster plan.

DEVELOPING THE WRITTEN PLAN

The existing organizational structure should be utilized as much as practicable for the written emergency plan. The regular supervisory authority and the technical skills and materials at hand should form the foundation for emergency responses. When the methods and materials used are familiar to the employee, the emergency organization will not be seen as a separate entity or as a threat by the remainder of the organization. The following factors should be considered in the development of the written plan:

1) The conditions requiring the activation of the emergency or disaster control program should be listed.

2) The person or persons with the authority to declare an emergency should be identified.

3) Maps and blueprints of the facility to be protected should be provided.

4) An emergency operations center and alternate sites should be designated.

5) Communication facilities between the operations center, the major sections of the facility and the community should be established. Alternate methods of communication (radios, sound-powered phones, cellular telephones, etc.) should be provided.

6) An emergency organization hierarchy should be developed and a list of the employees and their emergency duties should be available to all participants.

7) Emergency shutdown procedures should be developed and lists made of critical property and records that are to be especially safeguarded. This includes computer facilities, files, tapes, disks, and back-up material.

8) Emergency evacuations should be planned.

9) Shelters should be identified and supplied with food, medical supplies, water and disaster equipment.

10) An augmented security force should be planned.

11) Damage assessment and repair teams should be designated.

12) Emergency power, fuel, and utilities should be ready to be activated as needed.

13) Plans for cooperation with federal, state and local police, firefighters, and emergency preparedness officials should be developed. Mutual aid pacts should be set up.

14) Records should be kept of all activities that take place during the emergency in order to aid in satisfaction of legal liabilities and possible revision of the emergency-disaster plan.

A sound emergency and disaster control plan is the result of thorough advance planning, testing, revision, and updating. An adequate emergency plan must contain detailed and timely information about the resources that can be utilized in the most efficient and expeditious manner. The development of such a plan is time consuming. One west coast utility company reported that it took their emergency planning team more than two years to prepare their written plan. They learned that their investment in time and personnel was worthwhile when within months an earthquake struck and few adjustments had to be made to their original plan.

The plan for emergency control must consider the goals, products, and personnel within the facility. Goal changes, shifting responsibilities, and personnel turnover may require frequent updating of the basic plan. Therefore, emergency planning must be a continuous process if the best safeguards possible are expected.

All planned emergency control measures must be arranged so that they complement and supplement one another and the regular security force and the primary goals of the parent organization. Poorly integrated emergency control measures may result in a waste of human resources, funds, and equipment. Of greater importance, a lack of integration in the plans may jeopardize the safety and security of the facility.

THE ROLE OF SECURITY

Security forces have a crucial role during emergency operations. Little reference has been made with regard to the regular security forces up to this point because emergency or disaster planning for any type of an organization entails the orderly and efficient transition from normal to emergency operations by the regular workforce. The energy and power of the regular workforce is many times greater than what security personnel could provide. Although no known security force could provide all the services heretofore described in this chapter, the role of security is crucial in that a greater degree of personal involvement is expected during a crisis.

TRAINING FOR EMERGENCIES

The size of the guard force available to an organization during an emergency is usually the same as under normal conditions (if all the guards show up for work when called). There are few proprietary or contract guard services that have large numbers of reserve personnel who wait for an emergency or disaster to occur. Because of the limited number of guards available to a firm, security force roles usually do not differ greatly during normal and emergency operating conditions. Yet because of the aura of authority associated with the guards, most people expect them to be thoroughly trained in every aspect of the emergency operation. This means that the guard forces should know and understand every aspect of the emergency or disaster program, even though their role remains security-oriented.

Cross-training the security personnel with the fire or safety personnel will provide for added confidence in the capabilities of all involved. Fire or safety rescue operations might be learned by security personnel, but it must be remembered that rescue operations are best conducted by those forces that are provided with specialized equipment, training, and in-depth knowledge of the unseen dangers of the facility, such as high-voltage power lines, hazardous materials, or dangers of explosion.

1. DISSEMINATING CURRENT INFORMATION

During an emergency, the security force should be kept abreast of changing conditions and the emergency response so they can be a source of information for other employees. Communication with other emergency forces, the community emergency operations center and even television and radio stations will allow the guards to provide updated information to the employees. When internal communication equipment malfunctions, bulletin boards or town crier methods of dissemination can be effective. Employees need to be advised of the conditions outside the facility so they can make contact with their families, make plans for their return home via a safe route, and become aware of any especially dangerous situations or areas that they should avoid.

2. RESTRICTING ACCESS

Security personnel have the responsibility to ensure that only authorized personnel are admitted to the facility, that restricted zones are for limited personnel only, and that personnel entering and leaving the plant should be properly accounted for and monitored. The logging of employees and visitors in and out of the facility may seem unnecessary, but during emergencies the log may be of inestimable value in locating persons, identifying those in certain areas or establishing the identity of bodies in the event that deaths occur. The liability of an organization is not lessened during emergencies if authorized or unauthorized personnel claim injury after access was gained to a dangerous area or situation. Records of those within certain areas of the facility may protect the organization from false or fraudulent claims.

The guard service must be organized in such a way that they can be deployed to protect areas of high vulnerability. Temporary measures to secure areas from intrusion by the use of barbed wire, vehicle emplacement, trespass signs, and various alarm systems should be considered. Another important point is to ensure the availability of guard personnel and transportation to respond promptly to calls for assistance. When the facility remains in full or partial operation during an emergency, there are certain areas that will need extra guard help to facilitate the movement and control of employees (e.g., gates and parking lots). During an emergency, security duties will increase beyond the capability of the available personnel, so plans should be made for augmenting the security force with persons selected from the regular workforce. Employees with previous police or military experience would require little training or supervision to provide needed support services to security efforts. Provided with a special armband or a stenciled hard hat, they might be employed as secondary members of a guard patrol.

3. ARMING SECURITY PERSONNEL

Finally, the question arises about arming the security personnel. Many security forces are not armed; some have arms available to them via their guard supervisors or in arms lockers; others are armed at all times. The value of equipment or merchandise, the danger to life or property, recent criminal attacks in the area, and other factors will dictate the armaments necessary. Highly visible armed guards employed during civil disturbances may save businesses from losses incurred by looting and burning. The emergency and disaster control committee should resolve the question of arming personnel in consultation with the organization's legal officer and the local police and the prosecutor's office.

4. TRAINING FOR EMERGENCIES

The objective of a training program is to ensure that all the emergency force personnel are able to perform their special duties quickly and efficiently. The extent and type of training required to properly prepare emergency control forces will vary according to the importance, vulnerability, size, and other unique factors affecting the particular facility.

Thorough and continuing training is the most effective means to obtain and maintain the maximum proficiency of the emergency force personnel. Regardless of how carefully emergency personnel are selected, seldom will they initially have all the qualifications and experience to be effective team members without interactive training. Furthermore, new and revised emergency requirements frequently necessitate that personnel be retrained. The gap that exists between the job requirement and personal ability can be bridged by training.

Not all of the personnel selected for the emergency force will have the same training needs. It would be a waste of valuable time to require all personnel to sit through the training for the other participants when the training is specialized or has little relationship to everyone's assignments. Thus, the past experience, education, training, acquired skills, and interests of each emergency force member should be taken into consideration.

Thorough training has many benefits for both the organization and the emergency control program. Supervisors realize benefits because the trained personnel are easier to supervise: there is less wasted time and fewer mistakes are made. The resultant economies are of benefit to the organization. The confidence instilled by training affects the morale and welfare of the entire organization. Individual emergency personnel also benefit from training in terms of increased knowledge and skills, increased opportunities for personal advancement and a better understanding of their relationship to the emergency program and the parent organization.

5. TESTING THE PLAN

When the emergency plan has been completed, provisions for its implementation and testing must be made. This is the time when deficiencies and unrealistic features of the plan are discovered and corrected. The main goals of such a test include the following:

1) To familiarize all personnel in the emergency force with the overall plan and acquaint each person with his or her own emergency duties and responsibilities.

2) To evaluate the workability of the plan and identify deficiencies.

3) To make the necessary adjustments to the plan for future testing and implementation.

There are different ways to test an emergency disaster control plan. The most comprehensive method is to test the plan in three phases. The first phase is testing the key individuals separately. Then the plan is tested in each section or department within the facility. The third phase is a test of the response of the entire facility. Various conditions could be simulated for each phase or, if one threat is considered more likely than the others, one type of emergency could be simulated for all three phases. After the emergency control coordinator and the planning committee are satisfied that they have a workable plan, they might coordinate further testing with local emergency preparedness exercises to determine the plan's compatibility with the local effort.

There is no hard-and-fast rule as to how often an emergency plan should be tested. There must be a continuing and concerted effort to upgrade the response capabilities of the personnel selected for the emergency operation. In order to keep personnel acquainted with the plan and to familiarize new personnel with their responsibilities, further individual, departmental and facility testing should be conducted as needed, at least annually and possibly semiannually.

6. MOCK DRILLS

After the individual, departmental, and facility training has been determined to be satisfactory by means of testing, periodic, semiannual, or annual testing could take place in the form of mock drills. The drills should be arranged to simulate various types of natural or person-caused emergencies. Realism may be achieved by preparing appropriate simulations of damage to property, injury to role players, and deaths. Prior knowledge of the specific target of the mock drill should not be disseminated to the participants. They will then be required to "solve" their problems spontaneously, based upon their training.

Those conducting the mock drill should delimit the target area to one building or area in such a way as to interfere with normal organizational operations only minimally. Markers can be placed around the target area denoting damages and hazards. Role players might be provided with artificial replicas of injuries or have parts of their bodies painted with food coloring to resemble blood, while others represent dead or dying victims. The emergency control personnel and their supervisors would be provided with an instruction booklet that describes the individual problems that each participant would be required to solve. Persons who are not directly involved in the emergency control program (and possibly not even organizational employees) should act as judges to assess the appropriateness of the responses made by the participants.

The mock drill must be long enough for the participants to be informed of their roles, gather the necessary equipment, make judgments about the simulated damages and injuries, and take appropriate action. The mock drill should culminate in a session in which the participants and judges evaluate the actions taken and observed.

SUMMARY

Modern communications media constantly bring to our attention reports of emergencies and disasters. Death and destruction by natural, accidental, and human-caused events have alerted us to those ever-present dangers. We have learned that there are ways to reduce or eliminate losses of life and property. Recent experiences with disasters have vividly demonstrated that those people or facilities that had made appropriate preparations sustained the least amount of losses. It also has been learned that during emergencies and disasters, there are never adequate numbers of security personnel to perform all the necessary emergency tasks. The response to emergencies is an organization-wide responsibility.

In order to plan for emergency operations, an assessment of the physical plant and personnel involved must be undertaken to establish what needs to be protected. Secure areas must be sought in which to prepare and equip an emergency operations center and protect personal and critical property. Specific authority must be developed and given to certain personnel to make decisions in the absence of other management superiors. The augmentation of security personnel must be considered from internal and other sources. Emergency repair and life sustaining supplies should be identified, acquired, and maintained. Training should be conducted to ensure that personnel are able to perform the required activities. Tests and mock drills are some methods to encourage participation within the organization as well as in cooperation with a community disaster-preparation plan (Higgins, 1990; Rosenthal, Charles & Hart, 1989).

DISCUSSION QUESTIONS

1.   Discuss the major aspects of planning for emergency situations and how they interrelate.

2.   What specific written authority should the emergency plan include in order to direct the emergency force operations and personnel?

3. Identify the major phase of a vulnerability assessment for emergency or disaster operations.

4. Discuss the advantages and disadvantages of limiting the discretion of responses taken by personnel in the emergency force.

5. Identify some of the problems that will limit the use of all in-house personnel during emergencies.

6. Discuss the advantages and disadvantages of mutual aid agreements for assistance during emergencies.

7. List several benefits associated with training the emergency force.

8. List the different ways an emergency or disaster plan can be tested.

REFERENCES

(1998). *Annual Intelligence Summary 1997*. Encino, CA: Pinkerton's Inc., Pinkerton Global Intelligence Services, 1998.

(1997). *Annual Risk Assessment 1996*. Encino, CA: Pinkerton's Inc., Pinkerton Risk Assessment Services, 1997.

Arata, M. CPP (1995). "Where Access Control Meets the ADA." *Security Management*, September, 1995, 69-72.

Arata, M. CPP (1995). "Finding Order Amidst Chaos." *Security Management*, September, 1995, 48-53.

Arata, M. CPP (1995). "The Best Laid Plans." *Security Management*, March, 1998, 73-76.

Atlas, R. CPP (1995). "Security and the ADA: With Liberty and Justice for All." *Security Management*, September, 1995, 65-67.

Barber, H. (1997). "Political Violence 1996: Charting the Landscape." Encino, CA: *Pinkerton Solutions Magazine*, Vol. 2, No. 1, 21-23.

(1998). "Big Funds for Counterterrorism." *Security Directors' Digest*, July 8, 1998, 1.

Brubaker, A.F. (1996). "Preparing for a Twist of Fate." *Security Magazine*, May, 1996, 43-45.

(1995). "Clinton Anti-Terrorism Plan Backed, But GOP Wants Additional Measures." *Security Directors' Digest*, May 3, 1995, 1-4.

Cochran, M. CPP (1995). "Minimizing Mayhem." *Security Management*, September, 1995, 56-61.

(1995). "An Explosion of Terrorism?" *Security Management*, February, 1995, 9.

(1997). "Federal Buildings Getting Increased Security Measures in Wake of OK City Bombing." *Security Directors' Digest*, July 30, 1997, 7-8.

(1996). "Federal Facility Update." *Security Management*, June, 1996, 16.

Higgins, C. (1990). *Utility Security Operations Management: For Gas, Water, Electric and Nuclear Utilities*. Springfield, IL: Charles C Thomas, 1990.

Hinman, E. (1995). "Lessons from Ground Zero." *Security Management*, October, 1995, 26-35.

Jackson, J. (1997). "Business Continuity: Give Your LAN a Hand." *Security Management*, August, 1997, 44-52.

Jacobson, R. CPP (1995). "A Computer Security Self-Test." *Security Management*, July, 1995, 118-121.

Johnson, L. and Laird, D. (1995). "Growing Terrorists." *Security Management*, December, 1995, 58-63.

Joyce, E. CPP and Delp, G.E. CPP (1995). "Before the Smoke Clears." *Security Management*, November, 1995, 68-70.

Joyce, E. CPP and Hurth, L. CPP (1997). "Booking Your Next Disaster." *Security Management*, November, 1997, 47-50.

Kaplan, D. (1998). "On Terrorism's Trail." *U.S. News & World Report*, November 23, 1998, 31-34.

(1997). "Latest Data on Terrorism." *Security Management*, April, 1997, 10.

Miller, K. (1998). "Weather." *Life Magazine*, August, 1998, 38-52.

(1996). "Oil Firms Study Risks on International Work." *Security Directors' Digest*, August 7, 1996, 4.

Popinski, J. CPP (1995). "Five Principles of Computer Protection." *Security Management*, July, 1995, 116-117.

(1998). "Putting Terrorism on the Table." Alexandria, VA: *ASIS Dynamics*, July/August 1998, 1 and 31-32.

Reid, K. CPP (1996). "Testing Murphy's Law: A Contingency Plan Is Only as Good as the Company's Last Drill." *Security Management*, November, 1996.

Rosenthal, U., Charles, M. and Hart, P. (1989). *Coping with Crisis: The Management of Disasters, Riots, and Terrorism*. Springfield, IL: Charles C Thomas, 77-83.

Sniffen, M. (1998). "FBI's High-Tech Center Can Handle up to Five Crises Simultaneously." *Grand Rapids Press*, November 22, 1998, A7.

Stolovitch, D. CPP (1995). "Drawing Security into Building Design." *Security Management*, December, 1995, 69-75.

(1998). "Terrorism Casualties Drop." *Security Management*, April, 1998, 12.

(1994). *Terrorism in the United States 1994*. Washington, DC: Federal Bureau of Investigation, 1995.

Zalud, B. (1994). "Desktop: A Bomb Next?" *Security*, February, 1994, 5.

SECTION III
CRIME PREVENTION PRINCIPLES

Crime and the
Threat Environment

$$\boxed{8}$$

INTRODUCTION

Crime and the threat environment may be understood in a variety of ways. These will be viewed from an individual and organizational perspective in this text. Theories of crime and types of crime will be examined using an individual perspective. The threat environment will be examined using an organizational perspective for both internal and external threats.

CRIME

Crime is behavior that violates the criminal law. Criminals are citizens in society who have engaged in acts that have been socially and officially defined as exceeding the limits prescribed for legally acceptable behavior. Virtually all modern societies have enacted criminal laws to cover certain basic violations, such as homicide, injurious assault, incest, and violations of property rights. However, there is often considerable variation as to the exact definition of offenses, circumstances accepted as extenuating, severity of official reaction and societal sanction. The United States alone has 51 (state and federal) legal jurisdictions, each with its own set of criminal statutes.

Crime is one of the principal threats facing all citizens of the United States. An enormous variety of acts make up the crime problem. Crime is not just the street-tough teenager snatching an old lady's purse. It is a professional thief stealing cars "on order." It is a well-heeled loan shark taking over a previously legitimate business for organized crime. It is a polite young son who suddenly and inexplicably murders his family. It is a corporate executive conspiring with competitors to keep prices high. It is a bright young socialite who, for a perceived cause, can participate in violent acts of terrorism and destruction. No single theory, formula, or definitive generalization can explain the vast range and scope of human behavior called crime. Its causation is multiple and complex, and to begin to understand its intensity and scope, one must study and evaluate the threat environment, the criminals, and their functional roles within a given frame of reference.

Individual or group actions that can be classified as crimes are divided into two basic groups: (1) crimes against persons; and (2) crimes against property. Crimes against persons include murder, kidnapping, rape, assault, robbery, etc. Crimes against property include burglary, arson, vandalism, sabotage, shoplifting, auto theft, etc. Crimes are also classified as misdemeanors or felonies. A misdemeanor is a less serious act, usually defined as a crime with a penalty of a fine and/or up to one year in jail, while the penalty for a felony is a fine and/or one or more years in prison or the death penalty.

The major divisions of the law are civil and criminal. Civil law deals with legal liabilities between individuals, while criminal law deals with crimes that the government prosecutes in its own name. Private security personnel, while not expected to be lawyers, must be familiar with the law—civil and criminal—as it relates to the performance of duties. The manner in which private security personnel perform their duties has a direct bearing on the attainment of industry goals and professional status.

Criminal acts must be understood from the standpoint of corresponding legal definitions. The following are generalized definitions of some of the more common criminal acts that are of primary concern to security personnel. However, be aware that crime definitions may vary somewhat from state to state, particularly as to degree and penalty.

> **Robbery**—The stealing or taking of something of value from the custody or control of a person by force, threat of force, or putting that person in fear of his or her welfare.
>
> **Burglary**—The unlawful entry of a building or structure to commit a theft, even though no force may have been used to gain entry.
>
> **Larceny**—The unlawful taking or stealing of property or something of value without the use of threat, violence, or fraud.
>
> **Arson**—The willful, malicious burning of a dwelling, building, or other property with or without the intent to defraud.
>
> **Fraud**—Intentional misrepresentation to induce another to give up or part with something of value or to surrender a legal right.
>
> **Vandalism**—The intentional or malicious destruction, injury, or disfigurement of property.
>
> **Shoplifting**—The removal of merchandise from a store with the intent to deprive the owner of property without paying the purchase price.
>
> **Homicide**—The killing of one human being by another human being.
>
> **Assault**—An attempt or threat, with force or violence, to do corporal harm to another.

Criminal Trespass—Disturbance of possession of the premises of another.

Embezzlement—Fraudulent appropriation of property.

Computer Crime—Unauthorized system access, software piracy, theft of computer services, and the alteration or theft of electronically stored information.

The means by which these crimes and others can be perpetrated are varied and complex, but one can reduce the risks of being victimized by being aware of some of the factors involved. For example, one should be aware of how types of business, places of business, types of items carried, nearness and responsiveness of police protection, and types of protective hardware and procedures employed are determining factors in inviting or deterring criminal attacks.

No one can be certain, regardless of the steps taken, that they will be totally safe from crime. After all, there will always be some deviant behavior in every society. Still, the human-generated hazards classified as crime can be reduced to an acceptable level if appropriate measures are taken to deter, detect and/or deny the activities that are detrimental to all. Later chapters will deal with specific techniques of deterring and preventing certain crimes.

THE CRIMINAL

Individuals identified as criminals (i.e., those that have been found guilty of a crime) are not readily identifiable in appearance, speech, manner, background, attitude, behavior, skills, or method of criminal operation. However, there are some identifiable factors that can be utilized to deter or thwart a criminal's attempts to commit a crime—regardless of his or her personal or physical characteristics.

In the past, various criminological theories have been proposed to explain why people commit crimes. These explanations have been physiological, sociological, psychological, and even religious and political. However, current thought seems to accept the idea that an individual is a product of his or her own psychological makeup and the environment to which he or she is exposed. Thus, there is no typical criminal because each person acts and reacts according to his or her own inherent and acquired characteristics and capabilities.

The primary objective of most criminals is personal or financial gain; thus, currency, objects easily convertible to cash and objects taken for personal use are the items most often stolen. Other criminal objectives, though not as common as the above, are the destruction of property, social or political change, revenge, and the satisfaction of mental or psychological compulsions. The property owner, then, must evaluate what he or she owns in terms of how it can best be protected against the criminal who may desire it. For example, cash or property easily converted to cash is more desirable to the criminal than something that cannot be sold or used easily.

It is in this way that homeowners, business proprietors, and others must take steps to remove or decrease the opportunity for criminal activity. Most criminals do not want to get caught. Targets of opportunity for robbery, burglary, and other crimes exist where it is readily apparent that the criminal's objectives are easily accessible and relatively unprotected, and that there is little danger of being detected or apprehended.

The extremes of criminal proficiency and expertise are evidenced by the amateur and professional. The amateur does not depend on crime for a livelihood. Instead, most amateur illegal deeds are committed spontaneously as the opportunity presents itself. While no one knows for sure, it is assumed that professional criminals account for only a small percentage of the total criminal population. If this is true, then most crimes are committed by amateurs and most crimes are crimes of opportunity. Put another way, it is the inexperienced, nonprofessional "crook" who commits the majority of criminal acts. In fact, current crime statistics show that more than 50 percent of those arrested for criminal acts are juveniles.

The professional criminal, on the other hand, is one who makes a living through crime. This type of criminal usually has one particular type of crime considered to be his or her specialty. Of course, all professionals begin their careers as amateurs, but are able, through luck or intelligence, to develop the skills necessary for being successful criminals.

Given sufficient time and proper conditions, a highly skilled and determined professional criminal can successfully penetrate nearly any protective system—regardless of how complex or strongly fortified. In general, however, if a residential or commercial facility is secured by strong locks, hardware and other perimeter barriers, is well-lighted, and is protected by an appropriate type of alarm system, most criminals—whether amateurs or professionals—will seek other, easier targets.

It must be recognized that many criminal activities are initiated from within the environment being protected. The threat represented by the employee requires the owner/manager to evaluate protection needs from both within and without. Employee thieves range from those who steal a little money or small items every now and then, to those who systematically steal and deplete the company of huge amounts of money or inventory. Some will steal only when inadequate security seems almost to invite it, while others will manipulate and seek ways to steal regardless of what controls are in effect. The majority of dishonest employees will use straightforward techniques of stealing, while a few will utilize very sophisticated methods of draining off company assets. It is the employee who has the greatest exposure to company assets and the opportunity to engage in numerous types of behavior detrimental to the company.

The reason or combination of reasons that motivates one employee to commit a criminal act may or may not motivate another employee to do the same. While no company wants to think of its own employees as being dishonest, it must take steps to deal with employee crime as a condition of doing business. In order to protect property, the owner must, in effect, view company belongings from the perspective of a criminal looking for an easy "hit." The view from the criminal's perspective should reveal both the weaknesses and the strengths of existing security measures. Effective countermeasures can be taken only after the situation is understood. Though not an easy task, it is one that must be taken if goals and objectives are to be attained. Current information suggests that losses to employee crimes are increasing each year and are much larger than losses due to robbery, burglary, and shoplifting.

THEORIES OF CRIME

CRIME CAUSATION THEORIES

There are various reasons given to explain why people commit crimes. The following disciplines provide the basis for causation theories of violent crime: biology, sociology, and psychology. These causation theories are useful in trying to understand workplace crimes of violence, for example. The following summarizes the various types of crime causation theories:

1. General Theory of Self-Control—Many of the offenders appeared to have reached their frustration threshold and their typical self-control was no longer sufficient to keep them from committing an act of violence.

2. Routine Activities Theory—Routine activities theory is relevant to the workplace victims in that the whereabouts of the victims were known by the offenders and the victims were going about their normal duties when the acts of violence occurred. This might also explain why the incidents of domestic violence occurred in the workplace. The offender knew where their intended victim could be found and sought them out at the workplace.

3. Containment Theory—For those employees who use their position to gain the necessary information from which to commit robbery, the motivation appears to be greed. The lethal violence in such types of cases may result from a desire of the offender to protect himself or herself from detection or to keep from being apprehended at the scene.

4. Strain Theory—Most of the employees and all of the customers who commit workplace violence believe they have been mistreated by the organization and/or specific members within.

5. Parricide Theory—Employee violence against those in the workplace *or patracide* has several similar characteristics to those found in studies of parricide.

6. Domestic Violence Theory—Domestic-related offenders most often express a loss of control over the individual who has rejected their "love" or who appears to have "rebelled" against their authority. Committing the act of violence in the victim's workplace gives the offender a substantial degree of control over the fate of their intended victim. (Southerland, Scarborough & Collins, 1997:24-25).

THREATS

Threat may be defined in numerous ways according to various disciplines and often include both natural and manmade events. From a security perspective, threats are often classified into one of two broad categories: threats that occur naturally in the environment, and those that are generated by humans, either accidentally or intentionally. Naturally occurring threats such as fire, wind, and floods are discussed in greater detail in Chapter 7: Emergency and Disaster Preparedness. For purposes of this chapter, threats will refer to those involving an intentional human act.

Internal crimes and threats represent one of the major ways an organization loses supplies, parts, equipment, merchandise, money, information, and organizational vitality. Statistics indicate that the employee represents a greater threat to the organization than the robber or burglar. Internal theft prevention programs cannot be viewed in a one-dimensional manner: they must involve an extensive, in-depth evaluation of the organizational environment and cultural contrasts; they must utilize the potential of the workforce to solve its own problems; and they must be conducted so that each activity interfaces with and relies upon the strengths of the other program activities. Employers must be aware of the potential harms of drugs in the workplace and the need to have proactive programs designed to identify and assist employees with substance abuse problems.

External threats and crimes, though not representative of as large a dollar loss as internal threats and crimes, are very important to businesses. External threats and crimes also involve a greater risk of injury, potential injury, or death than do internal threats and crimes.

Many businesses today operate in areas in which research and technology are changing operations at a rapid pace. A competitive edge in one of the high-technology areas may be easily lost through crime. In fact, the potential for a financial disaster from a single incident of espionage or sabotage may be greater than from a crime of any other kind.

INTERNAL THREATS

The impact of internal threats (and other problems initiated by employees) on business and governmental organizations has reached alarming proportions. Fraud, embezzlement, pilferage, and other types of employee-initiated crimes have been the subject of numerous research projects, noted frequently by the media and discussed in company board meetings, yet many companies simply refer to internal losses as "shortages" rather than trying to discover and explain how and why these losses occurred. Until companies and top administrators decide that ethics and honesty are keystones to efficiency and effectiveness in the workplace, crime and criminal activity are likely to increase rather than diminish. Measurable success of employee crime reduction efforts will happen only when such undertakings have the full support and cooperation of top management.

According to *The Hallcrest Report II*, annual losses due to employee crime, white-collar crime, economic crime, etc., are estimated at $200 billion (Cunningham et al., 1990). Hefter (1986) refers to employee theft as "the crippling crime," detrimental and often devastating to four distinct and important areas of business concern:

1) Insurance costs rise. Losses have caused fidelity underwriters to drastically increase their premiums to insure against employee dishonesty. Costs in some areas have reached epidemic stages.

2) Increased funds invested to prevent losses. The security protection needed (and costs thereof) will increase, especially in the areas of deterrent devices, crime prevention methods, crime investigations, and criminal prosecutions.

3) Increased prices for goods and services. Increased prices due to internal thefts have caused many retailers to lose their competitive position. In fact, the need to increase prices and the loss of customers as a result of the increases have caused many businesses to go bankrupt.

4) Employee productivity and morale decline. Employees involved in thefts or associated with employees involved in thefts will have a decline in both productivity and morale. Quality of service declines if the business is service-related, and errors occur if the business is producing a product. In either case, the reputation of the company declines (Hefter, 1986).

EMPLOYEE EMBEZZLEMENT

One of the major internal theft categories is embezzlement. Embezzlement is defined as the "fraudulent appropriation of property by one lawfully entrusted with its possession" (*Black's Law Dictionary*). Embezzlement is common-law larceny extended to cover cases that do not include trespass, or cases in which an individual may abstract or misapply funds or property of another person or entity.

The statutes defining the crime of embezzlement do not make a distinction between a cash loss and a property/merchandise loss. However, according to several insurance groups, losses from embezzlement of cash reserves are seven to 10 times higher than losses from property or merchandise embezzlement. Even though losses from cash reserves far outweigh the losses from merchandise, merchandise loss is still a significant embezzlement problem.

In order to properly ensure that the risks of embezzlement are reduced, an employer must be familiar with the human and physical elements generally present in an embezzlement. These elements and their components are need, rationalization, and opportunity.

1. Need—A physical condition (e.g., sickness) may be the cause of unusual debts and may cause an employee to think seriously about how to convert merchandise or money to his or her own use. Bad health coupled with the stressful necessity of having to pay a large

debt may trigger an employee into committing an embezzlement act. Other personal acts of any employee, such as overcharging on one or more credit cards, or financing several items over a period of time with different due dates, may cause an employee to initiate a theft. Even though the desire for personal gain is far more common than the need for revenge or philanthropy, the latter certainly cannot be disregarded in considering the component parts of the element of need.

Personal financial gain represents the primary reason why persons embezzle from their employer. The psychological needs of an individual are difficult to discover and may change over a period of time, so it is not usually possible to identify an unmet need at any given time in order to prevent an act of embezzlement.

2. Rationalization—This represents the state of mind of an individual before and after a theft has occurred. Rationalization is the psychological state that provides explanations or excuses for one's own acts, usually without the individual being aware that such explanations may not be the real motives. These false motives are psychological defense mechanisms that allow an individual to face his or her actions on a day-to-day basis. These rationalizations are usually categorized in four ways: (1) "borrowing, not stealing," (2) lack of moral restraint, (3) moral right, and (4) reward within the work group. The "borrowing, not stealing" rationalization occurs when the employee thinks that he or she will return the money. Indeed, the employee may return the money in the beginning, but the amount taken over a longer period of time is usually too large to pay back at any one time. Time and need will work against the embezzler. The "lack of moral restraint" rationalization happens when employees observe other employees involved in larcenous acts, and after assessing the risk, tell themselves that it is all right for them to do it too. The "moral right" rationalization occurs when employees believe more pay is deserved and that they are only taking what is rightfully theirs. The last rationalization category involves the individual who sees other workers stealing and not getting caught. This worker rationalizes that it must be all right because no one is notifying the supervisor, and the dishonest employees are not rejected socially by the work group.

3. Opportunity—Certain conditions must exist for the act of embezzlement. Opportunity is usually afforded by management through the omission of controls or the inadequacy of existing controls. The control of opportunity is the key to controlling the elements of need and rationalization. The lack of opportunity certainly does not eliminate the need to embezzle, but it does prevent the act from happening.

An employer should be observant and watch for the following behavioral conditions in an employee and/or significant changes in personal spending habits. First of all, employers should be observant for employees who exhibit sudden changes in spending habits that seem to be above the employee's regular standard of living. Such changes could include the purchase of a new house, car, boat, or expensive clothes, parties or trips. However, there are obviously some very legitimate reasons for such expenditures, e.g., an inheritance from a wealthy relative, a lottery win, the sale of property, and so on. A rash mentality can alienate an honest employee. Second, an employer should pay attention when an employee has had a major illness or a member of their immediate family has had such an illness and a large debt has been incurred, or when an employee simply has financial difficulties. Third, an employer should observe an employee who has an apparent and unusual devotion to his or her work. This should be especially true of an especially trusted employee who may handle large amounts of money or who may be approving purchases or vendor contracts. Funds or services belonging to the company may be channeled "under the table" to the employee without the company knowing about the transaction. Fourth, an employee in a fiduciary position who strongly objects to procedural changes or closer supervision should be audited or observed. This resistance may be fear of the discovery of an illegal act.

One employee will not steal or be dishonest under any condition, while another may turn to stealing company property for almost any reason. Great care should be taken to assure that the personal integrity of the individual is afforded every courtesy, while the welfare and protection of company property is maintained.

EMPLOYEE FRAUD

Fraud is an essential element of various statutory offenses involving theft, misappropriation, and inventory shrinkage. These offenses, while having the same or similar elements, are given different names in various jurisdictions and are scattered throughout statute books under various theft offense headings.

Fraud is an intentional perversion of truth for the purpose of inducing another, in reliance of it, to part with some valuable thing owned or to surrender a legal right (*Black's Law Dictionary*). Fraud includes all acts, omissions and concealment that involve a break of legal or equitable trust or confidence justly reposed, and that are injurious to another, or by which an undue or unconscionable advantage is taken of another.

Embezzlement (sometimes called fraudulent conversion) may be defined as the unlawful taking of the property of another by one to whom the property has been entrusted. This contrasts with theft, which is simply the unlawful taking of property by someone to whom it has not been entrusted. A common form of embezzlement takes place when money is paid by a third person to a clerk for the clerk's employer and the clerk appropriates it before it is put in the cash register. Another variation is when goods are delivered by a shopkeeper to a carrier for delivery and the carrier appropriates the goods for personal use. Embezzlement requires a relationship of trust and confidence between the person taking the property and the owner, combined with fraudulent (unlawful) intent.

EMPLOYEE PILFERAGE

Pilferage is the stealing of property in small amounts over a period of time. The dollar value of the items taken in each incident is small, but when taken together, incidents of pilferage can amount to enormous dollar losses to the victim. The pervasiveness of employee theft has not been established because no one actually knows what portion of inventory shrinkage can be attributed to dishonest employees. Because only a small percentage of employees have the opportunity to embezzle or be involved in a fraudulent action in the workplace, the greater number of employees who steal do so by committing simple acts of pilferage.

While pilferage is also a form of embezzlement (as it occurs while in a position of trust and/or responsibility), it is not usually seen as a means of substantial financial gain. Instead, employees are often impervious to the dollar value of what they are taking and have little difficulty in rationalizing their dishonest act.

Most acts of employee pilferage are likely to be very simple because little planning and preparation is needed for the actual theft of company property. This assumption can be based on the following:

1) Worker theft generally is presumed to be largely undetected, unreported, unrecorded, and unprosecuted—with the result that the vast majority of perpetrators are unknown and go unpunished.

2) The actual act of pilferage by employees is usually accomplished by simply walking out of the workplace during the lunch hour, at closing time, or after hours with the item in their possession either concealed in clothing, packages, lunch boxes, etc., or taken when concealment is not even necessary.

While the taking of a pencil, a pad of paper, or nuts and bolts may be considered insignificant by both the employer and the employee, one has but to multiply these individual incidents by thousands of occurrences committed by a multitude of employees every day of the year. The kinds of items and materials that employees steal from their employers include a variety of both finished and unfinished products, office and maintenance equipment, and, of course, money.

Numerous studies have shown that people are more likely to steal from businesses and organizations than from other people. There is strong indication that employers are beginning to realize that worker theft is a real problem, and that proper steps must be taken to deter, prevent, and detect its occurrence.

To reduce losses through pilferage, many employers use in-house security, contract guard services and various types of detection equipment, surveillance equipment, security hardware, and security procedures. Other measures are those that can be designed to monitor or restrict the movement of company personnel in an effort to limit access to certain areas or operations of the facility, thereby denying—or least making it more difficult to have—the opportunity to steal. This can be accomplished through closer supervision, enforcement of procedural and access controls, increased use of security hardware devices, and increased emphasis of security at all levels of the workforce. The following discussion of theft control procedures points out some of the basic methods and means utilized to control employee theft.

THEFT CONTROL STRATEGIES

Most case studies and literature on internal thefts indicate that a positive step that must be taken by an employer is to make all employees aware that internal thefts are a serious problem and that the employer, in the interest of the business and its honest employees, must take some action on a regular basis to thwart dishonest acts by employees. The employer should develop and implement various strategies for reducing and controlling internal theft losses including screening of applicants, procedures and/or devices that make theft more difficult or apprehension easier, improvement in employee satisfaction, and the policy and process of apprehension and prosecution. Careful screening of applicants has long been accepted as a way of reducing employee problems. The employer should investigate the following areas: prior employment, credit references, and personal references. Many employers fail to do an adequate job of screening applicants either because of the time involved or because they do not know what they can or cannot ask an applicant. The verification of employee applicant information and the employee background check are considered the most important elements of a good screening process. In addition to federal laws, many states (if not most) have statutory provisions regulating pre-employment and employment processes and procedures. The restrictions imposed by the states have not been included in the above recommendations for a potential employer. It is recommended that the personnel office review the statutes in the respective state, and if applicable, check employee contracts for prohibitions before embarking on any technique or process to test a job applicant or employee with regard to honesty and integrity.

Frequently the problem of employee thefts can be solved by either installing new security detector devices or modifying or adding to the anti-theft procedures of the organization. Unfortunately, the theft problem cannot be solved by a simple set of procedures or detector devices. The problem should be approached by utilizing both procedures and detectors. For example, in an industrial situation, the equipment and merchandise open and available to the employee at any time should have a relationship to the amount of inventory needed to do a job, as well as to the efficiency and effectiveness of getting the parts to the workstation. Completed merchandise should be inventoried and placed in a storage area as soon as possible after the assemblage has been made. A direct flow of parts from the stockroom to the workstation with no intermediate stops will greatly facilitate control of those parts. Also, for maximum inventory control, after completion, the finished product should be taken directly from the workstation to a secure storage area when it is operationally efficient to do so. Allowances would necessarily have to be made for breakage, unusable parts, and other common reasons for parts loss; however, one would not expect differences between the number of completed products and the number available for shipment to a customer.

An organization experiencing "shortages" should require that employees be available for either a personal search, property search, or both before entering or leaving the premises. Because the use of alcohol and other non-prescription drugs on company premises has become a serious problem, the entry search of person and property should reduce the flow of such items onto company property. Exit searches are made primarily to stop the unauthorized flow of parts and merchandise from the facility. Security personnel usually have the responsibility of conducting entry and exit searches.

It is strongly recommended that the input and support of employees be solicited prior to the implementation and development of organizational policies regarding employee searches. Employees must be made aware of the need for such a measure; they must be notified well in advance that they will be subject to such searches; and must be assured that searches will be done on a regular and equitable basis, i.e., all employees (office and plant, salaried and hourly) will be subject equally to entry and exit searches. Inasmuch as possible, the support and input of all employees should be solicited for any procedure that questions their integrity and loyalty to the company (or even seems to). Various electronic devices may be utilized to assist security personnel, especially if the items likely to be stolen are metal. If the parts or products are cloth, rubber, or plastic, different methods must be employed.

The security procedures and devices utilized by any organization—whether it be a manufacturing plant, bank, retail store, or hospital—must be directed to reducing the opportunity for crime. An organizational environment, regardless of its function, is not safe or secure if it is subjected to employee theft. Yet security procedures and controls that are too strict or harsh can have a negative effect on employees. Such programs should be balanced so that the negative effects on employee morale and productivity do not offset the recognized gains through reduced company loss.

During the last few years, numerous studies have indicated that job satisfaction and morale are extremely important. Positive job satisfaction and morale have been linked to reduced levels of thefts and inventory shrinkage, with the opposite being the case for negative factors. The implications of works such as those of Abraham Maslow and Frederick Herzberg on the problem of thefts indicate that individuals operate on a "needs priority" basis, meaning that the elimination of an employee's financial "need" by paying a good wage should discourage theft. This might be an oversimplification of a major problem but the implications certainly suggest that many recognized causes of employee thefts are reduced or eliminated when an organization takes positive action to improve job satisfaction. Even though job dissatisfaction may not directly relate to thefts, the root causes of both job dissatisfaction and thefts seem to the same or similar.

The policy of apprehension and prosecution is a viable control strategy, especially if all alternatives have been explored by the organization. Any control strategy involving apprehension and prosecution must have a solid security program as its foundation. However, some organizations question whether the cost involved in a solid security program is worth the deterrent effect. Even when good cases have been made against a dishonest employee, the rate of prosecution is not always made by the organization. Busy prosecutors and overburdened courts may discourage and perhaps even refuse to handle cases that can be remedied outside the court, e.g., via termination of the employee or restitution.

Still, a decision not to prosecute may often be for the best. A decision to prosecute requires a legally sound security program plus a willingness to withstand possible bad publicity; to defend against libel and malicious prosecution of civil suits and false arrest cases; to bear the expense of having security employees, supervisors, managers, and witnesses available in court for criminal prosecution of cases; and to support any employees included in a case that involves them in a personal manner. Several security authorities have stated that a decision to prosecute an employee caught stealing by one organization might not have a deterrent effect, whereas decisions to prosecute dishonest employees by all organizations certainly would have a strong deterrent effect.

An organization may be required either by the statutes of a particular state or by the provisions of an employee contract to reinstate an employee who has been found not guilty to his or her original job with all back pay, raises, and seniority that would have occurred during the employee's absence. This, plus the expense and other ramifications, may cause an organization to want an apprehension and prosecution policy that will allow the organization to thoroughly review each case before deciding which course of action it will take.

A substrategy of apprehension and prosecution is a company-imposed restitution program. Restitution may provide an opportunity to rehabilitate an experienced and productive employee. If an organization decides on this approach, two basic questions must be considered. First, who will be involved in deciding the penalties to be imposed. Second, will a restitution program be sufficient punishment and penalty to deter other employees from committing the same act? It is generally accepted that any restitution program must involve both labor and management in imposing penalties and overseeing the program. A restitution program that is accepted by employees certainly helps control present and potential violators. The question of the deterrent effect of a restitution program is more difficult. One must either look at the success or failure of other programs, or test the program for a period of time and evaluate the results.

ALCOHOLISM

For our purposes, an alcoholic is defined as a person who cannot function on a daily basis without ingesting an alcoholic drink. Once a person reaches the point of excessive, compulsive drinking and dependence on alcohol, that person is considered an alcoholic, and their condition a disease.

What are the problem indicators or progressive signs of alcoholism? The first indicator is generally that the person cannot stop after one drink, and will usually get drunk every time he or she takes a drink. Once a person has reached this stage, a significant change in personality is noticed after drinking; a person may become troubled by public intoxication and/or domestic problems. This type of behavior may be followed by drinking in the morning and sneaking drinks during the day. Frequent absenteeism from the job is often one of the first signs that a supervisor may notice about an alcoholic.

Why should an organization be concerned about the habits of alcoholics? First, the increased absenteeism that frequently accompanies alcoholism causes a decrease in production, and a decrease in production means lost earnings and profits. Second, a person suffering the effects of alcoholism cannot work at maximum efficiency. Third, an organization has a social and moral obligation (and sometimes a legal one, if it is so stated in the employee contract) to assist an employee with such a problem.

ILLEGAL DRUG ABUSE

The abuse of illegal drugs is a serious problem for organizations as well as society as a whole. It is not a recent phenomenon, nor will it disappear in the foreseeable future.

A drug is generally defined as a substance which, by its chemical composition and action, alters the structure or function of a living organism. Drugs are currently divided into six classifications: (1) narcotics, (2) depressants, (3) inhalants, (4) stimulants, (5) hallucinogens, and (6) cannabis.

Narcotics include opium and its derivatives (generally morphine, heroin, codeine, or methadone), which are used legally to induce sleep and relieve pain. Heroin is the most common illegally used narcotic in the United States.

A depressant or sedative is a drug that affects the central nervous system, slowing a person's actions and calming anxieties. Sedatives have a wide variety of medical uses, notably to control hypertensive activity. A person affected by depressants usually is disoriented, staggers, and has difficulty concentrating. Among the more common and widely used depressants are alcohol, barbiturates, and tranquilizers.

Inhalants comprise those substances that are usually ingested by inhaling. In addition to nitrous oxide (laughing gas), chlorohydrocarbons, such as those found in aerosol paints and cleaning fluids, and hydrocarbons, which include gasoline, glue, and paint thinner, are easily obtainable substances inhaled for the possible effects of euphoria and giddiness.

A stimulant is a drug that affects the central nervous system by increasing the activities of specific areas of the nervous system. A person affected by stimulants is usually excessively active, nervous, and talkative. The most widely used stimulant is caffeine, found in coffee, tea, and cola drinks. Other commonly known and used stimulants are cocaine and amphetamines.

A hallucinogen is a drug that produces dream images and psychedelic reactions in an individual. Hallucinogens are generally recommended for clinical use and research and do not have any recognized medical utility. A person affected by hallucinogens may exhibit irrational behavior and may appear to be frightened or in a trance. Some of the hallucinogens are lysergic acid diethylamide (LSD), methyl dimethoxy (STP), mescaline and D-methyltryptomine (DMT).

Most employers obviously are concerned with employee drug abuse as it relates to the health and safety of the workplace and the quality of its services or products. The substance-influenced employee is impaired both mentally and physically. The task of identifying such employees cannot be left to security. It is the front line supervisor who has the primary and ongoing responsibility for evaluating the conduct and performance of a subordinate on a daily basis. It is recommended that supervisors, in particular, be trained to recognize the symptoms of drug abuse, i.e., changes in an employee's work habits, attitude, and job performance that may reflect drug abuse. Supervisors should be guided by documented procedures for dealing with an employee who abuses alcohol and/or drugs. Company policies and personnel procedures regarding alcohol and drug abuse should be very clear to employer and employee alike. If the company has requirements regarding employee drug testing, all related polices and procedures of the program should be within the framework of current legislation and fair management practices.

Many companies have established employee assistance programs to aid employees who have developed drug abuse problems. It is not always cost-effective for employers to simply fire any employee who has a drug dependency.

EXTERNAL THREATS

Even though crimes committed by employees generally have a far greater impact on the organization than do crimes committed by individuals outside the organization, there are numerous external threats that can result in enormous dollar losses.

ROBBERY

Robbery is the taking or attempting to take anything of value from the care, custody, or control of a person or persons by force, threat of force or violence, or by putting the victim in fear. Most experts agree that robbers generally plan their crimes to some extent. The first step is the decision to commit a robbery. The robber usually wants easy money, quickly, and will look for a target that offers little resistance and a minimum of exposure and risk. Any business that is located in a remote area or neighborhood, operates at times of the day or night with little or no pedestrian or street traffic, is easy to enter and exit, or has only one employee is very vulnerable to robbery. For example, a robbery target with most of the above conditions might be a convenience store or gas/service station located on a major street or thoroughfare, operating late at night and staffed by a single employee.

Apart from the loss of money, the most serious aspect of a robbery is the threat to the operator or employee's life. Statistics indicate that as many as one in five commercial robbery victims suffer injury or death at the hands of robbers. In the cases that could be verified, the person being robbed offered some degree of resistance in the majority of the injury or death cases.

What should be done by a business to reduce the likelihood that a robbery will be committed at their location? First, the amount of cash on hand should be kept as small as possible. Making daily or timely bank deposits and placing unnecessary cash in a safe that cannot be opened by the employee are common and acceptable practices. Advertise this practice with signs both outside and inside the premises. Second, operate the business with at least two employees. There may be businesses that cannot economically afford to operate with two employees at all times, but even in that case, any business that does not operate 24 hours a day should at least be opened and closed with two people. Third, money should not be carried between the business and the home of the operator or employee. Doing so gives the robber two targets. Fourth, the operator or employee should not open the business until the money for operating has been taken from the safe and all procedures for doing business are ready. After the doors are opened, preparations for doing business should always be limited to non-money types of actions such as stocking counters. Fifth, cash registers should be located near the front of the building with a good view of the entrance(s) and exit(s). Nonessential business doors should be kept locked. Windows and doors should be unobstructed so that it is possible to view the checkout area and cashier from the outside, e.g., they should be visible to pedestrians, passing motorists, and the police. Sixth, a telephone should be made available on the premises at a location other than the cashier area. Very often, telephones visible to the robber are disabled; an auxiliary telephone provides a backup or means for another employee to call the police without being observed by the robber. Another option in this regard is to have a robbery alert system in conjunction with an intrusion detection/alarm system. Signaling devices should be located at the cash register and at least one other location. Any attempt to activate the signaling device or use the telephone should occur only when it is safe to do so. Seventh, interior and exterior lighting should make it possible to see both inside and outside the premises. Good lighting will serve as a psychological deterrent to would-be robbers who weigh the risks of being seen and identified during the robbery. Persons and/or vehicles remaining in the area should be observed and reported to the police as appropriate. It is significant for the operator or employee to observe and greet customers as they enter the business to let them know their presence has been noted. Eighth, the presence of visible surveillance equipment will most often act as a deterrent to would-be robbers. The nature and complexity of the camera or CCTV, e.g., whether there are also hidden cameras, where or how the picture is being recorded or received, etc. are generally unanswered questions of sufficient strength that the individual considering the robbery decides that the risks are too great for a crime to occur.

In order to reduce the crime of robbery, a business must plan and implement robbery prevention policies and procedures. Robbery prevention not only reduces financial losses, but also may save lives and prevent serious injuries.

BURGLARY

Burglary is the unlawful entry of a structure to commit a felony or theft. Burglary is usually categorized as: forcible entry, unlawful entry where no force is used, and attempted forcible entry. Burglary is the second most prevalent property crime in the United States and represents a substantial financial loss to the victims.

As with robbery, the impulse to commit a burglary begins with the need or desire for money or merchandise. Reducing the likelihood that a burglar will select a particular target is a complex problem. For most businesses, the best overall strategy is to ensure that likely entry points are safely guarded by physical and visible means of discouragement such as lights, locks, fencing, and alarms, making entry appear to be difficult. This is called "target hardening." The would-be burglar should see a comprehensive security program, e.g., good lighting, perimeter barriers, high-quality locking hardware, well-constructed doors and windows, alarm devices, etc. Hopefully, this will deter any attempt at entry. However, no false assumptions should be made regarding deterring burglars. Deterrence is obviously a desirable goal, but not always obtainable.

A well-designed burglary prevention program should be a planned sequence of steps to deter, delay, detect, and possibly even deny the crime of burglary. It must include an awareness of facility vulnerabilities and the proper measures to take for its security and protection. Assuming that all of the aforementioned encompasses the first step of a burglary prevention program, the second step is to be sure that the lighting, fencing, locks, and alarms are of sufficient quality and quantity to make it extremely difficult and time-consuming to burglarize the building. Any delay in entering a building in a lighted area will increase the risk of being detected and apprehended. The third step is the use of a silent alarm, which, when activated, signals a remote respondent (usually a contractual or proprietary central station) that a break-in is in progress. A local alarm signaling device may also be used, either by itself (in which case no remote notification of the intrusion would be made) or in conjunction with the silent alarm capability. The property owner must make a decision as to the orientation of the intrusion detection system, i.e., a local alarm signaling device designed to scare the intruder away or as silent alarm signal oriented to apprehension. The fourth step is to use locking mechanisms and hardware that make it difficult to exit the premises any way other than through the point of entry. For example, double-cylinder deadbolt locks require that a key be used from the inside to unlock the door. The fifth preventive step involves securing merchandise and property, when feasible, in such a way that is difficult to gain access to it or remove it from the premises. Small valuable merchandise can be secured in a safe and some items (such as computers and typewriters) can be secured to furniture with specialty locks. In addition, internal target-hardened rooms can be used to house high-value items. While there are numerous other proactive steps that can be taken, a final suggestion is to mark property and merchandise so that it is easier to trace and identify, and thus more difficult for the burglar to fence.

SHOPLIFTING

While no type of retail business is entirely immune from shoplifting, the retail stores most frequently affected by shoplifting are those selling small and concealable items. Grocery, hardware, drug, and general merchandising stores are the most vulnerable in terms of items that are easy to shoplift.

In contrast to burglary, shoplifting occurs as a part of ordinary customer behavior, at least up to the point at which the customer conceals merchandise or alters the price tag. In general, it is difficult to identify a particular trait or define an approach that characterizes the common shoplifter. Usually, shoplifters are amateurs who operate alone and are likely to steal at any time of the day or day of the week. Studies have shown that shoplifters like to operate when stores are most crowded or in a store where they believe that the employees are not trained and/or are unfamiliar with shoplifting techniques. Friday and Saturday are usually peak times for shoplifting, as are holiday seasons when stores are crowded and store personnel are especially busy.

The behavior of shoplifters begins to differ from that of ordinary customers after merchandise has been removed from displays. First, shoplifters tend to concentrate on areas of the store where they cannot readily be observed from the cashier's area or by store personnel on the floor. Notably, they look for anything that obstructs vision or reduces visibility; high sales counters, tall displays, free-standing signs and poorly lighted areas. A shoplifting technique used by shoplifting teams (called "rounders") is to take advantage of such conditions to hide their shoplifting actions. These shoplifters operate in pairs, e.g., one member of the team blocks or distracts the view or attention of store personnel and customers while the other is concealing merchandise.

Shoplifters are legendary for their ingenuity in hiding items. While most use purses, pockets, or underclothing, some develop elaborate special-purpose equipment to increase their capacity to conceal merchandise. This equipment ranges from coats with extra pockets sewn into the lining to devices such as "hooker belts" that permit an array of merchandise to be hung around the shoplifter's waist under a bulky coat. Some even equip themselves with slings that permit them to carry comparatively large items (such as radios or turkeys) between their legs.

The two most serious problems associated with shoplifting are detecting the crime and dealing with the apprehended shoplifter. Most owners or managers agree that it is much better to have a program to reduce the opportunity for shoplifting than to place emphasis on the detection and apprehension phase of a complete shoplifting program; however, detection and apprehension of shoplifters must be a part of a comprehensive anti-shoplifting program. Most detection and apprehension techniques involve some combination of undercover security personnel, store employees and electronic surveillance equipment, such as CCTV and electronic article surveillance tags. Usually there is an integration of overt and covert methods designed respectively for deterrence and detection. Detection techniques and corresponding decisions to apprehend a shoplifter must be guided by good training programs that provide employees with the knowledge and capability to effect safe and legal apprehensions.

There are three critical points that offer the greatest opportunity for preventing and/or controlling shoplifting: (1) when potential perpetrators enter the store, (2) when they pick up the merchandise, and (3) when they leave the store. At the entrance, steps should be taken to project a store-wide attitude of shoplifting awareness: signs warning of prosecution and perhaps a procedure requiring customers to leave parcels with a cashier (which limits the means of concealment available to the shoplifter). When shoplifters are in the vicinity of their target merchandise, the courteous intervention of store employees offering assistance can put shoplifters on notice that they are being watched. Alert, observant employees will have a significant impact on the deterrence of shoplifting. Finally, when shoplifters have concealed merchandise and are preparing to leave, a device such as an electronic article surveillance tag attached to the merchandise, which can be removed properly only with a special tool, will cause an alarm signal to be generated if an attempt is made to take the merchandise (with the tag still attached) out of the store. If no such devices are being used, the detection and subsequent detainment of shoplifters will depend upon the act of concealment being observed by employees and/or security personnel, and unbroken surveillance affected to the point of detainment. Caution and care must be taken in regarding the handling of shoplifters and shoplifting incidents so that any potential litigation against the business is avoided. The requirements of the laws regarding shoplifting in a particular jurisdiction must be the standard by which shoplifting prevention programs are measured and accomplished. The following is representative of the sequential steps that should be followed in a shoplifting incident:

1) The shoplifting suspect must be seen taking the item;

2) The act of concealing the item must be observed—evidence of intent to steal negates the argument that the perpetrator forgot to pay for the item;

3) There should be no break in the surveillance of the suspect—no time in which the suspect could discard the item;

4) There must be no question that the item was not paid for; and

5) The suspect should be apprehended beyond the point of payment, preferably outside the store (this is not required by law but it strengthens the argument that the suspect had no intention of paying for the item).

Businesses can pursue the prosecution of shoplifting cases through the criminal justice system, and many still choose to do so, but the recovery of losses is generally not accomplished when this route is taken. Criminal court proceedings are usually a time-consuming headache for businesses because of the time and effort required for successful prosecution. Shoplifting cases in overburdened courts often take a backseat to the more serious crimes, such as murder, rape, drug offenses, assault, etc.

BAD CHECKS

Each year, businesses in the United States lose millions of dollars as a result of "bad" checks. Most states classify bad checks as theft by deception. This includes checks written against non-existent accounts, checks written with insufficient funds, forgeries, or stolen checks. The dollar amount of the check usually determines whether the offense is a misdemeanor or a felony. Most criminal cases result from forgeries, stolen checks, or checks written on "no account."

Any business or organization that receives checks on a regular basis can develop guidelines to reduce the risk of cashing a bad check and of not being able to identify and locate those who do pass worthless checks. The following are suggested general guidelines for employers to reduce risks associated with bad checks:

1) Always insist on proper identification. The best identification is one with a photograph, such as a driver's license. If a person does not have a driver's license, a secondary identification that gives certain specific information will suffice, i.e., a company identification card for an employee.

2) Check-cashing cards for a specific store. Many stores require a person who wishes to cash a check to fill out an application and receive a check-cashing card. Most stores that use this system will not cash a check without such a card.

3) Compare name, address, and telephone number on check with those on identification. Make sure to compare first, middle, and last names as well as the address on the check with the same information on the identification.

4) Record identifying information from identification on check. Record the driver's license number or other identifying number on the back of the check.

5) Check numerical amount against written amount. A bank is obligated to honor the written amount on a check. Make sure that the two amounts are the same.

6) Be cautious of "stale" dates; never accept post-dated checks. Question a person about a check with a date that is more than one month old. Never accept a post-dated check. It is best to take only those checks written and dated (current) by the individual at the time of the purchase.

7) If signature is questionable, have the person sign again. If the signature is illegible, and the person signs again and it is still illegible, have the person print his or her name.

8) Verify account at bank. The magnetic numbers on the lower left bottom of the check represent the banking information. The last set of digits is the account number.

A business should establish a firm check-cashing policy and advertise it. Strict dollar limits, requirements that checks be written for the amount of purchase only and the use of courtesy cards for check cashing are all good business practices.

CREDIT CARD FRAUD

Credit card fraud includes all fraudulent type offenses involving the use/and or theft of credit cards. Credit card fraud is an area that causes enormous dollar losses for certain business enterprises. For example, many banks are faced with greater dollar losses due to credit card fraud than to bad checks. At a recent security conference, a director of security for a large metropolitan bank stated that his bank was reassessing their policy on the issuance of credit cards, and that a major effort was underway to encourage retailers to do a more thorough job of checking both the card and the cardholder before accepting it. At least one major card company requires retailers to verify the current status of the card with the company prior to each transaction.

Current estimates seem to indicate that losses due to credit card fraud are well in excess of $1 billion each year. As with several other business-related crimes, there is no reliable data base on which to estimate annual losses. Credit cards often are fraudulently obtained from issuers with the intent to defraud. They frequently are stolen from mailboxes, homes, offices, and individuals, and then are used to obtain merchandise from an unknowing merchant. Other methods of fraudulent use include using a counterfeit or altered credit card, using a credit card previously canceled by the issuer and providing a false credit card number. When the credit card of another is illegally obtained and used to effect transactions, the crime of forgery is committed.

Methods of preventing credit card fraud in retail operations are similar to the techniques for protection against bad checks. Store personnel should use "hot lists" (issuers' lists of lost or stolen cards), be aware of established purchase limits and insist upon proper user identification.

TELECOMMUNICATIONS FRAUD AND ABUSE

Telecommunications involves the utilization of technology for the transmission of information, e.g., telephones and computers. Readily available equipment and technology make it possible for someone with the right tools to monitor and/or manipulate telecommunicated information and related transmission equipment. (See discussion of espionage later in this chapter.) Professional criminals penetrate private (telephone) branch exchanges (PBXs), voice mail systems and related equipment, stealing billions of dollars worth of telephone service. In a recent case, hackers broke into the computer systems of Sprint Corporation, Southwestern Bell, and GTE and illegally obtained long distance calling card numbers. Had the hackers been successful in carrying out their scheme, they would have sold the long distance calling card numbers.

VOICE-MAIL FRAUD

One of the newest high-tech telecommunication crimes is voice-mail fraud. A voice-mail computer operates like an answering machine and is commonly attached to a toll-free telephone number. When the person being called does not answer the phone, the caller is transferred to the voice-mail computer, which explains how to leave a message or transfer to another telephone line for assistance. The operational functions of the computer are initiated and controlled by appropriate numerical commands entered on the telephone keypad, or in the case of a hacker, the link and response is a telephone modem and computer. Voice-mail fraud works in the following manner:

1) Using an outside telephone line, a hacker calls into a business voice-mail system and gets into the message "mailbox."

2) Utilizing a personal computer and specialized software, the hacker attempts to break the mailbox pass code and gain access to the voice-mail operating system.

3) Once inside the system, the hacker, who is now committing fraud, can change the voice mail pass codes to lock out legitimate users, set up message boxes to pay automatically for third-party and collect phone calls (including those to foreign countries) or direct dial an unlimited number of long distance numbers, leaving the voice-mail box owner to pay the bill.

COMPUTER FRAUD

The rapid technological developments of the computer age have created a high technology environment vulnerable to a new kind of crime: computer crime. Within the span of a few years, the computer has become a commonplace yet vital fixture of business and industry. Perhaps no single factor in business or industry can surpass the computer in its potential to harm or destroy an entire organization. A compromised computer, whether by direct or remote manipulation, by theft of storage tapes or disks, by sabotage or accident, affects the ability of the user and owner to operate efficiently and effectively. The confidentiality and integrity of information and data stored in the computer is in many cases absolutely essential to continued, competitive operation. The theft, destruction or manipulation of information and data can destroy the capacity to simply stay in business. Moreover, computer crime cannot be approached via the traditional methods of detecting, investigating, and preventing losses.

Computer crimes and computer-related crimes are increasing at an alarming rate. Congress in 1984 and 1986 enacted two pieces of computer crime legislation. Computer criminality is generally classified as an "occupational" form of white-collar crime that benefits the perpetrator by victimizing an individual or organization and is usually committed during the course of one's occupational activity (Clinard et al., 1973). The Computer Fraud and Abuse Act of 1986 provides penalties for fraud and related activities in connection with access devices and computers. It addresses the unauthorized computer access with the intent to defraud, malicious damage via unauthorized access, and trafficking in computer passwords with the intent to defraud. Computer crimes include network intrusions to alter, steal, or destroy information or to disable systems; financial crimes over the Internet; transmission of sexually explicit material including child pornography via computer; and intellectual property crimes facilitated by computer. Financial crimes using computers has also become an area of concern. These type of crimes include attempts to illegally transfer funds from financial institutions. One of the more noteworthy cases involved the Citicorp's Citibank of New York, which was attacked by Vladimir Levin, a Russian hacker in 1994. Levin was able to break into the bank's computers and transfer $12 million. The bank detected the fraud after the first $400,000 was withdrawn, but allowed Levin to continue in order to track his whereabouts. He was ultimately arrested and prosecuted for the offense.

The FBI has responded aggressively to threats of computer fraud and crime. They completed a national assessment of computer crime problems in 1992, and, from that, established the Infrastructure Protection and Computer Intrusion Squad. This Squad is responsible for investigating unauthorized intrusions into major computer networks belonging to telecommunications providers, private corporations, United States Government agencies, and public and private educational facilities. According to IPCIS, there are several trends that have emerged with regard to computer fraud:

1. An increasing number of juveniles who are responsible for serious network intrusions costing tens of thousands of dollars;

2. An increasing number of employees, former employees, and contractors using their trusted relationships to harm their current or former employer; and

3. A rise in the sophistication and complexity of intrusions (IPCIS, 2000)

INTELLECTUAL PROPERTY

Intellectual property is classified as either industrial property or copyright property. Industrial property refers to inventions, trademarks, industrial designs, and appellations of origin. Copyright refers to literary, musical, artistic, photographic, and audiovisual works. Estimates by the American Society for Industrial Security indicate that intellectual property losses from foreign and domestic espionage may have exceeded $300 billion in 1997 alone. A 1996 Economic Espionage Act made theft of proprietary economic information in the United States a felony punishable by a $10 million fine and 15-year prison sentence. The 1997 survey disclosed that high-tech companies, especially in Silicon Valley in California, were the most frequent targets of foreign spies, followed by manufacturing and service industries.

BOMBS AND BOMB THREATS

The target of a bomb usually is not selected at random. Target selection often is based on some type of gain or revenge for the person or persons responsible.

Explosive devices generally are set for detonation at a time that allows the person responsible to be a considerable distance away before the threat is made and the device detonated. It is, however, becoming more common for terrorist groups to detonate a device at a specific location and announce at a later date that they were responsible.

Management personnel—especially of large multinational corporations—must consider both bombs and bomb threats as serious problems. Three factors must be examined in any bomb-related policy: the degree of risk and danger of injury or death to personnel; the consequences of damaging or destroying materials in a facility; and the total cost or loss from a bombing or a bomb threat. The risk factors associated with bomb threats must be balanced against the consequences of evacuating a facility every time a threat is received. A preplanned cursory search may be a more acceptable alternative than evacuation in a situation in which the known risks are not great.

If a business receives a bomb threat, the person receiving the call should try to obtain as much information about the bomb threat as the caller will give. In most cases, however, the caller will neither remain on the telephone for a long period of time nor answer questions. Second, the person receiving the call should notify the security director or person responsible for security at the facility. The director will make a decision to call the police department, the fire department, or both, and to search and possibly evacuate the facility. A decision to search will generally be made according to a prearranged plan and may be limited to specific areas of the facility, depending on the information given by the caller.

A decision to evacuate a facility usually is made only when there has been a history of having found bombs either in the area or at the facility, or when the caller gives enough information to the receiver to warrant an evacuation. The tone or urgency of the conversation and the possible identity of the caller (e.g., a teenage caller with giggling friends in the background) will provide a clue as to the credence of the call. In most cases, a decision to evacuate on a limited basis is both practical and feasible.

TERRORISM

There are varying definitions of terrorism, due in part to the fact that acts of terrorism are perceived differently by the victim, the perpetrator, and various others. For example, disorders and terrorism have common characteristics and specific differences. Both are forms of extraordinary violence that disrupt the civil peace; both originate in some form of social excitement, discontent and unrest; both can endanger massive fear in the community. Disorders and terrorism constitute, in varying forms and degrees, violent attacks upon the established order of society. However, the focus, direction, application, and purpose of the terror and fear are different.

Disorders do not necessarily have political overtones; they may arise simply from excessive stimulation and exuberance during an event such as a football game or rock concert. Disorders are often haphazard, with no planned events or directed objectives. They are collective discharges of human behavior that range from abusive language and resistance to destruction of life and property.

Terrorism is characterized by planned, calculated acts aimed at manipulating society toward defined objectives. The message of fear is deliberate and is the very purpose of the terrorist activity. Without an audience, terrorism is an exercise in futility.

The difference between terrorism and "terrifying" criminal acts lies in the technique and purpose of the violent act. Terrorism is coercive, designed to manipulate the will of its victims and larger audience. Similarly, the fear generated by a criminal act such as rape is aimed at overcoming the will of the instant victim, not the minds or resistance of others. Thus, a criminal act must be qualified before it can be called "terrorism"; however, an act of terrorism would in every case be considered a criminal act.

The Private Security Advisory Council's Committee on the Prevention of Terroristic Acts defined terrorism as "criminal acts and/or threats by individuals or groups designed to achieve political or economic objectives by fear, intimidation, coercion, or violence." Further, the committee identified five distinctive categories or kinds of terrorism: (1) political terrorism; (2) nonpolitical terrorism; (3) quasi-terrorism; (4) limited political terrorism; and (5) official or state terrorism (Private Security Advisory Council, 1976).

Political terrorism in its fully developed form is revolutionary in character; whether it is a realistic tactic or not, its purpose is the subversion or overthrow of an existing government. It is characterized by: (1) a violent, criminal nature; (2) an impersonal frame of reference; and (3) the primacy of its ulterior objective, which is the dissemination of fear throughout the community for political ends or purposes.

Nonpolitical terrorism includes a vast area of true Terroristic activity that cannot be termed political. Such terror may affect society and its patterns of behavior on a considerable scale, but the objectives of those involved are individual or collective gain, rather than the achievement of political ends. Organized crime, street gangs, and cult groups (akin to the "Manson family") characterize some of the types of nonpolitical terrorism.

Quasi-terrorism is the use of "terroristic techniques or tactics in situations that are not true terroristic crimes, such as the taking of hostages during the course of a commonplace crime like bank robbery. Another example is skyjacking, in which the aircraft and hostages are threatened subject to the payment of ransom for private gain.

Limited political terrorism involves acts of terrorism committed for ideological or political motives that are not part of a concerted movement to capture the government. Singular acts committed by a lone terrorist or acts limited to a particular social context constitute limited political terrorism.

Official or state terrorism involves situations in which opposition between the oppressive policies of a state (government) and the will of the people leads the state to use violence and this reciprocally causes the people to react by violent means. Frequently, terroristic behavior by individuals and dissident groups is claimed to be a response to acts of terrorism sponsored by the state.

Thus, terrorism is a serious and complex problem of national and international concern that defies easy, conclusive solutions. Acts of terrorism—including assassinations, kidnapping, bombings, and personal assault—are frequent and widespread. Modern terrorists have been assisted by the ease of intercontinental travel and mass communications. Acts of terrorism have gained immediacy and diffusion through television, which conveys the terrorist message to millions worldwide. The modern terrorist has been magnified, enlarged beyond his or her own powers, by others.

EXECUTIVE (PERSONAL) PROTECTION

The threat of a kidnapping or extortion varies from area to area, both in the United States and other countries of the world; therefore, assessments of the likelihood of their occurrence must be definitive and specific to localized situations. The political climate and regional conditions around company facilities and areas frequented by company personnel should be determined and documented. Because the risk level and exposure of company executives and employees will vary, the most vulnerable facilities and personnel should be afforded a higher degree of security.

Given the past occurrences of political kidnapping and hostage situations in various parts of the world, it is obvious that extremists view such acts as an effective tactic toward accomplishing specific goals. Political extremists and/or terrorists utilize the violence and suspense of the kidnapping or hostage situation to exert pressure on those in authority to comply with their demands and cause the public to recognize their power. Such incidents attract the attention of the public and the media, and require minimal commitments of terrorist personnel and equipment.

TERRORISM AND AIR TRAVEL

The savagery and disregard for human life by international terrorists is quite apparent. However, the goals of international terrorists are often difficult to discern because, in many cases, they are fanatics with obscure personal and/or political agendas. They tend to seek to drive Western influence from the developing world, and frequently favor despotic political systems over plural representative democracy.

American citizens are principle targets of terrorists. A significant percentage of terrorist attacks have been directed at United States citizens or installations abroad. Terrorist incidents within the United States have been decreasing and represent less than one percent of the worldwide total. The effective work of the FBI, tighter controls at points of entry, and a pronounced aversion to foreign-inspired violence have had an effect.

The following are a few suggestions for safe travel at all locations, not just while at an airport or aboard an airplane:

1) Plan for worst-case scenarios—leave copy of itinerary and other information such as airline ticket numbers and credit card numbers with relatives or friends. Have an emergency source or means of obtaining additional funds. Plan for any special health considerations.

2) Select airlines and flights carefully—avoid airlines that have experienced recent problems and flights with layovers in high-risk areas. U.S. airlines are usually preferable. Contact the U.S. State Department regarding any special travel advisories relative to civil unrest, natural disasters, and health epidemics in foreign countries.

3) Move directly to the gate—avoid lingering in the airport lobby or other uncontrolled areas. Have your ticket and boarding pass with you when you arrive at the terminal and move directly from luggage check-in to the gate. There, you will be in one of the terminals where passengers and luggage have been screened and X-rayed.

4) Avoid expensive-looking luggage and dress—in the event of hijacking, such items tend to label one as a "rich American." Try to avoid appearances that are out of the ordinary.

5) Avoid the aisle seat—hijacking victims seated near the aisle have fared worse than those near the window.

6) Avoid first class—passengers traveling first class are seen as being wealthy, and terrorists most often set up their headquarters in the first-class compartment. Keep a low profile.

7) Car rentals—rent inexpensive local cars to remain as inconspicuous as possible.

8) Restaurants and hotels—avoid sitting near front windows, which are the most vulnerable to bombing attacks. Avoid restaurants that specialize in traditionally American food or are known to be frequented by Americans. Select hotels with security and fire safety in mind. If feasible, stay in facilities located near U.S. Embassies.

9) Identification cards—official U.S. government ID cards or military service IDs should be left at home or stored in luggage. Terrorists more frequently prey on those holding official governmental identification.

10) Contact U.S. embassies and consulates—in cases of emergency, you should contact the nearest American embassy or consulate for assistance.

Affirmative actions to avoid and discourage kidnapping or extortion attempts must be undertaken prior to the occurrence of such incidents. An organized effort of planning and preparation must consider that any response to terroristic acts requires policies, resources, analysis, communications, and decisionmaking that go beyond the usual boundaries of a single organizational function. The concept of the "crisis management team" offers a means to draw together the necessary areas of management to obtain a viable defensive strategy.

ESPIONAGE

Some corporations worth hundreds of millions of dollars owe their existence to trade secrets that can be written on a few sheets of paper. Such corporations go to great lengths to keep trade secrets and confidential information out of the hands of competitors. However, this is especially difficult for international corporations, because trade secrets illegally obtained in this country may be perfectly legal in a foreign country that does not recognize our laws pertaining to such incidents. An American-controlled multinational corporation assembled through a series of mergers may find that it is practically impossible to control the actions of a foreign component. Any trade secrets held by a foreign subsidiary may be compromised, and legally so in that country, by disloyal employees. Multinational corporations routinely have employees from a variety of nations. Some employees' loyalty to the company may pale in comparison with their loyalty for their native country. Finally, most equipment used in business espionage, such as cameras, copy machines, and electronic listening and recording devices, are not licensed or registered. The buying, possession, and use of this type of equipment would not place a person in a suspect position in many foreign countries.

While most foreign governments—including those friendly to the United States—can and do collect competitive business information from open source literature as well as from human and electronic intelligence-gathering methods and techniques, so do competing companies in American industry. In fact, a new term, "competitive intelligence," has been coined to replace the stigma attached to what has commonly been referred to as traditional espionage. In essence, espionage (or competitive intelligence-gathering) appears to have reached a new level of acceptance in American industry.

Common targets of intelligence-gathering include research and development, manufacturing and production techniques, and processes, marketing strategies and pricing information, and human resource information. Information regarding these areas can provide significant and valuable insight about a competitor's immediate situation and/or plans for the future. Such knowledge may mean beating a competitor in the marketplace by introducing products first, offering lower prices, undercutting contract bids, etc.

Thus, the control and security of organizational information is of vital importance, and steps must be taken to ensure that its confidentiality is uncompromised. The following areas, common to most organizational settings, should receive special attention.

1) Employee access and information awareness. Employees should be trained in the proper handling of sensitive information. They must be aware of information significance and how to ensure its integrity.

2) Document classification and control. A program to ensure that documents are properly classified and secured.

3)   Physical security of office settings.

4)   Access control security and monitoring regarding maintenance, vendors, visitors, etc.

5)   Security and integrity of meeting rooms and offices from eavesdropping.

6)   Communications equipment security. Usage of cellular or cordless phones to discuss sensitive business information should be prohibited.

7)   Electronic mail or voice mail. Sensitive documents should be sent only on high-level encryption fax machines. Fax copies should be well secured. Voice-mail information and operational programming should preclude any potential access to sensitive information.

8)   Teleconferencing regarding sensitive information should be avoided.

9)   Corporate telephone exchanges (PBXs) should be physically secured. Operational features and programming aspects should reflect security of codes, exchange capabilities, user identification procedures, etc., from unauthorized use and penetration.

10)   Computer security relative to equipment, processing, storage mediums, information destruction, etc., should be matched to the level of information involved.

11)   Trade shows and employee presentations. Employees should be instructed on the nuances of information transfer and competitive intelligence techniques (Tanzer, 1992).

SABOTAGE

A business must be concerned with two types of sabotage: (1) actions that could cause disruption of vital services, and (2) actions that threaten (or could threaten) human life. Many acts of sabotage, such as disruption of communication or computer systems, may not directly affect human life; however, other actions, such as arson or bombing, may have an immediate impact on human life.

Sabotage can be defined as the willful destruction of property. The saboteur, whether a trained professional or an amateur, may be anyone within or outside the organization. A saboteur may work alone or in concert with others. There are numerous methods and devices used to accomplish sabotage. Generally, the techniques of sabotage can be classified as follows:

1)   Explosive Devices—Various explosive devices (bombs) containing either low or high explosives can be used to partially or totally destroy a facility or vital component of it.

2)   Mechanical Sabotage—Motors and machinery can be rendered inoperative by a variety of methods: breakage, insertion of abrasives into machinery, adding contaminants to fuel, acts of omission (failure to do proper maintenance), placing false information on maintenance charts, etc.

3) Fire—Fire is one of the oldest and simplest forms of sabotage. Whether the saboteur sets a simple fire or uses a timing device, fire is one of the most effective methods of sabotage because it can destroy both the property and any evidence of criminal action.

4) Electrical (Public Services) Sabotage—Almost every facility is dependent on public services for continued operation. Interruption of such services can be accomplished in a variety of ways. For example, electrical power liens, substations, or generating facilities can be rendered inoperative by cutting lines, bombing generators or substation units, or mechanical means.

5) Chemical Sabotage—Chemical sabotage can be accomplished by the introduction of various materials into fuel supplies, service water, or drinking water. The magnitude and effect of this method of sabotage is limited only by the sophistication of the saboteur.

6) Psychological Sabotage—Creating a negative situation or confrontation between employer and employees can often accomplish the objectives of the saboteur. While property is not destroyed, the employer's ability to produce may be disrupted or destroyed. For example, work slowdowns, walkouts, or general strikes can be instigated by one individual bent on creating unrest and disruption.

Thus, sabotage is a real threat to government, industry, and even individuals who have been targeted by someone wishing to cause them harm. Whether the motivation is criminal, political, or personal (revenge, mental imbalance, etc.), the results are equally destructive.

SUMMARY

In order to be comprehensive and complete, security must be approached systematically. Analysis of all real and potential threats, whether human-generated or natural, is a mandatory step that must be taken before effective preventive or deterrent action can be accomplished.

Current developments in detection and alert systems have made it possible to have advance warnings of many probable or actual hazardous environmental conditions. With proper planning and adequate preparation, property losses and life-threatening events can be minimized. The foreseeability of some events can be determined with some degree of certainty. Consequently, the relative effectiveness of proactive measures taken today is self-evident.

The current crime situation is a social problem of serious proportion that threatens the welfare and integrity of all people, homes, institutions, and places of business in the United States. The heavy burden of preventing and deterring criminal acts—whether committed by the professional, the amateur, the terrorist, the drug abuser, the employee, or even the employer—falls on everyone.

Crime prevention, for purposes of this text, has been divided into three zones of protection: primary, secondary, and tertiary zones. Primary zones refer to perimeter areas of protection and represent the furthest exterior of a property. For example, if the facility is a warehouse, then the property line and accompanying fence line would represent the primary zone in need of protection. The secondary zone refers to the building itself and includes the exterior walls, doors, and windows in need of specific target-hardening devices such as locks or access control devices. The third, or tertiary, zone refers to the interior of the facility, which can be subdivided further into areas with varying degrees of security. Protection here begins with intrusion detection systems that are commonly placed at entry points, but can also be used for areas in need of higher levels of security.

DISCUSSION QUESTIONS

1. Elaborate on the concept of foreseeability.

2. List some of the more common natural hazards and the locations in which they are most likely to occur.

3. Why does fire continue to be such a destructive force in a society having such technological and engineering capability as ours?

4. List several of the indirect losses associated with fire.

5. Identify and give examples of the two basic types of crime.

6. Define crime and discuss its range and scope.

7. What is the difference between criminal law and civil law?

8. Why is it not possible to "profile" most types of criminals?

9. Describe the differences between the amateur and the professional criminal.

10. Why is computer security and protection so important?

11. What have been some of the major effects of terrorism on the private security industry?

12. How can employee drug abuse affect the workplace?

13. What is embezzlement and how significant is it today?

14. What key business areas are affected most by embezzlement?

15. What are the human and physical elements generally present in an embezzlement?

16. What are the various strategies for reducing and controlling internal theft losses?

17. Explain how workforce pilferage occurs. How significant are the total annual losses due to pilferage?

18. What are some of the procedures that can be used to deter internal theft?

19. Discuss some characteristics of a business environment with high fraud potential.

20. Identify some of the problem indicators of alcoholism.

21. List the six types of drug classifications.

22. Outline what a business should do to prevent robberies.

23. What are some of the preventive measures that reduce the occurrence of burglaries?

24. Describe the critical points to prevent or control shoplifting.

25. What are some of the steps an employee should take when accepting checks?

26. List some of the more common methods by which credit cards are fraudulently obtained.

27. Identify several techniques of both telecommunications fraud and voice-mail fraud.

28. What are the current trends regarding computer fraud?

29. List the two types of intellectual property,

30. What three factors are critical to bomb threat policy?

31. Outline the various types of terrorism.

32. List four suggestions that should be given to air travelers to reduce their risk of becoming victims of terrorism.

33. Define and describe the difference between espionage and sabotage.

REFERENCES

Black's Law Dictionary, 6th ed., S.V. "embezzlement."

Clinard, Marshall B. and Richard Quinney (1973). *Crime Behavior Systems: A Typology* (2nd ed.). New York, NY: Holt, Rinehart and Winston.

Cunningham, W.C., Strauchs, J.J. & Van Meter, C.W. (1990). *Private Security Trends, 1970-2000: The Hallcrest Report II*. Stoneham, MA: Butterworth-Heinemann.

Hefferman, R.J. (1998). *ASIS Trends in Intellectual Property Loss Survey Report*, 4th ed.

Hefter (1986). "The Crippling Crime," *Security World*, March.

Hertzberg, Frederick, *Work and the Nature of Man*. New York, NY: Thomas Y. Crowell (1996).

Maslow, Abraham, "Motivation and Personality." New York, NY: Harper and Row, 1954.

Southerland, M., Scarborough, K. & Collins, P. (1997). *Workplace Violence: A Continuum from Threat to Death*. Cincinnati, OH: Anderson Publishing Co.

"Task Force Report on Disorders and Terrorism." Washington, DC: U.S. Government Printing Office, 1976, 3-6.

Tanzer, Mark (1992). "Foiling the New Corporate Spy," *Security Management*, September 1992, 38-42.

Washington Field Office Infrastructure Protection and Computer Intrusion Squad (2000). http://www.fbi.gov/programs/ipcis/ipcis.htm

Crime Prevention and Primary Zones of Protection

9

INTRODUCTION

Crime prevention is an area that has received a great deal of attention over the last two decades. From that analysis, a better understanding of how to prevent crime and reduce the risks associated with it have evolved. Crime prevention has been defined by the Crime Prevention Coalition of America as:

> . . . a pattern of attitudes and behavior directed both at reducing the threat of crime and enhancing the sense of safety and security to positively influence the quality of life in our society and to help develop environments where crime cannot flourish (Crime Prevention Coalition, 1990:64).

All effective crime prevention efforts must begin with a planning model that defines the process to be undertaken. Generally, that process involves a systematic analysis of the crime problem and the conditions that generate it, a review of the services and activities in place to tackle those conditions and ways to improve them, rigorous implementation of the program, and evaluation of the impact of the program on crime and its implementation so that improvements can be made (Waller & Welsh, 1998).

This chapter will focus primarily on Crime Prevention and Primary Zones of Protection. Primary Zones of Protection refers to those areas that represent the first lines of defense for the facility being protected. Within a primary zone is the perimeter, which can include environmental factors and manmade factors—both of which are used to provide crime prevention capabilities.

PERIMETER SECURITY

The ability to protect and secure any facility or building depends a great deal upon the environment and general location of the structure(s) to be protected. That is, the area contiguous to the facility must be secure if the facility itself is to remain secure. The surrounding area, immediately adjacent to and encircling a facility, is the perimeter. Most often, the value of the goods, the nature of the operation, the desired confidentiality, and existing threats to assets of a business or industrial process require that the perimeter be secured. This may be accomplished through the installation of alarms, barriers, and lighting; the security of the structure itself; and the introduction of procedural controls and security personnel.

In many instances, the security of a facility declines as accessibility to that facility increases. Also, as security precautions are increased, the cost to management increases—as does the inconvenience to employees, patrons, and management. Therefore, the efforts taken to secure a facility perimeter should depend in large measure upon that which is being secured. The value and related vulnerability (openness to attack) of the asset(s) being protected should be significant determining factors. Security does not operate in a world of its own. Retailing and merchandising techniques for retail stores that stress customer accessibility and convenience require trade-offs in terms of the amount and type of security with regard to costs, inconveniences, and aesthetic qualities. The ultimate selection and deployment of a security procedure, technique, or device is, therefore, dependent upon management's approval of security's requests for monies, resources, and programs.

This chapter examines some of the attributes, problems, and solutions regarding perimeter security. Topical areas include: site layout, perimeter barriers and protection, building surface security, cooperative issues, perimeter security hardware, and security personnel applications.

SITE LAYOUT

Too often, security is only of minor concern during the planning and construction of a facility. Frequently, management is more interested in other requirements—such as safety, economy of construction, operation, and convenience. Only after the facility has been constructed and put into operation does management consider security. However, by this time, the security problems are much more difficult and expensive to solve. Therefore, in order to enhance security, security specialists should have input during the initial architectural planning stages. This way, there can be a pre-construction compromise between cost, convenience, and security issues.

One of the most critical factors with regard to site layout is the positioning of the facility on the land and/or building lot. Great care should be taken to ensure that every structure receives maximum exposure from adjacent thoroughfares. The more isolated it is from public view, the more likely that a structure will be viewed as being susceptible to unauthorized entry or exit. Trespassers generally select properties and points of entry that have the least visibility and exposure. Robberies also can become a problem when there is limited visibility. Would-be robbers tend to select targets that are isolated or not easily viewed by pedestrians and vehicular traffic.

In most cases the facility should be constructed in the middle of the building lot so that movement around the facility is unimpeded and all sides can be easily observed. When this is not possible and the structure must be located immediately adjacent to another structure, special security precautions must be taken to guard against surreptitious entry or exit. Obviously, there is great variety in buildings and the land on which they sit (e.g., the 70-story high-rise on a downtown street, the corner drugstore, the multi-structure manufacturing facility occupying hundreds of acres, etc.), but in every situation security can be complemented if it receives its due regard at the earliest possible moment.

LANDSCAPING

The arrangement and types of trees, shrubbery, and other plantings around a facility can play an important role in reducing burglaries and inventory shrinkage. In most cases, management will want to make the facility as attractive as possible in order to enhance the appearance and image of the business. This usually entails the introduction of shrubbery, trees, and other vegetation or ornamentation. Although appealing to the eye, landscaping makes it easier for security to be compromised. If possible, large quantities of vegetation should be avoided and should not be located within 50 feet of any buildings. This will increase visibility, provide limited cover for concealment, and help deter illegal activities.

Special care should be taken with regard to where merchandise, supplies, and materials enter or leave the facility. These areas should remain free from obstruction to decrease the possibility of employees or carriers hiding goods and merchandise and later retrieving them. This is especially important around loading docks and rail entrances.

Finally, an integral part of landscaping is lighting, which is used to beautify the area as well as increase security. Frequently, management uses lighting for advertisement without regard to security. In most cases, however, the two can be blended to achieve some of the objectives of both. Security lighting is addressed later as a tool of security regardless of its value in landscaping.

The initial design and placement of a structure will have considerable bearing on future security efforts. Buildings, facilities, and perimeter areas must not only have utility and be pleasing to the eye, but should also be constructed so that illegal entry and activities would appear to be difficult—if not impossible—to achieve.

CRIME PREVENTION THROUGH ENVIRONMENTAL DESIGN

The environment to which one is exposed is fundamental in determining how an individual acts and perceives the surroundings. Thus, it is both natural and imperative that one should seek to understand its influence upon both crime and the fear of crime within society.

In 1974, a major program of Crime Prevention Through Environmental Design (CPTED) was launched by the National Institute of Law Enforcement and Criminal Justice. Residential, commercial, and school environments, and the predatory, fear-producing crimes within them, were the focus of this program.

The basis of using CPTED concepts to achieve security can be found throughout history. For example, moats and fortress walls were built around medieval cities to reduce external threats. Lighting programs also have a historical precedent: in the seventeenth century, some 6,000 lanterns were installed on Paris streets as part of a crime reduction program.

The CPTED concept is focused upon the interaction between human behavior and the "built environment," including both natural and constructed elements. The physical design of an environment can facilitate surveillance and access control of an area and can aid in creating a sense of property awareness (territoriality). Proper space definition through the design or utilization of barriers can:

1) extend the area over which one feels a proprietary interest and responsibility so that this area overlaps that of other responsible citizens or entities;

2) increase the ability to perceive when one's territory is potentially threatened and permit action on that perception; and

3) provide a potential offender or intruder with a perception that he or she is trespassing on someone else's domain, thereby deterring the individual from criminal behavior.

When possible, the CPTED approach emphasizes natural access control and surveillance created as a by-product of the normal and routine use of the environment. It seeks to deter and prevent crimes and attendant fears by careful design of the environment. Various security techniques and procedures can be added to complement and/or supplement the natural aspects of security accomplished with CPTED.

TYPES AND UTILITY OF PHYSICAL BARRIERS

Physical barriers are of two primary types: natural and constructed. Natural barriers include bodies of water, mountains, cliffs, deserts, canyons, swamps, or other types of terrain that are difficult to travel through or over. These features of nature can be utilized to serve as primary or secondary barriers to unwanted or unauthorized entry. Constructed structural barriers include fences, walls, grills, and bars.

Regardless of type, properly used barriers can effectively accomplish the following security objectives:

1) define property boundaries;

2) deter entry;

3) delay and impede unauthorized entry;

4) channel and restrict the flow of persons and vehicular traffic; and

5) provide for more efficient and effective utilization of security forces.

PERIMETER BARRIERS AND PROTECTION

Perimeter protection is considered the first line of defense against unauthorized intrusions and the last line of defense against unauthorized exits. When constructed and operated properly, a perimeter barrier is a physical and psychological deterrent to unauthorized movement to and from the facility. While a perimeter barrier deters thefts, intrusions, and vandalism, it should be remembered that it will not stand alone as a total defense, but must be supplemented with security personnel, alarms, cameras, and other measures. Sometimes walls are constructed, but most often fences are used as perimeter barriers. Solid or semi-solid walls can be constructed out of wood, stone, cement blocks, or concrete. The advantage of walls over fences is that they are stronger and usually more resistant to forcible intrusion (especially stone or concrete). They generally can be constructed to any desired height, and they can be designed to add aesthetic qualities to the facility. Disadvantages of walls include the restriction of perimeter visibility (which negatively affects security unless restricting visibility is the objective, e.g., in a high-security research and development compound) and the fact that they are usually more costly to construct than conventional fencing. Additionally, the type of barrier selected for security may be dependent on, or at least tempered by, the presence of natural barriers such as waterways and cliffs, or by the proximity of adjacent properties and activities. If, for example, the property being protected borders a public sidewalk or is located in a shopping center, physical barriers would be inappropriate and perhaps impossible because of legal and/or code restrictions.

A perimeter barrier should be constructed in as straight a line as possible. This is particularly critical if a solid wall barrier is used, as any angle or turn would offer a place of concealment for a would-be intruder. At least 50 feet on either side of the barrier should be clear of structures and obstructions so that there are no possible places of concealment for persons, burglary tools, or property. Such a clear zone provides for adequate observation on either side of the barrier. The integrity of the barrier must be assured by regular inspection and required maintenance, and supplemented by other security measures appropriate to its location and usage.

It is not uncommon to find the presence of a double line of perimeter barriers surrounding a facility. This is particularly true for facilities requiring high security. The spaced, double-perimeter barrier line allows for a clear zone between the barriers, increases the physical and psychological deterrence relative to intrusion, permits a confined area for patrol by security personnel and/or security dogs, and facilitates the utilization of various intrusion detection and alarm devices.

Even though perimeter barriers are obvious definitions and identifiers of property boundaries and restricted areas, appropriate postings should be affixed to the surface of the barrier at regular intervals. Postings might read "Keep Out," "Private Property," "Danger," etc. In any case, the added psychological deterrent value of the sign is worth the effort. Perimeter barriers are perhaps the best example of a security device that has an equal, and often greater, value as a safety device. There are numerous situations and activities in industrial manufacturing that require the presence of barriers for the primary purpose of channeling and keeping people out of unsafe environments. Very often such barriers are required by law, regulations and—in some cases—the insurance carrier. In general, the owner/manager of property has a legal and moral duty regarding the safety of persons on or about the premises under their control. Proper utilization and placement of barriers and postings are key components in satisfying such requirements.

TYPES OF FENCING

Fencing is generally used to secure larger areas. There are three basic types of fencing that are traditionally used to secure areas: chain-link, barbed wire, and barbed tape (concertina wire). The type used will depend on the permanence, appearance, and degree of security desired and/or needed. Chain-link fencing is usually used to secure permanent facilities; barbed wire is used for less permanent facilities or to mark perimeter boundaries; and barbed tape is used for emergency or short-term situations, or in combination with other types of fencing. Other, less common, types of metal fencing utilized for security include: welded mesh (each intersection of the mesh or link is welded, meaning that every wire must be cut to gain access), balustrade fencing (vertical metal spaced posts topped by a rail) and various other configurations of fencing designed to identify property lines and deter entry/exit.

CHAIN-LINK FENCING

A properly installed and maintained chain-link fence is attractive due to its clean, neat lines. Chain-link fencing poses less of a safety hazard than some other types of fences because it does not have barbs, yet its small openings still prevent intrusion. In addition, it is easily and inexpensively maintained.

Where a chain-link fence is used, it should be constructed of No. 1 or heavier gauge wire with mesh openings no larger than two inches across. The fence should be at least eight feet high. The fence should be topped with a "V" top guard, or 45 percent shaped arm bars and three strands of barbed wire attached on both sides to inhibit unauthorized entries or exits (see Figure 9.1). A variation of the barbed wire top guard is barbed tape, a thin ribbon or strand of metal to which razor-like projections of metal are attached. The fence should be permanently attached to metal posts anchored in concrete. When possible, the fencing should be buried at least two inches (this is especially true if the soil is soft or sandy), or a strong wire should be woven through the lowest sections of the wire mesh to inhibit attempts to go under the fence. Where the fence crosses rugged terrain such as streams, hills or ditches, precautions must be taken to ensure that there are no unprotected openings beneath the fence. Chain-link fencing is normally constructed of galvanized steel or aluminum.

Figure 9.1
Chain-Link Fence with "V"-Shaped Topguard

BARBED WIRE FENCING

Barbed wire is seldom used to secure perimeters due to its unsightliness and the danger of inflicting wounds on those who come into contact with it. When barbed wire is used to mark boundaries, it should be approximately five feet high and consist of three or four tightly stretched strands attached to firmly embedded posts standing from six to 10 feet apart.

On occasion, barbed wire has been used to secure restricted areas. When used, great care should be taken to ensure that it is not vulnerable to compromise. Barbed wire fences, when used for security:

> . . . should be not less than seven feet in height plus a top guard, tightly stretched and firmly affixed to posts not more than six feet apart. Distances between strands should not exceed six inches . . . the bottom strand should be at ground level to impede tunneling and the distance between strands should be two inches at the bottom gradually increasing to six inches at the top (Mombossiee, 1968:88).

Barbed wire is not recommended for securing perimeters, due to the aforestated drawbacks. However, it is useful on occasion in supplementing natural barriers. For example, barbed wire can be installed along the side of a cliff to further deter intrusions. It also can be used to add security to roof lines or as a top guard on wood, concrete block, or brick walls. Barbed wire, like chain-link fencing, is constructed of galvanized steel or aluminum.

Barbed Tape (Concertina Wire)

Finally, barbed tape (concertina wire) can be rolled into a two- to five-feet diameter coil, clipped together at intervals and used as a barrier to secure a perimeter or roadway. When used as a barrier by itself, effectiveness can be increased by laying one roll on top of two other rolls or laying two rolls side by side, giving the barrier added height and/or width. Regardless of how it is used, the roll(s) of barbed tape should be anchored to the ground periodically with ground stakes, and if more than one roll is used in conjunction with another, they should be attached together. For the most part, barbed tape is one of the most difficult barriers to penetrate because it is extremely flexible and affixed with an ample supply of exceedingly sharp barbs (see Figure 9.2).

Barbed tape is unsightly and hinders ground maintenance. Thus, it is not usually recommended for use as a permanent on-ground barrier. However, barbed tape has its advantages and can play an important role in perimeter security. It can be laid and picked up rather easily by one person; thus, it is an extremely mobile barrier that can be deployed very quickly with minimal effort in emergency situations. For example, if the permanent barrier, such as a chain-link fence, is damaged as a result of an automobile accident or a tree falling onto the fence, barbed tape can be used to hinder intrusion until the permanent barrier can be repaired. Also, it can be used to temporarily block roads or paths, e.g., in emergency crowd control or traffic control situations. However, considerable care must be taken in the on-ground usage of barbed tape, particularly in high activity areas or where children might be present.

Figure 9.2
Barbed Tape (Concertina Wire)

Provided Courtesy of American Security Fence

Barbed tape is commonly used as a top guard atop a chain-link security fence in lieu of barbed wire. When used in this manner, it retains its value as a psychological and physical deterrent, has the utility of permanence, and is not a danger to the typical passerby. It also can be found as an on-ground barrier either to the interior of a fence or solid perimeter barrier, or between a double perimeter fence or solid barrier line.

In contrast to other security tools that can be blended with the surroundings, barbed tape is dangerous and it looks the part. Because of its inherent value as a psychological deterrent and emergency tool of considerable utility, though, it is worthy of being kept in stock.

BUILDING SURFACE SECURITY

The second line of defense against intrusion is the building itself. A separate perimeter barrier may not be feasible, and even if present, may not always deter the determined intruder. As in every situation regarding the protection of assets, various contributing factors will come into play to determine the appropriate degree of security.

A building or structure should be considered an entity that can be intruded from at least six different directions: the roof, the flooring, or any of the sides. Thorough efforts should be made to completely secure the exterior of the structure with primary emphases on roof access, doors, entrances, windows, and miscellaneous openings such as fire escapes, vents, delivery areas, and trash portals.

ROOF

One of the most vulnerable sections of any structure is the roof. Roofs, especially flat roofs, are difficult to observe, thus giving intruders ample time to make an entry. In addition, roofs are generally constructed of easily compromised materials such as wood, tar, and shingles. If possible, roofs should be constructed with a high pitch, which makes them difficult to maneuver on and easy to observe from the ground. Second, the number of attachments to the structure (such as fire escapes) should be kept to a minimum, making it more difficult to gain access to the roof. Finally, the area immediately adjacent to a structure should be clear of obstructions so that it would be difficult to hide ladders, ropes, and other tools of entry. If points of potential access are reduced, the probability of illegal entry is reduced.

WINDOWS

A large percentage of illegal entries and exits occur through windows. Because windows are probably the most vulnerable part of any structure, if possible, the number of windows should be reduced to an absolute minimum and all windows on the ground level eliminated. Of course, this is not possible or even desirable for certain businesses. In such cases, efforts should be taken to "target harden" the windows, that is, make it as difficult as feasible to gain entry through the windows.

One common practice is to install metal grates or bars over windows. However, these precautions are frequently inadequate because of flaws in installation. When installed improperly, bars or grating can easily be pried from the face of the building. Proper installation includes the use of steel connector bolts that extend completely through the wall and connect with the bolts on either side via a piece of flat steel and nuts with lock washers (see Figure 9.3).

Many factories and businesses rely on steel-framed windows with steel strips holding each window pane. If such windows are used, care should be taken to ensure that the lock cannot be maneuvered from outside through a broken pane of glass. Moreover, these windows only offer minimum resistance to a good prying device.

For the most part, protective windows and window coverings are helpful in deterring the nonprofessional criminal. The Federal Bureau of Investigation's Uniform Crime Reports consistently point out the large numbers of burglaries and larcenies that are committed by juveniles and nonprofessional criminals.

Figure 9.3
Protective Metal Grate on Ground-Level Windows

DOORS

Doors, too, are used frequently to obtain illegal entry. Wooden doors, unprotected doors, and unlocked doors are the primary targets. All doorways should be adequately lighted and free from obstructions. Metal or metal-over-wood doors are best because they are most difficult to penetrate. When a wooden door is used, door construction should be heavy to prevent intruders from kicking or smashing a hole in the door. Doors should be installed properly and, when possible, secured with a standard deadbolt lock and a horizontal retaining bar. Retaining bars should be installed on all doors except those used most often.

Finally, special precautions should be taken with door frames and hinges. Frequently, fire codes require that doors open outward, which causes the hinges to be exposed to the outside, making the door vulnerable. In this case, special hinges or hinges that have been welded or pinned should be used to thwart illegal entry (see Figure 9.4). If the door frame is constructed of wood or similar materials, it may be possible to pry the door open by springing the door loose from the frame near the locking mechanism. A common automobile jack can be used to spring a door from a lightly constructed frame. Therefore, the door frame should be constructed of solid materials and supplemented with an intrusion detection device.

Figure 9.4
Pinning a Door to Prevent its Removal

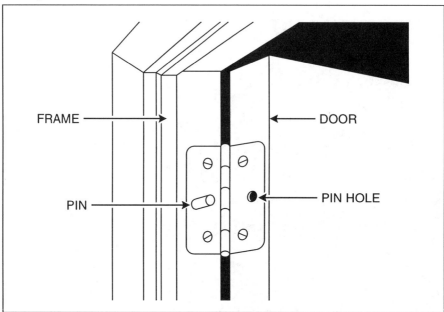

Garage or overhead doors not controlled by electric motors should also receive special consideration. These doors should be constructed of metal when possible. The lock should consist of solid sliding metal bars on either side of the door that are secured with padlocks to inhibit unauthorized exits and entries.

With any structure there are always a number of miscellaneous openings such as fire escapes, vents, storm sewers, or trash portals. These openings also should be secured. Even the smallest opening may jeopardize security for a building. For example, a common practice of intruders is to find or make a small entry point and allow a small juvenile or adult to go into the facility to facilitate access for others. This is a primary reason why all exits—safety permitting—should utilize locks that require keys on the inside as well as the outside.

Finally, special precautions must be taken where buildings adjoin other structures. Wherever this occurs, it may be possible to gain entry to a second, connecting building by knocking a hole through the common wall. This frequently occurs where a low-security structure adjoins a high-security structure containing valuables. The entry usually occurs during the evening hours or weekend when the intruders have ample time to work unnoticed. If this situation exists, then security must be supplemented either by reinforcement of the common wall, installation of intrusion detection devices, or particular attention to the adjacent structure.

PERIMETER ACCESS CONTROL

Perimeter security measures, in addition to and in concert with perimeter barriers, must satisfy the needs and goals of the organization being protected.

By its very nature, an organization depends on people for its success and existence. Any effort to restrict or control the movement of people through its gates, turnstiles, and doors must complement the daily activities and operations of the facility. Perimeter security controls must allow for authorized—and preclude unauthorized—entries and exits.

Effective and efficient access control (i.e., controlling the coming and going of people and vehicular traffic) requires a blend and balance of people, equipment, and procedures. The ways in which access control can be accomplished vary from very simple to highly sophisticated, depending on the level of security required, ranging from a lock and key, to a security employee checking identification badges, to magnetically encoded cards that operate electronic locking devices, to closed circuit television monitoring individuals.

Thus, a corollary to the need for access control is the need for a system of identification to determine who is authorized for entry and who is not. Access lists, personal recognition, security identification cards and badges, badge exchange procedures, and automated electronic devices are among the methods used to identify and control the movement of employees, vendors, visitors, and clients.

The determination of what perimeter security device or procedure to use, and where, when and how to use it, is dependent on the following considerations:

1) Existing perimeter barriers—fencing; walls; natural barriers; number, location, and type of perimeter openings.

2) Organizational type—manufacturing; retail; healthcare; transportation; etc.

3) Organizational attributes—size; location; schedule of operation; goals.

4) Management—philosophy of management; managerial guidelines and policies; managerial support.

5) Employees—employee acceptance; employee training; number of employees.

6) Risk factors—environmental variables; crime problems; vulnerability assessments; criticality factors.

7) Resources—money; equipment; human resources.

Obviously, there is no universal solution to perimeter security and access control. For example, a hospital environment has different needs and objectives than a manufacturing facility. While there will be a similar application of basic security principles and concepts in both locations, the manner and measure of their utilization will be very different. Several of the following chapters will include discussions relative to the application of personnel, equipment, and procedures to perimeter security and access control.

Parking

When a business or facility maintains a perimeter barrier and provides parking for clientele and employees, the parking area should be located outside the perimeter barrier. This greatly reduces the chances that undesirable persons will enter the facility because it is easier for security personnel to monitor persons when they must pass through a security point on foot. Such an arrangement provides for excellent security and maximum control.

When management provides parking facilities, they should be immediately adjacent to the perimeter barrier and security personnel posts. Even though outside the facility proper, parking areas can be enclosed by perimeter barriers. This allows for better security of employee vehicles and enhances the personal security of employees and others going to and from the workplace. The parking area should be well illuminated, and in high-risk situations, monitored by closed circuit television and/or secured by an electronic access control system. This allows security personnel maximum observation over the facility and deters thefts and vandalism without the need to deploy additional personnel to the parking area. Moreover, if mobile patrols are used at the facility, they should periodically patrol employee parking lots to enhance deterrence.

Vehicular Traffic Control

It is extremely important not only to control the comings and goings of employees, but also to control all vehicular traffic within the facility. The fewer entrances there are, the easier it is for security to control the perimeter. Thus, only those entrances necessary to the facility should be opened. In most cases, perimeter barriers have primary entrances (those used on a regular basis) and secondary entrances (those used for special occasions such as deliveries to isolated warehouses, maintenance activities, or emergencies). Security personnel should be posted at primary entrances unless those entrances are otherwise secured. Secondary entrances should remain secure or locked, and be patrolled on a regular basis to guard against intrusion. It is seldom necessary to post permanent security personnel at a secure secondary entrance.

Entrance or gate security is especially important in relation to shipping, receiving, and disposal. When receiving shipments, gate security is particularly helpful in directing facility traffic. Additionally, if there is need for tighter security, an escort can be provided for incoming carriers at the gate until they reach their destination or leave the facility. Security personnel also can be used to monitor shipping by comparing shipment invoices with loads, either on a continual or random basis. This is especially important in a facility where expensive and easily convertible goods are produced. Such a procedure inhibits drivers and plant employees from falsifying invoices. For example, this may have offset an incident in which employees in a Kentucky firm used such a method to steal truck axles. The axles were obtained through falsified invoices and sold to coal trucking firms.

Another problem area that confronts security is the disposal of waste and trash. Frequently, employees or other persons hide merchandise, goods, etc., in trash bins where it is later retrieved. Therefore, periodic security checks should be made of trash and disposal areas, and vehicles carrying trash should be checked periodically as they leave the facility. Such precautions will reduce employee thefts and aid in maintaining control over the facility compound.

At all times, security must work closely with management to marry the needs of management with those of security. It is important for the security staff to constantly monitor the facility's operations so that adjustments can be made in security as changes in facility operations occur.

PERIMETER SECURITY PERSONNEL

In most cases, perimeter barriers are supplemented with security personnel. They serve to boost the deterrent effects of the perimeter barrier and to monitor the barrier for defects. The posting of sentries or stationary personnel and the use of mobile patrols are largely dependent upon the nature of the facility being secured and the degree of security desired. In cases where the perimeter barrier encloses an extremely large area, it may not be efficient to post stationary personnel to observe the total barrier structure. In isolated or semi-isolated areas, protection may be reduced to infrequent mobile patrols or only an occasional maintenance check. However, if a high degree of security is desired, it may be necessary to increase patrols and/or stationary posts, or might be more cost-effective to construct a second or inner perimeter barrier closer to an area requiring a higher level of security.

Although security personnel are highly reliable as a means of enhancing security, they are extremely expensive compared to many other security measures. Therefore, if possible, the security personnel force should be reduced to the lowest effective level via the use of other security devices such as perimeter/interior alarm systems, clear zones, high deterrent barriers, and security lighting. It must be remembered, however, that security personnel are invaluable when a situation requires an immediate and/or innovative counteractive response.

PERIMETER CLOSED CIRCUIT TELEVISION (CCTV)

While not an intrusion detection system, closed circuit television (CCTV) is very useful in accomplishing physical security. Placement of television cameras at critical locations can provide direct visual monitoring from a centralized vantage point. In manufacturing and industrial settings, CCTV can be used to monitor gates, employee entrances, loading docks, receiving areas, parking areas, and hazardous operational areas. It is particularly applicable to retail settings, where various arrangements of cameras—visible and concealed—can be used to observe customers to check for shoplifting, employees for dishonest or improper cash/merchandise transactions, and areas outside the store (e.g., parking lot, receiving docks, etc.) for various illegal activities. A visible camera serves as a psychological deterrent to would-be thieves and intruders alike. A CCTV system ordinarily consists of a television camera, monitor, and electrical circuitry. Additional equipment might include a pan and tilt unit that gives remote control of the camera, an automatic scanning mechanism or a videotape unit to record on tape what the camera sees. The videotape can serve as a valuable tool of evidence in trial proceedings because it portrays the actual crime as seen by the camera. A CCTV system may be composed of one camera and one monitor, or several of each. The sophistication of the system can be enhanced by utilizing various kinds of camera lenses, full color equipment, and/or cameras that have the capability of producing clear images under minimal light conditions. Additionally, CCTV systems can be used in conjunction with various types of intrusion detection devices to complement their effectiveness level.

Because the primary means of providing perimeter protection is most often personal observation, CCTV offers a means of increasing the surveillance capability of security personnel. The presence of visible CCTV camera units increases the perceived risk for the potential intruder that any attempt to enter the facility will be observed. CCTV is discussed in more detail in Chapter 11.

PERIMETER INTRUSION DETECTION

Perimeter intrusion detection systems are used to provide electronic surveillance and monitoring of established perimeter lines. Such systems can be employed to provide continuous surveillance of perimeter lines to signal the entry or attempted entry of persons into a protected area. The decision to use perimeter intrusion detection will depend upon various factors:

1) the characteristics of the environment to be protected;

2) the vulnerability and criticality of the area to be protected;

3) the desired level of protection;

4) other security measures currently being used;

5) availability of personnel; and

6) cost-effectiveness.

There are several alarm and sensory devices applicable to perimeter intrusion detection. Given the proper environmental and operational conditions, various alarm system devices that are primarily used for internal purposes are adaptable to external usage. However, factors such as weather conditions, animals, birds, blowing objects, etc., must be considered prior to selecting a perimeter intrusion detection system. The level of effectiveness and reliability of the equipment with respect to the environment in which it is to be used must be determined prior to its purchase. Some of the systems currently being used to provide perimeter protection and access control include: electromagnetic capacitance devices, narrow-beam radio frequency devices (which operate similar to a photoelectric system), infrared or laser beam photoelectric systems, vibration/movement detection devices, and seismic devices.

PERIMETER SECURITY LIGHTING

Security lighting systems form an illuminated psychological barrier through which a would-be intruder must pass. They attempt to reproduce at least some measure of semblance of daytime conditions during the hours of darkness. It is a fact that intruders and criminals do not want to be caught in the act, and lighting, more so than any other type of security hardware, raises the risk factor of being observed, identified, and/or apprehended. Lighting used in concert with perimeter barriers significantly improves the effectiveness level of intruder deterrence and detection. A security lighting system that has been properly selected, installed, and operated is perhaps the most efficient (both in usage and costs) and effective tool available to the security manager. Without it, he or she is "in the dark"—an environment well suited to crime and criminal acts.

Figure 9.5
Street Light Innovations

Date	Place	Light Source/Lamp
1558	Paris, France	Pitch-burning lanterns, followed by candle lanterns
1690	Boston, Massachusetts	Fire baskets
1807	London, England	Gaslights
1879	Cleveland, Ohio	Brush arc lamps
1905	Los Angeles, California	Incandescent
1935	Philadelphia, Pennsylvania	Mercury vapor
1937	San Francisco, California	Low-pressure sodium
1952	Detroit, Michigan	Fluorescent
1967	Several U.S. cities	High-pressure sodium

The effectiveness of perimeter security measures is weighed and balanced by the potential intruder's discernment of the perimeter barrier, the lighting system, the CCTV camera, the intrusion detection system, and the security personnel as being significant or minimal psychological deterrents, physical impediments, and/or detection devices. If the security system is properly designed within the context of the environment and potential threats to its integrity, it will be effective in accomplishing the objectives for which it was intended.

The first street lighting system was initiated in Paris, France in 1558 when pitch-burning lanterns were placed on some of the main streets. An ordinance was passed requiring citizens to keep lights burning in windows that fronted streets (Tien, O'Donnell & Barnett, 1979:3). In 1805 the National Light and Heat Company started using gas lighting in London; two years later gas lamps were used to illuminate public streets.

Today, even the smallest communities provide for street lighting in their budgets. As protective lighting in the public sector has developed, it has come to serve many functions. The National Evaluation Program on Street Lighting Projects outlines the varied uses:

- Impact Objectives of Street Lighting Systems (Tien et al., p. 3)

- Security and Safety
  —Prevent Crime
  —Alleviate Fear of Crime
  —Prevent Traffic (Vehicular and Pedestrian) Accidents

- Community Character and Vitality
  —Promote Social Interaction
  —Promote Business and Industry
  —Contribute to a Positive Nighttime Visual Image
  —Provide a Pleasing Daytime Appearance
  —Provide Inspiration for Community Spirit and Growth

- Traffic Orientation and Identification
  —Provide Visual Information for Vehicular and Pedestrian Traffic
  —Facilitate and Direct Vehicular and Pedestrian Traffic Flow

While the above goals are obviously the concerns of law enforcement, they are also the concerns of security management, because the same situations and/or problems exist within this area of responsibility.

PLANNING CONSIDERATIONS

For the most part, protective lighting serves three distinct purposes. First, for the facility owner or manager, it can serve to advertise the business product or service during the evening hours. In terms of security, this frequently causes problems because the security manager is more interested in protection of the facility than in aesthetics. For example, a security manager would probably prefer flood lamps mounted near the roof, out of reach of potential intruders, and directed downward exposing a large area immediately adjacent to the structure, whereas a business or facility manager would prefer flood lights mounted at ground level and directed upward toward the building surface, illuminating its exterior and possibly an identifying sign. When protective lighting must also be used for advertising purposes and aesthetics, it most often can be integrated effectively with the overall design of the total system.

Second, protective lighting is used to facilitate pedestrian and vehicular traffic within a compound. For example, roads, entrances, exits, pathways, and parking facilities should be illuminated during the hours of darkness. Again, a conflict may arise when the same lighting is used to promote both safety and security. A pattern of lights adjacent to a structure that is used to provide visibility for vehicular traffic may not be the best arrangement to promote security for the structure itself.

Finally, security lighting is deployed to deter unauthorized entries and exits from the facility. When it does not deter, it should aid in the subsequent discovery and apprehension of intruders. The commission of a crime includes three elements: desire, ability, and opportunity. Protective lighting affects desire and opportunity. It serves as a psychological barrier—reducing a perpetrator's desire and decreasing opportunity by aiding apprehension.

Thus, protective lighting serves a number of purposes. In order to achieve the most advantageous use of lighting, a considerable amount of joint planning by facility managers, security managers, and engineers must take place. Plans should be inclusive of a preventive maintenance program designed to ensure that inoperative luminaires (units producing the light) will not be tolerated. A common method of preventive maintenance for a protective lighting system is a systematic group replacement program of luminaires at 70 to 80 percent of normal rated life.

PROTECTIVE PERIMETER LIGHTING

Protective perimeter lighting is an essential element of a complete, integrated physical security program. The application, placement, and level of security lighting depends on the specific location and structure to be protected. The type of perimeter (e.g., a fence line, a building wall, isolated or semi-isolated) is a determining factor in deciding which lighting system to utilize (see Figure 9.6). Good perimeter lighting, wherever it might be located, is achieved by adequate, even light upon bordering areas, glaring lights in the eyes of potential intruders, and relatively little light on security personnel and their patrol routes or stationary posts. Protective security lighting should enable security personnel to observe activities around and inside the facility without being "in the spotlight" themselves.

The lighting used for perimeter security will not be the same as that used for illuminating streets, roadways, or work areas. While almost any level of lighting is helpful, proper levels of intensity, coverage, and placement are necessary to maximize the effectiveness and efficiency of lighting types and sources. Lighting units should be placed in positions that offer maximal coverage and security for the unit being used. For example, lighting for perimeter fence lines should be located inside the facility, directed outward, and located so as to achieve the needed level of coverage both inside and outside the perimeter. Such placement also provides a measure of security from vandalism and sabotage for the lighting unit itself.

Figure 9.6
Perimeter Lighting Requirements

Type of area	Type of lighting	Width of lighted strip (ft)	
		Inside fence	Outside fence
Isolated perimeter	Glare	25	200
Isolated perimeter	Controlled	10	70
Semi-isolated perimeter	Controlled	10	70
Non-isolated perimeter	Controlled	20-30	30-40
Building face perimeter	Controlled	50 (total width from building face)	
Vehicle entrance	Controlled	50	50
Pedestrian entrance	Controlled	25	25
Railroad entrance	Controlled	50	50
Vital structures	Controlled	50 (total width from structure)	

(Department of the Army, 1979:91)

As previously stated, lighting is inexpensive to maintain and can sometimes be employed to negate or reduce the need for more expensive security measures. However, the nature and substance of protective lighting is that it serves to deter potential intruders. As such, it cannot stand alone. It must be supplemented by other security measures.

VISUAL FACTORS

In planning for an effective protective lighting layout, there are four visual factors that must be taken into consideration—size, brightness, contrast, and time (Healy, 1968:136-139). The lighting layout depends on the desired degree of security and the nature of the objects and environment being secured.

Size—Generally, larger objects require less light than smaller objects. The larger the object, the more light it will reflect, thus requiring less illumination.

Brightness—Brightness refers to the reflective ability of the object or structure being illuminated. Light colors such as white reflect more light than dark colors such as black or brown. Thus, a building painted white would require less light than a comparable building constructed of dark brick. Additionally, the texture of the objects under observation affects needed light intensity. Coarsely textured objects tend to diffuse light, whereas smooth-surfaced objects tend to reflect light, reducing the need for higher intensity protective lighting.

Contrast—Contrast refers to the relative shapes and colors of objects under observation in relation to the total environment. If there is contrast between the objects being secured and the immediate environment, observation is much easier than if there is little relative contrast.

Time—Time refers to the fact that greater illumination is required for areas that are visually complex or crowded. If there are many objects, a lot of very dark objects or a limited number of contrasting backgrounds, it will be more difficult to scan an area quickly—particularly for extended periods of time. Open, uncluttered spaces, on the other hand, require less light because the observer has more time to observe and focus on seemingly foreign objects.

In planning protective lighting patterns, it is important to consider all four of these visual factors. During the planning stages, various data should be collected (Department of the Army, 1979:83):

1)   descriptions, characteristics, and specifications of the various incandescent, arc, and gaseous discharge lamps;

2)   lighting patterns of the various units;

3)   typical layouts showing the most efficient height and spacing of equipment; and

4)   minimum protective lighting intensities required for various applications.

LIGHTING TERMINOLOGY

When comparing various lighting systems, it is important that one be familiar with the terminology used in rating the effectiveness of various lighting units or sources of illumination. Some of the more commonly used terms are:

Candlepower: One candlepower is the amount of light emitted by one standard candle. This standard has been established by the National Bureau of Standards and is commonly used to rate various systems.

Lumen: One lumen is the amount of light required to light an area of one square foot to one candlepower. Most lamps are rated in lumens.

Foot-candle: One foot-candle equals one lumen of light per square foot of space. The density or intensity of illumination is measured in foot-candles. The more intense the light, the higher the foot-candle rating for the light.

Brightness: Brightness refers to the ratio of illumination to that which is being observed. High brightness on certain backgrounds causes glare, and low brightness levels on some backgrounds makes observation difficult. Brightness, therefore, should not be too low or too high relative to the field of vision.

On a clear day during the middle of summer the sun supplies approximately 10,000 foot-candles to earth. This intensity can be measured in clear, non-shadowed areas such as open fields. At the same time, the amount of illumination under a shade tree is approximately 1,000 foot-candles. At night, the average living room is reduced to approximately five foot-candles.

TYPES OF PROTECTIVE LIGHTING

Protective lighting is divided into four general categories: (1) continuous lighting, (2) standby lighting, (3) movable or mobile lighting, and (4) emergency lighting. The type of lighting selected will depend upon the nature of the security problem and the characteristics of the situation to be protected.

CONTINUOUS LIGHTING

Continuous or stationary lighting is the most common type of protective lighting. Continuous lighting is the installation of a series of fixed luminaries so that a particular area is flooded with overlapping cones of light. There are two methods of deploying continuous lighting: glare projection and controlled lighting.

Glare Projection Lighting

Glare projection lighting involves lights aimed in the direction of the potential intruder so that observation is impaired when looking into the facility or structure. Figure 9.7 illustrates glare projection lighting on a perimeter fence line, but it also can be mounted on the surface of a building or other structure and directed outward. However, when using this method of lighting, regardless of where it is employed, particular caution must be taken to ensure that adjacent operations or traffic are not impaired. In most circumstances, glare projection lighting is limited to those areas of the perimeter that are isolated, where the desired area of coverage can be accomplished without interfering with facility or exterior activities. Glare projection lighting is a strong deterrent to potential intruders because observation into the secured area is difficult and security personnel cannot easily be seen in the comparative darkness of the facility proper. Utilization of a glare projection lighting configuration compounds both the physical and psychological deterrent effects of the perimeter barrier. Within appropriate limitations, this method can be useful in other applications because it increases the visual powers of security personnel while reducing that of potential intruders.

Figure 9.7
Perimeter Protection by Glare Projection Lighting

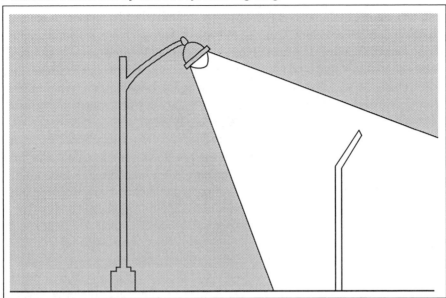

Floodlights, which can be arranged to illuminate a wide horizontal area, are the most common source of glare projection lighting. As already mentioned, the best location for installing perimeter lighting units is inside the facility where security for the fixtures is afforded by the perimeter barrier. However, it may be necessary to mount the lighting unit on posts or other apparatus along the fence, wall, or building surface. As always, the exact placement of lighting units will depend on the desired degree of security, the physical attributes of the facility being protected, and the nature of the immediate environment.

Figure 9.8
Perimeter Protection by Controlled Lighting

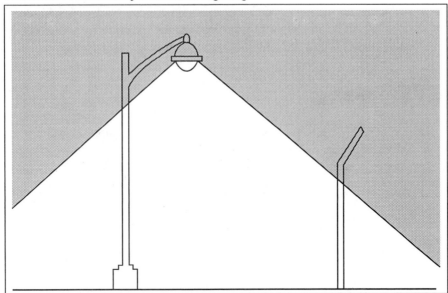

Controlled Lighting

Controlled lighting lights a particular area in a controlled fashion. It is used to light facilities or areas that cannot or should not utilize glare projection lighting. Frequently, outward-projected glare projection lighting cannot be used because it creates a dangerous situation for adjacent activities. For example, the structure may be adjacent to a highway, parking lot, or workplace. Where glare lighting may be dangerous or improper for the activities performed, some form of controlled lighting is appropriate (see Figure 9.8).

Controlled lighting is installed and located in the same manner as other perimeter lighting units, but is directed primarily downward and along the line of desired coverage, thus reducing the amount of glare. A common shortcoming of controlled lighting is that it often illuminates the facility being secured and thus the activities of security personnel.

STANDBY LIGHTING

Standby lighting configurations are similar to continuous lighting except that standby lights are not continuously lit, but instead are manually or automatically turned on in specific, predetermined situations. The lighting may be activated when suspicious activity is observed or when it is suspected that an intruder may be lurking about.

MOVABLE LIGHTING

Movable lighting is a manually operated, mobile system of lighting. Movable lighting should be available to supplement continuous or standby lighting. It also should be available to enhance security operations where a significant level of security is not normally provided. For example, it is particularly useful during an operation at an infrequently used loading dock facility or a short-term construction project having valuable on-site equipment.

EMERGENCY LIGHTING

Emergency lighting refers to a system that more or less duplicates all of the above systems. It is generally used in situations in which regular lighting is inoperable during power outages or emergencies. Such a system must include its own power source.

TYPES OF LIGHT SOURCES

The types of light sources most commonly used for security purposes are: incandescent (or filament) lamps and gaseous discharge lamps. Gaseous discharge lamps include mercury vapor lamps, sodium vapor lamps, metal halide lamps, and fluorescent lamps. The selection of a particular type of lamp depends upon the nature of the environment and the desired level of security. Figure 9.9 shows the historical development of light sources and some of the characteristics of various types.

Incandescent or filament lamps are common glass lightbulbs in which light is produced by the resistance of a filament to an electrical current. These bulbs are commonly used in homes and the workplace. Their use is somewhat limited in security systems because of their low rated life and their lower lumens per electrical watt rating (as compared to gaseous discharge units).

Gaseous discharge lighting sources are more efficient than incandescent lamps. Mercury vapor lamps, developed in early 1900s, emit a blue-green light and are commonly used to light both interior and exterior work areas because the light color is not as distracting to the human eye as is the light produced by other types of gaseous lamps. Sodium vapor lamps, similar in construction to the mercury vapor lamps, are the most efficient lamps in use today. As noted in Figure 9.9, high-pressure sodium lamps produce up to 140 lumens of light per watt and have a rated life of 15,000 hours. One problem with these lamps is that they emit a golden yellow light that is somewhat harsh and inappropriate for work areas. However, because of their efficiency of output and rated life, these lamps provide excellent perimeter security lighting. Today, many streets in high-crime areas use sodium vapor lamps. Metal halide lamps are similar in nature to sodium vapor lamps. They emit a harsh yellow light that can be extremely distracting. They contain sodium, thallium, indium, and mercury gases. Fluorescent lamps have a rated life of up to 14,000 hours, but they do not produce as much light as some of the gaseous discharge lamps. They are appropriate for work areas because the light is not as distracting as some of the other gaseous discharge lamps.

Although gaseous discharge lamps are the most efficient, one problem that qualifies their application for security purposes is the amount of time it takes them to reach full illumination. On the average it takes most gaseous discharge lamps approximately four minutes to warm up and become fully operative. If power is interrupted, it can cause the security lighting system to become ineffective for a short period. Incandescent lamps do not have this problem and fluorescent units reach full output in a matter of seconds.

Figure 9.9
Historical Development of Street Lighting

Lamp Description	Date	Rated Life for Street Lighting Service	Initial Lumens Per Watt
Arc			
Open carbon-arc	1879	Daily trimming	—
Enclosed arc	1893	Weekly trimming	4-7
Flaming arc			
Open	—	12 hours	8.5 (d-c multiple)
Enclosed	—	100 hours	19 (a-c series)
Magnetite (d-c series "luminous arc")	1904	100-350 hours	10-20
Filament			
Carbonized bamboo	1879	—	2
Carbonized cellulose	1891	—	3
Metallized (gem)	1905	—	4
Tantalum (d-c multiple circuit)	—	—	5
Tungsten (brittle)	1907	—	—
Drawn tungsten	1911	—	9
	1913	—	10
Mazda C (gas-filled)	1930	—	14-20
	1915	1,350 hours	10-20
	1950	2,000 hours	16-21
		3,000 hours	16-20
Mercury Vapor			
Cooper-Hewitt	1901	Indefinite	13
H33-1CD/E	1947	3,000 hours	50
H33-1CD/E	1952	5,000 hours	50
H33-1CD/E	1966	16,000 hours	51
H36-15GV	1966	16,000 hours	56.5
Low-Pressure Sodium			
NA 4 (10,000 lumen)	1934	1,350 hours	50
NA 9 (10,000 lumen)	1935	2,000 hours	56
	1952	4,000 hours	58
	1975	—	180
Fluorescent			
F100T12/CW/RS	1952	7,500 hours	66
F100T12/CW/RS	1966	10,000 hours	71
F72PG17/CW	1966	14,000 hours	68
F72T10/CW	1966	9,000 hours	63
High-Pressure Sodium			
	1965	6,000 hours	Over 100
	1975	15,000 hours	140

The selection of a particular type of light source depends upon a number of conditions. Some of these conditions are:

1) cleaning and replacement of lamps and luminaries, particularly with respect to the costs and means (e.g., ladders, mechanical "brackets," etc.) required and available;

2) the advisability of including manual and remote controls, mercury, or photoelectric controls;

3) the effects of local weather conditions on various types of lamps and luminaries;

4) fluctuating or erratic voltages in the primary power source; and

5) the requirement for grounding of fixtures and the use of a common ground on an entire line to provide a stable ground potential.

TYPES OF LIGHTING EQUIPMENT

Basically, there are four types of lighting equipment available: floodlights, street lights, fresnel units, and searchlights. The usage of a particular type depends upon the particular security situation or problem.

Floodlights are amenable to a variety of security needs because they can project a significant amount of light over both small and large areas. Floodlights are manufactured with a variety of beam widths, enabling one to select the appropriate light unit to meet the needs of the task at hand. Because floodlights emit a directed beam, they are appropriate for use in situations that call for glare projection lighting, i.e., the illumination of boundaries, buildings, and fences.

Street lights produce a diffused light rather than a directional beam. They generally produce little glare and are appropriate for use in controlled lighting situations. They are commonly used to light parking lots, thoroughfares, facility entrances and boundary perimeters where glare lighting is undesirable. Additionally, because of their efficiency, they can be deployed to light large areas at minimal cost.

Fresnel units emit a fan-shaped beam of light, covering approximately 180 degrees horizontally and 15 to 30 degrees vertically. When glare projection lighting is required on the perimeter line and the pattern of coverage is very restricted, fresnel units may be the only workable alternative. Additionally, fresnel units are very adaptable as the lighting unit of choice for areas between buildings and other structures. An inherent feature of the fresnel lighting unit is that little to no light is lost vertically.

Searchlights are lighting units that produce a highly focused beam of light. They can be stationary, mobile or handheld units, depending on the requirements of application. Because searchlights can be aimed in all directions and are often mobile, they are commonly used to complement existing lighting systems. Searchlights are commonly found on security vehicles.

DESIGNING A LIGHTING SYSTEM

Selection of a lighting system and fixtures depends upon the purpose of the system and the environment. For example, if a perimeter fence is at least 100 feet from structures or work areas and there is an adequate clear zone on the outside of the perimeter, then either controlled illumination or glare projection techniques are appropriate. Both techniques would adequately illuminate the barrier. If posted security personnel or patrol units are used, their positions and activities should be outside the interior illuminated areas. The same principles apply to semi-isolated and non-isolated perimeters. Lighting should be deployed to provide full illumination of the barrier and an adequate clear zone, but it must not interfere with the activities of security personnel, traffic, or other activities that take place in or around the perimeter.

In illuminating buildings, special care must be taken to ensure that operational activities are not inhibited. If the structure facade contains no windows, then glare projection toward the facility from ground or elevated units—or a combination of the two—perhaps would be appropriate because they would provide maximum exposure of the building surface and ground area to the structure. When this type of lighting is used, care should be taken to ensure that intruders do not sabotage individual units. If security personnel are posted, or there are windows or other openings that reveal work activities, then glare projection from roof-mounted units would be more appropriate. Additionally, glare projection lighting is not appropriate at vehicular or personnel entrances because the glare would create an unsafe condition. Here, controlled lighting is most appropriate. Efforts also must be made to ensure that the lighting coverage does not leave shadows in which intruders could hide.

Entrances for pedestrian and vehicular traffic should be illuminated with controlled lighting. The lighting should be intense enough to enable security personnel to recognize persons and examine credentials or other papers. If the entry point has a gate house, the level of illumination should be situated lower, projecting outward so that those approaching will have difficulty discerning the activities of security personnel.

All work areas within the facility, especially those where materials and merchandise are being loaded and unloaded, should be illuminated with some form of continuous lighting. If the work area and the immediate surrounding area are illuminated, it will reduce the probability of inventory shrinkage resulting from employees hiding the property there. Obviously, the areas having critical and valuable assets and those with the greatest vulnerability should receive particular attention for security lighting. Internally (within buildings) a system of appropriate "night lights" should be present for both security and safety.

Appropriate mechanisms and procedures for controlling the security lighting system must be in place if it is to be both efficient and effective. Normal control of an outside protective lighting system is accomplished either by manual or automatic means. Provided that adequate personnel are present, a manually operated system may be the least expensive and simplest method. In some cases it may be more desirable to control the system automatically. Automatic systems employ time switches, with or without automatic seasonable time correction, and photoelectric controls that operate as a result of change in the amount of light at dawn and dusk. Manual switches should be provided for systems that are automatically controlled, in case there is an equipment failure or emergency. There are a number of commercially available lighting control software programs.

OTHER PERIMETER BARRIER APPLICATIONS

As previously mentioned, in many facilities it is often necessary to construct perimeter barriers around equipment or operations that are especially hazardous or unsafe. These barriers serve to provide limited or restricted access into areas defined as hazardous. A prime example of a safety barrier is that of a fence surrounding the immediate area of an electrical substation. Only those people who have both the need and the level of expertise to enter the substation should be allowed to do so.

Another, perhaps more obvious, aspect of safety is derived from the perimeter barrier surrounding the total facility. Most industrial and manufacturing operations do not allow the general public to come and go as they please. The operations and equipment utilized are dangerous to the untrained and unaware nonemployee. The perimeter fence serves to deny free and unobstructed entry into what is essentially a hazardous environment. Freedom from interference by outsiders is assured and organizational liability for improper or inadequate safety measures is avoided.

Perimeter barriers are also utilized to complement and supplement fire prevention efforts. Areas containing very hazardous materials or processing operations can be separated from the larger facility, thereby allowing for more stringent control of fire regulations and standards. Mobile barriers are particularly useful when temporary conditions exist that are especially hazardous or unsafe. Barbed tape and other movable barriers can be utilized to block traffic lanes or isolate particular areas.

SUMMARY

This chapter has addressed some of the essential considerations for establishing Primary Zones of Protection. Perimeter security refers to factors such as the landscaping, physical barriers, fencing, building surfaces, windows, security lighting, and so on. Perimeter security represents the first Primary Zone of Protection for any type of facility because its is the first line of defense against intrusion and the last line of defense against inventory shrinkage. It is the responsibility of security personnel to evaluate both the natural and constructed elements of a facility and work with the features that reduce vulnerability to security and safety hazards. Paramount to the success of maintaining the Primary Zone of Protection is for security to be aware of new and important developments in technology and methods used to provide this first level of protection.

DISCUSSION QUESTIONS

1. Why protect the perimeters of property?

2. Relate the significance of asset values and vulnerability to perimeter security.

3. What are some of the security considerations relative to site layout and building placement?

4. What are the general rules regarding landscaping for security purposes?

5. Discuss the concept and attributes of CPTED.

6. What security objectives can be accomplished through the proper use of barriers?

7. List some of the attributes of chain-link, barbed wire, and barbed tape fencing.

8. Elaborate on the key areas of building surface security.

9. How and why should a person-identification system be integrated with perimeter barriers and access control?

10. What are some essential considerations regarding the selection of perimeter security devices and procedures?

11. In what ways can security be increased and/or improved in employee and customer parking areas?

12. Discuss both the advantages and disadvantages of using security personnel (as compared to other alternatives) to enhance security.

13. Why is security lighting an effective means of accomplishing a significant level of perimeter security?

14. In addition to security, what other applications and objectives can be satisfied with perimeter barriers?

15. What is the impact of street lighting on security and safety?

16. Briefly discuss the three purposes of protective lighting.

17. The commission of a crime includes three elements. List these elements and discuss the role of protective lighting in diminishing crime.

18. List and describe the four general categories of protective lighting.

19. Discuss some of the conditions that should be taken into consideration when selecting a light source.

20. What is the most advantageous position and location for a perimeter lighting unit?

21. Why should one be concerned about the relative size and color of objects?

22. Compare the utilization of incandescent lamps to gaseous discharge units for security purposes.

23. Discuss the aspects of controlling and maintaining a security lighting system.

REFERENCES

Crime Prevention Coalition. (1990). *Crime Prevention in America: Foundations for Action.* Washington, DC: National Crime Prevention Council.

Department of the Army. (1979). *Physical Security Manual FM-19-30.*

Healy, R.J. (1968). *Design for Security.* New York, NY: John Wiley and Sons.

Mombossiee, R.M. (1968). *Industrial Security for Strikes, Riots and Disasters.* Springfield, IL: Charles C Thomas.

Tien, J.M., O'Donnell, V.F. & Barnett, A. (1979). *Street Lighting Projects.* Washington, DC: National Institute of Law Enforcement and Criminal Justice.

Waller, I. & Welsh, B.C. (October, 1998). "Reducing Crime by Harnessing International Best Practice." *National Institute of Justice Journal.*

Crime Prevention and Secondary Zones of Protection

10

INTRODUCTION

The physical security of any property or facility relies very heavily upon locking and access control devices. These devices vary greatly in appearance, as they do in function and application. A lock, regardless of its type, is primarily a delaying device. The degree of delay presented by the lock depends upon its quality of construction and installation, and the skill of the would-be intruder. Access control includes the methods and procedures utilized to provide facility security by restricting and controlling the movement of persons into and/or within a protected area. Both of these technologies have become extremely sophisticated over the last 20 years.

HISTORY OF LOCKS

Archaeological digs have uncovered Egyptian pin locks that date back approximately 3,000 years. These ancient locks were wooden and required keys so large that they were carried over the shoulder. Although molded from wood and quite large by today's standards, the ancient locking devices of Africa, Egypt, and China utilized the same elements of alignment and positioning of component parts that are basic to modern locks (see Figure 10.1).

THE WARDED LOCK

Warded locks, the simplest of which has only three moving parts (i.e., the bolt, an arm that moves the bolt and the key that activates the bolt area) were in use as early as the first century, B.C. Warded locks of this same basic design can be found on the doors of many homes built prior to World War I and on cheap, low-quality padlocks (see Figure 10.2 and 10.3).

281

Figure 10.1
Types of Locks

Figure 10.2
Warded Lock

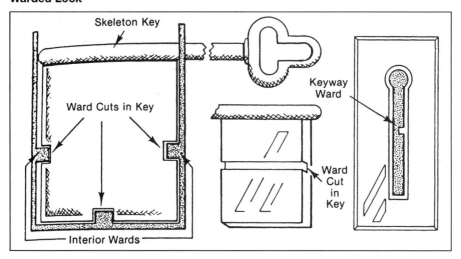

THE LEVER TUMBLER LOCK

The lever tumbler lock came into use somewhere around the turn of the nineteenth century. This device added one more step in the degree of security and protection afforded by locks. The introduction of the lever tumblers (movable pieces of metal between the key and the lock bolt) resulted in a locking device that was more complex and harder to pick or force open.

Figure 10.3
Low-Quality Warded Padlock

Figure 10-4
Early Lever Tumbler Lock

THE WAFER LOCK

Wafer locks, often referred to as disc-tumbler locks, were developed after the advent of the lever tumbler lock. Their development added yet another step in lock sophistication. Flat, spring-loaded metal discs in the plug of the lock bind the core of the cylinder shell to the cylinder housing. When the proper key is inserted into the keyway, the disc tumblers align and withdraw their protruding parts, allowing the plug to be turned. Today, wafer locks can be found on automobiles, desks, cabinets, padlocks and similar items.

THE PIN TUMBLER LOCK

In the 1850s, Linus Yale, Jr., developed what is known today as the pin tumbler lock. Based upon the ancient principles established by the Egyptians, Yale constructed an inner lock mechanism characterized by tumblers in the form of metal pins that rest vertically inside individual chambers housed in the cylinder shell. Today, the pin tumbler lock has become the most common type of mechanical locking device used for protection and security purposes.

MECHANICAL LOCK TERMINOLOGY

A prerequisite of lock security is a basic understanding of the terminology of lock security. The following terms are helpful in understanding the more common mechanical locks, locking devices, keys, functions, and lock features.

Astragal—A molding to cover the opening (gap) between two meeting doors.

Barrel key—A cylindrical, hollow key with a projecting bit. The hollow end fits over and turns around a post in the keyhole.

Bit key—A key with a bit projecting from a round shank. Similar to the barrel key but with a solid rather than hollow shank.

Blank—An uncut or unfinished key.

Bolt—The part of the lock that is moved into a locked or unlocked position.

Bottom pins—The lowermost pins of a pin tumbler cylinder.

Bow—The handle or head of a key.

Cam—The part of a lock that activates the bolt as the key is turned.

Code-operated locks—Combination locks in which no keys are used; operated by pressing a series of numbered buttons in the proper sequence.

Combination—The arrangement of numbers to which a combination lock is set, or the arrangement of cuts on a key.

Cremone bolt—A vertical throw lock that locks the door or the sash into the frame at the top and bottom.

Cuts—The indentations made in a key to make it fit the tumblers of a lock.

Cylinder guard—A covering or device used to protect the cylinder of a lock.

Cylinder housing—The external case of a lock cylinder (also called the shell).

Cylindrical lock—A lock set having the cylinder(s) in the knob (also known as lock-in-the-knob).

Deadbolt—A lock bolt having no spring action that becomes locked against end pressure when projected.

Dead-locking latch—A spring bolt with an anti-shim device, which prevents the latch from being retracted by pressure applied to it.

Disc tumbler—A double-acting, spring-loaded flat plate designed to slide in slots in the cylinder plug.

Double-bitted key—A key having cuts on two sides.

Driver—The uppermost pin in a pin tumbler lock.

Hasp—A fastening device consisting of a metal loop and a slotted hinged plate.

Header—Top cross member of a door frame.

Heel of a padlock—The stationary end of the shackle on a padlock.

Jamb—The vertical member(s) of a door or window frame.

Key—An instrument for operating a lock.

Keyhole—The opening in a lock to receive a key.

Latch—A device that secures or attaches but does not lock.

Lever tumbler—A flat piece of metal made to fit straight cuts in appropriate keys.

Lock—A device for fastening or engaging two or more objects that includes a means of manipulating the device into a locked or unlocked position.

Locking dog—The part of a padlock that engages the shackle and holds it in a locked position.

Locksmith—A person engaged in selling, installing, repairing, modifying, and designing locking devices and keying systems.

Master pin tumbler—Cylinder pins, usually flat on both ends, used to set a lock to accept more than one key.

Mortise lock—A lock with a bolt made for installing in a cavity cut in the edge of a door.

Padlock—A portable lock with a hinged or sliding shackle, normally used with a hasp.

Pin tumbler springs—Coil compression springs placed above or behind the driver pins in a pin tumbler lock.

Pin tumblers—Important parts of a pin tumbler cylinder, denoted as bottom pins, master pins, and drivers.

Plug—The round core of the lock cylinder, which receives the key and rotates when the key is turned.

Retractor—The part of a lock that is attached to the bolt that moves to an unlocked position.

Rim lock—A lock designed to fit on the surface of a door.

Shackle—The hinge or sliding part of a padlock.

Shearline—The area between the housing and the plug that is normally obstructed by the tumblers and becomes unobstructed by use of the proper key, allowing the plug to rotate.

Shoulder—The projection(s) on a key between the bow and the blade that prevents the key from passing too far into the cylinder.

Shell—The external case of a lock cylinder without the plug (also called housing).

Skeleton key—(See Warded key)

Spring bolt—A bolt that retracts upon contact with the lip of the strike and then extends into the hole of the strike to secure the door in a closed position.

Strike—A metal plate installed on or in a door jamb to receive the bolt.

Throw—The outward movement of a bolt; the distance it travels.

Wafer lock—A locking device utilizing a flat metal wafer tumbler.

Ward—An obstruction that prevents the wrong key from entering or turning a lock.

Warded key—A key used in warded locks that bypasses obstructions in the keyway (often called a skeleton key).

COMMON LOCKING DEVICES

Locking devices can provide varying degrees of security. A lock will go a long way toward discouraging burglars, thieves, or other would-be criminals; however, it must be the right lock selected on the basis of its use in conjunction with environmental activities and other security hardware.

The following is a discussion of various locking devices that are easily obtainable and frequently used in homes, businesses, and industry. However, it is important to point out that a locking device can be designed to operate in a specific manner, yet at the same time be any of a number of different types. For example, the single-cylinder locking device described below can be a lever lock, a wafer lock, or a pin tumbler lock, or it can be a rim lock, a mortise lock, or a cylindrical lock. Thus, the security function of the lock depends upon the type of locking device, and the desired level of security depends upon the kind of locking mechanism employed.

SINGLE-CYLINDER LOCKING DEVICES

Single-cylinder locking devices are installed in doors or placed on other objects that must be secured from only one side. They require a key to open them from one side. The most likely application of a single-cylinder locking device would be on a solid door far enough away from glass panels or windows to prevent an intruder from breaking the glass, reaching in and opening a locked door from the other side. Most locking devices of this type have a thumb turn on the inside of the door. This permits easy locking or unlocking of the door from the inside, which is sometimes important for reasons of safety or quick exit. However, the same ease of exit is available to any intruder who gains entry through a window, roof, or another door.

DOUBLE-CYLINDER LOCKING DEVICES

The double-cylinder locking device is installed on doors that must be secured from both sides. A key is required to unlock or lock the door from either side. A door with glass panels or next to glass panels would likely be fitted with a double-cylinder locking device. Such locking devices would not be feasible for use in schools, hospitals, fire exits, etc., where for reasons of safety their use would be prohibited.

EMERGENCY EXIT LOCKING DEVICES

These devices allow for quick exit without use of a key, usually by means of a horizontal "panic bar." The device locks the door against entry and in many instances no external hardware is apparent at all. Frequently these emergency exits have an alarm device that sounds when the exit is used.

RECORDING DEVICES

While not a locking device within itself, a recording device is a feature that can be incorporated into most locking devices, either mechanically or electrically, to provide for a record of door use by time of day and/or by key used.

VERTICAL THROW DEVICES

Several variations are available in vertical throw locking devices. While a vertical throw bolt can be found in a rim lock, single-cylinder lock, double-cylinder lock, and others, there are variations that do not require a key and can be opened or locked only from the secured side of the door. An example of this is the "police lock," which uses an angled bar that fits into a receptacle in the floor and is secured to the door at the other end. Another variation is the vertical bolt, which can be installed in the floor or on the bottom of the door in a recessed position, and is pushed down into a floor well to prevent the door from opening (see Figure 10.5).

Figure 10.5
Vertical Throw Cremone Bolt

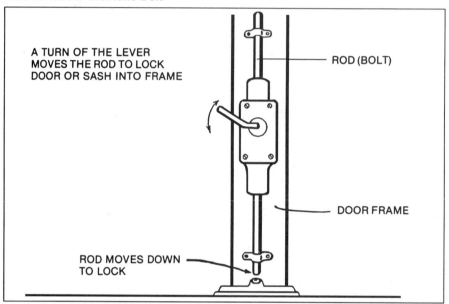

SEQUENCE LOCKING DEVICES

Sequence locking devices are used to ensure that doors are closed and locked in a predetermined order. Each door is locked in its sequence and no door can be locked until its designated predecessor has been locked. This locking system prevents the phenomenon of the forgotten unlocked door.

KEY-OPERATED LOCKS

A key is the standard method of accomplishing entry through a locked door and the normal way of locking it. Most key-operated locks are made to accept only one key that has been specifically designed and cut to fit it. Of course, a lock of any function, quality, or effectiveness is worthless if keys are not available to those who need them. Keys and keying systems are generally divided into control keys, submaster keys, master keys, grand master keys, change keys, and maison keys.

The process of master keying consists of splitting the bottom pin into two or more segments so that keys of different combinations (cuts) will raise bottom pins and master pins to a shearline (see Figure 10.6). As the number of locks in a master key system increases—and as the progressive stages of master keying increase—so does the number of master pins and shearlines. With each increase there is a resulting decrease in security, because the chances of arriving at or finding a shearline for each pin by picking is increased sharply. There can be progressive stages of master keying. The following keys are found in a simple master key system.

Control Key—A control key is used primarily for maintenance or replacement purposes. It is cut in such a way that it operates to remove the core from the housing. Another core requiring a different key can then be inserted in a matter of seconds. This method is particularly useful when security of the facility has been compromised by lost or missing keys.

Submaster—A submaster key will open all locks of a particular area or grouping within a given facility. The locks may be those of one floor of a multi-storied building, a particular operation (such as administration) or even one building out of several.

Master Key—The master key will open all the locks in the facility that are incorporated into the master key system.

Grand Master Key—The grand master key will open every lock in a keying system involving two or more master key groups.

Change Key—The change key is the standard type of key that fits a single lock within a master key system or any other single lock unnumbered by such a system. Numerous locks can be "keyed alike" to accept only one key.

Figure 10.6
Change Key and Master Key Illustrate Different Shearlines and Pin Alignment

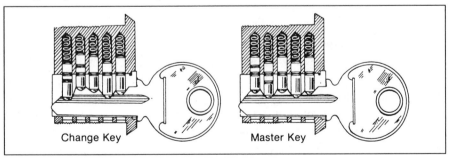

Change Key   Master Key

Maison Key—The maison key is a type of submaster key system very common in apartment houses and office buildings. Tenants are given a single key that operates both their apartment or office door and the main entrance door lock. This is done by using a lock having pin tumblers with many segments in each tumbler. The more tenants, the more shearlines there must be in the lock at the main entrance. This is usually a very insecure system of keying. A better and more secure practice would be to provide each tenant with one key for entrance to the building and a second key for entrance into the individual office or apartment.

KEY CONTROL

There must be a system that accounts for and controls every key and every lock. Thus, responsibility and authority must be given to someone (preferably the security department) to maintain records, provide for a key depository, control issuance and retrieval, and investigate any misuse or loss of facility keys and locks (see Figure 10.7).

Figure 10.7
Typical Keying System used in Industry

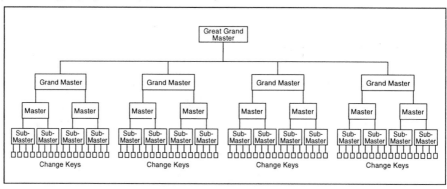

LOCK AND KEY RECORDS

A written record and log should be maintained on all keys and locks. The issuance of keys should be controlled to provide keys only to those persons who have been shown to need keys that allow entry into an area of the facility. When a key is issued, the record should indicate the key number, the name of the person to whom it is assigned, the holder's position within the company, the date of issuance and any other relevant data that might be beneficial.

A log should be kept regarding maintenance and repairs on locks, lost keys, and actions taken to remedy any problems detrimental to lock and key security. All keys should be identified and secured in a high-security key cabinet. All unissued and duplicate keys should be protected in this manner. As a general rule, the fewer keys issued, the more effective the security control.

KEY DEPOSITORY

It would be optimal if no keys to a facility ever left the premises. Though this is often not feasible or appropriate, the closer this goal is approached, the greater the degree of security a facility has over controlling access to its property. Keys taken off the property can be duplicated, lost, or used in other ways to compromise the security of the facility. An ideal method would be for all employees who were issued keys each day to turn in or deposit the keys with security personnel at the end of the work day. A log of daily issuance and return would ensure that all keys were accounted for and properly issued.

MASTER KEY CONTROL

Master keys must be treated with greater care and security than change keys. The loss of a master key can threaten the entire keying system. While a primary rule of key security is to minimize the number of keys given out, it is particularly imperative relative to master keys. Keys must not be issued for convenience, nor should they be issued on the basis of an employee's position. Indiscriminate issuing of keys is little better than having no locks at all.

Master and submaster keys should not be marked or inscribed in any way that would identify them as master keys. A coding system for purposes of internal identification should be developed that would be known only by the necessary personnel. Whenever a key is issued to an employee, a lock becomes vulnerable to being compromised through the theft, loss, improper use, or duplication of the key. The loss or theft of one master key can result in considerable cost of re-keying and extensive losses of property.

COMPUTERIZED KEY CONTROL

In a computerized key system, keys are secured in a wire panel linked to a computer. The system's data bank includes names, code numbers, and other identifying information that allows users to access certain keys as programmed. For example, a microcomputer-based key control system can be programmed for various levels of authorization and user access. A feature of the system is its accountability, as an automatic audit trail is made of each key transaction. Even unsuccessful attempts to access keys can be noted. A significant advantage of computerized key control is that it takes the guesswork out of who has what key and how long they have had it.

COMBINATION LOCKS

A combination locking device, provided it is of good quality and installed properly, generally affords a greater degree of security than most key-operated locking devices. Commonly found on safes, vaults, high-security storage cabinets, and high-security padlocks, dial-type combination locks do not require keys to operate the lock mechanism. Generally, the integrity and security of a combination lock can be more effectively maintained than a key-operated lock, though combination locks are capable of being compromised if the combination should fall into the wrong hands or the storage unit is improperly used. The combination must be subject to effective security procedures and controls, and must be restricted to an absolute minimum of personnel. Any written record of the combination must be afforded the highest security and, if feasible, no such record should even be kept. Combinations should be changed periodically as a matter of procedure and changed after the termination or transfer of any employee who knows the combination or has worked in close proximity to the storage unit. Naturally, a change should be made at any other time there is a suspicion that the security of the combination has been compromised.

PUSH-BUTTON COMBINATION LOCKS

Mechanical push-button combination locks are common fixtures in apartment complexes, industrial settings, and retail operations. They require no key, but instead are operated by pushing protruding buttons in the proper sequence and combination. They also can be fitted with a key to allow "by-pass" usage by maintenance workers and authorized personnel. The level of security afforded by push-button combination locks depends on the affected degree of security given to the combination and the relative quality of the lock purchased (see Figure 10.8).

Figure 10.8
Push-button Combination Lock

Provided Courtesy of Simplex Access Controls

PADLOCKS

Padlocks have a variety of security applications: perimeter fenceline gates, building doors, storage areas, equipment lockers, employee lockers, and tool chests. They can be incorporated into a master key system or they can be operated by a change key. A key-operated padlock has three basic parts: the key, the casing, and the shackle. The combination padlock, similar in construction except for the keyway, is fitted with a revolving combination dial. The casing houses the internal locking mechanism and the keyway (or in the case of a combination padlock, the revolving discs and gates). The shackle is the locking or holding part of the padlock (see Figure 10.9).

Figure 10.9
Parts of a Padlock

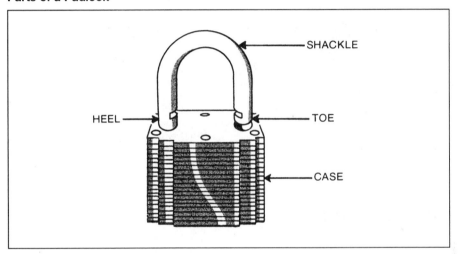

The internal locking mechanism of a padlock can be of the warded, lever, wafer, or pin tumbler type. It is generally agreed that a pin-tumbler padlock having at least five pins in the cylinder offers the greatest degree of security from manipulation. However, the secure padlock also must be constructed of case-hardened metal that is resistant to cutting and hammering. The padlocks shown in Figure 10.10 represent the more secure and government-approved padlocks.

Like other locking devices, a padlock is effective only when the surface on which it is installed is of solid construction. Care also must be taken that the hasp be case-hardened and installed properly (i.e., mounting screws or bolts should not be exposed when in locked position).

The procedures for the control and security of keys or combinations to padlocks should be incorporated into the total key control program. Routine inspection and maintenance of padlocks is important because padlocks are often exposed to the environment and isolated on seldom-used perimeter gates. Security personnel on regular patrol should routinely inspect such padlocks and the attached fastening device (e.g., a chain or manufactured lock bracket) for evidence of compromise or deterioration.

Figure 10.10
Government-Approved Padlocks

(Sargent & Greenleaf, Inc., 1990)

THE PIN TUMBLER CYLINDER SYSTEM

Most locks manufactured today utilize the pin tumbler cylinder system. Pin tumbler cylinders are constructed of five basic components, the most visible part being the shell or housing encompassing the entire cylinder. This shell contains three to seven cylindrical chambers drilled from the top down through to the smaller circumference opening near the bottom. This opening is filled with a cylinder plug, which has an equal number of cylindrical chambers aligned directly with those drilled in the shell. This plug is retained in position by means of a cam, or tailpiece, normally attached with two screws from the back. This cam is the activating lever for the lock itself. In order for the cylinder to function as a security device, a set of coil springs and pin tumblers are placed within each chamber, from the top of the shell down. They are sequenced with a coil spring applying pressure to the driver pin. Normally, the driver pin is flat on both ends; however, various configurations such as mushroom shapes or cone shapes are used to provide additional pick resistance. The driver pin is pressed against the top of the bottom, or combination, pin, which is flat on one end and tapered to a point on the bottom side. The point at which the driver pin meets the bottom pin is known as the shearline.

When the proper key is inserted within the lock, the springs force bottom pins downward into the cuts in the top of the key. The depth of each cut in the key is proportional to the depth of the bottom pin, which means the top of each bottom pin will align itself at the breaking point between the plug and the cylinder shell, allowing the key to turn the plug without resistance (see Figure 10.11).

The versatility and security provided by the pin tumbler cylinder make it applicable to the simplest or most complex keying system.

Figure 10.11
Standard Pin Tumbler Lock Mechanism Without Key

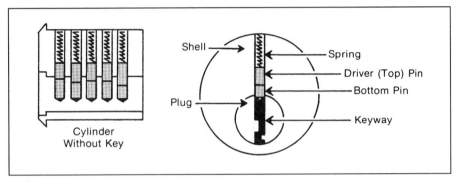

TYPES OF LOCK BOLTS AND LATCHES

The latch or bolt is the part of the lock that secures the door, window, gate, or other movable object to a stationary fixture. All bolts or latches, regardless of type, serve the same function. Bolts and latches can operate in two directions: horizontally across the door into a strike or vertically into a frame or floor receptacle at the top or bottom of the door.

DEADBOLTS

A deadbolt does not contain a spring, and must be moved manually into its locking position within the strike by turning a key or thumb turn. It does not automatically move into the strike and secure the door when it is shut, and when the bolt is thrown into a locked position, the door cannot be closed until the bolt is withdrawn. Deadbolts are usually rectangular in shape and provide a greater degree of security than latch devices. Quality of construction and the throw of the bolt are important determinants in the level of security provided by deadbolt mechanisms. The greater the outward movement of the bolt—whether vertical or horizontal, the greater the degree of security.

SPRING-LOADED LATCHES

There are two kinds of latches: the spring-loaded latchbolt and spring-loaded deadlatch. The spring-loaded latchbolt provides a minimum level of security because the latch can be withdrawn from the strike whenever force is applied directly to the latch itself. When the door is closed, the spring bolt automatically retracts upon contact with the strike and then extends into the hole of the strike, securing the door in a closed position. Spring-loaded latchbolts have a beveled end to allow this depression of the latch to occur. They are withdrawn from the strike by a turn of a key, thumb turn, or doorknob.

The spring-loaded deadlatch operates in the same manner as the spring-loaded latchbolt except it has an extra latch piece (bar) located on the side of the latchbolt, which when depressed against the edge of the strike, locks the deadlatch into position. These are sometimes called deadlocking latches or spring bolts with an anti-shim device.

LOCK VIOLATIONS AND PHYSICAL ASSAULTS

The most common method of gaining entry through a locked door or other fixture is to use a key. This is the expected and proper way to gain legal entry. However, numerous methods and techniques are utilized by would-be intruders to defeat locks. Surreptitious violations and physical assaults include picking, jimmying, prying, jacking, smashing, carding, and drilling.

Picking	A method by which the lock's tumblers are manipulated through the keyhole with small tools made for this purpose. Picking a cylinder is usually done in one of two ways. One method is by using a small tool called a **tension wrench**, which puts tension on the plug and hence on the pins that are impeding the rotation of the plug. With this tension tightening the pins, the pick is inserted to raise the pins, one by one, to the right level until the shearline is obtained for all the pins (see Figure 10.12). Another method is **raking**, by which a thin metal tool is inserted into the keyway and then quickly pulled out, jostling the pins into position.
Carding or "loiding"	The action of slipping or shimming a spring bolt with a piece of celluloid. The spring-loaded latch, which does not resist end pressure, is particularly susceptible to carding.
Jacking	The action of placing an ordinary car jack horizontally between the door jambs and applying pressure. A poorly constructed, insufficiently fortified door will spread, pulling the bolt or latch out of the strike and allowing the door to open.
Jimmying and prying	Activities accomplished by using tools such as crowbars, small jimmy bars, large screwdrivers, or other metal tools to

pry the door away from its frame or break the locking mechanism. Vertical locking devices will usually offer greater resistance to jimmying than horizontal devices.

Figure 10.12
Tools Found in Lockpicking "Kit"

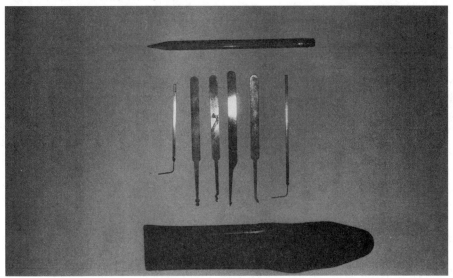

Smashing   A physical assault on the door. It can range from total destruction of the door to the breaking of a glass panel in the door to gain access to a thumb turn. Various tools can be used to smash a door. This technique, while not very common in heavily populated areas, frequently occurs when a building or other structure is located in an area so remote that the noise created by the smashing does not serve as a deterrent to forcible entry.

Drilling   This involves the use of a drill to destroy the locking mechanism, e.g., drilling a hole through the keyway destroying the pin tumblers, discs, wards, etc.

Wrenching   A technique used to force or break a key-in-the-knob lock device open. By using a pipe wrench applied to the knob, enough force can be exerted to break the locking mechanism. Key-in-the-knob locks are available that have a retaining device which, when broken, allows the knob to be free-turning so that no pressure is placed on the locking mechanism.

Hinge pin removal   Another method of bypassing a locked door. Hinges should be located on the interior side of the door, but if they are exposed, they should be welded in position or otherwise made nonremovable.

OTHER TYPES OF LOCKS

Basic Door Locks

Crime statistics indicate that approximately 50 percent of all illegal entries occur through a door. It is axiomatic, then, that doors should be secured against surreptitious violations and physical assaults. The same is true for windows, which are the point of entry in another 40 percent of illegal entries.

Windows and doors are chosen as points of entry because they are the most common openings in buildings, yet it is not always apparent why one building is broken into as opposed to another. Anyone desiring illegal entry into a building or facility, in many if not most cases, bases his or her choice on the perceived ease of entry and the level of risk involved. The perceived ease of entry has a direct relationship to the level of risk-taking, in that the easier the break-in, the lower the level of risk. It is in this regard that the level of security provided by locking devices is apparent. Some locks are simply more secure than others and present a more formidable barrier to surreptitious violations and physical assaults.

Key-in-the-Knob Locks

One of the most frequently used door locks today is the key-in-the-knob. However, unless a top quality unit is used, it is almost always the least secure type of door lock. The typical key-in-the-knob lock purchased in the hardware store is susceptible to failure or breakage when force is applied to the knob or to the lock cylinder (see Figure 10.13).

Figure 10.13
Key-in-the-Knob Lock

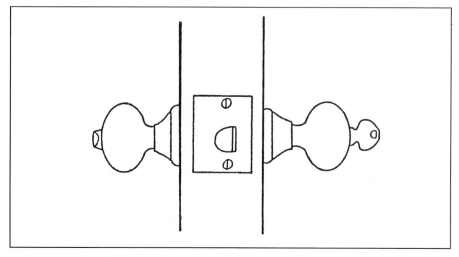

AUXILIARY LOCKS

Auxiliary locks are locks added to a door or other opening while the existing locking device is left in place. Adding an auxiliary lock is usually the simplest way to bolster the security offered by the primary door lock. Two types of auxiliary locks are used most often.

A **rim lock** with a vertical or horizontal bolt-throw is a common auxiliary lock. When properly installed, a rim lock of the single-cylinder or double-cylinder variety with a deadbolt provides a substantial level of security. It is resistant to jimmying, prying, carding, and jacking (see Figure 10.14).

Figure 10.14
Jimmy-Resistant Rim Lock

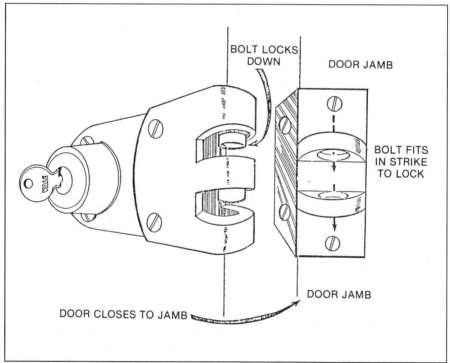

Another type of lock commonly utilized as an auxiliary lock is the **tubular lock**. The deadbolt variety, single or double cylinder, can be added with minimal difficulty and affords an improved degree of security over many primary lock types.

MORTISE LOCKS

To install a mortise lock, a cavity must be made in the door to receive the lock. The housing of the lock and bolt is made so that a hole must be cut in the edge of the door for proper installation. Mortise locks provide an acceptable level of security because most of the lock mechanism is encased in the door. They can be of the single- or double-cylinder variety and very often have additional functions, such as automatic locking capability from one or both sides of the door (see Figure 10.15).

Figure 10.15
A Standard Mortise Lock

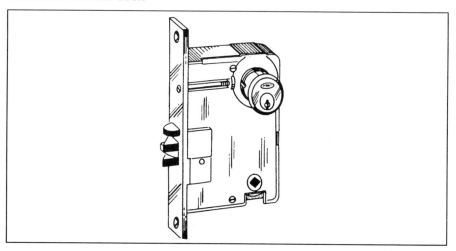

WINDOW LOCKS

There are a number of specialty locks available for windows. Most windows are provided with a latch when installed, but such latches offer little resistance to pressure. Most can be forced open from the outside with a minimal level of skill. There are both keyed and non-keyed devices that afford a greater level of security than the latch. These devices are particularly applicable to ground floor windows or those near accessible stairs, fire escapes, etc.

The sliding glass door found in many homes and offices is both a window and a door. Generally, the manufacturer-supplied locking mechanisms of these units do not afford a high level of security. There are a variety of locking devices available for complementing the primary lock, including keyed and non-keyed devices, bars, and pinning devices. These will make it more difficult to raise, slide, or force the unit open.

ELECTROMECHANICAL LOCKS

THE ELECTRIC STRIKE

The electric strike is an electrically operated device that replaces a conventional strike plate and allows a door to be opened by the utilization of electric control switches at remote locations. Many of these systems incorporate some means of communication and/or observation between the door being protected and the remote control site. Examples are intercom systems, closed circuit television, direct observation, and electronic access control systems. Various keying and/or coding systems can be used in conjunction with electric strikes. A preventive maintenance and testing program should be present and ongoing.

ELECTROMAGNETIC LOCKS

One of the oldest locking mechanisms utilizing electrical power as an element of its operation is the electromagnetic lock. Each lock consists of two non-moving parts: a magnet and a strike plate. The magnet typically mounts on the door frame and the armature to the connecting door (the input electrical current interacts with the magnetic field to produce an average holding force of more than 1,000 pounds). Exterior doors should have mechanisms with a holding force of 1,000 pounds or more, while interior doors can be equipped with less powerful units. Various keying and control systems can be integrated and used with electromagnetic devices and systems. If an electromagnetic lock is used on an exit door, it may need to be equipped with a fail-safe egress device that can be mounted on the door or door frame. Users must press or lean on the egress device for several seconds before the door will open. An on-site alarm will sound during the delay period, and if a master control system is present, a signal will be processed as to location and status.

MICROCOMPUTER LOCKING MECHANISMS

High security locks have been developed that can generate their own internal power enabling them to be used without external power sources. The U.S. government developed these locks in response to a request for a high-security locking device that used computer technology to enhance the overall security of these locks.

The company that was able to develop this technology is the Mas-Hamilton Group located in Lexington, Kentucky. They were the first company to be able to develop the technology that would enable an electronic lock to generate its own power. The name of the lock they developed is referred to as *The X-07*. The X-07 revolutionized the industry, which previously had relied upon post-antebellum mechanical combination lock technology.

The lock generates its own electricity every time the dial is turned, enabling a microcomputer to drive the functions of the lock. The end user merely dials directly to their individual combination without having to dial a specific number of revolutions before entering the combination. If the user misses the number, they do not have to start over, but simply continue to dial until their number appears. What makes this lock more secure than conventional combination locks is that numbers randomly appear in the LCD screen. There is no relationship between the number being dialed and the dial position.

ELECTRONIC ACCESS LOCKING SYSTEMS

ELECTRONIC ACCESS KEYPAD CONTROL SYSTEMS

An early application of an electronic access control (EAC) system was the utilization of a keypad. To gain entry through a door with an electronic keypad, the user must know the correct sequence of numbers to push on the keypad before the locking mechanism will release and allow the door to be opened. Keypad codes are easily transferred to other users and thus are not highly secured. Utilization of keypad controls are common in a variety of settings, particularly residential areas, motor vehicles, and interior applications where a high degree of security is not required.

ELECTRONIC ACCESS CARD CONTROL SYSTEMS

Electronic access card control systems employ a wide variety of equipment and devices designed for entry/exit control. Equipment and systems applications range from relatively simple stand-alone units at a single entry to complex computerized systems integrated with the entire management information system. EAC card systems are found in facilities with only a few doors and cardholders as well as in facilities with hundreds of doors and thousands of cardholders. Such systems can be incorporated with a significant range and scope of automated facility and energy management systems, i.e., heat, ventilation and air conditioning, elevators, etc., along with security, fire, audio, and CCTV systems. Because most EAC systems employ cards that are unique to the individual, accounting of card usage and card users can be accomplished for purposes of payroll, tracking locations and times of usage, evaluating traffic patterns, etc. Restricted entry by location and time can be easily accomplished through card encoding and programming. The modern EAC card system utilizes a computer and is essentially a powerful input/output control system that listens and talks to digitally controlled devices (card readers) based on information/inputs from some form of identification credential (card). When the cardholder presents a valid card, the computer activates a device such as an electric strike or a solenoid in a turnstile or gate motor to allow access.

EAC CARD TYPES

Many different access control cards and encoding technologies are on the market today. They all perform the same basic function, i.e., they generate an encoded message for the system's computer to interpret and act accordingly. Although various technologies produce similar results, they vary in their relative level of security and susceptibility to moisture, heat, cold, and copying. Correspondingly, there are differences in the types of cards by construction, data capacity, flexibility, reliability, convenience, and price. Manufacturers of EAC cards may use different coding formats, but in general, the card code consists of a site code and a personal identification number. The site code identifies the location of the card reader station and the personal identification number (PIN) tags the holder of a specific card. Software in the access control system tells the computer or microprocessor what to do when a card is passed through the reader and a specific code is transmitted. The following provides an overview of the cards and operating characteristics currently being used for EAC card systems (Mourey, 1989:17A-20A):

Hollerith—One of the earliest card technologies, the punched paper or plastic card, is now most widely used as an encoded key for hotels/motels and controlled parking areas. The Hollerith card uses a series of punched holes to code information. It can be read by light passing through the holes to photo sensors or by pins dropping through the holes. It has limited storage capacity and can be as small as a credit card. Compared to others, Hollerith cards are relatively inexpensive, but quite susceptible to damage and wear from usage. Card security is minimal because they can easily be duplicated and forged. The card reader has a simple construction and experiences some problems with reliability when dirt and foreign objects obstruct the light, photo sensors, or pins.

Bar Code—The use of bar code cards for access control is limited, primarily because of poor security. They can easily be duplicated and are very susceptible to damage, requiring the user to be careful with storage and usage.

Magnetic Strip—The magnetic strip card has been in use for a number of years. A strip of magnetic tape applied to one side of the card can store large amounts of information. It is commonly used for credit cards, automatic teller machine (ATM) cards and airline ticket applications. The plastic card is relatively inexpensive (90¢ to $2.50), but is susceptible to tampering. A high coercivity magnetic strip (which has an increased capability to retain its properties) is available that reduces the possibility of card tampering. Magnetic strip readers are usually of the swipe variety, employing a reader head similar to that used in a videocassette recorder or tape recorder.

Wiegand—The Wiegand card, named after its inventor, uses a series of small-diameter wires assembled and embedded in a coded strip laminated into the card. When the card is moved through a set of magnetic fields, each wire sends an electrical pulse that is read in binary code. Most Wiegand card readers are of the swipe variety. The cards are factory encoded and are very difficult to copy, counterfeit or alter. Both cards and readers retain significant reliability through both usage and varying environmental conditions. Depending on the number of wires, the Wiegand card has tremendous capacity for information storage.

Barium Ferrite—To produce the barium ferrite card, bits of barium ferrite are magnetized and located in specific areas of a plastic card. The magnetized bits and their polarity and location determine the code. Each magnetized bit contains one bit of data, and a card usually contains 20 to 40 bits. The cards are factory-encoded and somewhat difficult to copy or alter. Readers have traditionally been of the insertion type. The average cost per card is $2.50.

Proximity—Proximity cards permit the transmission of a code simply by bringing the card near the reader. Card reader technology is complex, but units are reliable and easy to maintain. A primary problem, however, can arise if the presence of conductive materials between the card and the reader disrupts the signal transmission. Proximity cards are factory-encoded and quite difficult to copy. They are considerably more expensive than other card technologies, but offer the ultimate in convenience. The most common proximity card contains a passive or tuned circuit with an embedded antenna and chip that is energized by the radio frequency of the reader. The current cost of a proximity card is around $6.00.

Laser—Laser card technology is available but in the developmental stage as of the early 1990s. The cards are factory-encoded and can hold a wealth of data. A scanner reader unit is utilized for the laser card.

Infrared—Infrared cards are not in widespread use for security purposes. The cards are factory-encoded and considered quite secure. Encoding is accomplished by creating a shadow pattern within the card. It is passed through a swipe or insertion reader that uses an infrared scanner. The cost of the card is moderate to expensive when compared to other technologies.

"Smart" Card—Smart card technology is relatively new and quite expensive. Currently, a card costs around $20.00. It is essentially a mini-computer, i.e., a memory chip or microprocessor with enormous capacity for information storage is embedded or laser-written on plastic. Card information can be changed or added as needed. Reading and coding devices are expensive and technically advanced, making forgery and copying unlikely.

Card access systems are thus available with a variety of functional attributes, levels of sophistication, and cost considerations. The card is the "key" and the card reader is the "lock." A card access system may not be the best solution for every situation. A mechanical locking system may be just as appropriate. The advantages of an EAC card system are:

1) Card access systems can be programmed to open entrances at specified times of the day and/or week, and for specified individuals;

2) Lost cards or stolen cards can be electronically canceled by telling the system they are invalid; mechanical keying systems require the installation of new locks or new cores and the issuing of new keys;

3) Logging and tracking of card usage by location and time are easily obtained;

4) Functional attributes of card systems allow for immediate and simple resolutions to problems or situations requiring change and flexibility.

EAC SYSTEMS AND BIOMETRICS

Biometric technology consists of a validation comparison of personal physical and behavioral characteristics. The physical characteristics include retinal screening, finger imaging, hand geometry, iris recognition, face recognition, and esoteric diometrics. Behavior-based biometrics include signature dynamics, voice verification, and keystroke dynamics (Woodward, 1998:20-26).

Physiological Biometrics	Behavior-Based Biometrics
1. *Retinal Scanning:* The retina, or inner-most layer of the wall of the eyeball, is electronically scanned. The eye blood vessel pattern is mapped.	1. *Signature Verification:* Computer technology is used to record pen/stylus speed, pressure, and direction in signature and related characteristics.
2. *Finger Imaging:* An optical scanner reads the unique lines and grooves on a person's finger, then compares them to stored images.	2. *Esoteric Biometrics:* These are still in the early development stages. Examples include vein measurement, skin-pore mapping and analysis of body-odor composition. An infrared light and a special camera capture animage of the blood vessels, in the form of a tree pattern, which is then converted into data and stored in a template.
3. *Hand Geometry:* A three-dimensional record of the length, width, and height of the hand and/or fingers is made. This digital map of the outline of the hand is compared against the stored image.	3. *Speaker/Voice Verification:* The acoustic signal of a person's voice is recorded and converted to a unique digital code, which is then stored as a template.
4. *Iris Recognition:* The iris or colored circle that surrounds the pupil of the eye is recorded using video technology.	

An EAC system utilizing biometric technology typically scans or replicates the personal characteristics to be measured and compares that information to data that has been stored previously. A computer then processes, analyzes, and validates the inquiries before permitting access. Physiological biometrics deal with static, generally unchanging personal characteristics, e.g., fingerprints, hand geometry, and the retina of the eye. Being individually unique, each can be used for identification and validation purposes.

Behavior-based biometrics discern differences in the way individuals present themselves each time they write their signature, type a password on a keyboard, or speak. Again, these characteristics are uniquely personal to the degree that, at least in theory, no one else has the exact same characteristics.

Biometric access control systems can stand alone or be incorporated with card access systems. "Biometric cards" can emulate Wiegand, magnetic strip, or other card formats. The biometric data storage or template necessary for comparison can be on a card, in a biometric reader device or in a host computer (Miller, 1991:32-35). Though acceptance of biometric technology has been somewhat slow, it appears that its usage is increasing and will be an integral component of many EAC systems in the future.

VIDEO CARD IMAGING SYSTEMS

An emerging and advancing technology is video imaging, which incorporates photograph identification cards, CCTV and/or a computer video database. A computerized video database of employees and cardholders is created with a photograph of each person and corresponding information unique to the individual (e.g., name, social security number, workstation code, biometric information, etc.). A cardholder desiring access inserts his or her card into a recognition device that triggers the database to bring up the appropriate card for photograph and information comparison. The disc—video or compact—used to store the data can also be used to develop map and pictorial imaging of rooms, building, and site layout for immediate screening. A CCTV system can be used in conjunction with the system for a live comparison of a cardholder to what is in the database. The uniqueness of video imaging is apparent. Presently, the cost is considerably higher than other card access systems.

SUMMARY

Locks and access control systems are critical to establishing the Secondary Zone of Protection. The choices are tremendous and the security professional must have a fundamental understanding of their use and appropriate application for their particular situation. One of the best ways to stay informed is to attend conferences such as the International Security Technology Conference, the Exhibits at the American Society for Industrial Security's annual conference, and the International Computer Security Association. Independent labs such as Sandia National Laboratories are also useful in providing independent analysis and research of various security and computer technologies.

DISCUSSION QUESTIONS

1. Differentiate between pin tumbler locks, wafer locks, and lever tumbler locks.

2. Describe the elements of a master key system.

3. Outline and describe the responsibilities of the key control officer.

4. What are some of the important considerations regarding the use of combination locks (such as those found on safes or vaults)?

5. Describe the workings of a pin tumbler lock.

6. When should a double-cylinder locking device be used instead of a single-cylinder locking device?

7. What is the shearline?

8. Describe the parts of a padlock and the security considerations regarding its usage and installation.

9. Why is a deadbolt more secure than a spring-loaded latch?

10. Describe the operation of a push-button lock.

11. List and describe some of the ways that locks can be manipulated or bypassed.

12. Describe a typical early EAC system.

13. How does an electromagnetic lock work?

14. Describe a modern EAC system arrangement.

15. Why is a Wiegand card more functional and secure than a magnetic strip card?

16. What are the attributes of a proximity card EAC system?

17. What are at least three advantages of an EAC system over a mechanical keying system?

18. What is biometrics? How is it related to EAC?

19. What kind of advantages and positive features are offered by the computerized EAC system?

REFERENCES

Miller, B. (Sept. 1991). "The Nuts and Bolts of Biometrics." *Security Management.* Arlington, VA: American Society for Industrial Security.

Mourey, R.L. (July 1989). "It's in the Cards." *Security Management.* Arlington, VA: American Society for Industrial Security.

Sargent & Greenleaf, Inc. (Oct., 1990). *Security Products Catalog.*

Woodward, J. (Feb. 1998). "Believing in Biometrics." *Information Security, Vol. I, No. 3.*

Crime Prevention and Tertiary Zones of Protection

11

INTRODUCTION

The Tertiary Zone of Protection represents the last defense against the intruder. This zone is most often characterized by the use of electronic protection systems and/or a safe or vault. Although alarm systems are often used in both the Primary and Secondary Zones of Protection, these tertiary intrusion detection systems represent a multifaceted system designed to integrate and interface a variety of sensory and surveillance components to provide the highest level of defense.

Yet even with the advances in electronic systems and devices, physical security and protection of people and property is still a matter of degree. Given enough knowledge, equipment, and time, the determined criminal can achieve almost any objective. Many times the electronic system chosen for a given environment and/or task fails to provide the expected level of security—the burglar is not detected, the robbery alert system fails to function or the access control system is easily compromised. The selection of a proper electronic system is not a simple task, particularly if the purchaser is not a security professional and/or is unfamiliar with electronic security systems and their applications to given environments and problems. The complexity of today's electronic devices, systems, and applications can be very confusing because the average user lacks the technical background and knowledge to make an educated purchase. Thus, there is great dependence placed on the security expert and/or the representative of an electronic systems company to recommend the proper system.

Any electronic system, whether it be for intrusion detection, surveillance, environmental monitoring, or emergency alert, must be balanced against the nature and value of the property to be protected, the cost of the system, the presence and/or availability of police protection or security personnel, the integration of the system with the total environment and the desired level of security. An evaluation of the total security program and its objectives must be made so that the three major component areas of security (i.e., personnel services, security equipment, and hardware) and security procedures will be balanced for maximal utilization and effectiveness. Overdependence in one area may increase costs far beyond benefits, whereas underdependence may result in the creation of a "weak link" in the total security system.

Any protection system—whether personnel services, equipment and hardware, procedures, or some combination thereof—must satisfy two practical tests in any organization. The system must: (1) work the way that it was planned and implemented without major problems, and (2) be economically feasible for the assets and facility being protected. Any protection system that does not work properly or is not economically feasible should be evaluated for improvement or elimination.

ELECTRONIC ALARM SYSTEMS: FUNCTIONS AND SELECTION

In general, electronic alarm devices are used to detect, monitor, or react to abnormal or predetermined security or environmental conditions in a facility. The function of an electronic alarm system can be viewed as one or more of the following: (1) detection of fire, (2) detection of intrusion, (3) emergency notification, (4) monitoring of facility environment for access control, criminal activity or procedural compliance, and (5) monitoring of equipment or environmental conditions of the facility. (Please note that CCTV, which is used primarily for monitoring, is covered in this chapter.) Any one system may or may not incorporate all of the above. When utilized for any of these functions, the electronic system is operating as a machine and is performing a mechanized task. While various system components or devices may be better suited to certain protection tasks than humans, and their use may be an improvement in protection at less cost, the role of personnel in the total protection program cannot be eliminated. The human factor must remain so that intelligent judgment can be used to react and respond to environmental exceptions and problems signaled by the electronic system.

Thus, no inference should be drawn that either electronics or personnel is superior to the other. Obviously, routine, rote-like tasks should be relegated to electronic devices whenever possible, and activities requiring reasoning and judgment should be performed by security personnel. The requirements, in terms of electronics, equipment, personnel, or even procedures of a particular security program can best be determined after such factors as the following have been considered:

- The threat environment—what must the system protect against?

- The type of security needed—personnel, perimeter, access control, information—what is to be protected?

- The methods of security to accomplish given objectives or levels of security—what works best?

- The methods of coverage and response—what is to be the relationship of security equipment and electronics to security personnel?

- The resources available for security—what are the short-term and long-term costs?

Planning, then, is an essential and important element of the decision-making process of selecting the best combination and arrangement of people, procedures, equipment, and electronics for accomplishing protection and security objectives. The successful operation of any system depends on the proper integration, arrangement, and relationship of its parts.

An electronic alarm system must be viewed as one of the defensive layers surrounding the assets to be protected. It should be considered in the context of its fit, relative to perimeter barriers, locks, storage containers, lighting, personnel, procedures, etc. Such questions as when, where, and how the alarm system components are to deter and detect entry must be answered with regard to the location and vulnerability of critical assets and their physical protection. Most often, the electronic alarm system should be viewed as having multiple layers, e.g., perimeter alarm devices, door/window alarm devices, interior space/volume protection devices, etc. If one part of the system is breached without detection, a subsequent layer will work as planned. However, multiple-alarm device layers should be utilized to improve detection capability, not to compensate for a weak or ineffective system.

TYPES OF ALARM SYSTEMS

Regardless of its operational features, an electronic alarm system will be effective only if there is a response to any signal initiated. Therefore, the termination of the electronic alarm signal, which indicates system reaction to an abnormal or problem condition, must be planned so that the proper audience and/or personnel are alerted and a timely response is made. There are four basic types of terminating alarm system signals: local alarm system, central-station alarm system, proprietary central control system, and auxiliary alarm system.

The purpose, orientation, cost, and operational features of the electronic alarm system will generally determine which of the four basic types of signal termination should be utilized. For example, if the primary purpose of a system is to detect fire, it would be foolhardy to install only a local alarm system in a remote, isolated area where no one would hear the signal (e.g., siren, horn, bell) and respond to the fire. A local alarm system designed to detect an intrusion to a facility having immediate response capability would frighten most intruders away. To be efficient and effective, an alarm system must be designed to meet the needs of the environment and the purposes for which it was intended. Decisions must be made regarding the orientation of the system. For example, should it be oriented to catching the intruder via utilizing a silent alarm signal to a remote location? Would it be best to just scare the intruder away? Or should the system have both local and remote signal termination capabilities?

LOCAL ALARM SYSTEM

A local alarm system generally has signal termination on the premises at either a central control station or near the vicinity of the activated sensor. The sensor activates either a visual signal, audible signal, or both. This system requires that someone be present at, or least very near, the facility at all times in the event that an immediate response is necessary. Local alarms that do not have monitoring personnel at or near the facility are usually undesirable for the following reasons:

1) Local alarms are generally simple in design and complexity, allowing an opportunity for the amateur to compromise the system.

2) Audible alarms usually will not deter a person if the person knows the facility and location relative to alarm response variables.

3) Audible alarms act as a fear mechanism only for persons who are surprised by the alarm. Even when surprised by the audible alarm, intruders are rarely apprehended as a result.

4) Frequent false alarms (sirens, horns, or bells) do not build goodwill between the company and police or neighbors.

If an outside audible alarm is used by a company or private individual without plans for direct around-the-clock response to the alarm on the part of a company employee or neighbor, it should be set on a timer so that the alarm will shut off after a reasonable period of time. If there are other homes or businesses in the immediate area, common courtesy dictates such a feature. System rearm/reset may or may not be possible once the alarm shuts off. This depends on the operational features of the system and the condition of the sensory device(s) initially activated.

CENTRAL-STATION ALARM SYSTEM

A central-station alarm system is composed of fire, intrusion, and/or monitoring and sensory devices capable of activating either a telephone, receiving module, or screen at a location away from the facility the system is protecting. Several alarm systems are generally monitored at a central location by trained personnel. The monitoring function generally requires that personnel observe the various alarm indicators 24 hours a day, seven days a week. The physical location of the central station may be in the same geographic area as the facilities being monitored, or it can be several hundred miles away. In either case, telephone transmission lines usually provide the link between the central station and the protected facility. In some locations, however, the communication of alarm system messages is by long-range radio signal transmission. Ademco, a manufacturer and supplier of security products and services, provides radio transmission of alarm signals to subscribers in 15 major metropolitan areas in the United States. Generally, the facility being protected pays a fee to the central-station company for system monitoring, officer response, and system maintenance. Several varieties of service and monetary arrangements are common.

Most central-station alarm companies are privately owned, one of the largest being the American District Telegraph (ADT) Company. Upon receiving an alarm from an activated sensor, the person monitoring the alarm panel will notify either the fire or police department, dispatch a security officer, or do both.

An activated fire sensor requires that the fire department be notified. If the activated sensor is an intrusion alarm, security personnel should proceed to the facility and, if there is the possibility that an intruder may be inside, wait on the outside of the building for police personnel before entering. The security officer who has been dispatched by monitoring personnel from the central station can alleviate the need for police response in cases in which an employee set off the system or a malfunction occurred in the equipment. Contributing factors regarding alarm response situations include whether the alarm signal was received only by the central station or if a local alarm signal was also present.

PROPRIETARY CENTRAL CONTROL SYSTEM

A proprietary central control alarm system is one that is privately owned and controlled. This system is very similar to a central station system in that the monitoring of the alarm system is done at a central location, but the station is within the facility rather than at a distant location. A central control center is usually staffed 24 hours a day, seven days a week, and the response to any alarm is handled by dispatching facility personnel to the location of the alarm. These are in-house systems that serve only the owner. In some cases they may protect more than one facility owned by the company.

In most cases, the response time to the activated alarm is less for a proprietary central control center alarm than for a central station alarm system. Alarm signals can be silent, local, or both. However, for all but the largest facilities, the proprietary system will cost more to operate than will the contractual service of a central station system. This can be somewhat mitigated by the fact that proprietary central control systems can be multifaceted systems receiving and monitoring signals and communications relative not only to security but also to safety, fire, production processes, etc. Signal transmission lines may be direct (inside the facility circuits) or telephone lines where several separate facilities are monitored by the same proprietary central control system.

AUXILIARY ALARM SYSTEMS

Auxiliary alarm systems include all other means of signal termination to police departments, fire departments, or other designated locations. These methods include the programmed tape dialer, the digital dialer, and the "dry line" direct connect.

Auxiliary alarm systems involve notification directly to either the police station, fire department, or other designated telephone numbers. They are usually silent alarm systems, but can incorporate local alarms if such is dictated by the circumstances of the facility being protected. Direct notification systems necessitate either hard-line or wireless communications between the alarm system and the notification point. The usual transmission circuit is a telephone line leased for that specific purpose.

> **Tape Dialer**—The tape dialer alarm system is designed to dial a programmed telephone number when the alarm system is activated. The activation of the sensory device, via the control unit, releases the dialer and causes the programmed telephone number to be dialed. Once the telephone number has been answered, a recording gives a receiver a coded message, i.e., the type and location of the alarm. The recorded message will repeat itself for a given number of times if the contact is not broken. A broken, cut or malfunctioning telephone circuit usually will cause the system to fail. Line fault circuit monitors can be installed to alert the system control unit of an inoperative transmission line. This will automatically cause the system to revert to a local alarm system.

> **Digital Dialer**—Instead of sending a programmed message, this unit transmits a coded message to a special receiver located at the police department, fire department, or other location. The coded message, usually numerical, indicates the location and type of alarm so that an appropriate response can be made. A line fault circuit monitor is also appropriate for this system.

> **Direct Connect**—Direct connect alarm systems employ a telephone transmission circuit called a "dry line," which is an exclusive circuit connecting the alarm system directly to a specific location. The alarm signal is received by a module alarm receiving unit, which is usually capable of indicating both alarm activation and circuit malfunction.

While very common, auxiliary alarm systems have created problems for public services such as police and fire protection. Police and fire departments generally do not have the space for numerous direct connect module units, nor do they have the time or human resources to deal with the high rate of false alarms. Many police departments now refuse to monitor private alarm systems. Most of those that do monitor private alarm systems require that alarm systems meet certain qualifications for quality, installation, and service before they will monitor the unit and/or respond to its signals.

FUNDAMENTALS OF ALARM SYSTEMS

Alarm signal information, other than for the local system, generally is transmitted via a leased telephone line to a designated location. The regular telephone system in a facility, or lines specifically dedicated to transmission of alarm system information, may be used. Often, such dedicated lines can be adapted to handle the two-way transmission of special, preprogrammed supervised signals for the purpose of monitoring the integrity of the alarm circuit. The ability to monitor the status of the transmission line and its condition is essential to effective alarm system operation.

Another less common, but growing, means of transmitting alarm signal information is via radio waves. Radio telemetry, commonly referred to as wireless communication, is the transmission of data and information via radio signals to a distant station. It is an alternative to telephone lines, but the protected facility must have the necessary corresponding equipment (which is generally more expensive).

The internal features of alarm systems are composed of five basic components: (1) sensory device(s) that monitor and react to a change in the environment; (2) a control unit that acts as a signal processing unit; (3) an annunciator, either silent or local, that elicits human response; (4) a power supply from a commercial power source and/or alternative battery power source; and (5) circuitry—either hard wire or wireless—for transmission of signals. These five basic components are common to most alarm systems, regardless of their function or purpose. Whether an alarm system is designed for detection of fire, detection of intrusion, emergency notification, or monitoring of equipment or facility conditions, the operating principles of each are much the same. It is possible to construct a very simple alarm system without all of these components, but in the vast majority of situations it would be impractical to do so.

SENSORY DEVICES

Sensory devices initiate alarm signals as a result of sensing the stimulus or condition to which they are designed to react. Depending on the type of sensor, it may react to sound, motion, vibration, stress, heat, or smoke. When this sensing of a change in the environment or situation has occurred, a change in the flow of electrical current takes place to initiate a signal to the control unit.

CONTROL UNIT

The control unit is the terminating point for all sensors and switches in the alarm system. It can be designed to have a variety of capabilities from a simple on-off switch to a complicated set of sensors and switches divided into zones and functions. Control units are usually housed in heavy, steel, tamper-resistant containers. Elements of the control unit are arranged to receive signals from the sensors and to relay signals to the appropriate termination point. System control can be accomplished by an exterior shunt lock to allow entry to the control unit to turn the system on or off, or by an entry-exit time delay component that allows enough time to get to the control unit to turn it on or off.

Annunciator

The annunciator is a visual and/or audible signaling device that indicates activation of the alarm system. Selection of the appropriate annunciation for an alarm system depends upon two factors: (1) the circumstances and location of the alarm system site, and (2) the desired or required orientation of the alarm system. Very often the location of a facility or the availability of alarm services mandate that either a local alarm or remote, silent alarm be employed. When choosing the type of annunciation, particularly with an intrusion detection system, one must make the choice between an apprehension-oriented system (the silent alarm) and the deterrence-oriented system (the local alarm).

Power Source

The primary power source for alarm systems is obtained from commercial power sources. The 110-volt alternating current is transformed, rectified, and filtered to provide direct current of the proper voltage to the alarm system. Thus, alarm systems are totally dependent upon an electrical power source for proper operation. In the event that the commercial power source is disrupted, an adequate backup power source (either dry cell or rechargeable storage batteries) is an essential element of any alarm system.

Alarm Circuits

The alarm circuit transmits signals from the sensors to the control unit, which in turn transmits signals to the local or remote annunciator/receiving unit. Alarm systems are wired as either "open" or "closed" circuits. The open circuit system is a line that does not have an uninterrupted flow of current present until a switch or relay is closed to complete the circuit. The closed circuit system is a line with current flowing through it; any change in this flow may initiate an alarm signal. Alarm circuits also can be installed by two different methods of circuit arrangement, i.e., the direct circuit connect and the McCulloh Loop. The direct method of wiring an alarm system is to connect each sensor or system to the control or receiving unit by an exclusive circuit. The McCulloh Loop is a circuit that has two or more sensors, switches, or systems on the same circuit. Various components of an alarm system may incorporate remote control capability by means of a transmitter that sends radio or microwave signals to a receiver device on the control unit. A remote control device can be a hand-held emergency signal actuator or a transmitter incorporated with the sensory device to transmit a signal from a sensor back to the control unit.

SELECTION OF ALARM SYSTEMS

Each type of alarm detection or notification system is intended to meet a specific type of problem. The necessity and feasibility of any alarm system must be determined before installation begins. The following elements need to be considered:

1)   importance of the facility, materials, and processes;

2)   vulnerability of the facility, materials, and processes;

3)   appropriateness and feasibility of using specific types of alarm systems;

4)   initial and recurring costs of the alarm system compared to cost (in money or security) of possible loss of materials or information;

5)   savings in human resources and money over a period of time;

6)   response time by security personnel or other respondents; and

7)   improvement over current security methods. Decisions to utilize electronic alarm systems should lead to economy and improvement over existing security practices and methods.

ALARM SYSTEM SENSORS

Alarm system sensors and devices are usually classified in three general categories according to the type of physical protection provided: (1) point or spot protection, (2) area or space protection, and (3) perimeter protection. An electronic security system can provide the desired type and depth of protection by a combination of two or more of these categories. The following discussion of alarm devices and sensors will be directed to the coverage, purposes, and functions that the alarm system is to provide, and the types of devices, switches, and sensors that will satisfy those objectives.

Intrusion detection alarm systems provide deterrence against and detection of unauthorized entry into a facility, building, or other structure. The situations and conditions at a particular site to be protected determine which devices and sensors would be the most efficient and practical. Following are some of the more common sensory devices and the principles upon which they operate.

ELECTROMECHANICAL DEVICES (PERIMETER OR POINT)

The most commonly used alarm sensors are electromechanical, i.e., sensors that operate on the principle of either breaking or closing an electrical circuit. Generally, the system operates in a way that requires a current-carrying conductor to be placed in a position between a potential intruder and the place to be protected.

Switches are commonly utilized in electromechanical alarm systems. The two most common types of switches are the **simple contact switch** and the **magnetic contact switch**. The simple contact switch requires only that the two halves of the switch device touch in order to complete a circuit. Any action to disconnect the switch will activate the alarm. The standard type of magnetic switch consists of a magnetically activated switch unit and a magnet. The magnet is usually attached to a movable fixture and the switch unit is attached to a permanent fixture. When moved, the magnetic portion of the unit will cause the switch component to either make or break the electrical circuit connection.

Another common electromechanical device is metallic window foil that can be applied to the glass in windows or doors. The foil tape cemented on the glass forms a complete circuit and if broken will activate the alarm system. A basic advantage afforded by window foil is the psychological deterrence it has on would-be intruders, as it is obvious to outsiders that an alarm system appears to be present.

Electromechanical devices are used primarily to provide perimeter protection for buildings or other structures. Individually, the devices provide point protection of a window, door, or other opening, but taken together they can create a perimeter line of alarm protection.

Advantages of electromechanical sensor devices are:

1) once installed, they provide relatively maintenance-free service (environmental conditions will affect switches and exposed wire on outside units);

2) simplicity of operation allows them to operate without excessive numbers of nuisance alarms; and

3) they provide good perimeter security in low-risk situations.

Disadvantages of electromechanical sensor devices are:

1) electromechanical devices can be compromised relatively easily;

2) they are costly to install in a facility with numerous openings;

3) lack of local standards on installation and maintenance of various systems and keen alarm company competition may result in low-quality equipment; and

4) they will not detect "stay-behinds" until they leave premises.

PHOTOELECTRIC DEVICES (SPACE, POINT, OR PERIMETER)

The photoelectric intrusion detection device uses a light-sensitive cell and a projected light source. The light beam is projected from a transmitter unit to a receiving unit that houses a photoelectric cell. When an intruder crosses the light beam, the contact with the photoelectric cell is broken and the alarm is activated. The transmitter and receiver can be arranged in such a way that reflectors (mirrors) can be used to obtain a crisscrossed pattern of coverage. The light source can be white, infrared, or laser. Infrared light is used most frequently because of its invisibility and ease of purchase. Coverage from infrared units can include point, perimeter, or area, depending upon their arrangement.

Advantages of photoelectric detectors are:

1) they are useful at entrances, exits, and driveways where obstructive devices cannot be used;

2) when properly installed and used, they can provide reliable security; and

3) they may be used to activate other security and/or safety devices, i.e., cameras and fire extinguishing systems.

Disadvantages of photoelectric detectors are:

1) when used outdoors, rain, fog, dust, and smoke can interfere with light beam;

2) they must be used in locations where it will not be possible to go over, under, or around the light beam; and

3) requires frequent maintenance inspections of units and the grounds.

AUDIO DEVICES (SPACE OR POINT)

Sensitive microphones are installed in the protected area and are adjusted to tolerate the ambient sound levels in the environment. Attempts to force entry into the area generate sounds and noises that actuate the alarm. Audio devices can be used as audio monitors that provide the capability of listening in on the environment being protected. Contact vibration detectors are considered to be audio devices because they detect vibration of sound in the structure being protected. Audio devices are particularly suited to protection of structures that are solid-walled and reasonably insulated from exterior noise.

MOTION DETECTORS (SPACE)

The protection of an enclosed space can often be effectively accomplished by the use of a class of alarm protection devices referred to as space alarms. Such systems generally derive their operating principles from a phenomenon known as the "Doppler Effect." There are several types of space alarms—the most common being the ultrasonic motion detector, microwave motion detector, and passive infrared detector.

The ultrasonic motion detector generates high-frequency sound waves that fill a given enclosed area with a pattern of waves. Any motion within the protected area will compress or expand the transmitted sound waves, causing the reflected waves to differ in frequency from the original transmission. This change in frequency is detected and the alarm signal is activated.

The principles of operation for the microwave motion detector parallel those of the ultrasonic unit with one important exception. Microwave units utilize radio waves rather than sound waves. They are highly penetrating and are not easily confined within closed spaces. Buildings or rooms constructed of light materials would not be suitable to the utilization of a microwave motion detector.

The passive infrared detector measures the level of infrared energy radiated from objects and looks for any changes in its field of coverage. The passive infrared detector does not transmit a signal as such, but is a receiving device capable of detecting relative changes in radiation temperature, such as a human body moving through the field of coverage. Open areas such as offices and hallways are particularly appropriate for passive infrared detectors.

Dual technology sensory devices are available that incorporate both microwave and infrared sensors. Such devices combine two technologies and require the activation of both sensors to signal an alarm. The result is high sensitivity and fewer nuisance (false) alarms.

Space protection devices are usually at or near the last line of defense. They are particularly useful where other types of devices cannot be used or would not be appropriate for the type of desired coverage. Additionally, they can be installed so that they are not obvious to the untrained observer. If perimeter and building surface devices are bypassed successfully, space protection devices offer the next—and possibly the last—layer of protection against intruders.

PRESSURE/STRESS DEVICES (POINT)

Pressure-sensitive devices are usually placed in a location where an intruder is likely to walk, i.e., in front of a door, under a window, in a hallway, or on a stairway. Usually these devices have the appearance of rubber mats, in which alarm circuit wires are placed. When sufficient weight (about 40 pounds) comes to bear on the mat, circuit wires come into contact and an alarm signal is activated. Pressure mats can be disguised and used on bare floor, or they can be installed beneath carpets or rugs, thereby remaining hidden from intruders.

Other forms of pressure-sensitive or stress-sensitive devices can be used to detect changes or shifts in weight. Contact stress or vibration detectors can be placed under stairways or on floor joists to detect weight or stress changes. Pressure devices are also applicable to placement under art objects, store merchandise, and other such items in order to detect removal, and on window frames, doors, safes, and walls in order to react to vibration or shock.

CAPACITANCE DEVICES (POINT)

The electromagnetic or capacitance-type device can be installed on a metal fence, safe, file cabinet, or other metallic object. The protected metal object acts as part of the capacitance of a tune circuit. If a change occurs in the proximity of the protected object (such as the approach of a person) there is sufficient change in the capacitance to upset the balance of the system and trigger an alarm. Unlike space alarms, the protective field around the protected object can be adjusted down to a depth of a few inches from its surface. In this way, objects can be protected day or night, even during business hours. Capacitance devices have a high degree of security, but are restricted in application because they can only be applied to ungrounded metal objects.

GLASS BREAKAGE SENSORS (POINT OR PERIMETER)

Glass breakage sensors are shock/sound sensing devices that are attached to glass and sense its breaking by the corresponding vibration or frequency of sound waves. The sensor mechanically responds to the breaking of glass and can be used to protect perimeter windows, glass storage units, and similar objects.

VIBRATION DETECTORS (POINT)

Vibration detectors are normally mounted on fixed, stable surfaces. When the sensitivity of the vibration device is properly adjusted, any shock to the surface beyond the set tolerance level will cause the contacts to touch or separate, signaling an alarm condition.

To discuss all possible types and varieties of intrusion detection devices is beyond the scope of this text. However, those presented represent the devices that are most commonly utilized to detect or deter unwanted intrusion. A basic understanding of their respective principles of operation is essential to the selection and application of an appropriate electronic intrusion alarm system.

PERIMETER FENCE SENSORS

To complement the deterrence and delaying attributes of perimeter fence lines, various types of sensor systems can be added to detect intrusion. A brief overview of the more common systems in use today is provided. The **strain-sensitive cable sensor** is a specially treated coaxial cable and associated signal processor. The sensor cable is woven across the fabric of the fence and attached at intervals. Attempts to cut, climb, or otherwise move the fence are "heard" by the sensor, which initiates an alarm signal. Inherent in the system is an audio listen-in capability for monitoring assessment. The **mechanical fence disturbance**

sensor uses a weight or other inertia-based device that moves in response to fence movement, thereby sensing and reacting to fence motion. The weight is typically a part of a closed circuit and movement causes it to jump off its contacts. **Electro-mechanical fence disturbance sensors** are mounted directly to the fence or fence posts to detect corresponding motion. Fence motion is translated into electrical signals that are proportional to the amount of motion in the fence. Piezo-electric crystal devices or geophones (pressure/vibration sensitive devices) are used as the sensing mechanisms. **Electric field** and **capacitance sensors** consist of a number of wires arrayed horizontally along the fence line. The wires are insulated from the fence and ground to create an invisible electrical field, which, when disturbed, generates an alarm. **Taut wire sensors** consist of a series of wires arrayed across the fence. Each wire is under considerable tension and is connected to one or more vertical sensor posts along the fence line. Deflection or cutting of one or more of the wires will result in an alarm condition (see Figure 11.1).

Figure 11.1
Taut Wire System Configuration

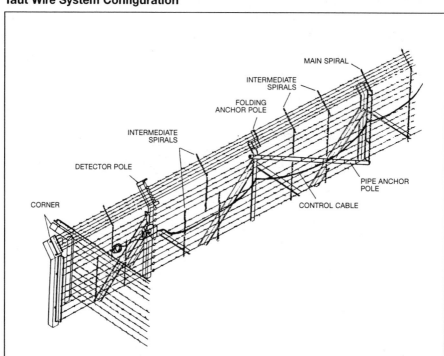

Provided Courtesy of Safeguards Technology, Inc.

The microbending or breaking of a fiber optic cable sensor device is detectable and alarm-generating. The fiber optic sensor cable is arrayed along and coupled to the fence to react to excessive movement in the fence. There are various types of **buried cable sensor** devices that can be used in conjunction with a perimeter line. Most such devices react to pressure, stress, or vibration (e.g., geophones), exerted on the ground over or near the buried cable (Vitch, 1992:50-54).

An obvious consideration regarding any kind of sensory device or system utilized for perimeter protection is its exposure to the outside environment, e.g., wind, snow, rain, birds, animals, etc. All of the aforementioned perimeter sensor devices and systems have discriminatory and tolerance functions. That is, the systems can be adjusted to accommodate the ambient environmental conditions. However, a perimeter alarm system still must be selected with great care.

FIRE DETECTION SYSTEMS

Fire is one of the most destructive forces humankind faces. Whether its initiation is artificial or natural, potential losses of life and property can be enormous. Of course, steps to prevent the occurrence of fire precede the steps taken to detect or suppress fire. However, the detection of fire, if and when it occurs, is a necessary step that must be taken in the home and in business and industry.

Alarm systems and devices designed to detect fire may be incorporated into or parallel intrusion alarm systems. Methods and types of signal transmission and system components are generally the same, except for the respondents to fire alarm signals and the detection devices employed.

The fire department or fire brigade is the ultimate respondent to a business/company fire. Local alarms should always be included in a fire detection system even if a central station, proprietary central control station, or auxiliary system is also used. The objective of fire detection systems is generally to alert as many people as possible, as quickly as possible.

FIRE DETECTION DEVICES

Heat detectors are of two general types: those that operate at a predetermined temperature (fixed-temperature devices) and those that operate when there is an unusual increase in temperature (rate-of-rise devices). The **fixed-temperature detector**, the more commonly used of the two devices, is similar to a common thermostat and employs the principle of different coefficients of expansion in metals as they react to heat and cold. By arranging electrical contacts so that a circuit opens or closes according to the difference in length of two strips of different metals, an alarm signal will occur at a predetermined temperature. Other types depend upon heat expanding a metal disc until electrical contact is made, or on the melting of heat-sensitive plastic insulation.

Rate-of-rise detectors react to a sudden, rapid change in temperature and can be set to operate more readily than fixed-temperature detectors. There are two principal types of rate-of-rise heat detectors. The first has a pneumatic tube that reacts to changes in air pressure caused by heat; the second uses the principle of the thermocouple.

SMOKE DETECTORS

In many fire situations, detection can be more rapid if smoke detectors are present. The two most common types of smoke detectors are the photoelectric unit and the ionization unit. The photoelectric smoke detector is activated by smoke passing through a photoelectric beam. Sufficient concentrations of smoke will interrupt the beam and cause activation of the alarm. The ionization smoke detector reacts to hydrocarbons that develop in the chemical processes prior to actual ignition.

Other fire detection devices include the rate compensated detector, laser beam fire detector, and ultraviolet or infrared flame detector. Each fire detection device should be selected on the basis of its appropriateness to the environmental conditions in which it is to be used.

EMERGENCY NOTIFICATION SYSTEMS

Instead of being triggered by intruder or fire, an emergency notification system is used for security and safety in unusual or dangerous circumstances. Perhaps the most common example of this is the robbery alert system used by businesses and most financial institutions.

A robbery alert system is usually a component of the intrusion detection alarm system. For this to be possible, the master control unit must have day circuits and night circuits, which allow zoning of alarm devices and alarm circuitry. Intrusion detection devices that would interfere with daytime business activities are on the night circuit and those designed to be utilized for the robbery alert system are on the day circuit. By setting the control unit on the day circuit and by strategic placement of hold-up buttons or other devices around the facility, one can alert the police or others to a robbery in progress. Robbery alert signals should be silent and used only if it is safe to do so.

Another example of an emergency notification system is the kind utilized by business and industry to alert employees and others that an emergency has occurred or is pending. Such alarms must be audible or visible to everyone if effective action is to be taken. Steam whistles, bells, sirens, and other devices are utilized to warn people to take cover, evacuate, or take some other action. Such systems and devices are used to warn of fires, explosions, tornadoes, hostile attack, or any other situation with hazardous potential.

THE PROBLEM OF FALSE ALARMS

Although alarm systems have been proven effective in deterring and apprehending intruders, they are subject to certain inherent problems. A traditional and still-to-be-resolved problem is that of false alarms. It is estimated that from 90 to 98 percent of all alarms transmitted are false. This high percentage can be attributed to three factors: (1) user error or negligence, (2) poor installation or servicing, and (3) faulty equipment.

Figure 11.2
Robbery Alert Device/Bill Clip, in Left Upper of Cash Drawer

More than one-half of all false alarms are estimated to result from user error or negligence. Users often do not understand how to operate their systems properly. Commonly, alarms are set off by users who fail to lock doors or windows or who enter a secured area when the system is engaged. Merchants have been known to use their alarm systems to summon the police to deal with bad checks or suspicious individuals. Some users even set off their alarms to time police response to their premises.

The second factor contributing to false alarms is poor installation or servicing. In order to function as intended, an alarm system must be properly installed and maintained. Equipment that is installed in an inappropriate environment or positioned, set, or wired improperly is more likely to produce false alarms. Likewise, if equipment is not adequately maintained, the chances of false alarms increase. Too often, installers and service personnel lack the necessary skills and knowledge for today's more sophisticated equipment.

Poor installation or servicing has caused states and local governments to develop standards for installing and servicing alarm systems. In addition to standards for both installers and installation procedures, the requirement of some type of bond is now commonplace. Future standards for the alarm business will probably be as stringent as those now in place for electricians and plumbers, e.g., systems must be installed according to a predetermined code of standards.

The third common cause of false alarms is faulty equipment. If equipment is electrically or mechanically defective, the alarm can be activated when, for instance, the equipment breaks or shorts out the circuit. The use of cheap, substandard equipment frequently leads to false alarms. Another claim for false alarms results from environmental conditions such as electrical storms, wind, rain, etc. Some would argue, however, that these false alarms are attributable to faulty or improper equipment and not to the environment.

In addition to false alarms that can be traced to the above factors, there are a certain number of false alarms for which the cause cannot be determined. Based on the results of various studies, roughly 25 percent of all false alarms fall into this unknown category. It is possible that they may, in fact, be the result of user error; faced with probable sanctions, a user may deny responsibility for a false alarm. Another possibility is that a burglary or other unauthorized intrusion may have been successfully prevented, leaving no visible evidence of intrusion or attempted entry.

The continued high incidence of false alarms—whatever the cause—has led to other problems. In the use of automatic telephone dialer alarm systems, a large number of storm-related false alarms simultaneously occurring can seriously hamper police capacity to respond to genuine emergencies. Malfunctioning of such systems may lock in, or at least tie up, police communication trunklines for considerable periods of time. In many communities, the police do not allow direct alarm system signal transmission to their communications center. Although telephone dialers offer effective, low-cost protection, these problems have created negative police reaction toward their usage—so much so that in many areas certain categories of facility alarm systems receive very low response priority.

A more serious problem, especially to police personnel, is the personal risk involved in false alarms. Any high-speed response to false alarms unnecessarily endangers the personal welfare of police, as well as other drivers and innocent bystanders. Many departments have adopted a policy of non-emergency response to routine alarm system calls. False alarms also bring to the scene alarm company respondents who may be armed, presenting a further threat to life and safety.

Another problem of false alarms is the burden of expense to alarm system users. When a system falsely alarms, servicing is usually required, resulting in increased costs that are eventually absorbed by users or passed along to consumers. Moreover, some local governments directly impose fines upon users whose systems repeatedly produce false alarms.

MONITORING/SURVEILLANCE SYSTEMS

There are many processes and pieces of equipment that are critical to the continued operation of businesses and industrial concerns. Often these need to be monitored by an electronic system capable of observing, sounding, or sending an alarm signal. The necessity of monitoring may be due to operational requirements, economic reasons, or the hazardous nature of the process or operation. The importance of this particular type of electronic alarm detection/monitoring system is best illustrated by the nuclear power industry, in which various operations and processes must be monitored by means other than the immediate presence of personnel (which is precluded by the hazardous conditions of the environment). The application of monitoring and surveillance systems for purposes of security includes various aspects of access control, detection of intrusion, and detection of crime or improper activities.

CLOSED CIRCUIT TELEVISION (CCTV)

Particularly applicable to monitoring/surveillance for purposes of security are closed circuit television (CCTV) and other types of photographic surveillance equipment, such as motion picture photography and still photography. While various types of photographic equipment can be used for purposes of monitoring and surveillance, the operational and functional features of CCTV have brought it to the forefront regarding its applications for purposes of security. CCTV allows for live and remote monitoring of an environment, equipment, or process without danger of exposure to personnel, and is particularly adaptable to various applications involving detection of intrusion and access control, and in retail operations as both a deterrent and detection device for shoplifting and employee improprieties. Today, CCTV systems are in wide use in retail stores and shopping centers, hospitals, motels and hotels, financial institutions, office buildings, manufacturing facilities, museums, schools, etc. A CCTV system basically consists of a television camera, a monitor, connecting circuitry, and a power source. An expanded system that has numerous cameras, monitors, VTR, remote control, etc., is expensive, yet may offer improvement and savings over existing security methods.

> **CCTV Cameras**—CCTV cameras come in two main varieties: **tube** and **solid-state** (chip). Tube cameras are generally less expensive and offer better resolution than chip cameras. The types of tubes differ and should be selected on the basis of planned usage. The vidicon tube camera is the standard general-purpose unit, used almost exclusively in well-illuminated indoor areas. Newvicon and ultracon cameras are more expensive, but can be used for lower light and outdoor applications. Silicon-intensified target and intensified silicon-intensified target camera units are even more expensive and can operate in full sunlight or starlight conditions. Microchip-based cameras use integrated circuits rather than tubes to provide a picture. Chip (CCD) cameras are lighter and more compact than tube cameras, usually have a longer life span and are more adaptable to situations requiring concealment and surreptitious usage.

> **Camera Housings**—Cameras are costly and often are a critical element of the security system. To protect them, various types of camera housing units are available. A protective housing is essential to outdoor camera applications. Wind, rain, snow, and sunlight can damage or otherwise diminish the effectiveness and continued operation of outdoor cameras.

Indoor housing units can add aesthetics, concealment, and dust protection. Other types of housing units can protect the camera against vandalism or provide for its safe operation in a hazardous environment.

Camera Lens—A camera lens has two primary functions: to collect light and to focus light on the camera's faceplate. A 16mm lens is normally used in CCTV. Variations of the 16mm lens include the wide-angle and telephoto (or zoom) lens. Other lens types that have unique security applications include the split-field lens, which divides the field of view into two or more parts (to look both ways down a hallway), a pinhole lens that is extremely small and applicable for covert surveillance (available in straight or right angle models), the gyro-stabilized lens, appropriate for usage on moving vehicles such as automobiles or boats, and so on. Obviously the correct lens must be used for each specific application.

Camera Control—Pan and tilt units allow the operator to remotely control the direction of the camera. Normally this is accomplished with a direct wire electrical circuit that connects the pan and tilt unit to the control point. Other methods of both receiving the picture of what the camera sees and exercising control over where the camera is pointing include microwave systems, lasers, and VHF or UHF signals.

Figure 11.3
Security Control Center with CCTV Monitors

Monitoring Units—CCTV monitors come in various sizes, the most common being 9-inch and 12-inch screens. Several factors must be considered with regard to effective and efficient monitoring of CCTV units. These include the number of monitoring personnel, the number and operational features of the monitors, the number of CCTV camera units and their operational features, and the nature of the functions and operations for which the camera units are being employed. For example, the physical number of monitors, the expected level and complexity of the activities to be monitored, and the relative criticality of each will determine how much one observer can monitor effectively. There are various monitoring options that allow for more effective viewing of multiple cameras. Manual switcher devices allow the operator to select the specific camera and site to be viewed. Automatic sequential switcher devices allow for viewing of multiple cameras in a sequence of time and duration determined by the user. Alternatively, a video motion detector can be employed to analyze the signal sent from a video camera and, if changes occur in the scene, the signal change will alert monitoring personnel. Another method of minimizing the number of monitors personnel have to watch is **quad multiplexing**, which allows for the viewing of four cameras simultaneously on one video screen. With this configuration, the operator can call up any one camera for full-screen viewing if needed.

ELECTRONIC ASSET PROTECTION (ELECTRONIC ARTICLE SURVEILLANCE)

Electronic article surveillance (EAS) tags have been a fixture in the retail industry for several years. Recently given a more generic name, because of various innovative adaptations and applications, electronic asset protection (EAP) tags now protect computer tapes, computer equipment, fax machines, babies (against kidnapping), hospital equipment, etc.

All EAP systems have two basic components: (1) a tag, and (2) a sensory system. When a tag passes through or past a sensor, the system is activated. The signal triggered can be a point-of-event light, audible alarm, or remote signal to a central station. The systems usually work in one of two ways—passive or active tag signal activation of the alarm mechanism. Passive tags react to a signal generated by transmitter units located at exits or control points. Active tags are transponders that return an intelligent signal to the radio frequency source at a control point or exit. Technology is available for individual and informational coding of the tags for purposes of people and asset tracking, audit trails, and integrated systems response (such as automatic locking of selected doors and exits). Tags can be worn, attached to equipment and materials either overtly or covertly, or (as in the case of protecting the maternity and nursery areas of hospitals) sewn into a baby's diaper. *The Hallcrest Report II: Private Security Trends (1970-2000)* has predicted that sales of EAP devices will increase to more than $1 trillion by the year 2000 (Cunningham, Strauchs & Van Meter, 1990:203-205).

UNDERWRITERS' LABORATORIES

Founded in 1894, Underwriters' Laboratories (UL) is an independent, non-profit service corporation that applies existing safety and testing standards to products submitted by manufacturers. A UL label on a product usually indicates that its design, and the manufactured item itself, have met certain Underwriters' standards. UL's findings and certifications are recognized by insurance rating bureaus and most federal, state, county, and municipal authorities. Thus, in order to satisfy the established criteria for electronic equipment and systems certification, protective devices, control units, circuitry, etc., must meet specific UL standards for operation and performance. In addition to certification of alarm and detection devices, UL certifies local and central station alarm service companies. Alarm installation companies and service companies must utilize UL-approved products, install alarm systems according to UL standards, provide maintenance and inspection as required, and satisfy certain performance standards for alarm responses. There is a trend toward increased utilization of UL-listed or UL-certified systems so as to preclude additional liabilities relative to the alarm system.

ALARM SYSTEMS AND DEVICES TERMINOLOGY

An understanding of the applications, operations, and principles of electronic alarm systems is essential to effective and efficient usage. There are a wide variety of systems and devices available, and technological advances occur almost daily. All have one or more functional weaknesses that can cause their operational effectiveness to be minimized or even completely disrupted, yet most will prove satisfactory if properly selected, installed, and maintained.

The use of electronic warning and/or detection systems and monitoring devices has proven to be very effective and beneficial in a wide variety of situations; however, individuals responsible for security planning and application must carefully analyze their security needs and the systems available before making any decisions regarding purchase, installation, and utilization.

Access Control—The control of pedestrian and vehicular traffic through entrances and exits via means of security personnel, equipment, and/or electronic means.

Active Sensor—A sensing device that detects a disturbance within the field of its transmitted signal.

Actuator—A switch that is manually or automatically activated to transmit a signal.

Alarm Circuit—An electrical circuit of an alarm system that transmits an alarm signal.

Alarm Condition—A sensory device or alarm component that has reacted or been activated to signal a threatening condition.

Alarm Discrimination—The ability of some alarm systems and devices to distinguish between the ambient (normal) and abnormal conditions of the environment being protected.

Alarm Drop—Alarm system has been activated and is in alarm condition.

Alarm Signal—A signal received and processed by the control unit to indicate an alarm condition.

Alarm Station—A device, installed at a fixed location, that can be activated manually to transmit an alarm signal.

Alarm System—An assemblage of components designed and arranged to monitor and signal an alarm condition.

Annunciator—The component of the alarm system that signals that an alarm condition has been received. The annunciator signal may be audible, visible, or both. Its primary purpose is to elicit human response to the alarm condition.

Area (Space) Protection—Protection of an area, other than perimeter or point. Sensory device is capable of protecting a large area or space.

Audible Alarm Device (Annunciator)—An annunciator device that makes noise, e.g., siren, horn, or bell.

Audio Detection System—An alarm system capable of monitoring and sensing sound in the area being protected.

Auxiliary Alarm System—All means of alarm system signal termination to police departments, fire departments, or locations other than central stations, proprietary control centers, and local alarm systems. Alarm signals are generally transmitted by means of tape dialer, digital units, or dry-line direct connect.

Bill Clip—A holdup alarm device, located in the cash drawer, that is activated when bills are removed, allowing contact to be made.

Bug—A microphone or other audio sensor used for the purpose of "listening in" or audio surveillance.

Capacitance Alarm System—A system in which the object being protected is electrically connected to a capacitance sensor. Intrusion into the capacitance field around the object causes a change in the electrical field and an alarm condition (sometimes called a Proximity Alarm System).

Central Station—A control center to which subscriber alarm systems are connected and monitored. Central stations are owned and operated independently of the facility being protected. Subscribers pay a fee to the central station according to the level or amount of alarm services being provided.

Circumvention—A means of bypassing or defeating the alarm system.

Closed Circuit—An alarm circuit that has a continuous flow of electrical current.

Closed Circuit Television (CCTV)—A self-contained system of electronic surveillance including camera, monitor, and circuitry. Additions to system may include pan-and-tilt to control coverage capability of camera, zoom lens on camera to obtain close-ups, etc.

Contact—A switch or relay that causes an interruption or completion of current flow by the touching or separation of its metallic parts.

Contact Microphone—A listening device (microphone) designed for attachment to the surface of the area to be protected.

Control Unit—The "brain" of the alarm system that functions to monitor, receive, transmit, and activate components to achieve system objectives.

Crossover—An insulated connecting path used to connect foil tape across dividers in multiple-pane windows.

Detection Range—The outermost distance at which a sensor will effectively detect an intruder.

Digital Dialer—A device used to transmit alarm signals to a special unit capable of receiving coded messages that indicate the location and type of alarm condition.

Direct Connector—An exclusive telephone transmission line connecting the alarm system directly to a specific location.

Door Cord—A short, insulated cable, with attaching block and terminals, used to conduct current to a device mounted on the movable portion of a door or window.

Doppler Effect—A change or shift in transmitted and received frequencies caused by movement within the protected area. Primary to the operation of motion sensors such as the ultrasonic and the microwave.

Duress Alarm Device—A device, normally manually activated, that produces either a silent or local alarm. Generally used to indicate a condition of personal stress or emergency, such as fire, robbery, illness, etc. (also called a "panic" alarm). The actuating device may be fixed or portable, wired or wireless.

Electromagnetic—Pertains to the characteristics and relationship between electrical current flow and magnetism.

Entry Time Delay—The amount of time between actuating a sensory device on an entrance and the transmission of an alarm signal by the control unit. The time delay allows a person with a control key to enter and turn off the control unit without triggering an alarm.

Exit Time Delay—The time between turning the control unit on and exiting a protected door without triggering an alarm signal. The delay is provided by a timer within the control unit that is set to accommodate the situation regarding both exiting and entering.

False Alarm—An alarm signal transmitted when no alarm condition exists. False alarms may be due to equipment failure or malfunction, environmental conditions, or human error.

Foil Tape—Thin metallic strips affixed to a protected surface, usually glass, and connected to an electrical circuit. If the tape is broken, e.g., by a crack in the glass, an alarm signal is initiated.

Foot Rail—A common holdup alarm device used by banks at teller windows. When confronted by a robber, a teller can activate the foot rail with foot pressure to initiate an alarm signal.

Glass Breakage Detector—Essentially a contact microphone attached to window glass to detect breakage of the glass.

Heat Sensor—A sensor that responds to a predetermined level of temperature or to a rate of temperature increase that is greater than a preselected rate of rise.

Holdup Alarm Device—A device, fixed or portable, used to signal a robbery. The device ordinarily initiates a silent alarm signal and may take the form of hidden buttons, footrails, hand-carried activators, bill clips, etc.

Infrared Detector—A passive sensory device that detects changes in radiation/temperature of the area being protected.

Interior Alarm Protection—An alarm system that provides protection of the interior of a building. Areas of coverage may include the interior perimeter, doors, file cabinets, safes, vaults, etc.

Intrusion—Any unauthorized or illegal entry into a protected area.

Ionization Smoke Detector—A sensory device that contains a small amount of radioactive material that reacts to smoke particles entering the ionization chamber. A sufficient amount of smoke in the chamber decreases the conductance of the ionized air; when a predetermined level of nonconductance is reached, the detector circuit is activated.

Lacing—A network of fine wire surrounding an area to be protected, such as a vault or safe. The network of wire forms a complete electrical circuit. Usually the wires are embedded or covered by concrete, paneling, or plaster so their presence is not obvious to a would-be intruder.

Line Supervision—The capability of monitoring an alarm circuit and/or transmission line to detect changes in the circuit characteristics.

Local Alarm System—An alarm system that produces a signal in the immediate area that is being protected. Such signals should be audible and/or visible for the purpose of eliciting human response to the alarm condition, and hopefully should be sufficient to deter the intruder.

Magnetic Alarm System—An alarm system capable of detecting a change in a magnetic field when ferrous objects (such as guns, knives, bombs, etc.) enter the area of coverage. One such device, the magnetometer (metal detector) can be used and designed to search for buried coins and metal or (in another form) to screen airline passengers for hidden weapons.

Magnetic Switch—A switch that consists of two separate parts: a magnet and a magnetically operated switch. The switch component of the unit is normally mounted on the stationary portion of a door or window directly opposite the magnet, which is mounted on the movable segment of the opening. When the movable portion of the door or window is opened, the magnet moves away with it, causing the switch to make or break its contact.

Mat Switch—A pressure-activated switch normally used under carpeting or disguised as an entry mat. May be designed for small or large areas of coverage.

McCulloh Loop—An electrical circuit having several devices on the same "loop."

Mercury Switch—A switch containing mercury, which when vibrated or tilted makes or breaks the electrical contact. Mercury contact switches can be used on doors, windows, safes, fences, stairs, storage units, etc.

Microwave Motion Detector—An active sensory device capable of detecting via the "Doppler principle." High-frequency radio waves are projected into an area of coverage and any penetration of the protected area causes the transmitted signal to be disturbed and subsequently detected by the unit.

Motion Sensor—A sensor that responds to motion.

Normally Closed Switch—A switch in which the contacts are in the closed position when the alarm system is "on" and in a secure condition.

Normally Open Switch—A switch in which the contacts are open (apart) when the alarm system is "on."

Passive Sensor—A sensory device that does not transmit a sensing mechanism, rather it monitors and reacts to changes in the environment. Examples include audio sensors, vibration sensors, and infrared sensors.

Perimeter Alarm System—An alarm system that provides coverage of the outermost boundary of the area being protected.

Photoelectric Alarm System—An active sensory device that uses a light beam (white, infrared, or laser) and photoelectric sensor to provide a specific line-of-sight protection. The beam of light may be constant or modulated, and the area of protection may be increased by using a series of reflectors. An interruption of the focused beam by an intruder is sensed by the photoelectric sensor and an alarm signal is generated.

Photoelectric Smoke Detector—A beam of light is projected to a photo-electric cell within the detector unit. A sufficient amount of smoke will interrupt the light beam and cause actuation of the alarm system.

Point (Spot) Protection—Alarm system protection of specific objects, such as doors, windows, safes, etc.

Proprietary Central Control—An alarm system similar to the Central Station, except it is owned and operated by the facility being protected. One or more facilities may be protected by the same proprietary central control station.

Radar Alarm System—An alarm system or tracking device that utilizes radio waves to detect motion and/or speed of motion.

Remote Alarm—An alarm signal that is transmitted to a location removed from the area being protected.

Seismic Sensor—A sensory device, generally buried in the ground, that responds to vibrations within the earth. It will react to an intruder walking within the detection area, or if designed to do so, will aid in the detection and measurement of earthquakes.

Sensor—A device designed to respond to given events or stimuli.

Shunt—A key-operated switch that isolates (turns off) a portion of the alarm system. Used most often for the purpose of entering or exiting protected doors.

Silent Alarm—An alarm signal transmitted to a remote location. The orientation of silent alarm signals is generally to the apprehension of the intruder. In some situations, such as a holdup, the initiation of a local alarm would be dangerous for the victims.

Smoke Detector—A device capable of detecting visible or invisible particles and products of combustion.

Spring Contact—A contact device using a current-carrying spring that monitors the position of the object being protected, e.g., door, window, file drawer, etc.

Standby Power—Equipment capable of producing sufficient electrical power to operate a system in the event the primary power source fails. May be supplied by batteries, generators, or some combination of the two.

Stress (Strain) Detector—A sensor capable of reacting to applied stress, such as the weight of an intruder walking across a floor or on a stairway.

Supervised Alarm System—A system that monitors conditions and procedures of system usage for variations or deviations from the norm.

Surveillance—Monitoring of premises through the use of various alarm system devices (particularly CCTV).

Tamper Device—Any switch or device constructed to detect any attempt to gain unauthorized access to the alarm system or manipulate its operation.

Tape Dialer—A device used to transmit alarm information via means of programmed telephone messages to designated locations. Activation of a sensory device and operation of the control unit releases the tape dialer to dial programmed telephone number(s) with a recorded message of the alarm condition and its location.

Trap Device—A device (usually a switch) installed to protect openings or situations not conducive to other means of protection. An example would be a cord stretched across a window air conditioner unit, with one end of the cord having a piece of nonconductive material between two metal contact points, which in turn are a part of the alarm circuitry. An attempt to remove the air conditioner would pull the cord away and the nonconductive wedge from between the two contacts, allowing for the activation of the alarm signal.

Trickle Charge—A continuous direct current sufficient to maintain a battery at full charge.

Trip Wire—A switch activated by breaking, removal, or release of pressure of a wire or cord stretched across an area.

Ultrasonic Motion Detection—An active sensor that transmits and receives ultrasonic sound waves. The device operates by filling a space with a pattern of sound waves and reacting to changes in the pattern of the waves caused by a moving object.

Vibration Detection Sensors—Contact microphones on vibration sensors are attached to fixed surfaces and react to excessive levels of vibration caused by sound, attempts at forcible entry and other vibration-causing forces. Such units must be adjusted to compensate for the normal conditions of the area being protected.

Volumetric Sensor—A sensor with an expanded detection zone, capable of protecting a large area.

Walk Test Light—A feature of most motion detectors that allows the user to set the sensitivity/coverage level of the unit. It also allows for routine checking of the units.

Zone—The different sections of an area being protected by an alarm system. Division into zones allows monitoring personnel to better pinpoint the location of an alarm condition, and zoning allows for flexibility in system usage.

SAFES

Because safes are expensive, great attention must be given to particular needs and corresponding features of security storage containers to ensure that a costly investment is not made in error. Safes are designated in two distinct categories to describe the type and degree of protection they provide: (1) fire-resistant, and (2) burglary/robbery-resistant. The ratings of safes for both fire and burglary protection are not mandated by any federal or state law, but instead are accomplished through specifications established by the Safe Manufacturers National Association (SMNA) and independent tests conducted by Underwriters' Laboratories (UL). Even though SMNA has ceased to be active, its specifications for security storage containers are still being utilized by UL and various insurance groups. The General Services Administration (GSA) also publishes specifications and guidelines for security storage containers relative to federal government applications.

FIRE-RESISTANT SAFES

The SMNA provides specifications for the manufacturing of fire-resistant containers; Underwriters' Laboratories does the independent testing. A UL label or rating means that the merchandise in that class meets the minimum fire specifications designed for that class by SMNA. Figure 11.4 contains listings for SMNA and UL labeled fire-resistant safe equipment.

The Class A fire-resistant safe, SMNA specification F 1-D, UL rating Class 350-4 hours, with a test feature of "Impact" means that this safe would withstand temperatures of up to 2000°F for a period of four hours. During the span of four hours (0-4 hours), the temperature of the interior of the safe would not exceed 350°F. Because 350°F is the ignition point of paper, any record or paper content would be considered to be protected under the above conditions. This same safe would also withstand an impact of being dropped 30 feet while still hot. This feature would be very important in a multi-storied building where fire damages the floor and allows the safe to fall through. A Class A or 350-4 hour fire-resistant safe provides the maximum fire protection available in a safe. It is recommended that this safe be used when the following conditions exist:

1) a facility is located in a remote area where response time will be lengthy and no firefighting personnel are available on the premises;

2) a facility has extremely valuable papers or records that either cannot be replaced or can be replaced only after costly delays;

3) a facility has materials, substances, or petroleum products that will cause a quick increase in temperature during a fire;

4) a facility has any unique features that would make it difficult to extinguish a fire easily and quickly, e.g., a grain elevator building; or

5) a facility has multiple floors and the safe is stored on an upper level.

Figure 11.4
Safe Manufacturers National Association Fire-Resistant Labeled Equipment

Product Classification	SMNA Spec.	SMNA Class.	UL Rating	Test Feature
Fire-Resistant Safe	F 1-D	A	Class 350 - 4 hr.	Impact
Fire-Resistant Safe	F 1-D	B	Class 350 - 2 hr.	Impact
Fire-Resistant Safe	F 1-D	C	Class 350 - 1 hr.	Impact
Insulated Filing Device	F 2-ND	D	Class 350 - 1 hr.	No Impact
Insulated Filing Device	F 2-ND	E	Class 350 - 1/2 hr.	No Impact
Insulated Record Container (Ledger File)	F 1-D	C	Class 350 - 1 hr.	Impact
Insulated Record Container	F 2-D	C	Class 350 - 1 hr.	Impact
Insulated Record Container	F 2-D*	Class 150	Class 150 - 4 hr.	Impact
Insulated Record Container	F 2-D*	Class 150	Class 150 - 2 hr.	Impact
Insulated Record Container	F 2-D*	Class 150	Class 150 - 1 hr.	Impact
Fire-Insulated Vault Door	F 3	6 hour	Class 350 - 6 hr.	—
Fire-Insulated Vault Door	F 3	4 hour	Class 350 - 4 hr.	—
Fire-Insulated Vault Door	F 3	2 hour	Class 350 - 2 hr.	—
Fire-Insulated File Room Door	F 4	1 hour	Class 350 - 1 hr.	—

NOTE:

Class A	protects paper records from damage by fire (2,000°F) up to 4 hours.
Class B	protects paper records from damage by fire (1,850°F) up to 2 hours.
Class C & D	protects paper records from damage by fire (1,700°F) up to 1 hour.
Class E	protects paper records from damage by fire (1,550°F) up to 1/2 hour.
Class 150	protects EDP records from damage by fire and humidity for rated period.
The Drop or Impact test:	The Drop or Impact test is used to determine whether or not the fire resistance of a product would be impaired by being dropped 30 feet while still hot. Fire-resistant equipment is designed specifically to resist fire, and consists of a metal insulation.

*Impact tested when unloaded.

(Holcomb, 1977:17)

Class B and C fire safes provide two-hour and one-hour protection, respectively, and both have the impact feature. The Class C fire safe costs less than either the Class A or B and is the most popular and commonly used fire-resistant safe. The Class D, insulated filing device, SMNA specification F 2-ND, UL rating Class 350-1 hour, with a test feature of "No Impact," will withstand temperatures of up to 1700°F for a period of one hour. During the span of one hour, the temperature of the interior of the safe would not exceed 350°F. This unit would not withstand an impact or drop. Other types of storage units with various fire-resistant classes and ratings are noted in Figure 11.4.

Fire-resistant safes and storage units are double-walled containers. Between the relatively thin (as compared to burglary-resistant safes) outer and inner metal walls, is a layer of moisture-impregnated insulation. When the unit is exposed to heat, the moisture is driven off as steam, allowing for dissipation of the heat. Locking devices for both fire-resistant and burglary-resistant units are similar: key locks, combination locks, and time locks. However, the locking device does not have anything to do with determining whether the unit is a fire-resistant container. The construction features and performance standards of the fire-resistant safe, filing device, or records container are such that very little protection is provided against the safecracker.

Once exposed to a fire, a fire-resistant safe does not have the degree of protection for which it was originally rated. Exposure to heat will drive off moisture from the insulation and reduce its future protection capability.

BURGLARY-RESISTANT SAFES

Burglary-resistant mercantile safes, commonly known as money safes or money chests, are classified by SMNA specifications, by UL ratings and by design features of the door, walls, and lock. They are listed by insurance underwriters in mercantile safe policies according to these specifications. Figure 11.5 gives some of the more basic UL safe classifications, and Figure 11.6 shows the incorporation of UL labeling into insurance specifications.

The following are construction features common to burglary-resistant safes.

1) Safes and chests are constructed of laminated or solid steel.

2) Laminated steel is defined as two or more sheets of steel with the facing surfaces bonded together with no other material between the sheets.

3) Each door of each safe, chest, or security locker must be equipped with at least one combination lock, except a safe, chest, or security locker equipped with an Underwriters' Laboratories, Inc. labeled key lock.

4) Doors. Thickness of steel is exclusive of bolt work and locking devices. If a safe has more than one door, one in front of the other, the combined thickness of the steel in the doors, excluding any door with less than one inch of steel, must be used in applying the classifications referred to in Figure 11.6.

5) Combination Lock. Each safe, chest, cabinet, or vault must be equipped with at least one combination lock, except a safe or chest equipped with a key lock and bearing the label, "Underwriters' Laboratories, Inc. Inspected KL Burglary."

The proper selection and use of a money safe will provide for the effective protection of valuables, reduce insurance premiums, increase employee efficiency and morale, and deter or prevent losses. Because money safes have unique design and construction features, the manner in which one is to be used must be given every consideration before the decision to purchase is made.

Figure 11.5
Underwriters' Laboratories Burglary-Resistant Safes

Classification	Description	Construction
TL-15	Tool-Resistant	Weight: 750-pound minimum Body: Minimum 1" steel or equal Resistance: Door and front of unit must withstand attack with common hand and electric tools for 15 minutes.
TL-30	Tool-Resistant	Weight: 750-pound minimum Body: Minimum 1" steel or equal Resistance: Door and front of unit must withstand attack with common hand and electric tools, plus abrasive cutting wheels and power saws for 30 minutes.
TRTL-30	Torch- and Tool-Resistant	Weight: 750-pound minimum Resistance: Door and front of unit must withstand attack with common hand and electric tools, abrasive cutting wheels and power saws, and/or oxy-fuel gas cutting or welding torches for 30 minutes.
TRTL-30X6	Torch- and Tool-Resistant	Weight: 750-pound minimum Resistance: Door and entire body must withstand attack with tools and torches listed above plus electric impact hammers and oxy-fuel gas cutting or welding torches for 30 minutes.
TXTL-60	Tool-, Torch- and Explosive-Resistant	Weight: 1000-pound minimum Resistance: Door and entire safe body must withstand attack with tools and torches listed above, plus eight ounces of nitroglycerine or equal for 60 minutes.

NOTE: Various combinations of classification ratings are available according to safe construction, design features, and performance standards.

Figure 11.6
**Commercial Lines Manual—Insurance Service's Office
Burglary- and Robbery-Resistant Equipment**

Safe, Chest or Security Locker Classifications	Construction	
	Doors (Combination Locked)	Walls
A	Steel less than 1" thick, or iron	Body of steel less than ½" thick, or iron
B	Steel at least 1" thick	Body of steel at least ½" thick
	Night depository — steel at least 1½" thick	Body of steel at least 1" thick
BR	Steel at least 1½" thick	Body of steel at least 1" thick
	Safe or chest bearing the label: "Underwriters' Laboratories, Inc. Inspected Tool Resisting Safe TL-15 Burglary."	
	Night Depository — Receiving safe to be equal to at least Class "BR"	
	The receiving safe and chute to be encased in at least 6" of reinforced concrete.	
C	Steel at least 2" thick	Body of steel at least 2" thick
	No longer manufactured	
	Night depository — Receiving safe to be equal to at least Class "BR." Depository head to bear UL inspected label. Receiving safe and chute to be encased in at least 6" of reinforced concrete.	
D	Steel at least 2" thick	Body of steel at least 2" thick
	When contained within a safe:	
	Steel at least 1" thick	Body of steel less than ½" thick or iron
	No longer manufactured	
E	Steel at least 2" thick	Body of steel at least 2" thick
	When contained within a safe:	
	Steel at least 2" thick	Body of steel less than ½" thick or iron
	No longer manufactured	
F	At least two: Steel aggregating 5" or more in thickness — no door less than 1" thick	Body of steel at least 2" thick
	No longer manufactured	
G	Round lug-type, steel at least 1½" thick	Body of steel at least 1" thick
	If this safe is outside of a vault, this safe is to be encased in at least 6" of reinforced concrete and the door is to be equipped with at least a two-movement timelock.	
	Safe or chest bearing one of the following labels: 1. "Underwriters' Laboratories, Inc. Inspected Tool Resisting Safe TL-30 Burglary"	

Figure 11.6, *continued*

	2. "Underwriters' Laboratories, Inc. Inspected Torch Resisting Safe TR-30 Burglary"
	3. "Underwriters' Laboratories, Inc. Inspected Explosive Resisting Safe with Relocking Device X-60 Burglary"
H	Safe or chest bearing one of the following labels:
	1. "Underwriters' Laboratories, Inc. Inspected Torch and Explosive Resisting Safe TX-60 Burglary"
	2. "Underwriters' Laboratories, Inc. Inspected Torch Resisting Safe TR-60 Burglary"
	3. "Underwriters' Laboratories, Inc. Inspected Torch and Tool Resisting Safe TRTL-30 Burglary"
I	Safe or chest bearing the following label:
	"Underwriters' Laboratories, Inc. Inspected Torch and Tool Resisting Safe TRTL-15x6 Burglary"
J	Safe or chest bearing the following label:
	"Underwriters' Laboratories, Inc. Inspected Torch and Tool Resisting Safe TRTL-30x6 Burglary"
K	Safe or chest bearing one of the following labels:
	1. "Underwriters' Laboratories, Inc. Inspected Torch and Tool Resisting Safe TRTL-60 Burglary"
	2. "Underwriters' Laboratories, Inc. Inspected Tool Resisting Safe TXTL-60 Burglary"

The decision to purchase a particular classification of safe should depend on a thorough examination of such factors as:

1) Where the safe will be used (e.g., jewelry store, movie theater, department store, etc.);

2) What types of valuables will be stored in the safe (e.g., cash, precious gems, etc.);

3) How many items will be stored in the safe;

4) The design features required to incorporate the safe into a reasonable and secure procedural usage; and

5) The risk factors applicable to the safe and its contents (e.g., employees, burglars, robbers, etc.).

SAFECRACKING METHODS

Many safes in use today cannot withstand the efforts of the modern-day safecracker equipped with high-quality cutting and burning tools. Once the safecracker has defeated or bypassed the perimeter barriers and alarm system (if present), there are several techniques available to attack the safe.

Drilling or **Punching**—Many locking mechanisms for safe doors can be defeated by knocking off the combination dial or by drilling a small hole near the combination dial to expose the locking device. A safe without relocking devices (which jam the locking mechanism in place) offers little resistance to this technique.

Burning—To burn a safe is to cut an opening in the wall or door of the safe with high-temperature oxyacetylene torches or "burning bars." This attack is intended to create an opening large enough to expose the locking mechanism or to remove the contents of the safe. A burning bar or thermic lance is a device consisting of a hollow metal bar into which are packed ferrous alloy rods. To one end is attached an oxygen tank that feeds through the ferrous alloy rods. When lit at the burning end with an acetylene torch, tremendous heat is generated, which is capable of burning through the toughest steel safe (and destroying the contents of the safe).

Peeling—Sometimes safe doors and walls are constructed of thin steel plates laminated or riveted together to form the total thickness of the door or wall. The safecracker attacks the seams of these metal plates with pry bars and other tools to peel back the layers of metal, exposing the locking mechanism or the interior of the safe.

Ripping—Ripping is similar to peeling, with the difference being that ripping can be accomplished against a solid, metal-walled container having a very thin outer and/or inner wall.

X-ray—X-ray examination of the locking mechanism can expose the position of the combination, and reveal what type of manipulation is necessary to open the safe. While this is not a common technique of safecracking, many safes are constructed with shields that protect the combination from X-rays.

Explosives—The use of explosives as a means of safecracking has decreased greatly in recent years because more efficient, safer tools and techniques are now available. However, nitroglycerin, plastic explosives, and other materials still can be used to "crack" a safe.

Power Tools—Power-driven rotary devices, hydraulic tools, and power drills can be utilized to pry, cut, spread, and drill openings into the door or body of the safe.

Manipulation—Few safecrackers have the skill to manipulate a safe's combination without some prior knowledge or condition being present. Most often, manipulation is the result of the "safecracker" having discovered or stolen the combination to the safe.

Although no safe is impenetrable, the old axiom "you get what you pay for" certainly applies to safes. The burglary-resistant properties provided by a safe are in direct proportion to its cost. A safe, then, is not totally "safe," and other measures must be taken to provide for its protection. Perimeter barriers, adequate locking hardware, electronic alarm systems, and security procedures must be apparent if the desired level of security is to be accomplished. How the safe is used is just as important as its quality of construction and performance. Hiding the safe in the back room, being careless with the control of its combination or keys, or depending too much on its protective capability all invite theft of its contents.

Additionally, the security of a safe can be (and often should be) improved by taking steps to reduce its vulnerability. For example, any safe that weighs less than 750 pounds should be anchored to the building structure, thereby making its removal from the premises very difficult. This also can make it more difficult to attack the bottom or rear of the safe. This is why fire-resistant safes are frequently encased in concrete. This not only adds to their fire-resistant qualities but also makes them less vulnerable to most safecracking techniques. Some safes are designed to be installed in-ground (in concrete), thereby increasing both the security and fire-resistive attributes of the unit.

Once the decision is made to purchase either a fire-resistive or burglary-resistant storage container, consideration must be given to its utilization and function as a protective device. Business practices, risk factors, and environmental conditions can change to the point that a safe currently in use is no longer adequate for the needed level of security.

VAULTS

Designed for the secure storage of valuables, a vault is a room of a size and shape sufficient for entrance and movement within by one or more persons. A vault is different from a safe in that it is larger, a part of the building structure and constructed of different materials.

Vault walls, floors, and ceilings should be made of reinforced concrete at least 12 inches thick. The vault door should be made of steel (or other torch- and drill-resistant material) and be equipped with a combination lock, fire lock, and lockable day gate. The door also should be designed to afford an appropriate degree of fire resistance.

Ratings for vaults are established by the Insurance Services Office. The ratings are based on the type of construction materials utilized, their relative thickness, applicable construction standards, and equipment features. Materials—whether concrete, stone, or steel—must be of an appropriate thickness for each rating category. Materials must be fabricated and installed according to set methods and guidelines. Construction standards must be such that the rating of the vault will not be invalidated by such variances as excessive openings in number or size. Equipment features must be met in certain rating categories, such as inclusion of combination locks and time locks. Safety deposit boxes, for the convenience of customers, are a common feature of most bank vaults.

A recent innovation in vault construction and installation techniques is the modular, all-metal unit. Used primarily for satellite facilities, such as small branch banks, the modular vault arrives at the construction site in sections, to be

Figure 11.7
Safety Deposit Boxes Within a Vault

lifted and fitted in place. The technique saves time and installation costs and such units are classified by Underwriters' Laboratories according to their design and construction features.

Vault walls can be steel, concrete, or stone. Figure 11.8 compares the different kinds of wall materials. Electronic alarm protection of vault walls, ceilings, and floors is generally accomplished by audio microphones or vibration detectors that sense attempts to penetrate the vault structure. Vault doors are protected by means of door contact switches and heat sensors. Some vault doors have a built-in wire grid that causes an alarm if the wires are cut or melted. Additional protection of the vault can be provided by area or space devices such as the motion detector, which reacts to anyone moving into the area around the vault.

Figure 11.8
Vault Wall Material Equivalents

Steel Lining		Nonreinforced Concrete or Stone		Reinforced Concrete or Stone
¼ inch	=	12 inches		
½ inch	=	18 inches	=	12 inches
¾ inch	=	27 inches		
1 inch	=	36 inches	=	18 inches
1¼ inch	=	45 inches		
1½ inch	=	54 inches	=	27 inches

(Commercial Lines Manual, 1985)

DISCUSSION QUESTIONS

1. What are some of the key considerations in deciding upon the utilization of any alarm system?

2. Briefly describe the functions of alarms and alarm systems.

3. List and describe the basic components of an alarm system.

4. Discuss the utility and benefits of using security personnel versus security equipment and hardware.

5. Explain the differences between a tape dialer system and a digital dialer system.

6. In terms of coverage, what are the three categories of alarm system sensors?

7. What are the basic components of a CCTV system?

8. Describe at least three types of perimeter alarm systems.

9. Explain why false alarms are such a problem with alarm systems.

10. What are the two types of safes and what are the purposes of each?

11. Describe the circumstances that may dictate the use of a maximum fire protection safe.

12. Discuss the differences between safes and vaults.

13. Outline the steps to be taken to protect information.

14. Describe the three methods of protecting information.

15. Describe at least three safecracking techniques.

16. Explain why the security of computers is important to organizations.

17. Describe some of the differences in the construction features of a safe designed to be fire-resistive and one constructed to resist direct forcible attack.

18. List and discuss the sequential levels of computer security and information resource security that must be accomplished.

REFERENCES

Commercial Lines Manual. Insurance Services Office, 1985.

Cunningham, W.C., Strauchs, J.J. & Van Meter, C.W. (1990). *Private Security Trends 1970-2000: The Hallcrest Report II.* Stoneham, MA: Butterworth-Heinemann.

Holcomb, R.C. (Dec. 1977). "Rating of Safes: Part 1." *Keynotes.*

Vitch, M.L. (July 1992). "Sensing Your Way to Security." *Security Management.* Arlington, VA: American Society for Industrial Security.

SECTION IV

PRINCIPLES OF PUBLIC AND PRIVATE SECTOR LAW ENFORCEMENT

Legal Aspects of Private Security

12

INTRODUCTION

Our legal system attempts to strike a balance between the rights of persons and private organizations to protect themselves and their property, and the rights of private citizens to be free from the power of others. The attempt to balance conflicting interests is nowhere more apparent than in the field of private security.

On the one hand, the private sector uses security employees to protect personnel, property, and customers from the mugger, shoplifter, pickpocket, hijacker, embezzler, arsonist, vandal, terrorist, and other threats. On the other hand, all citizens are entitled to be free from assault and battery by others, unlawful detention or arrest, injury to reputation, intrusion into personal privacy, and illegal invasions of one's land, dwelling, or personal property.

In order to perform effectively, private security personnel must, in many instances, walk a tightrope between permissible protective activities and unlawful interferences with the rights of private citizens. The precise limits of the authority of private security personnel are not clearly spelled out in any one set of legal materials. Rather, one must look at a number of sources in order to define (even in a rough way) the dividing line between proper and improper private security behavior. These sources are briefly discussed below.

COMMON LAW

The United States derives its law from the common law of England. Having been influenced by the Germans, Celts, French, feudalism, the Canon Law of the Church, and the Natural Law of the Romans, English common law was shaped by various monarchs, the demands of the barons, the decisions of circuit judges, and the demands of citizens. While English common law was still maturing, the "New World" was being settled by people from various European countries. It was the early English settlers and their colonial philosophies that determined the direction and content of the American system of law and justice. Thus, it was common law that provided the basis for such legal concepts as mens rea, civil liability, self-defense, self-help, etc. (Bilek, Klotter & Keegan, 1981:1-5).

English common law considered human life more important than property and held the right of self-defense—even forceful self-defense—for one's person and others to be right and proper. In fact, the vassal (servant) under the feudal system had a fundamental obligation to protect and defend his lord. This is the origin of the present right to contract for the protection of oneself or another. However, in the United States the common law has held that, in general, a private person has no legal obligation or duty to protect another from criminal attack by a third person unless it can be shown that a special relationship and affirmative duty exists between the parties involved. For example, this exception would require a private person to protect another if the other person placed himself or herself under the person's care and control, thereby subordinating protection of self to the care and responsibility of another. Areas generally covered by this exception are innkeeper-guest, common carrier-passenger, business-business patron, hospital-patient, and employer-employee. *Kline v. 1500 Massachusetts Avenue Apartment Corporation,* 439 F.2d 477 (D.C. Cir. 1970), became the focal point for such control and protection cases. In this case, two important legal theories evolved. First, a landowner may be liable where the ability of one of the parties to provide for personal protection had been limited and this particular party submitted to the control of the other. Second, liability against criminal acts may arise where the criminal act was reasonably foreseeable by the landowner. Thus, the legal tenet that certain property owners and possessors have a special duty to exercise reasonable care (see "Tort Law") or higher than ordinary care to prevent foreseeable dangers from harming their guests, passengers, patrons, patients, employees, etc., has been well established through the evolution of the English common law, case law, legislation, and tort law.

CONSTITUTIONAL LAW

The federal Constitution places many limitations on the conduct of government officials, including police and quasi-police agencies and other components of the total criminal justice system. The Constitution does not protect citizens from private actions, *Burdeau v. McDowell,* 41 S. Ct. 574 (1921). Most constitutional rights of an individual relate to governmental or state action and not to activities of other private persons or corporations. Constitutional limitations can, however, apply to the conduct of private security personnel who act in concert with public law enforcement officials or as agents of such officials to obtain evidence with the intent of furnishing it to such officials for use in prosecution. While the Constitution does not protect against the actions of private citizens, general tort theories may.

Basically, a security officer may possess one of three kinds of power and authority. An authority identical to that possessed by a citizen or a property owner is by far the most common power held by security officers. Less common is an authority obtained by deputization or commissioning from a public law enforcement agency. The third type of authority possessed by some security officers is a mixture of the powers of a civilian with certain special prerogatives added by statute, ordinance, or governmental regulation. A full-time police officer working as a part-time security officer would be in this third area. Deputization is the most frequent legal action that vests the private citizen or private security official with full police powers (as well as the restrictions and limitations on such powers). The extent of permissible deputization is limited. In Maryland, for example, the governor is able to appoint "special" police officers to work for private businesses with full police power limited to the property of the requesting business (Md. Ann. Code art. 41, 60). Oregon has a similar code but only in the railroad and steamboat industries (O.R.S. §§ 148, 210). Deputization does not always give full police powers, and it usually subjects the deputized individual to constitutional restrictions (Bird, Kakalik, Wildhorn et al., 1972:13).

As constitutional restrictions normally apply to state actions only, they generally do not pertain to private security activities. Only in rare instances are private security actions classified as a state action. The question of whether the licensing of private security personnel constitutes state action is raised in *Weyandt v. Mason's Store Inc.,* 279 F. Supp. 283 (W.D. Pa. 1968). The argument was the same as that in *Burton v. Wilmington Parking Authority*, 365 U.S. 715 (1961), in which the Supreme Court held that there were sufficient grounds for a restaurant owner to be liable for racial discrimination, because the state granted a lease to the restaurant. That reasoning was not followed in *Weyandt*. It was held that, although a private detective of a store was licensed under the Pennsylvania Private Detective Act and was acting under "color of the law," the law is not a deputization law and does not invest the licensee with the authority of state law. Thus, the private detective of the store was only acting with the authority of a "private citizen." When private security personnel are hired on a contractual basis by a public authority, they are in fact acting with authority of state law and have the imposition of constitutional restrictions upon the exercise of power. *Williams v. United States*, 341 U.S. 97 (1951). This applies to the area of arrest as well as other categories of legal involvement of private security officials.

CRIMINAL LAW

Criminal codes offer both a source of power and restraint for the private security officer. In criminal law, a crime is a "social harm" for which the offender is answerable to society and is punishable by fine or imprisonment (Perkins, 1969:23). Criminal law operates as a deterrent to the extent that the law is known, the consequences of being convicted are sufficient, and the criminal justice system operates effectively in imposing sanctions. Because intent to commit a crime is required, crimes are carefully defined and the prosecution must prove guilt beyond a reasonable doubt. Criminal law can be best seen as the establishment of outer limits on behavior rather than a day-to-day regulatory device.

Two concepts are important if private security personnel are to acquire a working knowledge of criminal law. First is the legal maxim that everyone is presumed to know the laws of the state and nation. Of course, this legal premise is not valid when tested on a nonlegal, practical basis. Even lawyers are not able to recite all of the laws of a state. Nevertheless, this rule prevails and is applied in courts of law. The second legal concept is that a law must be clear and understandable so that an ordinary person will know what conduct is prohibited.

Before a person can be convicted of violating one of the specific laws of the state, the prosecution must establish beyond a reasonable doubt each of the elements of the offense. The state must prove that there was *mens rea*, or intent, and an *actus reus*, or an act. For example, burglary is generally defined as the breaking and entering of a dwelling or other building for the purpose of committing a felony therein. If one element is not proved, even though the others are shown beyond a reasonable doubt, there can be no conviction of that offense. If the government can prove a breaking and entering (*actus reus*), but cannot prove the intent to commit a felony (*mens rea*), the proof is insufficient to prove the crime of burglary. There is a possibility, however, that the person could be convicted of a lesser included offense.

TORT LAW

[handwritten margin note: Tort - Civil wrong, other than breach of contract for which the law will provide a remedy. ① negligence ② intentional. Accidents vs. meant]

Tort law is the primary source for the authority of private security officers and the limitations on such authority. The law of torts is found in both legislation and court-developed common law. There is no single body of tort law; it varies from state to state. However, there is an ongoing attempt to achieve some conformity through various model laws and the "Restatement of Torts," published by the American Law Institute. Tort law is defined as a body of law that governs the civil relationships between people (Prosser & Smith, 1967:1-2). It defines and creates causes of actions permitting one person to remedy the wrongs committed against him or her by another, and has the effect of restraining conduct by making the wrongdoer aware of the one injured. These remedies may be either equitable (the enjoining of certain conduct) or legal (the recovery of money damages for injuries received). Tort law differs from criminal law in that private parties do the suing, and the suing party seeks relief, e.g., compensation for damages incurred, and possibly punitive damages to "punish" the defendant for a serious wrong.

To a certain extent, tort law defines privileges and immunities that offer a source of authority for private conduct. Early rules of arrest, prevention of crime, self-defense, defense of others, and defense of property have their bases in common law tort principles. Further, tort law protects an individual's person and property from injurious conduct, a reputation from disparagement, privacy from unreasonable exposure, and mental well-being from emotional distress. Conduct that harms another and violates norms of reasonableness is generally actionable if engaged in without privilege or immunity. For example, the courts have generally held that businesses and commercial enterprises are expected to make reasonable efforts to protect visitors from known or reasonably discoverable defects. Those that do not attempt foreseeability of injurious and harmful events and situations may be held financially accountable for the losses incurred.

Tort law does not provide specific authority for private security officers, but does define some limits on the conduct of private security personnel. It allows for an injured party to bring a lawsuit for damages and injuries caused by the tortious conduct of private security officers and/or any businesses and organizations associated with the situation in question. The courts follow precedents when established, and create remedies to fit novel cases. Typically, these remedies come from common law. Thus, tort law restrains the authority of private security officers only by the threat of a subsequent lawsuit, and provides general parameters on reasonable conduct through case law precedents.

Tort law provides that a civil action for damages may be maintained by one party against another whenever the former has suffered a compensable injury or loss by reason of the act of the latter. Therefore, an act or omission that causes such injuries or losses to another is known as a civil action or tort. In order for the injured party to recover damages from the tortfeasor, the injured party must prove that the tortfeasor either intentionally, or through negligence, caused damages.

The purpose of a civil action is to provide reasonable compensation to an injured party for damages incurred due to the acts of another. Therefore, as opposed to criminal prosecutions where the intent of the accused is a major element of the offense, civil actions require less proof. The burden that a plaintiff (the person raising a claim of injury) must bear is to prove by a preponderance of evidence that the act occurred. The major concern is that the person or corporate entity be required to pay for the damages caused to another. In negligence cases, the victim need not prove that the tortfeasor intentionally damaged the victim.

Most civil actions are based on a claim that the defendant was negligent in conduct and that it was this negligence that occasioned the loss for which recovery is sought. Negligence (or the absence of due diligence) is the key to most cases involving security personnel and/or security issues. The law requires that all persons conduct themselves with due regard for the safety and rights of others; the failure to do so constitutes negligence. The standard by which particular conduct is tested to determine whether it constitutes negligence is that of the "reasonable person." That is, would a reasonable person of ordinary prudence have acted similarly under the same or similar circumstances? Common law torts have traditionally established four conditions or elements for a negligence lawsuit to succeed: (1) that an established link or duty to a plaintiff exists; (2) that the defendant breached this established duty; (3) that the breach of duty by the defendant was the proximate cause of damage or injury; and (4) that the breach of duty by the defendant resulted in the occurrence of actual damage or injury to the plaintiff.

Of course, the standard is higher when the conduct of certain professionals is in question. If one holds oneself out to the public as an expert in a particular field, one thereby assumes the duty to conduct all activities in accordance with the generally accepted standards of others in the same profession. Therefore, someone who claims to be a professional, having special knowledge or expertise in a particular field (private security, for instance), will have his or her conduct measured against this higher standard rather than by the standard of the ordinary person who professes no such expertise.

CONTRACT LAW

There are several types of contractual arrangements that are important to the scope of authority of private security personnel and the component areas of service offered by a full-service security agency. The performance of the security officer has been the dominant concern of contract law regarding security services since World War II. In addition, improvement in electronic alarm systems and seemingly reduced costs have led many businesses to install them in the last decade. This movement toward more sophisticated electronic alarms (as well as their sometimes extravagant advertising claims) has focused attention in contract law to the various alarm applications and their relationships to a business enterprise.

The terms of a contract between a business enterprise and a security service may limit the private security officer's authority and define more stringent standards of behavior than are defined in other bodies of law. The contract between the security agency and the employing company usually will define the respective liabilities of all parties. If there is harm to a third party, the contract usually will establish who is to be responsible and who is to carry insurance for which risks. However, in some suits by third parties, the courts have held one party liable even though a contract said that another party was to be responsible. (See Annotation, "Liabilities of One Contracting for Private Police or Security Services for Acts of Personnel Supplied," 38 A.L.R. 3rd 1332 (1971)). In addition, union contracts may impose restraints on employers (and thus on private security personnel) with regard to such areas as search of employee lockers or belongings and the conduct of investigations into employee wrongdoing.

STATUTORY PROVISIONS

Restraints on the conduct of private security personnel may also be found in a variety of state and local statutes, rules, ordinances, and regulations. Much of this legislation is in the form of licensing or registration statutes that place requirements on qualifications of security personnel to obtain or retain a license or permit. To some extent, these statutes also delineate proper and improper forms of conduct.

Many of these regulations provide for suspension or revocation of a license and include provisions requiring the posting of surety bonds and/or evidence of appropriate liability insurance. Special privileges, such as the right to carry a concealed weapon, may be granted by such regulations to private security personnel. The statutory provisions vary by state and locality, and enforcement procedures vary even more.

Special attention needs to be given to four problem areas in private security: (1) use of force, (2) interrogation and questioning, (3) search, and (4) a comparison between public and private police.

USE OF FORCE

Any activity performed by a security officer that interferes with the rights of other persons, unless there is privilege or consent, places the security officer in a position of possibly being held liable for such interference. The primary legal basis for many activities performed by a security officer is consent. If a security officer asks a person to do a certain act, i.e., leave an amusement park, and the customer does so voluntarily, the customer has consented to leave the park. Consent cannot be coerced, however, and it also may be limited in its scope. When consent is not given, there are various privileges that usually provide the legal basis for enforcement activities.

Two important privileges are the right of a real property owner to prevent trespasses on owned property and the right to self-defense. A person may use reasonable force against someone who appears to be about to inflict physical harm. Generally, however, only that amount of force reasonably necessary to realize the legitimate purposes of the privilege is allowed. If excessive or unreasonable force is used, not only is one liable for the torts resulting from this excessive force (usually battery), but one forfeits the original privilege.

There are no clear rules as to what degree of force is allowable in given situations. Usually, the concept of "reasonableness" controls, and what is reasonable depends on the nature of the interest being protected, the nature of the act being resisted and the particular facts in a given situation. To add to the confusion, the amount of force allowed is different depending upon which privilege is being invoked. Where property rights are involved, a request for voluntary cooperation (consent) should precede the use of any force. Similarly, when only property is at stake, the use of deadly force (e.g., a gun) is impermissible unless the threat to property also threatens life. The law places a higher value upon human safety and life than upon rights inherent in property, and it is the accepted rule in law that there is no privilege to use any force calculated to cause death or serious bodily injury to repel the threat to land or chattels, unless there is also such a threat to the property owner's (or representative's) personal safety as to justify self-defense. This rule, for example, would likewise apply to the privileges granted in all shoplifting cases.

INTERROGATION AND QUESTIONING

As long as a person is legally detained, there is no absolute ban on asking questions. Courts have held that an improper interrogation is not itself a tort, whereas an illegal arrest or an illegal search or seizure may be. However, there are still certain limits imposed by state law on the methods of interrogation. For example, a suspect has the right to remain silent and is under no legal obligation to answer questions. At the same time, however, the private security officer who is not operating under special sanctions and commissions of a state is not obligated to advise the suspect of these rights.

Some indirect control over interrogation methods is exerted by virtue of contract law: any releases, promises, or agreements signed or entered into as a result of coercion or duress would be unenforceable. Indirect control also exists by virtue of decisions by some courts that confessions or admissions obtained by coercion, force, and (sometimes) promises are inadmissible in subsequent criminal proceedings against the suspect. *Arizona v. Fulminante*, 111 S. Ct. 1246 (1991).

The use of physical force or threats of physical force to coerce answers is prohibited. Such threats or force would be tortious, either directly (as assault or battery) or indirectly (as constituting unreasonable exercise of the detention or arrest privilege involved). The legality of any interrogation or questioning will turn on the manner in which the questioning is conducted. The standard for the manner of questioning is whether a reasonable person would feel that their will to resist was overborne by the interrogator. *Brown v. Mississippi*, 56 S. Ct. 461 (1936).

SEARCH

There is a vast difference between searches conducted by law enforcement officers and searches made by private persons. For example, unless a private security officer is acting in concert with police officials or under the authority of state or local laws that confer the authority of a "quasi" police officer, the private security officer has the same rights as any other private person in this regard.

A police officer is most often concerned with whether the results of a search will be admissible as evidence in a criminal prosecution. The Fourth Amendment and its companion, the exclusionary rule, require that such governmental searches be based on probable cause. A police officer may be held liable civilly for damages to the victim of an unlawful search on the basis of a Constitutional tort (42 U.S. Code, Section 1983).

The Fourth Amendment does not apply to searches by private persons. As long as they were not acting under the advice of law enforcement officers, evidence discovered by means of a private search is ordinarily admissible in a criminal prosecution, even when there was no basis at all for the search other than mere curiosity or snooping. A private security officer, though, must be more concerned with possible civil (and sometimes criminal) liability that may result from an illegal or unreasonable search. Tort actions against private security would generally follow a theory of invasion of privacy.

The legality of a search, like the legality of interrogation or questioning, is usually inseparable from the legality of the initial detention of the suspect. Following this logic, if there is no probable cause for the detention, then any search incident to the detention also would be illegal. Assuming a legitimate basis for detention, the question is whether a private security officer has the legal power to search a suspect's person, purse, briefcase, or other items the suspect is carrying.

Often, consent will render the search valid, particularly if the suspect physically cooperates in the search at the request of the private security officer. Without consent, some legal privilege or right must be found to justify a search. However, the privileges that might allow searches to be made by private security are not clear-cut, nor is any single privilege, like self-defense, expansive enough to sanction a wide range of searches in a number of different situations. The law regarding searches in the private sector has simply not been developed as it has in the public police sector.

The common law right of self-defense might justify reasonable searches for weapons, but only where there are reasonable grounds to fear imminent attack by use of a concealed weapon. Under common law, the arresting individual is empowered to search a suspect who is already under detainment if the arresting individual "has reason to believe that the suspect has on or about their person any offensive weapons or incriminating articles." (See Perkins, supra, note 304 at 261, Warner, "The Uniform Arrest Act," 28 Va. L. Rev., 315, 324 (1942); *United States v. Viale*, 312 F.2d 595 (2d Cir. 1963); Restatement of Torts (2d) 132, comment d.) However, this power was limited to cases of formal arrest (i.e., in which the person will be turned over to the authorities), not mere detention. A similar right is provided by state statutes that specially authorize private citizens to seize weapons from the arrested person when making an arrest. The common law privilege of recapturing chattels (property) wrongfully taken seems to support a search about the person for such goods or chattels in a nonarrest situation; however, in states that allow this practice, its use is quite limited. Most merchant detention privileges would not support such a search, and some states even prohibit it by statute.

COMPARISON BETWEEN PUBLIC AND PRIVATE POLICE

Under state tort laws and statutes, public police officers have significantly more powers than nondeputized private security officers. Public police officers can obtain and serve a search or arrest warrant. Even without a warrant, police officers may arrest or detain a suspect in all of the situations in which a private citizen could, and many more. For example, police officers can arrest for the commission of a felony that was not committed in their presence as long as there is probable cause for believing a felony has been committed. In contrast, private citizens usually may arrest for a felony only when, in fact, the felony has been committed. Further, not only are public police officers usually vested with the same powers as merchants (or their agents) to detain shoplifters, they are often empowered to stop or temporarily detain persons suspected of other crimes, and to frisk any temporarily detained person for a weapon if reasonable suspicion exists to believe they are armed and dangerous. (*Terry v. Ohio*, 88 S. Ct. 1868 (1968)). Incident to a lawful arrest, police officers are allowed to conduct a search of the person for weapons and contraband.

Moreover, public police officers have at least the same powers as private security officers to take actions short of arrest, such as expelling intruders or persons causing disturbance from private property. They are as capable of acting on behalf of the owner as any other agent of the owner. In addition, public police officers are often given specific statutory authority to take such action in particular situations.

As a practical matter, enforcement of restrictions on the activities of the public police officer by means of a civil or a criminal lawsuit is difficult, and a police officer is likely to encounter much less resistance to requests for voluntary cooperation. Finally, in most states it is a crime to resist an arrest by an officer of the law, even if the arrest is illegal.

On the other hand, the public police officer is subject to various restrictions imposed by the federal Constitution which, so far, generally have not been imposed upon private security personnel. In those areas controlled by the Constitution, a private person may be less restricted, and thus have more latitude than a public police officer.

First, the Fourth Amendment restricts a public police officer's power to arrest without a warrant. For example, to arrest a suspect in his or her home, an officer must have an arrest warrant in order to enter and make the arrest.

Second, the Supreme Court has held that warrantless searches incident to a valid arrest may extend only into the area within which an arrestee might reach a weapon or destructible evidence. *Chimel v. California*, 89 S. Ct. 2034 (1969). While the court in *Terry* sanctioned the warrantless "stop and frisk" of a person engaged in suspicious activities, the court strictly limited the searches incident thereto to a frisk, or pat-down for suspected weapons. *Sibron v. New York*, 88 S. Ct. 1889 (1968). These constitutional limits upon the scope of searches incident to arrests and detentions have not yet been imposed on private searches. Tort law governing private searches of the person are neither clear nor well developed, but will most likely follow a theory of invasion of privacy. Thus, since both the Supreme Court's Fourth Amendment decisions and tort law rely heavily upon "reasonableness," the two areas of law may well coincide without directly imposing constitutional standards upon the activities of private security officers. It is possible that tort law will eventually impose more restrictive standards on private security than are now applied by constitutional law to public police.

Third, the Supreme Court has placed restrictions upon police methods of interrogating suspects to ensure that any confessions are voluntary and not "coerced." The court has enforced these standards by excluding evidence obtained by improper interrogations from subsequent criminal prosecutions of the suspect. Many courts have rendered these constitutional standards applicable indirectly to private persons by excluding any "coerced" confessions from criminal prosecutions, regardless of whether the source of coercion was public or private. *Fulminante*, 111 S. Ct. 1246 (1991).

However, in *Miranda v. Arizona*, 86 S. Ct. 1602 (1966), the Supreme Court imposed an additional requirement for the admissibility of incriminating statements. Before interrogation, the suspect must be informed of the right to remain silent and to obtain the assistance of counsel. This requirement clearly goes beyond what is required of private security personnel by virtue of tort law or by the admissibility standards applied in such decisions.

In summary, the public police may have greater arrest, search, and interrogation powers under state law, but they are also subject to constitutional restrictions which, so far, have not been imposed upon private security. Nevertheless, these constitutional restrictions sometimes are not significantly different from the restrictions imposed on private security by tort law.

CURRENT LEGAL TRENDS

Security-related lawsuits have increased tremendously during the past several years. They have multiplied not only in terms of total numbers but also in terms of payments awarded to litigants. These lawsuits have affected a wide range of businesses and organizations, ranging from retailers, health care facilities, financial institutions, schools, hotels/motels, civic groups, and municipal governments. It appears that the majority of cases revolve around the question(s) of inadequate security, improper security practices, and failure to prevent crimes. The litigants bringing suit for negligent actions include victims of criminal acts that occurred in parking lots, motel rooms, hallways, bars, restaurants, apartments, etc.; employees claiming that they were subjected to improper security actions by their employer; customers charging that they were subjected to improper security procedures, including searches and seizures, slander, harassment, etc.; and lawsuits by customers, invitees, and others over failure to perform adequate employment practices such as training, pre-employment selection procedures, and employee controls.

Without question, organizations of many types are being forced to consider and recognize that certain acts and/or omissions with regard to adequate security controls can result in a major lawsuit. In the years since the *Kline* ruling, most courts have eased the plaintiff's burden of proving foreseeability by acknowledging its existence even in the absence of identical or similar crimes previously occurring on the property.

Since most tort actions in private security are brought in state court, the theories of liability are as varied as the states. Three general theories—prior criminal conduct, totality of the circumstances, and reasonable risk—define the foreseeability of crimes.

The prior criminal conduct theory requires that there must have been prior crimes on or near the premises in order to foresee that a particular crime may occur. States that follow the prior criminal conduct theory range in their interpretation as to what criminal conduct makes crimes foreseeable. Generally, the prior crime must be the same or similar to the instant crime to be foreseeable. Also, the crimes must usually occur in or around the area with an amount of frequency, or recently to be foreseeable.

Under the totality of the circumstances theory, foreseeability is not dependent on a prior crime or crimes, but looking at a totality of the circumstances. Prior similar crimes, prior dissimilar crimes, the frequency of crimes, the type of business, etc., are taken into consideration when determining whether or not a crime was foreseeable.

The reasonable risk theory looks at several broad factors to determine foreseeability. First, is there a foreseeable probability of harm or injury? In this determination, one could look at a wide range of conduct as in the totality of the circumstances. Second, is there alternative conduct that the premises owner could engage that is feasible? This allows the exploration of various means to prevent the commission of a crime. Third, what is the usefulness of the safer conduct? If we could make a building impenetrable, what is the feasibility of doing so? Does the risk of not applying certain security features outweigh the cost of a lawsuit? In the absence of a duty to protect under one of the aforementioned theories, a duty to protect may arise from statements made to a visitor to the property. Telling a tenant there has been no crime on the property when in fact there have been crimes on the property, is an example. A prospective tenant, in reliance on the property owner's statement, which the property owner knew, or should have known, to be misleading, will most likely result in liability against the property owner. Advertising statements, such as "lighted security parking" or "security patrols," entice people onto the property but also point to assuming a duty to protect. When an incident occurs, plaintiffs will point to these statements as proof of the existence of a duty.

The following cases are cited to provide a brief overview of lawsuits in selected areas.

Foreseeability

Prior assault in parking lot sufficient to raise issue of foreseeability of second assault. *Haskins v. Lau's*, 402 S.E.2d 58 (Ga. App. 1991).

Prior crimes on premises made assaults foreseeable. *Doud v. Las Vegas Hilton*, 864 P.2d 796 (Nev. 1993)

There is no liability where there is no evidence of frequent or recent criminal acts. *Miller v. South County Center*, 857 S.W.2d 507 (Mo. App. 1993).

There is no foreseeability of an assault when there was no notice of similar prior crimes even though there were some incidents of vandalism and theft. *Karp v. Saks Fifth Avenue*, 639 N.Y.S.2d 575 (A.D. 1996).

Absence of prior similar crimes on premises does not render assaults unforeseeable. *Sharon P. v. Arman, Ltd.*, 55 Cal. App. 445 (1997).

Duty to Protect

Duty to protect is voluntarily assumed when advertising "lighted security parking" for patrons of nightclub. *Scott v. Harper Recreation*, 480 N.W.2d 270 (Mich. App. 1991).

Owners of parking garages have a duty to protect because parking garages are "inherently dangerous places." *Sharon P. v. Arman, Ltd.*, 55 Cal. App. 445 (1997).

State law imposes no duty to protect based on prior crimes on the premises. A business invitor will not be liable for criminal acts unless he has knowledge that the crime is occurring or about to occur. *Folmar v. Marriott, Inc.*, 918 P.2d 86 (Okl. App. 1996).

Businesses have a duty to protect against foreseeable criminal assaults. The test to determine liability will weigh severity of possible harm to patrons against the burden of providing security measures. *McClung v. Delta Square Ltd.*, 937 S.W.2d 893 (Tenn. 1996).

Liability can be found where landlord knew of defective locks, failed to repair the locks, and tenants were not allowed to make the repairs. *Stubbs v. Panek*, 829 S.W.2d 544 (Mo. App 1992).

Landlord had no duty to provide security absent express contract with tenants to provide security. *Potter v. 1st Federal S&L*, 602 So.2d 675 (La. App. 1993).

SUMMARY

While arrest or police powers generally are not conferred on private security personnel by state statute, in some states there is some enabling legislation (or county and local ordinances) that grants special police powers to licensed private security personnel under specific conditions. In addition, 45 states, through state statute or common law, permit arrests by private citizens, and the majority of states have enacted antishoplifting statutes that permit detention of suspected shoplifters by private security agents of a merchant. In all of these instances of special police powers, citizen arrest privileges, and shoplifting detention statutes, there is great variation among states as to the privileges conferred and the legal restraints imposed on the conduct of private security officers.

In recent years, there has been an explosion of civil suits over inadequate and/or questionable security practices. Such cases have revealed a critical need for a compendium of standards that can serve as a prescriptive guideline of reasonable, consistent measures of security to be utilized by property owners, courts, and security personnel.

DISCUSSION QUESTIONS

1. What are the types of power and authority that a security officer may possess?

2. Briefly discuss the significance and relationship of tort law to the security officer.

3. What is the difference between the purpose of tort law and that of criminal law?

4. Briefly outline and discuss the four problem areas of private security that are relevant to the practitioner.

5. Define *mens rea* and its relation to tort and criminal law.

6. Discuss the "standards of security" suggested by Dr. Lawrence W. Sherman.

7. What is common law? What is its origin?

8. What is the relationship between foreseeability and the duty to prevent crime?

9. What are three theories of foreseeability?

10. Does constitutional law apply to the actions of security personnel?

REFERENCES

Bilek, A.J., Klotter, J.C. & Keegan, R. (1981). *Federal, Legal Aspects of Security.* Cincinnati, OH: Anderson Publishing Co.

Bird, W.J., Kakalik, J.S. & Wildhorn, S., et al. (Feb., 1972). *The Law and the Private Police, Vol. II* Santa Monica, CA: The RAND Corporation.

Perkins, R.M. (1969). *Criminal Law, 2nd ed.* Mineola, NY: Foundation Press.

Prosser, W.L. & Smith, Y.B. (1967). *Torts, 4th ed.* Mineola, NY: Foundation Press.

Private Security
Career Orientation

13

INTRODUCTION

In a free enterprise system, the best indicator of success is sustained growth. By this criterion, private security is a success. The best data available indicate that private security grew at an annual rate of 10 percent per year during the 1970s. Few segments of the American economy were able to maintain such a growth rate during the same period.

Two broad hypotheses have been used to explain this growth. One is that the private security industry has grown because of the increase in crime in the United States and the inability of public law enforcement to stop this increase. The second is that the quality of private security services has improved and that this has been recognized by industry, which has resulted in greater utilization of private security services.

The truth probably lies somewhere in between. For example, an argument often used to explain data showing increases in the crime rate is that better reporting of crimes accounts for much of the increase. On the other hand, some argue that the quality of private security has not really improved, but has simply become an increasingly necessary part of doing business.

Another position is that government regulation is the real factor in the growth. The security requirements for doing business with the government (primarily federal) have increased, and industry has responded by increasing security for the simple reason that without it they could not obtain government contracts. With the ending of the Cold War there are officials in the private security field who predict that, in some industries, the need for security will decrease because of the shift away from needing to maintain security to meet government regulations. On the opposite side are those who feel that security will increase because companies will need more security to compete in the global economy of the future. Looking to the future, if crime continues to increase and the quality of private security continues to improve, then the growth rate will continue.

PUBLIC VS. PRIVATE SECURITY—SOME DATA

Throughout this text many references have been made to the important contributions of private security in the overall effort toward crime prevention. A significant contribution of data is contained in *Private Security and Police in America: The Hallcrest Report I*, by William C. Cunningham and Todd H. Taylor. Extensive research was conducted in making their projections.

Figure 13.1
Hallcrest Estimated Private Sector* Security Employment in the U.S. 1982.
*Excludes Government (Civil and Military) Security Workers

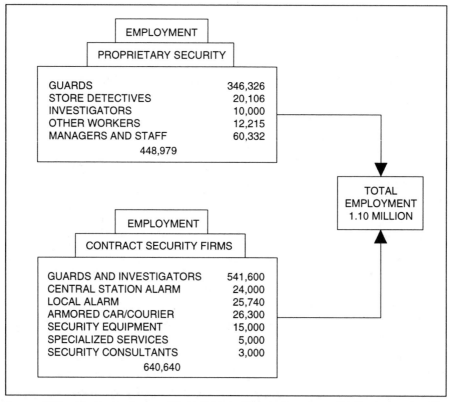

Source: William C. Cunningham and Todd H. Taylor, *Private Security and Police in America: The Hallcrest Report I* (Stoneham, MA: Butterworth-Heinemann, 1990), Figure 8-2.

Two major findings further supported research conducted by the RAND Corporation in the early 1970s and the Private Security Task Force in the middle 1970s. These were concerned with the number of private security personnel and total expenditures of private security compared to public law enforcement. The projections were based on analysis of data collected by the Bureau of Justice Statistics, the Bureau of Labor Statistics and the Bureau of the Census.

Estimated private-sector security employment in 1982 was 1.10 million. Figure 13.1 provides detailed information about the number of persons in proprietary and contract security at that time. It does not specifically include employment data for public police, but other research indicated that the total was under 600,000.

Detailed information about the estimated annual expenditures for protection services provides another perspective on the issue. For example, 1979 expenditures for police protection were estimated at $13.8 billion, while estimates for private protection in 1980 were $21.7 billion. Figure 13.2 provides additional detailed information.

Figure 13.2
Summary of Estimated Annual Expenditures for Protected Services

POLICE PROTECTION (1979)[1]		$ BILLION	%
Federal		$ 1.0	14.1%
State		2.1	14.4%
Local		9.8	71.5%
	TOTAL	$13.8 billion	100%
PRIVATE PROTECTION (1980)[2,3]			
Industrial/Manufacturing		$ 5.9	27.6%
Retailing		3.8	17.4%
Government Installations		3.3	15.9%
Financial Institutions		1.9	8.8%
Healthcare Facilities		1.4	6.3%
Educational Institutions		1.4	6.3%
Utilities/Communications		1.1	5.1%
Distribution/Warehousing		.92	4.2%
Hotel/Motel/Resort			3.3%
Transportation		.29	1.4%
Other		.87	4.0%
	TOTAL	$21.7 billion	100%
	GRAND TOTAL	**$35.5 BILLION**	

[1] *Sourcebook of Criminal Justice Statistics*, 1981 U.S. Department of Justice, 1982.

[2] "Key Market Coverage," *Security World*, 1981.

[3] Note the absence of the residential contingency, a major user of locks, alarms, fencing, and security patrols.

One of the best projections for the decade from 1980-1990 is contained in *Private Security and Police in America*. See Figure 13.3.

Figure 13.3
Projected Growth in Protective Service Workers[2]

	1980	**1990**	**Ten-Year Increase**
PUBLIC SECTOR			
State and Local			
Police Officers	92,981	108,642	16.8%
Patrol Officers	92,972	458,922	16.8%
Sheriffs	22,276	26,601	16.8%
Police Detectives	42,705	49,913	16.8%
	550,504	643,438	16.8%
Parking Enforcement Officers	7,379	8,653	17.3%
Guards and Doorkeepers	25,170	42,428	68.6%
TOTAL STATE & LOCAL	563,053	694,619	23.4%
Federal			
Police Officers	9,179	9,905	7.9%
Police Detectives	20,635	22,267	7.9%
Guards and Doorkeepers	8,987	9,608	7.9%
All Other Workers	1,825	1,969	7.9%
TOTAL FEDERAL	40,356	43,839	7.9%
TOTAL PUBLIC SECTOR	623,409	738,438	18.4%
PRIVATE SECTOR			
Guards			
Proprietary	271,308	369,964	36.4%
Contract	341,102	443,594	30.0%
Store Detectives	18,279	27,365	49.7%
Fitting Room Checkers	8,864	11,790	33.0%
Security Checkers	230	260	13.0%
Railroad Police	2,165	1,944	[10.2%]
All Other Workers	2,395	3,976	[7.9%]
TOTAL PRIVATE SECTOR	644,343	858,893	33.3%

Source: *National Industry-Occupation Matrix*, 1980-1990, Bureau of Labor Statistics, 1982. From William C. Cunningham and Todd H. Taylor, *Private Security and Police in America: The Hallcrest Report I* (Stoneham, MA: Butterworth-Heinemann, 1990), Table 8-3.

    The trend toward greater reliance on the private sector was most recently reported in *Private Security Trends 1970-2000: The Hallcrest Report II*. This report concluded that the movement toward greater utilization and allocation of resources continued through the decade of the 1980s and will continue until the end of the century. Chapter 4 provides additional information and a perspective in support of this trend.

    Figure 13.4 provides an excellent summary of the projected employment and expenditures from 1980-2000. The significance of all this data is that there has been no major study or report that has concluded a pattern other than continued growth of private security employment and expenditures, and a stagnant or declining pattern of employment and expenditures for public law enforcement.

Figure 13.4
Hallcrest Estimates and Projections 1980-2000
Summary of Private Security and Law Enforcement Employment
and Expenditures

Year	Private Security Employment (Millions)	Law Enforcement Employment (Millions)	Total Protective Services Employment (Millions)	Private Security Expenditures (Billions)	Law Enforcement Expenditures (Billions)	Total Expenditures (Billions)
1980	1.0	0.6	1.6	$20	$14	$34
1990	1.5	0.6	2.1	$52	$30	$82
2000	1.9	0.7	2.6	$103	$44	$147

Source: William C. Cunningham, John J. Strauchs, and Clifford W. Van Meter (1990). *Private Security Trends 1970-2000: The Hallcrest Report II*, Table 7.1, p. 229. Stoneham, MA: Butterworth-Heinemann, 1990.

Two major conclusions seem obvious about the future of protective services. First, private security employment opportunities and overall expenditures for private security will continue to grow. Second, public sector employment and expenditures will grow, but at a rate much slower than that of private security. The results will be greater reliance on the private sector in the overall effort for crime prevention as well as better employment opportunities for persons seeking careers in private security.

PROFESSIONALISM

A factor in the evolution from an occupation to a profession is a viable code of ethics for practitioners. The Private Security Task Force recognized this, as did the Private Security Advisory Council to the Law Enforcement Assistance Administration. Working cooperatively and in concert with private security professional associations, two codes were developed: one for management and one for employees.

CODE OF ETHICS FOR PRIVATE SECURITY MANAGEMENT

As managers of private security functions and employees, we pledge:
I   To recognize that our principal responsibilities are, in the service of our organizations and clients, to protect life and property as well as to prevent and reduce crime against our business, industry or other

organizations and institutions; and in the public interest, to uphold the law and to respect the constitutional rights of all persons.

II   To be guided by a sense of integrity, honor, justice and morality in the conduct of business; in all personnel matters; in relationships with government agencies, clients and employers; and in responsibilities to the general public.

III   To strive faithfully to render security services of the highest quality and to work continuously to improve our knowledge and skills and thereby improve the overall effectiveness of private security.

IV   To uphold the trust of our employers, our clients, and the public by performing our functions within the law, not ordering or condoning violations of law, and ensuring that our security personnel conduct their assigned duties lawfully and with proper regard for the rights of others.

V   To respect the reputation and practice of others in private security, but to expose to the proper authorities any conduct that is unethical or unlawful.

VI   To apply uniform and equitable standards of employment in recruiting and selecting personnel regardless of race, creed, color, sex or age, and in providing salaries commensurate with job responsibilities and with training, education, and experience.

VII   To cooperate with recognized and responsible law enforcement and other criminal justice agencies; to comply with security licensing and registration laws and other statutory requirements that pertain to our business.

VIII   To respect and protect the confidential and privileged information of employers and clients beyond the term of our employment, except where their interests are contrary to law or to this Code of Ethics.

IX   To maintain a professional posture in all business relationships with employers and clients, with others in the private security field and with members of other professions; and to insist that our personnel adhere to the highest standards of professional conduct.

X   To encourage the professional advancement of our personnel by assisting them to acquire appropriate security knowledge, education, and training.

Code of Ethics for Private Security Employees

In recognition of the significant contribution of private security to crime prevention and reduction, as a private security employee, I pledge:

I   To accept the responsibilities and fulfill the obligations of my role: protecting life and property; preventing and reducing crimes against my employer's business or other organizations and institutions to which I am assigned; upholding the law; and respecting the constitutional rights of all persons.

II To conduct myself with honesty and integrity and to adhere to the highest moral principles in the performance of my security duties.

III To be faithful, diligent, and dependable in discharging my duties, and to uphold at all times the laws, policies, and procedures that protect the rights of others.

IV To observe the precepts of truth, accuracy, and prudence, without allowing personal feelings, prejudices, animosities, or friendships to influence my judgments.

V To report to my superiors, without hesitation, any violation of the law or of my employer's or client's regulations.

VI To respect and protect the confidential and privileged information of my employer or client beyond the term of my employment, except where their interests are contrary to law or to this Code of Ethics.

VII To cooperate with all recognized and responsible law enforcement and government agencies in matters within their jurisdiction.

VIII To accept no compensation, commission, gratuity, or other advantage without the knowledge and consent of my employer.

IX To conduct myself professionally at all times and to perform my duties in a manner that reflects credit upon myself, my employer, and private security.

X To strive continually to improve my performance by seeking training and educational opportunities that will better prepare me for my private security duties.

Commentary

A serious problem that has plagued private security for years is the perception that it does not operate in a professional manner and attracts low quality personnel. The following examples are presented not as an attempt to cover all of the unprofessional activities, but to indicate some of the incidents which lead, right or wrong, to the perceptions of many citizens.

- *The Grand Rapids Press*, April 26, 1998, reported a case of a 32-year-old security guard who played out a "suicide-by-cop plan" which resulted in his death.

- *Security Director's Digest*, November 27, 1996, reported that Illinois regulators had rid the industry of more than 2,000 guards with criminal records in the past year.

- *Security Management*, June 1998, reported that from 1995 to 1998 there have been more than 200 arrests of security officers for crimes. In 1997, there were 38 arrests of security officers and five had previous criminal records. This data was presented at a meeting of the Private Sector Liaison Committee (PSLC) of the International Association of Chiefs of Police.

> 12 on assault charges
> 8 for theft
> 4 for arson
> 4 for murder or attempted murder
> 3 for bank robbery
> 2 on drug charges
> 2 for sexual offenses
> 1 for kidnapping
> 1 for weapons charges
> 1 for racketeering

However, it must also be recognized that private security employees also make positive impacts. Two examples, one individual and one of a group, may be typical of many others that have gone unreported.

- In Grand Rapids, Michigan a private security guard risked his life to save a person who was about to be hit by a train.

- *Reader's Digest,* Large Edition, January, 1998, highlighted the fact that the New York Times Square Business Improvement District hired 40 private patrolman, who were hooked up by radio to the police department. Prostitution was chased out and street crime plummeted 47 percent.

SALARIES

Security Director's Digest, March 27, 1996 reported a study sponsored by the American Society for Industrial Security which provided some salary information. The study involved 506 companies and some of the findings were:

- Unarmed security officers/ guards have an average income of $17,154 per year.

- Security loss prevention directors and vice presidents as a group have an average income of $67,617 per year.

Of course, overall figures vary because of location, type of employer, size of organization, size of security budget, level of education, length of service, and other similar variables.

Another study, reported in the August, 1996 issue of *Security Management* focused on salaries by size of organization:

Size of Organization	Average Annual Income
25,000 or more	$90,391
10,000-24,999	$87,225
5,000-9,999	$70,565
2,500-4,999	$65,324
1,000-2,499	$60,664
500-999	$58,058
100-499	$52,920
Less than 100	$61,372

Career Opportunities in Security (date of publication not listed) published by the American Society for Industrial Security provided some additional data on the typical manager based on type of organization, education, years in security, and salary ranges:

Organization	Education/Years	Salary Range
Educational Institution	BS/BA or grad/12	$40-65,000
Financial Services	BS/BA or grad/10	$40-125,000
Government Security	BS/BA/5	$30-55,000
Healthcare Security	BS/BA/15	$45-75,000
Lodging Security	BS/BA/10	$30-50,000
Manufacturing Security	BS/BA/15	$50-150,000
Retail Security	BS/BA/13	$35-60,000
Security Sales	BS/BA/15	$40-100,000
Transportation Security	BS/BA/20	$40-100,000

PRIVATIZATION AND OUTSOURCING: CONCEPTS FOR THE FUTURE

In *Issues for Today's Security Director: 1997 Fortune 1000 Survey Report* published by Pinkerton Service Corporation, the study reports that there is an increased emphasis on security outsourcing. The majority of the companies (61%) are not increasing the amount of outsourcing, but the number of companies expanding outsourcing outnumber the number reducing their outsourcing by more than four-to-one. Obviously, if this trend continues, the use of outsourcing will continue to increase during the next decade.

Another study reported in *Security* (September, 1997) reported that most organizations with security officers contract some or all of their labor. For example, 35 percent were proprietary, 29 percent contract, 27 percent hybrid (using both contract and proprietary), and 9 percent surveyed had no security force.

Ira S. Somerson, CPP, in an article titled "The Next Generation" appearing in the January, 1995 issue of *Security Management*, comments that the shrinking workforces will lead to more outsourcing and better and more efficient use of nonsecurity personnel in an organization.

It is important to understand that outsourcing is the process that is used to replace one type of security, normally proprietary, with another type, normally contract. However, another process is in progress and that is the concept of privatization which is a process whereby law enforcement functions and services are replaced or eliminated by organizations using private security personnel.

The late Robert Trojanowicz, a pioneer in community policing, made the following comment regarding the need for closer cooperation between public and private law enforcement at a conference held at Loyola University in 1991. He said " One question that need not be asked is whether the trend will persist. We are already too far down the road to turn back. Therefore, the ultimate question is not whether this change is good or bad, but whether these changes will occur piecemeal and poorly or thoughtfully and well."

One of the fastest growing areas of privatization is in the field of corrections. The National Institute of Justice, in 1998, made research and evaluation of this activity a priority. In the *Solicitation for Research and Evaluation on Corrections and Sentencing* (1998) they sought applications to study the impact of privatization. Some of the specific topics in the proposal included:

- What is the extent of privatization?

- What types of services and operations are the most developed and extensive?

- What new privately provided services and operations are emerging?

- How do supervision issues differ between public and private facilities?

- What are the incentive structures for privately funded services?

- How and for what performance measures are contractors held accountable?

- How do private facilities and/or services compare to public facilities/services?

- How do the costs of public and private facilities compare and what criteria and/or performance measures are used to make this comparison?

- Does any cost advantage occur over time?

Although these questions are specifically directed to privatization in corrections they could, with some minor revisions, be used to evaluate law enforcement services performed by private security.

PRIVATE EMPLOYMENT OF PUBLIC POLICE

Another aspect of the delivery service for security services in the use of public police as private police. The common term applied is "moonlighting" which, during the work of the Private Security Task Force in the 1970s, was a cause for conflict between public and private agencies. The importance of this issue, at that time, can be seen by reviewing the standards developed by the Task Force. These standards are in Appendix H.

By the 1990s, public law enforcement officers were, in many areas of the country, routinely involved in the providing of services traditionally assigned to private security.

Obviously, there is a potential for conflict when public officers take business away from private security companies. *Security,* January, 1997, reported one case, in Virginia, where four private security companies filed a lawsuit against 23 law enforcement agencies citing federal and state anti-trust laws by allowing officers to use their uniforms, vehicles and police facilities for off-duty security work.

Albert J. Reiss, Jr. in a December, 1988 *National Institute of Justice Research in Brief* article titled, "Private Employment of Public Police" presented many of the issues. The policy and management issues raised were:

- Employee injury

- Liability for actions

- Control of work

- Supervision

- Dealing with misconduct

- Fraudulent misrepresentation

- Extortion

- Use of coercion

- Complaints

- Conflict of interest

Additionally, issues regarding competition with private security firms included:

- Authority and limits

- Who should bear the cost?

- How should public police relate to private needs?

- Fairness

Professor Reiss presented two models for off-duty police employment that are being used in various locations.

Officer Contract Model

- Each officer finds own secondary employment

- Officer independently contracts conditions of work, hours, pay

- Officer then applies for permission to accept off-duty job

- Department grants permission provided job meets minimum standards

- Employer pays officer in cash (work is called "cash detail") Union Brokerage Model

- Union, guild, or association finds paid details

- Union assigns officers who have volunteered

- Union sets assignment conditions for paid details

- Union bargains with the department over status, pay, and conditions of paid details

Department Contract Model

- Police agency contracts with employers

- Agency assigns officers and pays them from reimbursements from employers

- Agency assigns an Off-Duty Employment Supervisor to receive employer requests, issue off-duty work permits, and assign officers to paid details

- Agency negotiates with union or guild on pay, conditions, and regulations governing employment

One of the unique contributions of Private Security and Police in America (Hallcrest I) was the section called "Blueprint for Action," specifically the findings, conclusions, and recommendations regarding privatization.

PRIVATE SECURITY'S CONTRIBUTION TO CRIME PREVENTION AND CONTROL

The research material presented in this project demonstrates the complex and far-reaching scope of private security programs in business, industry, and institutions, as well as the utilization and growth of a broad range of purchased security goods and services. Based on the sheer preponderance of evidence presented, it is clear that private security makes a sizable contribution to crime prevention and control. Crime, however, is just a part of a broad range of threats addressed by the loss prevention programs of private security (including fires, accidents, information security, materials movement, etc.). Law enforcement has become increasingly aware of the presence of private security, but the substantial impact of proprietary and contract security on the overall safety and security of their communities has not been fully recognized by administrators or operational personnel. Law enforcement executives rate the overall contribution of private security and the reduction of direct dollar crime losses by private security as only somewhat effective. They tend to see private security's contribution to reducing the volume of crime, apprehending criminal suspects and maintaining order as ineffective. These assessments are influenced to a great extent by law enforcement's poor ratings of private security in 10 areas of performance:

(1) quality of personnel, (2) pre-employment background checks, (3) training received, (4) supervision, (5) personal appearance in uniform, (6) reasonable use of force, (7) proper use of weapons, (8) familiarity with legal problems, (9) reporting criminal incidents, and (10) responding to alarms. Law enforcement's low opinion of private security in most areas is perceived accurately by private security managers and employees: less than one-fourth of security employees think police officers view them as even performing a valuable service.

One major contribution of security personnel is their integral part in asset protection and loss prevention programs that sustain the viability and profitability of companies. In manufacturing, for example, guards prevent goods from being stolen, from burning in fires and from other forms of loss that affect the profitability of the company. Guards also protect raw materials, precious metals, production machinery, and proprietary information—all of which have a direct bearing on the ability of the company to produce new goods at a profit. Private security personnel thus stimulate the economy.

THE SHIFT TO PRIVATE PROTECTION RESOURCES

The origins of modern policing have their roots in private policing or security initiatives of the early nineteenth century, when there were few paid police yet thousands of "watchmen." The societal mission of prevention and control of crime gradually became associated with public law enforcement. The growth of modern policing and its expansion through the 1960s was a result of the redistribution of private property protection responsibilities to the public sector.

The current research documents a stabilization (and often a decline) of public law enforcement resources in recent years and simultaneously notes the growth of all segments of both proprietary and contract security. Some law enforcement administrators recognize the dramatic growth of private security in the past decade, but seem to feel that this growth is a result of the failure of law enforcement and criminal justice to do its job. In other words, if law enforcement were given adequate resources, there would be no need for widespread use of private security. These law enforcement executives see an erosion of their "turf" to private security. *The Hallcrest Report II* views the recent decline in law enforcement resources, increased use of private security and increased citizen involvement in crime prevention programs as signs of a return (a century later) of the primary responsibility for protection to the private sector.

The private sector will begin bearing more of the burden for crime prevention, while law enforcement will narrow the focus of police services to crime control. Thus, law enforcement is viewed as assuming an increasingly reactive role even as it has expanded crime prevention programs in recent years. Hard economic realities and strained property tax bases will force law enforcement agencies to seek alternative ways to reduce their work loads. The traditionally proactive orientation of private security is well-suited to assuming the non-crime-related police workload. Proprietary and contract security managers indicate a willingness to accept more responsibility for criminal incidents occurring on property being protected by them (e.g., burglar alarm response, completion of misdemeanor incident reports and preliminary investigation). In general, law enforcement administrators are open to discussing the transfer of responsibility for criminal incidents occurring on property protected by private security, and have identified a number of police tasks as "potentially more cost effectively performed by private security." Contract security companies have expressed an interest in contracting for these non-crime-related police services, e.g., public building security, parking enforcement and court security. Many of the activities were listed as potential areas of business growth in the next five years by national and regional contract security firms; some firms currently perform some of the candidate activities.

The smaller law enforcement agencies (which are most affected by budget cuts) and departments noting a decline or stabilization of resources are most receptive to transfer of police activities. Industry (which is frequently located in smaller communities with limited public safety services) may be willing to play a greater role in the protection of its facilities, especially if tax relief (property or corporate) is involved. The greatest law enforcement interest is in transfer of burglar alarm response: nearly 70 percent of large police and sheriffs' departments in jurisdictions of more than 500,000 population wish to be relieved of the "false alarm burden'' on the police workload.

It is clear that the law enforcement workload could be significantly reduced, and redirected more toward "street" crime, and that the dynamics and structure of protective services delivery could be greatly changed by a realignment of public and private protection responsibilities. As long as law enforcement maintains the posture that they should bear the primary burden for protection of the community, however, creative alternative solutions will be limited in the midst of dwindling public resources.

RECOMMENDATIONS

Strategic Planning for Transfer of Selected Police Services to Private Security

The interests of the public may be best served through constructive dialogue and creative planning by law enforcement and private security to facilitate transfer of minor criminal incident responsibility and contracting of certain non-crime activities. Energy wasted on debating the quality, performance, and contribution of private security could be better utilized in the identification of areas for contracting out, research on required legal mechanisms and the development of tightly prescribed contract specifications of performance. The dynamics of supply and demand in the marketplace will produce a sufficient number of qualified firms, independent of any stimulus from regulation or licensing.

Some private security personnel have been shown to have salaries comparable to some police officers, as well as substantial training and experience. Contract security company business practices and standards for security personnel would be a paramount issue in the consideration of these alternatives by government.

"Brokering" Alternative Policing Arrangements

In addition to the transfer of responsibility for minor criminal activity on private property to private security, a broader range of linkages of private security and police services should be explored. Well-defined and homogeneous commercial and industrial districts, as well as residential developments, developers, property owners, and residents, should have an opportunity to "broker" the mix of protective services that best suits their protection needs and ability to pay. Private patrol services, for example, might be permitted to respond to certain citizen calls for service routed to the security officer through the technical support of the police communications center.

Similar support might be provided to a volunteer citizen patrol trained and supervised by an area or zone police supervisor. Police administrators themselves might become "brokers" of policing service throughout the community, negotiating a variety of public and private protective arrangements in different areas of the community on a cost-effective basis. These efforts could be a logical extension of the progress of many law enforcement agencies in securing community involvement in the crime prevention process through neighborhood watch and citizen alert groups.

Police Involvement in Community Growth Planning

While the fire services component of public safety has a long record of proactive involvement in the zoning and subdivision approval process of local government, law enforcement agencies have traditionally had little involvement in these processes. Police planners, crime prevention personnel, and experienced security consultants could contribute to the review process of city and county planning and zoning departments. These activities would include recommending Crime Prevention Through Environmental Design (CPTED) concepts for individual buildings and small subdivisions, and examining larger developments for potential impacts on police services and needs for private security resources. This is presently being done in some departments on a limited scale.

The concept envisioned here, however, would also include (1) imposition of certain standards (e.g., requiring monitored alarm services and/or private security patrols for certain densities and types of commercial developments), (2) integrating security and police services in planned urban developments (PUDs), and (3) facilitating special assessment or taxing districts with needs for greater or lesser levels of police services for funding both police and security services at desired levels.

Special Police Officer Status for Private Security

With special police officer status (SPO), a majority of minor criminal incidents can be resolved by security personnel prior to police involvement. Establishment of preemptive state statutes on special police officer powers would allow standardized training and certification requirements to be developed, thus assuring uniformity and precluding arbitrary use of special police and deputization powers for security personnel.

In the Baltimore case study site used in Private Security and Police in America, many of the retailers and some of the industrial security operations opted to have certain of their security personnel designated as special police officers. The State of New York has a similar provision (for proprietary security only) and requires the security personnel to complete an approved training curriculum. In New York City, for example, some retailers utilize a 35-hour SPO training program sponsored by the Security Management Institute of John Jay College of Criminal Justice. Police officers no longer have to perform tasks of apprehension, prisoner transport, report writing, evidence presentation, and court testimony for the large volume of shoplifting, trespassing, vandalism, and other criminal offenses against the major retailers who use SPOs. In such situations, the private business, rather than the general public, would bear the expense for certain police services required on its property.

Security Expenditure Tax Credits

To enhance national crime prevention efforts, continued efforts should be directed toward enactment of a federal tax credit for certain security expenditures. One of the recent attempts at federal legislation made provision for a direct offset to taxes similar to the energy tax credit. If, in fact, there is validity to the crime prevention literature supplied to the public and the deterrent capabilities of certain security technology (e.g., alarm systems), then investments in security hardware in time could result in reduced police workload. Unless the tax credit amounts to at least $500, there is not much incentive to purchase reliable and sophisticated alarm systems or locking systems. On the other hand, if the tax credit is too low it could encourage the purchase of systems ill-suited for particular security applications, which could, in turn, exacerbate the false alarm problem.

Efforts also should be directed at the state and local level to reduce corporate and property tax on significant expenditures on security goods and services that offset the need for additional police services. Within the context of alternative policing arrangements, companies and organizations should have the opportunity to broker a specified level of public and private services with which they will be satisfied. If the alternative arrangement reduces the cost for—and burden on—public police, then some offset to taxes should be allowed.

Determining Which Activities Require Police Authority

While studies on police workloads have consistently shown that about 80 percent of police work is non-crime-related, there never has been an empirical examination regarding which police activities require the sworn authority of a police officer with accompanying levels of training and skill. With local budgetary constraints forcing many law enforcement executives to practice "cutback management" and make difficult choices about the types and levels of service to be provided, attention should be focused on defining nonessential tasks, with private security as a viable alternative for many non-crime-related tasks. The greatest improvement in police resource efficiency will occur when sworn personnel are performing only those activities that they are uniquely qualified to perform, or that could not be performed on a lower unit cost basis by the private sector with the same level of community satisfaction.

ALTERNATIVE MODES OF POLICING

An assessment should be made of (1) the basic police services the public is willing to support financially, (2) the types of police tasks/activities most acceptable to police administrators and the public for transfer to the private sector, and (3) which tasks/activities might be performed on a lower unit cost basis by the private sector with the same level of community satisfaction. An analysis should then be conducted of the organizational, environmental, and legal dynamics of public and private linkages in community protection. The alternative modes or linkages with public police services should include, but not be limited to, contract security, proprietary security forces, contracts for limited police services, use of special police officer status, private developer and property management companies, and residential, neighborhood, and citizen associations. For the latter group, the variables of "self-help" programs may help identify the key determinants of public willingness to assume greater responsibility for their own protection by undertaking traditional policing tasks. Relationships between cost, quality, and effectiveness need to be explored for various activities and services and alternative delivery modes. Points of resistance by law enforcement administrators, government officials, private business and organizations, and citizens also must be examined.

KANSAS CITY, MISSOURI

An excellent example of how cooperation and privatization can be combined is the research, initiated in 1989 by Larry Joiner, former Police Chief in Kansas City, Missouri, in which a departmental study group was appointed to review law enforcement tasks that could be handled by private security organizations. The Kansas City Police Task Force concluded that:

> . . . most, if not all, of the non-law enforcement activities carried out by our department could be handled by private security organizations. The tasks in question could be handled just as effectively, at a lesser expense, and would not require a diminution of overall service to the public. The accomplishment of these tasks requiring relatively unskilled personnel could be met with the cooperation of the private sector. This would produce the desired effect of freeing up police officers for true law enforcement functions and would require less training for those private security personnel assigned to carry out the perfunctory tasks.

The task force recommended that one patrol division within the city be used as the test site for a two-year experiment for three types of contracts encompassing 22 separate tasks. The first is a special-request contract for tasks that occur at irregular times, such as assisting with traffic and crowd control at special events and guarding prisoners at hospitals. The second contract type would initially include only one task: response to all intrusion alarms in the test patrol division, estimated to be about 30 per day. The third contract type would involve performing 19 support tasks within one patrol division. The tasks proposed for unarmed private security personnel are the following:

1) Transport prisoners

2) Provide standby for owner on open window or door

3) Provide standby for vehicles to be towed

4) Assist at traffic, medical, or other emergencies

5) Assist stranded motorists

6) Perform school crossing guard duties

7) Provide standby on road hazards

8) Direct traffic on lights out or at barricaded positions

9) Respond to 911 hang-up calls from outside pay phones

10) Assist elderly and disabled people on minor problems (e.g., lockouts)

11) Transport citizens (e.g., victims, witnesses, etc.)

12) Assist lost juveniles or elderly people

13) Deliver intradepartmental paperwork

14) Respond to parking complaints

15) Recover found property not involved in crimes (e.g., bicycles, purses, etc.)

16) Take walk-in reports (e.g., minor traffic accident)

17) Guard crime scenes

18) Provide standby for arrival of police officers (e.g., traffic accident, injured person)

19) Perform routine tasks (e.g, obtain building listings, provide community and crime prevention information, etc.)

In 1990, the Kansas City Police Department submitted a federal grant application to the National Institute of Justice for financial assistance for implementation of this privatization experiment. For a number of reasons including changes in the senior administration of the Department, the program was not implemented. However, the thinking and planning shows the types of opportunities for utilization of private security resources.

At the Michigan State University Golden Jubilee for the School of Criminal Justice in 1985, three speakers commented on the issue of use of private security in the future. Donald Bennett, Director of Security, Michigan National Bank, stated that Michigan has a joint committee of public and private security and urged that police set up several demonstration programs to use private security for police services. William Hegarty, Chief, Grand Rapids, Michigan Police Department, stated that he saw a trend toward neighborhood associations incorporating and contracting for protection services from police or private security. Wayne Hall, Director of Security, Ford Motor Company, remarked that he saw increasing private sector activity in the criminal justice system through privatization. He feels this concept will be expanded.

One of the most intriguing views on privatization is contained in the doctoral dissertation of William L. Tafoya based on a Delphi Study. In the study, a panel of experts reached a majority opinion that in the year 2035, private security agencies will assume more than 50 percent of all law enforcement responsibilities.

The Institute for Law and Justice and the Hallcrest Division of Science Applications International Corporation prepared a report entitled "A Literature Review of Cooperation and Partnerships Between Law Enforcement and Private Security Organizations" for the Bureau of Justice Assistance, U.S. Department of Justice. The authors are Edward H. Connors, William C. Cunningham, and Peter E. Ohlhausen. It is pending publication by the Bureau of Justice Assistance, U.S. Department of Justice. The following sections: Types of Cooperation, Trends, and The Future are based on information contained in this report. It is important to recognize that these sections do not comprise the entire report. Readers must also understand that the following information is an edited version of these sections, and persons wanting to see the entire report should obtain one when it is formally published.

TYPES OF COOPERATION

Cooperative programs fall into the following broad, somewhat overlapping categories: informal, formal, contractual, familiarity/goodwill, topic-specific, and umbrella.

Formal versus Informal

Setting up by-laws, sectors, committees, and funding is very difficult and time-consuming. For that reason, some groups of law enforcement and private security officials opt to cooperate informally. For example, a New Jersey partnership created by AlliedSignal, Inc., is informal and unnamed. An article by David R. Green, *Security Management,* (May, 1998) stated "Begun in 1996, the partnership has evolved into an informal network that allows local, state, and federal law enforcement officials based in the area to meet with security professionals and top executives in some of the county's [Morris County, NJ] Fortune 500 companies." The partnership holds three to four breakfast meetings or other get-togethers per year. "The sessions have no formal agenda. [After a speaker speaks, participants] can give or receive advice on security projects or discuss how corporate security professionals can help police solve or prevent criminal activity. . . . The meetings have also been used by security professionals to discuss common problems, such as how several companies with employees overseas could work together if their workers had to be suddenly evacuated from international trouble spots."

By contrast. some groups opt to organize formally, usually in the hope that structure will increase longevity. One such group is the Virginia Police and Private Security Alliance (VAPPSA), which sponsors educational presentations at its meetings, works to apply problem-solving approaches to public safety issues, conducts shared training programs, maintains a public/private information and resource network, and tracks and tries to influence legislation. VAPPSA features by-laws, membership dues, voting and nonvoting membership categories, a board of directors, and one-half dozen formal committees. Interestingly, "the VAPPSA members who initiated the group did not realize how much time it would take to establish by-laws, create a formal structure, remedy legal entanglements, and create momentum. . . . The founders realized early on that their attention could easily be diverted from the original vision and get lost in the swamp of organizational development." On the plus side, VAPPSA has remained in existence since 1991.

Contractual

Some cooperative programs go beyond being formal to being literally contractual. Such programs are typically business improvement districts (BIDs) or other forms of privatization.

BIDs can be formed in several ways. James P. Murphy, *Security Journal,* (Volume 9, 1997) reported that "In New York, the formation of a BID can be initiated by property owners, by a local development corporation or a Chamber of Commerce, by a local Community Board or that area's City Council member, or by the mayor or a mayoral agency. Any commercial, retail, or industrial area in New York city may apply for BID status through any such sponsor." Once the

BID is approved by the government, a special assessment is added to the property tax bills of all businesses within its geographical area. The money is collected by the government, then returned to the BID for the purposes stated in the BID's official plan. Typically, BIDs use the money for capital improvements, marketing of the area, sanitation, and security. Often, the security contractor hired by the BID contacts the police when an arrest needs to be made, and its security officers serve as extra eyes and ears for the police. In return, the police sometimes provide training and crime information to the security contractor or to in-house security departments of businesses that belong to the BID.

Greene, Seamon, and Levy, in a 1993 paper, indicated BIDs divide public safety responsibilities in this way: "The public police have typically regulated social order outside of buildings, while the private police have typically regulated order within a building or within building complexes. More importantly, whether recognized or not, these groups interact in fundamental ways all of which contribute to the 'security net' within central business districts. In essence the 'horizontal and vertical' safety of any center city business area is greatly enhanced with cooperative public and private police arrangements."

In other cases, law enforcement agencies or local governments actually contract out work that was formerly performed by law enforcement. Such arrangements necessarily involve cooperation between law enforcement and private security. For example, to relieve its police department from the burden of investigating some 500 bad-check complaints each year, the city of Kentwood, Michigan, contracted with a private firm to do the work. The result is that investigations are no longer backlogged, merchants have an effective means for recovering their losses, and police have more time for their other duties. The Kentwood Program recently received a Webber Seavey Award.

Bob Stewart in the *Gazette* (December, 1997) notes that "contracting out enables police officers to concentrate on the tasks for which they are trained and can be most effective . . . [freeing up] a well-trained, professional police force from administrative and routine duties to concentrate on tackling crime. . . ."

Familiarity and Goodwill Programs

Some cooperative programs exist mainly to familiarize individual law enforcement and private security professionals with each other.

Law Enforcement Appreciation Nights

Typically, the liaison committee in a private security organization will host an annual law enforcement appreciation night. Ronald L. Kuhar and Jon C. Paul in *ASIS Dynamics* (July/August 1996) indicated that, for example, the Law

Enforcement Liaison Committee of the Greater Milwaukee Chapter of the American Society for Industrial Security (ASIS) holds annual law enforcement appreciation nights for about 100 police chiefs, sheriffs, and executives of federal law enforcement agencies in southeastern Wisconsin. The first benefit of such meetings is that key parties get to know each other. The second benefit is the actual cooperative work that develops from those relationships. For example, a member of the chapter assisted the Milwaukee County Sheriff's Department on security surveys, security policies and procedures, and security awareness to help the department in its new role of providing security at several county facilities.

Directories

The ASIS Greater Milwaukee Chapter publishes a directory of all Wisconsin police chiefs and state and federal law enforcement contacts. The chapter distributes the directory to ASIS members and law enforcement agencies.

Awards

An effort similar to law enforcement appreciation nights is the awarding of honors by security organizations to law enforcement. It is cooperation in the sense that security thereby encourages law enforcement to perform in ways that benefit private security. *Security* (July, 1997) stated that the John J. Duffy Memorial Award, given by the National Council of Investigation and Security Services to the Threat Management Unit (TMU) of the Los Angeles Police Department in 1997, "spotlighted the effectiveness of the police program. But it also underlined the necessary dialogue between law enforcement and private security and the complexities of stalking crimes." NCISS lauded the TMU for aggressively enforcing the anti-stalking laws on the books instead of working for the closure of public records, which would hinder private investigations.

Umbrella Programs

Many cooperative programs are best described as umbrella programs, as they are designed to develop law enforcement-private security relationships, teams, and task forces that address a wide range of concerns.

William C. Cunningham (*Security Management*, November, 1991) noted that one of the most notable is the Washington Law Enforcement Executive Forum, mentioned earlier, which, among other activities, funds a statewide loaned-executive program to enhance management of local police agencies; provides support for the *Law Enforcement Executive Journal*, the nation's first law enforcement business publication. It has also sponsored legislation on the regulation and training of private security personnel and on computer crime; and created an "Economic Crime Task Force to assess the nature and extent of white-collar crime in the state, develop strategies to reduce such crime, promote appropriate legislation initiatives and revisions, and collect and disseminate information on economic crime."

David R. Green, *Security Management* (May 1998) reported that the Business/Law Enforcement Alliance (BLEA), created in 1994, is a formal partnership between California businesses and city, county, state, and federal law enforcement agencies. An arm of the California Peace Officers Association, it includes some 200 participants from various industries and law enforcement and has a 10-member board of directors. BLEA's purpose is to create a link between the California business community and law enforcement so that both can work together to solve specific problems in the state. "The organization's leadership recognizes, for example, that some law enforcement agencies do not have the specialized expertise, tools, or time to investigate and prosecute certain high-tech offenders." BLEA is currently working on three projects: reducing check fraud, stopping the theft of rental equipment, and reducing false alarms. It may soon develop alliances with trade organizations to combat audio and video piracy.

Another umbrella program, as indicated in their April, 1990 newsletter, is the Baltimore County Police and Private Security Association, which meets once a month, has a newsletter, organizes joint training, works on legislation and reducing false alarms, addresses specific crimes (such as graffiti), organizes training of security officers to make better witnesses, and conducts other activities.

Anthony M. Voelker, circa 1988, in a New York Police Department document indicated that The Area Police-Private Security Liaison Program (APPL), formed in 1985, consists of high-ranking New York City Police Department members and respected security directors in New York City. "The program's main goals are to engage in cooperative efforts to protect people and property, exchange information to aid in the accomplishment of mutual goals, [and] eliminate the 'credibility gap' between police and private security." Police members provide information on local crime trends, patterns, and incidents; offer expertise to help private security protect assets and clientele; and provide an atmosphere conducive to trust and cooperation. Private security members learn how to cooperate with and help the police, and they offer expertise in technology, building security, and asset protection. The group holds quarterly regional meetings with speeches on specific topics. Members train each other and work together on legislation.

The *1991 Annual Report of The Creve Coeur,* Missouri Police Department indicated that the Creve Coeur Joint Crime Prevention Program consists of the Creve Coeur Police Department, Monsanto Corporate Security, and St. John's Mercy Medical Center Safety and Security Department. It has initiated a community-wide project to develop a mobile crime prevention display and command center trailer for the education and safety of the community. It holds Neighborhood Watch appreciation awards dinners to recognize citizens of the community for their efforts in assisting the police and preventing crime. Other activities include a bike rodeo with a crime prevention theme; crime prevention booths at local festivals; participation in National Night Out Halloween parties for children; crime prevention displays at program members' sites; one-day seminars at program members' sites on sexual assault, burglary prevention, drug and alcohol abuse, traffic safety, vacation safety, and security checks; and a phone notification system to alert neighborhood and business watch groups about crimes.

Some umbrella programs operate on the national level. For example, the Private Sector Liaison Committee of IACP has produced, for national distribution to law enforcement and private security practitioners, several resource and guideline documents. Examples include "Non-Sworn Alarm Responder Guidelines: Guidelines for Employers and Law Enforcement" and "False Alarm Perspectives: A Solution-Oriented Resource." Other papers have addressed product tampering, workplace drug crimes, and workplace violence. Recently, such efforts have been able to reach a wider audience by being posted on the Internet (www.amdahl.com/ext/iacp), which was itself an instance of cooperation, as the site space was donated by Amdahl Corporation.

Similarly, since the early 1980s, the Law Enforcement Liaison Committee (LELC) of ASIS has promoted cooperation by sponsoring seminars and presentations on (1) security and police issues, such as improving communications and working relationships; (2) trends in outsourcing and privatization; (3) training law enforcement personnel about private security functions; and (4) encouraging the establishment of law enforcement and security partnerships. In the late 1980s the LELC produced a video describing the roles and typical functions of private security. The video was distributed to virtually every major police training academy in the United States. The LELC has also worked to develop a closer association with such law enforcement organizations as IACP and the National Sheriffs' Association. In 1997, the LELC provided the initiative for a national project (supported by the Bureau of Justice Assistance, U.S. Department of Justice) to develop guidelines for establishing and improving partnerships between public law enforcement and private security.

Topic-Specific Efforts

Other cooperative programs focus primarily on a single topic or activity. The following section describes specific topics addressed by such programs or, in some cases, by umbrella programs.

Equipment

Sandy Moy in a February 8, 1998 e-mail message to the Private Sector Liaison Committee of the International Association of Chiefs of Police highlighted an effort, Project Blue Lights (named after its purpose: to get more "blue lights," or police, on the information superhighway) locates, obtains, and distributes usable, surplus computer hardware donated by private corporations to law enforcement agencies. The project's sponsor is the Washington Association of Sheriffs and Police Chiefs, which sent out letters to police departments and private companies to find out who needed computers and who had computers to donate. About one-third of police chiefs and sheriffs responded with their needs. United Parcel Service offered dozens of computers, which the company then shipped to any law enforcement agency in the state that needed one.

An article in *Security Concepts* (March, 1996) cited how an equipment transfer grew out of a rise in murders at San Diego's Balboa Park. Rangers felt they could not stop the problem. One ranger contacted a former coworker who had gone to work for Robot Research, a manufacturer of digital video products and CCTV control systems. Robot agreed to donate the multiplexing equipment necessary for a video surveillance system for the park. Then other companies (Pelco, Elmo, and Rainbow) donated the remaining needed equipment to create a five-camera system. Crime is now down in the park.

Incident News

R.H. Melton in an article in the *Washington Post,* November 21, 1995 reported that through the Hot Fax program in Bethesda, Maryland, the Montgomery County police, on learning of a crime, fax news of it to local business and community organizations. Those organizations then relay the fax to several hundred businesses and merchants. Fairfax County, Virginia, has a similar program, as do Buffalo, New York, Phoenix, Arizona, and Stamford, Connecticut. The Fairfax system reaches nearly 1,000 participants.

Terrorism and Overseas Safety

As stated in the *Proceedings of the 12th Annual Briefing* (date unknown) The Overseas Security Advisory Council (OSAC) consists of high-level corporate security directors and U.S. State Department representatives. OSAC provides an annual international security briefing for members. Its Research and Information Support Center provides international business intelligence to help American companies compete in the global economy.

High-Tech Crime

Local, state, and federal law enforcement agencies, along with corporations in the high-tech industry, have been working to establish networks of regional, specialized task forces. The approach has already been tested in some locales, formally and informally, with great success. Peter Olhausen in a study available on the web entitled "Combating High Tech Crime in California: The Task Force Approach," (see web citation in references) reported that The Sacramento Valley High-Tech Crime Task Force has coordinated the efforts of several law enforcement departments and federal agencies with the advice and support of local high-tech businesses, which lend expertise, donate equipment, and sometimes provide "buy money." In 1996, the task force investigated more than $13 million in property losses, recovering more than two-thirds. It performed 98 original investigations, assisted in 25 others, and conducted 53 forensic investigations. Those successes were largely due to several strengths of the task force approach: improved cooperation among different agencies, use of investigators who specialize in high technology, a focus on long-term investigations, and development of intelligence networks.

White-Collar Crime

An article by Chris A. Bradford and Clifford E. Simonsen (*Security Journal*, Volume 10, 1998) points out that private security and law enforcement have similar, though not identical, interests in preventing, investigating, and prosecuting white-collar crime. Opportunities for cooperation arise where those interests overlap. For example, to improve the likelihood of successful prosecutions, law enforcement investigators can teach private sector investigators how to gather evidence in accordance with police policies. Likewise, the private sector can teach law enforcement about computer security and other complex topics that arise in investigations of sophisticated white-collar crimes. Interest in such cooperation is not new. For example in 1978 the National District Attorneys Association held a conference that sought out potential areas of cooperation between the criminal justice system and private organizations in "detecting, investigating, and prosecuting organizational fraud and abuse."

Background Investigations

Terence J. Mangan and Michael G. Shanahan in the January, 1990 *FBI Law Enforcement Bulletin* indicated "In many states, thanks to cooperative law enforcement/private security initiatives, corporations are simply obtaining a release from applicants, submitting a fingerprint card, paying an established fee, and subsequently receiving a criminal history from the desired police agency. There has been no evidence of problems with these arrangements, and corporations that operate in multiple states have been willing to adjust their procedures to conform to applicable state laws."

Operations

Felecia Stratton (*Inbound Logistics*, March 1991) stated that over a period of many years, Conrail, Yellow Freight, American President Lines, Consolidated Freightways, and other shippers have teamed up with local law enforcement agencies to "wage war on cargo crime" by setting up sting operations.

Legislation

As indicated in the *Directory, ASIS and Wisconsin Chiefs of Police Association* the ASIS Greater Milwaukee Chapter has worked with the Wisconsin Chiefs of Police Association and a Wisconsin state senator on legislation regarding licensing of guards, private detectives, detective agencies, and armored car companies. The minutes of the first meeting of the Joint Council of Law Enforcement and Private Security Associations in 1986 identified, as a topic for immediate action, working for passage of legislation that gives access by corporations to conviction records of prospective employment applicants and developing model legislation model legislation.

Shared and Mutual Training

Bill Bruns in a November/December, *1989 NIJ Reports* reported on Operation Bootstrap by indicating it was "Launched as a pilot program by the International Association of Chiefs of Police, Operation Bootstrap now reaches into 40 states with support from private foundations and the National Institute of Justice. It offers state-of-the-art training and self-help programs that. . . cover subjects such as effective supervision, conflict resolution, group problem solving, and stress management. About 70 corporations donated over 800 seats in their executive education programs in 1988, absorbing tuition costs for law enforcement personnel and leaving participants responsible only for travel and per them expenses through their departments. At an average cost of $600 a course, corporations donated approximately $500,000 to the law enforcement sector [that] year."

Ronald L. Kuhar and Jon C. Paul in *ASIS Dynamics,* (July/August 1996) noted that police recruits in Wisconsin can take their elective classes at either the Milwaukee Area Technical College or the Milwaukee Police Department Academy. "Both agreed to allow representatives from the [ASIS] Greater Milwaukee Chapter to speak to their recruit classes as part of a pilot program in security/police cooperative efforts. Topics to be discussed will include the history and description of private security; comparisons between the private and public sectors; the professionalization of the security industry; interaction and cooperation; and developing sound relationships." The chapter then began working to get the Wisconsin Law Enforcement Training and Standards Board to make the ASIS orientation mandatory curriculum in all certified training academies throughout the state.

It is common for law enforcement and security professionals to speak at each other's conferences.

Trends

The literature reflects a number of trends that are affecting or will affect cooperation between law enforcement and private security.

The most powerful trend is the continued growth of the private security industry, both in real terms and relative to law enforcement.

Another trend is the change in law enforcement's approach to much of its work. The philosophies of community policing, neighborhood-oriented policing, and problem oriented policing all call on law enforcement to cooperate with the community, which includes private security.

In addition, increasing professionalism in private security has slowly been improving law enforcement's attitude toward security practitioners.

Another trend is the private sector's increasing need to prosecute. The entrance of the high-tech white-collar criminal, whose skillful predictions can prove disastrous for a corporation, will likely be the most significant catalyst bringing together the private sector and the various components of the criminal justice system for mutual assistance.

Also driving cooperation is the evolutionary loss of preexisting relationships. In 1986 at a Feasibility Conference on Private Security at the Federal Law Enforcement Training Center it was noted that "Informal levels of communication and cooperation are dissipating as private security firms promote managers more from within rather than from the field of law enforcement. The 'good ole boy' network cannot be relied upon for communication in future years."

The Future

An experienced participant in law enforcement-private security collaborations, Michael G. Shanahan, in "Private Enterprise and the Public Police: The Professionalizing Effects of a New Partnership" (Praeger, 1986) makes these comments about the possible future of cooperation:

> This interaction will probably produce different benefits for each participant, including enhanced professionalization of public law enforcement. Corporate people eventually will learn to operate more comfortably with some of the openness and public accessibility required of criminal justice agencies. Private sector executives will also learn to interact with people who are action-oriented, who show a great deal of initiative, and whose freshness in attacking problems is devoid of some of the intrigue and subtleties that frequently are found in the corporate bureaucracy.
>
> On the other side, law enforcement officials will be exposed to a higher degree of organizational sophistication. They will learn to view corporate problems through the eyes of chief executive officers, upwardly mobile corporate managers, and stockholders. . . . They will learn, too, that realistic planning and effective marketing are basic to survival. The police managers also will become sensitized to the fact that corporate entities, unlike police agencies, must measure up to competing firms or go out of business.

THE CERTIFIED PROTECTION PROFESSIONAL (CPP) PROGRAM

In 1972 the American Society for Industrial Security established the ASIS Institute. The combined efforts of the Society and the Institute resulted in the development of a Professional Certification Board that controls the Certified Protection Professional (CPP) program of the American Society for Industrial Security. Although this is a recent move in the professionalization of private security, it is a significant one.

In 1997, the twentieth anniversary of the program, more people have been certified as CPPs (6,000) than were active members of ASIS in 1977 (5,881). This amounts to approximately 10 to 20 percent of the total membership which has stayed fairly consistent over the last 20 years.

An article about the history of the CPP program in *Security Management* (September, 1997) provided information on the primary reason for seeking CPP designation. The following table presents the information.

Primary Reason for Seeking CPP Designation

Age	Increase Salary; Promotion	Increase Professional Advancement	Recognition Among Peers	Personal Satisfaction	Percent Each Age Group
30s	9%	75%	11%	19%	15%
40s	12	63	12	18	36
50 or over	8	51	27	30	49

Source: 1997 ASIS Survey of Certified Professionals, Applied Research Analysts, McLean, VA.

Additional information about this program was contained in a letter from F. Mark Geraci, CPP, President of ASIS, included with the *1999 Information Guide and Application*.

- 95 percent of CPPs have at least 10 years of professional security experience

- 78 percent of CPPs have obtained a post-secondary degree.

- 50 percent of CPPs hold an advanced degree from an accredited institution

- 58 percent of CPPs claim that professional advancement has been the primary benefit of the designation.

As this program grows, it is reasonable to assume that employers of private security professionals will require certification as a desirable attribute for applicants.

PROCESS FOR THE CPP EXAMINATION

Note: specific information about the test dates, locations, etc. can be obtained from the ASIS Web page: http://www.asisonline.org.

Applying for the Examination

Applications must be completed in full by the applicant and endorsed by an active CPP in good standing. Completed applications and fees must be received by the application deadline. Any application that is not completed in full will be returned to the applicant. Eligible candidates will be notified of their applications' approval. They will also receive information applicable to preparation for the examination. Within approximately three weeks of receiving the completed application, candidates satisfying the conditions of eligibility will receive written notices of authorization from ASIS to sit for the exam.

Testing Fees

Application fee: $100
Examination fee: $100

Test-Taking Procedures

Candidates satisfying the conditions of eligibility will receive written notices of approval to sit for the exam after completed applications are reviewed. Candidates will then be notified by ASIS approximately three weeks before the examination regarding the exact location of the exam site and other procedural information.

Exam Scoring

1. Exam scoring is performed by an independent service.

2. If a candidate fails to pass the exam, the candidate does not earn the CPP designation, and must wait a minimum of three months before taking the exam a second time, and six months before taking the exam a third time.

3. All details pertaining to requests and results concerning certification will be handled on a confidential basis. The awarding of certification to successful candidates will be published.

CPP Eligibility Requirements

Candidates wishing to take the CPP examination must first satisfy the following standards.

Experience and Education

- Nine (9) years of security experience, at least two (2) years of which shall have been in responsible charge of a security function; or

- An earned Associate's Degree from a regionally accredited college and seven (7) years of security experience, at least two (2) years of which shall have been in responsible charge of a security function, or

- An earned Bachelor's Degree from a regionally accredited college or university and five (5) years of security experience, at least two (2) years of which shall have been in responsible charge of a security function; or

- An earned Master's Degree from a regionally accredited college or university and three (3) years of security experience, at least two (2) years of which have been in responsible charge of a security function; or

- An earned Doctoral Degree from a regionally accredited college or university and two (2) years of security experience and responsible charge of a security function.

Note: Documentation for education is not needed if eligibility requirements based on years of experience are met. If education is used, official transcripts must accompany the application.

Applicant must not have been convicted of any criminal offense which would reflect negatively on the security profession and ASIS.

Endorsement

Certification candidates must be endorsed by a CPP in good standing. Endorsement of an application for certification shall signify that the person making the endorsement is satisfied that statements made by the candidate on the certification application are complete and accurate- and that in the judgment of the person making the endorsement, the applicant meets the requirements and is eligible to take the examination.

Successful Completion of Exam

An examination is required for all applicants who meet the experience and/or education and responsible charge criteria. A passing grade on the examination is necessary.

Preparing for the Exam

Study and preparation are key to successfully passing the CPP exam. To assist candidates in attaining their professional certification, ASIS provides reference materials and review courses, both available to members at discounted prices. By joining ASIS, CPP candidates can take advantage of the savings offered to members on the materials and review courses, as well as the valuable networking opportunities with more than 28,000 professional peers.

Chapter Review

Many of ASIS' 200 chapters assist members and prospective members by providing certification review courses locally to CPP candidates. Check with your local chapter for more information.

CPP Review Course

To fully prepare for the examination, candidates may take advantage of the ASIS CPP Review Course. Candidates benefit from:

- Knowledgeable instructors with expertise in content areas

A copy of the valuable study aid, *CPP Study Guide* an overview of the concepts found on the examination.

- A unique chance to have questions answered
- Personal counseling to assist in formulating a home study program
- Networking opportunities to learn from other CPP candidates and form valuable study groups

CPP Examination Structure

The CPP examination contains multiple-choice questions covering knowledge application in a wide range of security topics.

All U.S. and Canadian candidates will take an examination that includes questions covering the laws and jurisprudence of their specific countries. Candidates from other countries will not be tested on legal issues.

United States and Canada

The examination consists of 240 questions which must be completed within a four-hour period. Fifteen of the 240 questions are pre-test questions and will NOT count toward your final score. These 15 pre-test questions are placed randomly throughout the examination and are not identified. Your final score will be based on the 225 previously approved items.

International

The examination consists of 224 questions, which must be completed in three hours and 45 minutes (note: this represents an increase over previous year international examinations, which had to be completed in three hours and 30 minutes). Fifteen of the 224 questions are pre-test questions and will NOT count toward your final score. These 15 pre-test questions are placed randomly throughout the examination and are not identified. Your final score will be based on the total of 209 previously approved items.

CPP Examination Content

The CPP examination is comprised of six major subject areas, plus a seventh, Legal Aspects, for United States and Canada. The subjects covered are:

Emergency Planning
Implementation
Plan Development
Types of Emergency
Approximate percentage of test questions: 6 percent

Investigations
Investigative Resources
Methods of Investigation
Results and Reports of Investigation
Types of Investigation
Approximate percentage of test questions: 18 percent

Legal Aspects (U.S. and Canada only)
Administrative and Regulatory Agency Requirements Civil Liability-Torts
Civil Rights and Fair Employment
Contract Considerations
Crimes, Criminal Procedures, and the Criminal Justice System
Due Process and Constitutional Immunities
Approximate percentage of test questions: 7 percent

Personnel Security
Employment Selection and Retention Standards
Evaluation of Information
Screening Techniques
Security Awareness Programs
Disciplinary Action
Approximate percentage of test questions: 9 percent

Physical Security
Employee and Visitor Control
Alarms
Barriers
Facility Planning

Guard Patrols and Weapons
Materials Control
Mechanical, Electrical and Electronic Devices, and Equipment
Perimeter Boundaries, Gates, and Lobbies
Protective Lighting
Security Surveys
Parking, Traffic Control, Communications, and Security Transportation
Approximate percentage of test questions: 20 percent

Protection of Sensitive Information
Control
Identification
Sensitivity
Approximate percentage of test questions: 6 percent

Security Management (includes Liaison, Loss Prevention, and Substance Abuse)
Countermeasures Selection
Financial Management
Management Systems
Personnel Management
Planning, Organization, Leading, and Communications Management
Vulnerability Assessment
Risk Assessment
Countermeasures
Policies
Internal Relations
External Relations
Identification and Disposition of Abusers
Prevention Programs
Types of Solutions
Loss Prevention
Liaison
Substance Abuse
Approximate percentage of test questions: 34 percent

RECERTIFICATION

Recertification, earned through the accumulation of nine professional maintenance credits every three years, is required to maintain the CPP designation. Recertification is important for a number of reasons, including:

- Professional development and improvement.

- Continuing education and active participation in professional endeavors.

Recertification maintenance reports are due by December 31 of the third year of the original certification and every three years thereafter. ASIS will issue reminders in the third year of each CPPs' certification terms.

Recertification Fees

CPP recertification fees are $30 payable every three years. All checks must be made payable to ASIS in U.S. dollars and must be drawn on a U.S. bank. Fees are subject to change.

Code of Professional Responsibility

Applicants must adhere to the Code of Professional Responsibility to maintain standards of conduct. These standards are based on the ASIS Code of Ethics.

- I WILL ENDEAVOR to perform my professional duties in accordance with the highest moral principles.

- I WILL WORK VIGILANTLY and unceasingly to thwart the activities of individuals or groups who seek to change or destroy the democratic government processes by force or violence or by any other unlawful means.

- I WILL STRIVE to strengthen my government by the security protection of facilities and conserving of resources.

- I WILL BE FAITHFUL and diligent in discharging the duties entrusted to me, protecting the property and interests of employers, and safeguarding the lives and well-being of employees.

- I WILL OBSERVE strictly the precepts of truth, accuracy, and prudence.

- I WILL RESPECT and protect confidential and privileged information.

- I WILL PROMOTE programs designed to raise standards, improve efficiency, and increase the effectiveness of security.

Examination Oversight

Professional Certification Board

The ASIS certification program is administered by the Professional Certification Board (PCB), a panel appointed by the ASIS President with expertise on security matters. The PCB has full and final authority, pursuant to the policies of the American Society for Industrial Security to the qualifications of each candidate for certification. Independent testing services are retained to score and provide administrative functions for the examinations.

The PCB does not intend to determine who shall engage in security management. That a person is not certified by ASIS does not indicate that he or she is unqualified to perform security responsibilities, only that such person has not fulfilled the requirements or has not applied for certification. ASIS membership is not required for certification.

Revocation of Certification

A. Certification is subject to revocation by the PCB for any of the following causes:

1. The individual certified shall not have been eligible to receive such certificate, irrespective of whether or not the facts were known to, or could have been ascertained by, the PCB at the time of issuance of such certificate; or

2. The individual certified shall have made any misstatement of fact in the application for such certificate or any other statement or representation, connected with the application for certification, or

3. The individual certified has been found to have engaged in unethical practices or has been convicted of a criminal offense which would reflect negatively on the security profession and ASIS.

B. No certification shall be revoked unless the following procedures are followed:

1. A copy of the charges against the CPP and the information concerning the event or events from which such charges have arisen is sent by registered mail to the individual. Such notice shall state that no action will be taken against the CPP until after a hearing, unless the CPP fails to request a hearing or offer a defense within 15 days.

2. The CPP is given at least 15 days to prepare a defense.

3. A hearing is held on such charges, before a panel designated by the PCB, at which time the person is given a full opportunity to be heard in his or her own defense, including the right to be represented by counsel, the right to cross-examine witnesses appearing, and to examine documents material to said charges. Accommodation support will be provided to eligible individuals.

4. The panel shall initially determine whether or not the CPP's certification should be revoked. The initial determination of the panel, including all evidence submitted at the hearing, shall be reviewed by the PCB. Upon review, the PCB may affirm, reverse, modify, or remand the original determination of the panel.

5. If the initial determination of the panel is to revoke the certification of the CPP, and if a majority of the PCB in official session call on due notice shall affirm the panel's determination, after review, that the individual is not eligible for continued certification, then the PCB shall direct the Certification Program Director to issue such notice signed by the President of the PCB. No PCB member shall vote or take part in the review of any determination if he served as a member of the hearing panel.

Endnotes:

1. "Experience" shall mean that the individual has been personally engaged in security or loss prevention on a full-time basis or as a primary duty.

2. Generally, "Responsible Charge" shall mean that charge exercised by an individual in a supervisory position, who makes decisions for the successful completion of objectives without reliance upon directions from a superior as to specific methods or techniques. However, an applicant need not have absolutely held a supervisory position, as long as the positions on which the application relies shall have specifically included responsibility for independent decisions or actions. If Responsible Charge is not based on supervisory responsibilities, then the duties which qualify as Responsible Charge must clearly show security program management responsibilities and duties. Generally, this excludes such positions as patrolman or equivalent.

3. "Security Function" shall mean the protection of assets.

Examples of acceptable experience in a security function are:

1. Experience as a security practitioner in the protection of assets, in the public or private sector, criminal justice system, government intelligence or investigative agencies.

2. Experience with companies, associations, government, or other organizations furnishing services or equipment, including consulting firms, shall be considered as meeting the experience requirements, provided the duties and responsibilities substantively relate to the design, evaluation, and application of systems, programs, equipment, or development and operation of services for protection of assets in the private or public sectors. Direct sales experience alone will not be considered as qualifying experience.

3. Experience as a full-time educator on the faculty of an accredited educational institute shall be considered as meeting the experience requirements, provided the responsibilities for courses and other duties relate response primarily to knowledge areas pertinent to the management and operation of protection of assets programs in the public or private sectors.

SUMMARY

This text has presented material on a wide range of subjects from security lighting to locks to personnel selection. Thus, conclusions in the traditional sense cannot be made. However, the authors believe that it will have served an extremely useful purpose if the readers are encouraged to give serious consideration to pursuing private security careers and continue their efforts to obtain experience and education in the field. If this text raises more questions than it answers, it will have served a useful purpose in furthering the professionalization of private security.

DISCUSSION QUESTIONS

1. Discuss the probable future growth of private security.

2. Outline the criteria to be met for the Certified Protection Professional Program (CPP).

3. What activities best lend themselves toward privatization?

4. Which tasks in the Kansas City Police Task Force study are most appropriate for private security personnel?

5. Compare the advantages and disadvantages of privatization and outsourcing.

6. What are the important issues involved in the concept of private employment of public police?

7. What are the key ingredients involved in the programs of cooperation between public and private agencies?

REFERENCES

(1996). "Alarming Trends: Down." *Security Management*, April, 1996, 12.

(1994). "America's New Watchword: If It Moves, Privatize It." *Business Week*, December 12, 1994, 39.

Anderson, T. (1997). "Judicial Decisions: Security Officer." *Security Management*, June, 1997, 97.

Anderson, T. and Cannan, P. (1996). "Private Security Behind Bars." *Security Management*, October, 1996, 32-41.

(1998). "ASIS Aids IACP in Formulating Guidelines." *Security Management*, June, 1998, 103.

(1997). "ASIS CPP Program Participation Grows 243%." *Security Director's Digest*, January 15, 1997, 1&3.

(1998). "ASIS Introduces Computer-Based Testing For The Certified Protection Professional (CPP). *Security Director's Digest*, February 18, 1998, 10.

Bentley, W. CPP. (1997). "An Alliance is Born." *Security Management*, October, 1997, 77-80.

Berry, D., Mullen, M. and Murray, T. (1998). "Administering a Healthy Dose of Security." *Security Management*, June, 1998, 46-50 & 59-61.

Bradford, C. and Simonsen, C. (1988). "The Need for Cooperative Efforts Between Private Security and Public Law Enforcement in the Prevention, Investigation, and Prosecution of Fraud-Related Criminal Act." *Security Journal*, Volume 10, 1988, 161-168.

Bruns, B. (1989). "Operation Bootstrap: Opening Corporate Classrooms to Police Managers." *NIJ Reports*, November/December 1989, 2.

(undated). *Career Opportunities in Security*. Arlington, VA: American Society for Industrial Security.

Carter, T. (1998). "Locker Sniffers: Sixty-One School Districts in State Already Use Dogs to Detect Drugs and Gunpowder." Grand Rapids (Michigan) Press, April 4, 1998, A3.

(1998). *Certified Protection Professional (CPP): A Program for the Advancement of Professional Practice Information Guide and Application*. Alexandria, VA: American Society for Industrial Security, 1998.

Chaiken, M. and Chaiken, J. (1989). "Public Policing-Privately Funded." *Issues and Practices*. National Institute of Justice November/December 1989.

(1996). "Companies Look Askance at Employees' Criminal Pasts." *Security Director's Digest*, October 30, 1996, 4.

(1990). "Contracting Police Support Services to Private Security: Proposal Submitted to the Program on Public Safety and Security." National Institute of Justice by the Kansas City, Missouri Police Department.

Crawford, M. (1997). "CPP Comes of Age." *Security Management*, September, 1997, 129-138.

Cunningham, W. (1991). "Success Across America." *Security Management*, November, 1991, 43.

Cunningham, W. and Strauchs, J. (1992). "Security Industry Trends: 1993 and Beyond." *Security Management*, December, 1992, 27-36.

Cunningham, W. and Taylor, T. (1985). "Crime and Protection in America: A Study of Private Security and Law Enforcement Resources and Relationships: Executive Summary." Washington, DC: U.S. Government Printing Office, May, 1985.

Cunningham, W. and Taylor, T. (1985). *Private Security and Police in America: The Hallcrest Report I*. Stoneham, MA: Butterworth-Heinemann.

Cunningham, W., Strauchs, J. and Van Meter, C. (1990). *Private Security Trends 1970-2000: The Hallcrest Report II*. Stoneham, MA: Butterworth-Heinemann.

(1997). "Ex-Security Director Indicted." *Security Director's Digest*, February 19, 1997, 9.

(1997). "Five Indicted with $19 Million Public Housing Scam." *Security Director's Digest*, July 30, 1997), 6-7.

(1995). "Getting the Goods." *Security Management*, September, 1995, 21.

Green, D. CPP (1998). "Joining Forces Against Crime." *Security Management*, May, 1998, 95-98.

Greene, J., Seamon, T., and Levy, P. (1993). "Merging Public and Private Security for Collective Benefit: Philadelphia's Center City District." Paper, 1993, 5, 96.

(1998). "Guard Charged with Theft at Buick Plant." *Grand Haven (Michigan) Tribune*, July 24, 1998, 7.

Horn, J. CPP (1995). "Demographics of CPP Candidates." *Security Management*, February, 1995, 80.

Holmes, P. (1985). "Taking Public Services Private." *Nation's Business*, August, 1985, 20-22.

(1996). "Intel to Pay Police for Crime Investigation, Prevention." *Security Director's Digest*, August 7, 1996, 3&4.

Johnson, B. and McCatty, P. (1998). "Security's Amazing Recovery." *Security Management*, October, 1998, 31-38.

Johnson, L. (1997). "The Fall of Terrorism." *Security Management*, April, 1997, 26-32.

Kirch, J. (1995). "FBI Program Expands." *Security Management*, October, 1995, 12-13.

Kuhar, R. CPP (undated). "Private Security Orientation for Police Recruits." Milwaukee, WI: Milwaukee Area Technical College.

Kuhar, R. CPP (undated). "Private/Public Cooperation: The Milwaukee Experience." Milwaukee, WI: Milwaukee Area Technical College.

Kuhar, R. CPP and Paul, J. (1996). "The Milwaukee Experience." *ASIS Dynamics*, July/August 1996, 5-7.

Lapides, G. (1986). *CPP News Notes*, No. 4. Arlington, VA: ASIS.

Lewan, T. (1998). "Some Draw Unwitting Cops into Death Wish." *Grand Rapids (Michigan) Press*, April 26, 1998, A2.

Longmore-Etheridge, A. (1996). "CPP Candidates Multiply." *Security Management*, September, 1996, 179-180.

Longmore-Etheridge, A. (1998). "Special CPP Exam Administered." *Security Management*, July, 1998, 129.

Longmore-Etheridge, A. and Neeley, D. (1998). "The Jobs Are Out There." Alexandria, VA: *ASIS Dynamics*, 1 & 21-22.

Mangan, T. and Shannahan, M. (1990). "Public Law Enforcement/Private Security: A New Partnership." *FBI Law Enforcement Bulletin*, January, 1990, 18-22.

(1996). "Many Security Guards With Felony Convictions Remain on Job." *Security Director's Digest*, November 27, 1996, 3.

Melton, R. (1995). "Bethesda's Phone Posse." *Washington Post*, November 21, 1995, B1.

Michelmore, P. (1998). "Times Square Where We Greet the New Year." *Reader's Digest* (Large Print Edition) January, 1998, 55-62.

Murphy, J. (1997). "The Private Sector and Security: A Bit on BIDS." *Security Management*, Volume 9, 1997, 11.

(1995). "Nebraska Court Leaves Taxpayers Liable for Police Working as Security Guards." *Security Director's Digest*, November 22, 1995, 9.

Ohlhausen, P.(1997). "Combating High-Tech Crime in California: The Task Force Approach." iv, v, 17. Available at http://members.aol.com/pohlhausen/library/fa/fa.html.

Patterson, J. (1995). "Forging Creative Alliances." *Security Management*, January, 1995, 33-35.

(1998). "Private Problems, Public Service." Cambridge, MA: *American Police Beat*, May, 1998, 16.

(1998). "Protection One Leads Privatized Alarm Response." *Security Director's Digest*, April 1, 1998, 1.

(1996). "Public and Private Sector Unite to Fight Crime." *Security Concepts*, March 1996, 11.

Reiss, A. (1988). "Private Employment of Public Police." Washington, DC: National Institute of Justice, 1988.

Richards, D. CPP (1995). "Rules of Thumb for Biometrics Systems." *Security Management*, October, 1995, 67-71.

Satchell, M. (1998). "Crime: Holy Wail." *U.S. News & World Report*, May 4, 1998, 14.

Seamon, T. CPP (1995). "Private Forces for Public Good." *Security Management*, September, 1995, 92-97.

(1995). "Security Companies Hire Police Rejects for Florida Rest Stops." *Security Director's Digest*, August 30, 1995, 1&9.

(1997). "Security Companies Sue Police Agencies Over Free Lancing." *Security*, January, 1997, 75.

(1997). "Security Group Honors Anti-Stalking Police Unit." *Security*, July 1997, 7-8.

Shanahan, M. (1986). *Private Enterprise and the Public Police: The Professionalizing Effects of a New Partnership*, p. 452. New York, NY: Praeger.

(1998). *Solicitation for Research and Evaluation on Corrections and Sentencing (1998)*. Washington, DC: National Institute of Justice, March, 1998.

Somerson, I. CPP (1995). "The Next Generation." *Security Management*, January, 1995, 26-30.

(1995). "Spokane Police Want to Charge for False Alarms." *Security Director's Digest*, August 23, 1995, 10.

Stewart, B. (1997). "Breaking Barriers: Public Police and Private Security." *Gazette* (A Royal Canadian Mounted Police Publication), December, 1997, 10.

Stratton, F. (1991). "Cargo Cops: to Catch a Thief." *Inbound Logistics*, March 1991.

(1986). "Summary of a Feasibility Conference on Training Possibilities Addressing Private Security/Public Law Enforcement Relationships." Federal Law Enforcement Training Center, Glynco, Georgia 1986.

Tafoya, W. (1986). "A Delphi Forecast of the Future of Law Enforcement." Unpublished doctoral dissertation, Criminal Justice and Criminology, University of Maryland.

(1998). "10 Largest U.S. Security Guard, Patrol and Investigative Companies." *Security Business*, Vol. XXVIII, No. 12, June 15, 1998, 1.

(1997). *Top Organization & Professional Issues For Today's Security Director: 1997 Fortune 1000 Survey Report*. Encino, CA: Pinkerton Service Corporation, 1997.

(1998). *Top Security Threats Facing Corporate America: 1998 Survey of Fortune 1000 Companies*. Encino, CA: Pinkerton Service Corporation, 1998.

Trotta, L. (1998). "Guiliani Bids to Use Cops to Cut Crime in Schools." *The Washington Times*, March 15, 1998, 14.

Voelker, A. (circa 1988). "Area Police-Private Security Liaison Program." New York City Police Department document, circa 1988.

(1996). "White House Moving Ahead on Plan to Privatize Employee Security Checks." *Security Director's Digest*, July 10, 1996, 5.

Appendix A
Job Description: Security Programs Manager

Department: Security, Safety & Shuttle Services

Reports To: Security, Safety & Shuttle Services Manager

Purpose:

To develop and maintain security and safety programs and policies for designated members of the Executive staff and Board of Directors.

Responsibilities:

Define, develop, implement, and continually refine security and safety programs to provide reasonable protection of designated members of the Executive staff and Board of Directors, and their immediate families, from random or premeditated threats at all times (work, home, school, etc.).

Develop, implement, and continually refine a domestic and international Executive travel program to include all aspects of travel and associated event security. Position may require regular travel.

Maintain extremely sensitive and confidential personal information about designated members of the Executive staff and Board of Directors, and their immediate families, including health history, private routines and functions, work and travel schedules.

Develop and continually refine philosophy and design standards, and operational manuals relating to protection systems (i.e., burglar, fire, and duress alarms; video coverage, etc.), procedures (i.e., international and domestic travel; kidnap and ransom, event security, Company's Corporate Security emergency response, etc.), and building design (i.e., residential construction; landscape, etc.).

Provide physical audits of office(s) and residence(s), based on the developed standards, and provide recommendations based on findings; provide project management of improvements, and final approval upon project completion.

Market and promote Corporate Security, its services, programs, policies, and recommended practices, for designated members of the Executive staff and Board of Directors. Improve overall awareness of customer, and their immediate families, through education. Act as the point of contact on security-related issues for all designated members of the Executive staff and Board of Directors, their families, and domestic help and maintain regular contact with those affected, by e-mail and telephone, supplemented by periodic visits.

Review, develop, and continually refine policies to insure Company is meeting or exceeding the best practices in the areas of Executive protection, personal safety, and Corporate assumed liability.

Review, develop and continually refine security operation's operational manuals and procedures regarding monitoring of executive systems and response to incidents, and provide direction to the Security Operations Manager regarding resource support of the established executive protection programs, including the management of staff assigned to monitor executive residences.

Manage quality control and productivity of service providers. Review service provider practices and methodologies to insure that Company's objectives are being met, including method of delivery, quality of service, pricing, reporting, and customer (Executive) satisfaction.

Act as primary contact for all Executive security emergency issues and act in a primary role in the Emergency Operations Center during disasters. Position requires on-call availability 24 hours a day, seven days a week.

Develop and manage fiscal budgets for Corporate Security Executive operations totaling up to $500,000 annually.

Provide consulting to international Executives as needed.

Analyze and resolve non-routine problems. Advise Executive staff of proposed changes to policy/procedures as well as extenuating circumstances regarding security-related issues.

Complete required monthly operations report. Act as liaison between Executives, management, and service providers on security-related issues.

Contacts:

This position has regular contact with all levels of Company's Executives, Board of Directors, managers, and frequent contact with local, domestic, and international government agencies and outside service providers.

Qualifications Recommended:

The ideal candidate will have a four-year degree in criminal justice or related field, and a minimum of five years management experience in an Executive security-related capacity in a corporate/private setting. This position requires the ability to maintain extreme confidentiality. Must have the ability to work independently to achieve results. Excellent organization, communication, and interpersonal skills are required. Candidate must be able to work under pressure and within short time constraints. PC skills strongly preferred.

This position has been designed to indicate the general nature and level of work performed by employees within this position. The actual duties, responsibilities, and qualifications may vary based on assignment. A background investigation will be required prior to an offer of employment.

Appendix B
Job Description: Security Officer

Mission

The primary mission of a Security Officer is to help maintain a center where customers can shop comfortably in a friendly, safe, and secure environment.

General Description

The Security Officer works alone and with co-workers to provide, at all times, quality customer service (such as answering questions and providing other assistance), and to guard and secure the shopping center exterior and interior property (which at times might include tenant stores) against fire, theft, disruption, vandalism, illegal entry, and illegal activities. The Security Officer maintains center safety at all times, including emergencies. Each Security Officer follows general and detailed guidelines for doing the work; however specific activities may vary from guidelines in response to daily conditions. Security Officers prepare a variety of important reports and records. The Security Officer must maintain competence in the work by training throughout the year. Clean and neat appearance, pleasant demeanor, positive attitude, and commitment to quality customer service are as important to job success as is satisfactory performance of the essential functions of the job.

NOTE – This Position Description does not create an employment contract or an obligation for employment by either the Company or the employee. The employment relationship may be terminated by either party at any time for any reason or for no reason. This Position Description may be changed by the Company at any time.

ESSENTIAL FUNCTIONS

Listed below are the essential functions for this position and example duties for each function. These are the tasks that are fundamental, basic, primary, and necessary to the job. Every person in this position must be able to perform the essential functions. Essential functions do not include the marginal, minor, or incidental tasks that can easily be re-assigned to another job. Tasks assigned "at Supervisor discretion" are not considered essential functions.

FREQUENCY is rated in hours per week:
OCCASIONAL = 12 or less; FREQUENT = 13-24; CONSTANT = 25 or more

FUNCTION FREQUENCY

1. Provide customer service to the public, tenants, and center staff, observe and report security, safety, and other problems, answer questions give directions give assistance(such as entering/exiting center, carrying parcels, auto assists) control crowds, control vehicle traffic
    CONSTANT

2. Patrol, inspect; search the center interior and exterior, patrol the site interior and exterior, drive around the site exterior, observe people, objects, details, detect sounds, odors, inspect locks, equipment, alarm systems
    FREQUENT

3. Respond to incidents, problems, emergencies, communicate with public, tenants, co-workers, initiate helpful action, direct people to take proper action, maintain order and calm, obtain assistance from public, co-workers, agencies, follow instructions, maintain self-control
    OCCASIONAL

4. Gather, relay information; rile reports, report details of patrols, incidents, assistance rendered, etc., (for administrative and legal records), interpret and compile data for such records, write logical, coherent, accurate summaries, attend meetings, hearings, court sessions
    OCCASIONAL

    Maintain, enhance skills and knowledge, participate in training and education programs, demonstrate mastery of skills and knowledge in "test" situations, maintain current qualifications for certifications, licenses
    OCCASIONAL

I understand the 5 Essential Functions stated above for this position.

APPLICANT SIGNED: _____ DATE: _____

ESSENTIAL ACTIVITIES

Listed below are the essential physical and mental activities for this position. These are the activities that are involved in performing the essential functions of the job.

1. PHYSICAL ACTIVITIES
    walk, stand, lift, carry, push, pull, 0-20 pounds, excessive weight in emergencies, stoop, kneel, crouch, reach, handle, finger, see near or far details of objects, color, depth, field, speak, hear, smell

2. MENTAL ACTIVITIES
   understand, follow instructions, comprehend, convey detailed information with clarity, memorize, remember details and procedures, make judgments, and routine and emergency decisions, perform repetitive tasks, deal with people, perform effectively under stress

I understand the Physical and Mental Activities stated above for this position.

APPLICANT SIGNED: _____ DATE: _____

SCHEDULE and SUPERVISION REQUIREMENTS

Listed below are the work schedules, training and performance evaluation schedules, and requirements for supervision for this position.

1. WORK SCHEDULE
   Hours: full-time 40 hours per week – part-time flexible hours
   Shift: any of 3 shifts
           change shift on 24 hours' notice
   Overtime: with compensation
               without notice
   Attendance: comply with Attendance Policy

2. TRAINING and PERFORMANCE REVIEW SCHEDULE
   Training: ongoing during the year
   Performance Reviews: Probationary Period – 60 and 120 days
   Standard Reviews – April, October

3. SUPERVISION and DIRECTIONS
   Supervisors: 1st Level – Sergeant
                 2nd Level – Lieutenant or Assistant Security Director
                 3rd Level – Security Director
   Subordinates: NONE
   Directions/instructions: reading: department correspondence
                             department guidelines
                             rules and regulations
                             training manuals
                             task lists
                             logbooks
                      speaking/hearing: beepers, walkie-talkies
                                 alone or in groups with
                                 supervisors, co-workers
                      demonstration: by supervisors, co-workers
                                 alone and in groups
                                 audio-visual recordings

I understand the Schedule and Supervision requirements stated above for this position.

APPLICANT SIGNED: _____ DATE: _____

ABILITIES and PERSONAL TRAITS

Listed below are the minimum qualifications for abilities (education, skills, and experience) and personal traits required to commence work in this position.

1. ABILITIES (Education, Experience, Certifications)
Education level: reasoning: apply common sense
carry out directions
(in written, oral, diagram form)
solve problems involving several variables (in standard and emergency situations)
math: add, subtract, multiply, divide
all units of measure
fractions and decimals
American monetary units
compute rate and percent
measure quantities and time
Language:
read: journals, periodicals
manuals
rules, instructions
write: information into logbooks
coherent, logical summaries
detailed reports
speak: 1-on-1, and in groups
clearly and distinctly
well-modulated voice control
proper English
Experience: NONE.
Certifications, Degrees, Licenses: valid driver's license

2. PERSONAL TRAITS
honest
trustworthy
courteous
helpful (cooperative)
patient
careful, cautious
good common sense
operate well under stress
respect authority, laws
organized
service-oriented
detail-oriented
crisis-sensitive
rule-conscious
safety-conscious

3. OTHER: no record of criminal convictions which may be deemed to disqualify the person from employment. (Consideration of nature of the crime, date of conviction, and final disposition will be determinative.)

I understand the Abilities and Personal Traits stated above for this position.

APPLICANT SIGNED: _____ DATE: _____

TOOLS, EQUIPMENT, MACHINERY, AND WORK ENVIRONMENT

The person in this position must be able to properly select and skillfully use the tools, equipment, and machinery listed below, as well as be able to work in the environment described.

1. TOOLS, EQUIPMENT, and MACHINERY
    keys
    flashlight
    handtools
    First Aid/CPR equipment
    battery cables
    chemical extinguishers
    fire hose
    spotlight
    baton/nightstick
    writing tools
    tape recorder
    dictating machine
    office machines
    computer
    typewriter
    camera
    audio-visual equipment
    2-way communicating devices (beeper, walkie-talkie, telephone, radio, etc.)transport vehicles (cart, bin, etc.)motor vehicles

2. WORK ENVIRONMENT
    Location: indoors, outdoors, multi-level, rooftop
    Barriers: stairs, escalators, elevators, doorways, narrow passages, roof hatch
    Climate: regulated indoors
                  unventilated areas
                  outdoors
    temperature: extremes in emergencies

Possible Hazards:

Chemicals	Objects	Machines	People
Mace	carpeted floors	electricity	assault
Fumes	slippery floors	vehicles	diseases
Explosives	weapons	mechanical	bloodborne pathogens

I understand the Tools, Equipment, Machinery, and Work Environment requirements stated above for this position.

APPLICANT SIGNED: _____ DATE: _____

Appendix C
Crime Awareness and Campus Security Act of 1990

Crime Awareness and Campus Security Act of 1990—The Crime Awareness and Campus Security Act, passed by Congress in November 1990, required all post-secondary institutions receiving federal funding to initiate a program to disclose campus security policy and campus crime statistics. Beginning September 1, 1992, and each year thereafter, the affected post-secondary institutions began the task of preparing, publishing, and distributing, through appropriate publications or mailings, to all current students and employees, and to any applicant for enrollment or employment upon request, an annual security report containing at least the following information with respect to the campus security policies and campus crime statistics of that institution:

1) A statement of current campus policies regarding procedures and facilities for students and others to report criminal actions and emergencies occurring on campus as well as policies concerning the institution's response to such reports;

2) A statement of current policies concerning security and access to campus facilities, including campus residences, and security considerations used in the maintenance of campus facilities;

3) A statement of current policies concerning campus law enforcement;

4) A description of the type and frequency of programs designed to inform students and employees about campus security procedures and practices;

5) A description of programs designed to inform students and employees about the prevention of crimes;

6) Statistics concerning the occurrences on campus during the most recent school year, and during the two preceding years for which data are available, for murder, rape, robbery, aggravated assault, burglary, and motor vehicle theft;

7) A statement of policy regarding the monitoring and recording through local police agencies of criminal activity at or involving off-campus housing and student organization activities recognized by the institution;

8) Statistics concerning the number of arrests for the crimes of liquor law violations, drug abuse violations, and weapons possessions occurring on campus; and

9) A statement of policy regarding the possession, use and sale of alcoholic beverages and illegal drugs, and the enforcement of applicable laws.

Prior to the passage of the Crime Awareness and Campus Security Act Congress found:

1) The reported incidence of crime, particularly violent crime, on some college campuses had steadily risen for the past several years;

2) That about 80 percent of campus crimes were committed by one student upon another student;

3) That approximately 95 percent of campus crimes were alcohol- or drug-related;

4) That only 352 of 8,000 post-secondary institutions participating in federal student aid programs voluntarily provided crime statistics directly through the Uniform Crime Reports of the FBI; and

5) That current and prospective students and employees had the right to have access to crime and security information regarding that institution.

The impact of the Crime Awareness and Campus Security Act remains to be seen, but it is quite evident that the affected institutions are now being required to maintain and distribute crime data and security information with some degree of certainty and consistency. Institutions having significant crime problems may be forced—particularly if the bad news affects student enrollments—to improve the status of their campus security and law enforcement efforts. Additionally, the ever-present specter of litigation relative to campus crime will continue to provide an impetus for colleges and universities to assure that their campuses are in compliance with applicable laws and expected standards of safety and security.

Appendix D
School Safety Resources

School Safety Links

National Association of School Resource Officers
www.nasro.org

National School Safety Center
www.nssc1.org/home2.htm

Kentucky Center for School Safety
www.kysafeschools.org

Center for the Prevention of School Violence
www.ncsu.edu/cpsv

Missouri Safe Schools Homepage
http://cctr.umkc.edu/user/rthompson/safe.html

Guide for Prevention and Responding to School Violence
ww.theiacp.org/pubinfo/pubs/pslc/svindex.htm

National Association of School Resource Officers
www.nasro.org

Early Warning, Timely Response: A Guide to Safe Schools
www.ed.gov/offices/OSERS/OSEP/earlywrn.html

Violence Prevention Links

Violence Prevention Research Program
http://web.ucdmc.ucdavis.edu/vprp

Early Prevention of Violence Database
www.csnp.ohio-state.edu/glarrc/vpdb.htm

Violence Prevention Resource Center
www.crisisprevention.com

Center for the Study and Prevention of Violence
www.colorado.edu/cspv

CDC Division of Violence Prevention
www.cdc.gov/ncipc/dvp/dvp.htm

International Center for the Prevention of Crime
www.crime-prevention-intl.org/english/index.htm

Violence Prevention Initiative
www.accessarizona.com/partners/preventviolence

Community Violence Prevention Network
www.cvpn.org

Distance Education Links

Administrative Function of Planning in Distance Education
http://members.aol.com/_ht_a/esocollier/DEpresentation.html

Distance Education and Videoconferencing System Design
http://members.aol.com/_ht_a/tbrenneman/index.html

Distance Education Clearinghouse
http://www.uwex.edu/disted/home.html

Distance Learning Resource Network
http://www.wested.org/tie/dlrn/

Dave Feeney, Distance Education Project Director
http://members.aol.com/_ht_a/distanceed/default.htm

University of Washington Distance Learning
www.edoutreach.washington.edu/extinfo/dl_index.htm

Stanford Online
http://online.stanford.edu/main.html

Cornell Lecture Browser
http://www4.cs.cornell.edu/LectureBrowser/1.%20overview/default.htm

Caliber.com
www.caliberlearning.com/aboutus

Convene.com
www.convene.com/overview.asp

Community Policing Links

Community Policing Pages
www.concentric.net/~dwoods

Community Policing Consortium
www.communitypolicing.org

RICP
http://ricp.uis.edu/main_bottompage.htm

National Center for Community Policing
www.ssc.msu.edu/~cj/cp/cptoc.html

Threat and Risk Assessment Links

Dealing with White Collar Crime Risk Assessments
www.sarnet.co.za/comcrime/dwc3c.htm

Gavin de Becker Incorporated: Threat Assessment
www.gdbinc.com/threat.htm

Michael H. Corcoran, Ph.D & Associates, Inc.
www.workthreat.com/index.html

Computer-Based Training Links

UCDavis CBT
http://cbt.ucdavis.edu/

Web Based Training
http://cbt.netdirect.net/

The University of Memphis CBT Web Usage Guide
http://umvirtual2.memphis.edu/cbt.htm

N.C. State CBT Project
http://cbt-training.ncsu.edu/

Appendix E
Counterterrorism Security Checklist

BACKGROUND: ASSET IDENTIFICATION PROCEDURES
- Employee survey
- Accounting identification and valuation
- Outside consultants

EXISTING THREAT PROTECTION PROCEDURES
- Policies and procedures
- Disaster planning
- Training programs

VULNERABILITY COMPLIANCE AND ASSESSMENT
- Audits
- Costs/benefit analysis

ASSET AND LOSS RECUPERATION
- Recovery planning
- Emergency response
- Stabilization systems

SAFEGUARDS
Typical:
- Barriers
- Entry and visitor control systems
- Verifiable identification systems
- Clearance controls and limited access areas
- Monitoring systems
- Locks and key protection procedures
- Internal and external communications
- Shift and guard rotation

Extraordinary:
- Explosive detection devices
- K-9 Units
- Automatic notification for law enforcement
- Automatic notification for fire protection
- Offsite CCTV monitoring
- Evacuation planning

Appendix F
Terrorism Risk Assessment

Terrorism risk assessment is the process of the formal identification of assets that are in need of protection, determination of what controls are prudent given the costs and benefits of that protection and formalization of the procedures, including audits, that will help standardize these procedures. Automated software exists for terrorism risk assessment for both facilities and computer systems (i.e., Risk Watch,® Risk PAC,® etc.). These programs are based on the set of answers given to several hundred questions. These types of programs can provide counterterrorism security personnel with a formalized profile of the risks associated with particular facilities. The following checklist is an attempt to manually create a similar process for use by security professionals.

Such a survey should always be conducted in conjunction with a formalized security analysis (i.e., see general survey example elsewhere in this appendix). The justification for this combination analysis is simple—traditional security procedures should be considered a foundation where constructive counterterrorism procedures begin.

Author note: The plural "facilities" is used to provide some consistency in the survey. Some surveys may cover only one facility.

Counterterrorism Security Survey
for Commercial Facilities

Date of Report _____

Name of consultant or agency conducting survey _____

Name of surveyor _____ Name of report writer _____
      Signature   Signature

Name and address of facilities being surveyed _____

_____

Date survey conducted _____ Dates of previous surveys _____ , _____
                                  (If appropriate)

List of parties responsible for facilities

Contracting department or agent _____   Contract # _____

Phone number _____   E-mail _____

Address _____

Security supervisor's name_____   E-mail _____

Phone number _____

Address _____

Primary contact person _____   E-mail _____

Phone number _____

Address _____   E-mail _____

Secondary contact person_____

Phone number _____

Address _____

Brief description and history of business conducted at these facilities _____

_____

_____

Facilities Demographics

Buildings:

Total number of buildings? _____

Occupied buildings? _____

Unoccupied buildings? _____

Total building(s) size(s) _____ (total sq. ft/sq. mt.)

Occupied buildings' sizes? _____ (total sq. ft/sq. mt.)

Unoccupied buildings' sizes? _____ (total sq. ft/sq. mt.)

Estimated glass area of total vertical
building surface area _____ (% of surface)

Occupied buildings' glass area? _____ (% of surface)

Unoccupied buildings' glass area?_____ (% of surface)

Number of rooms?   _____

    Occupied buildings' rooms?   _____

    Unoccupied buildings' rooms?   _____

Height of tallest building?   _____ (stories)

Describe primary HVAC system(s) _____

_____

Describe primary fire suppression system(s) _____

_____

Describe primary emergency alarm system(s) _____

_____

Perimeter:

    Type of fence_____

    Height of fence _____ (ft./mt.)   Percent of total length _____%

    Length of fence _____ (ft./mt.)   Number of interruptions _____

    Topguard on fence?   Yes _____   No _____

        Outward facing?   Yes _____   No _____

        Inward facing?   Yes _____   No _____   Percent of total length _____%

        Dual facing?   Yes _____   No _____   Percent of total length _____%

    Describe _____

_____

    Lighting on perimeter _____   Describe _____

Access points:

    Number of vehicle access points:

        Primary roads _____   Est. length _____(miles/kilometers)

        Fire roads _____   Est. length _____(miles/kilometers)

        Other _____   Est. length _____(miles/kilometers)

Number of pedestrian entrances/exits _____

Rail spur?   Yes _____   No _____

Estimated length of rail spur
within the facilities grounds? _____ (miles/kilometers)

Is rail entrance and/or exit gated?   Yes _____   No _____

Is rail entrance and/or exit guarded?   Yes _____   No _____

Facilities geographics:

Land area? _____ (acres/hectares)

Brief description of facilities landscape _____

_____

_____

Brief description of facilities external topography _____

_____

_____

Vehicle access:

Employee parking spaces

   Secured   _____ (Number inside fenced perimeter)

   Unsecured   _____ (Number outside fenced perimeter)

Visitor parking spaces

   Secured   _____ (Number inside fenced perimeter)

   Unsecured   _____ (Number outside fenced perimeter)

Vendor parking/delivery spaces

   Secured   _____ (Number inside fenced perimeter)

   Unsecured   _____ (Number outside fenced perimeter)

Building entrances accessible to vehicles_____

Appendix G
Risk Identification Procedures

I. BACKGROUND

A. Employee survey
   1. Survey employees about areas of potential threats, risk areas, access problems, and solutions. Ask questions on local police and emergency response times, security issues for particular assets, special hazardous conditions (i.e., Haz-Mat, etc.), and other questions that are unique to these facilities.

B. Response agency survey
   1. Survey those agencies that would respond in the event of an attack on these facilities. Discuss areas of potential threats, risk areas, access problems and solution. Ask questions on existing or potential jurisdictional disputes, emergency response times, security issues for particular assets, special hazardous conditions (i.e., Haz-Mat, etc.), and other questions that are unique to their emergency response to a potential attack on these facilities.

C. Accounting identification of assets and valuation of assets:
   1. Use accounting records as an additional method to identify critical assets.
   2. Use accounting procedures to identify current valuations and replacement costs for these critical assets.
   3. Be prepared to justify counterterrorism security recommendations with a detailed cost and benefit analysis based on this information.

D. Review any previous surveys on facilities and/or security reports.

II. EXISTING PROCEDURES

A. Policies and Procedures

   1. Do security policies and procedures exist?

   2. Do these security policies/procedures directly identify terrorism as a threat to these facilities?   Yes _____   No _____

3. How often are these policies and procedures:

    a) Revised   _____(months)

    b) Audited for compliance   _____(months)

B. Disaster Planning

    1. Does disaster planning exist for these facilities?   Yes ____   No ____

    2. Does a procedure exist and describe the notification procedures for:

        a) Law enforcement.   Exists_____   Does not exist_____
            Describe: _____

        b) Fire protection.   Exists_____   Does not exist_____
            Describe: _____

        c) Emergency response.   Exists_____   Does not exist_____
            Describe: _____

        d) Facilities Management. Exists_____   Does not exist_____
            Describe: _____

        e) Security personnel.   Exists_____   Does not exist_____
            Describe: _____

C. Do training programs relative to terrorism awareness exist for the following?

    1. Security personnel.   YES_____   NO_____
        Describe: _____

    2. Management/executives.   YES_____   NO_____
        Describe: _____

    3. Employees.   YES_____   NO_____
        Describe: _____

    4. Local emergency responders.   YES_____   NO_____
        Describe: _____

III. COMPLIANCE AND ASSESSMENT

A.   Audits

1.   Do procedures exist for security audits?   YES_____   NO_____

2.   Do procedures exist for counterterrorism audits? YES_____   NO_____

3.   If yes to a or b, how often drills occur for:

   a)   Fire evacuations?   _____ (weeks/months)

   b)   Bomb threat evacuations?   _____ (weeks/months)

   c)   Other security procedures (locks, guard rotations, vehicle access?)
        _____(weeks/months)

   d)   Describe audit procedure, if applicable. _____

B.   Cost/Benefit

1.   Have the facilities done a cost/benefit analysis
     of existing security arrangements?   YES_____   NO_____

2.   Have alternative security arrangements
     received a cost/benefit analysis?   YES_____   NO_____

3.   Are any current changes in security
     arrangement under consideration?   YES_____   NO_____

4.   If yes, has a cost/benefit analysis been
     conducted on these procedures?   YES_____   NO_____

IV. RECUPERATION

A.   Recovery Planning

1.   Does a written plan exist for recovery
     in case of an emergency?   YES_____   NO_____

2.   Does this plan directly address terrorism
     recovery procedures?   YES_____   NO_____

   In particular, does it suggest procedures on how to:

   a)   Secure the crime scene?   YES_____   NO_____

   b)   Secure/preserve the crime scene
        evidence?   YES_____   NO_____

    (1) Notify law enforcement:

        (a) Municipal?   YES_____   NO_____

        (b) County?   YES_____   NO_____

        (c) State?   YES_____   NO_____

        (d) Federal?   YES_____   NO_____

B. Emergency Response

    1.   After notification, what procedures exist for a coordinated emergency response to a disaster/terrorism incident?

    2.   Do employees receive first aid training and are triage procedures in place?

        a)   General employee first aid?   YES_____   NO_____

        b)   Security personnel first aid?   YES_____   NO_____

        c)   General employee triage procedures?   YES_____   NO_____

        d)   Security personnel triage procedures?   YES_____   NO_____

    3.   Describe existing equipment for chemical spills? _____

        _____

C. Stabilization Systems

    1.   Do formal plans exist for business stabilization? YES_____   NO_____

    2.   Do formal plans exist for business continuation during extended disruptions due to investigative activities by law enforcement?   YES_____   NO_____

    3.   Describe any recovery/stabilization systems currently in place? _____

        _____

IV. SAFEGUARDS

A. Typical safeguards

    1. Barriers

        a)   Are vehicle barriers in place:

            (1) Next to main entrance?   YES_____   NO_____

            (2) At facilities vehicle entrances?   YES_____   NO_____

(3) At visitor check-in stations (vehicle)? YES_____ NO_____

(4) At visitor check-in stations (foot)? YES_____ NO_____

(5) At rail spur entrances and exits? YES_____ NO_____

2. Entry and Visitor Control Systems

    a) Are visitors issued passes or badges? YES_____ NO_____

    b) These passes/badged reconciled daily?
       (Accountability Procedure) YES_____ NO_____

    c) Are these passes/badged required
       to be displayed at all times? YES_____ NO_____

    d) Do passes/badges restrict access
       to only public areas? YES_____ NO_____

    e) Visitors sign in/exit procedure? YES_____ NO_____

    f) Visitor arrivals/departures recorded? YES_____ NO_____

    g) Are permanent records of visitations
       maintained? YES_____ NO_____

3. Mail and package procedures?

    a) Are packages inspected prior to being
       left/allowed entrance into the facilities? YES_____ NO_____

    b) Are mail/overnight packages reviewed
       prior to distribution within the facilities? YES_____ NO_____

    c) Do the facilities have isolation and
       safeguard procedures in place for
       suspicious packages? YES_____ NO_____

4. Employee identification systems

    a) Are employee identification
       cards/badges used? YES_____ NO_____

    b) Do they contain the employees':

       (1) Picture? YES_____ NO_____

           How often are pictures updated? _____ (months/years)

       (2) Finger/hand print YES_____ NO_____

       (3) Retina print YES_____ NO_____

    c) Are procedures followed? YES_____ NO_____

    d) Are procedures audited? YES_____ NO_____

    e) Is special clearance required for highly
       sensitive areas? YES_____ NO_____

f) Are employees required to wear
passes/badges at all times? YES_____ NO_____

g) Do procedures exist if an employee
pass/badge is lost? YES_____ NO_____

Describe _____

h) Do security personnel compare/verify
identify of pass/badge holder by
comparing with the person presenting? YES_____ NO_____

i) Are these employee identification items
controlled by an accountability procedure? YES_____ NO_____

j) Are passes/badges made invalid
at time of termination? YES_____ NO_____

k) Are security personnel advised of
terminated employees?

(1) Posted list of non-access or
terminated personnel? YES_____ NO_____

(2) Systematic deletion of passwords/access
allowances YES_____ NO_____

5. Clearance Controls/Initial Access Areas

a) Do controls exist? YES_____ NO_____

Describe _____

b) Are these procedures written? YES_____ NO_____

c) Are these procedures audited? YES_____ NO_____

6. Monitoring systems

a) Do these facilities have a video
monitoring system? YES_____ NO_____

b) Do these facilities have centralized
monitoring station? YES_____ NO_____

c) Is the monitoring station connected
to alarm systems? YES_____ NO_____

d) Do backup power supplies exist for:

(1) Cameras? YES_____ NO_____

(2) Monitoring station? YES_____ NO_____

(3) Alarm system? YES_____ NO_____

7. Locks and key protection. If the system is card access, or another system that does not primarily use keys, please indicate type of system and answer questions below accordingly. Type? _____

---

   a) Does a key/card control system exist?   YES_____   NO_____

   b) Who has control of masters/programming tools?

   c) Are keys/cards able to be duplicated?   YES_____   NO_____

   d) Is a key/card accountability procedure
      in place?   YES_____   NO_____

   e) Are locks/access changed when:

      (1) Keys/cards are lost?   YES_____   NO_____

      (2) Keys/cards are missing/stolen?   YES_____   NO_____

      (3) Employees are terminated?   YES_____   NO_____

   f) Are locks/access codes rotated withing
      the facilities on a periodic basis?   YES_____   NO_____

      How often? _____ (months/years)

8. Internal/external communications?

   a) Do these facilities have internal
      communications equipment?   YES_____   NO_____

      Describe _____

      (1) Do back-up systems exist?   YES_____   NO_____

      (2) Do written procedures exist
          in the event of problems?   YES_____   NO_____

   b) Do these facilities have external
      communications equipment?   YES_____   NO_____

      Describe _____

      (1) Do back-up systems exist?   YES_____   NO_____

      (2) Do written procedures exist
          in the event of problems?   YES_____   NO_____

   c) Do these facilities have procedures
      for notification of:

      (1) Facilities management?   YES_____   NO_____

      (2) Security management?   YES_____   NO_____

      (3) Fire department?   YES_____   NO_____

      (4) Emergency response?   YES_____   NO_____

       (5) Municipal police?   YES_____   NO_____

       (6) County police?   YES_____   NO_____

       (7) State law enforcement?   YES_____   NO_____

       (8) Federal law enforcement?   YES_____   NO_____

9. Shift/guard rotation

    a) Does a guard force exist?   YES_____   NO_____

    b) Are guard services proprietary?   YES_____   NO_____

    c) Are guard services contracted?   YES_____   NO_____

    d) Are guard services a combination of
        both proprietary and contracted?   YES_____   NO_____

    e) Is the current service generally
        adequate as a safeguard?   YES_____   NO_____

    f) Is it sufficient for current terrorism
        threat environment?   YES_____   NO_____

    g) Do procedures exist for increasing
        security during times of higher
        threat conditions?   YES_____   NO_____

    h) If audits exist do they measure:

       (1) Effectiveness?   YES_____   NO_____

       (2) Use of communications equipment? YES_____   NO_____

       (3) Arms training?   YES_____   NO_____

       (4) Counter-terrorism training?   YES_____   NO_____

    i) Are guards scheduled for fixed times? YES_____   NO_____

    j) Are supervisors scheduled for fixed times? YES_____   NO_____

    k) Are shifts rotated periodically?   YES_____   NO_____

    l) Are actual guards rotated periodically? YES_____   NO_____

    m) Are supervisors rotated periodically? YES_____   NO_____

B. Extraordinary measures

    1. Explosive detection equipment?   YES_____   NO_____

    2. K-9 units?   YES_____   NO_____

    3. Automatic local law enforcement notification? YES_____   NO_____

    4. Automatic Fire notification?   YES_____   NO_____

    5. Is monitoring of CCTV done at a location
       away from actual facilities?   YES_____   NO_____

    6. Does evacuation planning exist for local area? YES_____   NO_____

Appendix H
Selections from the Private Security Task Force Report

Standard 1.8
Minimum Preemployment Screening Qualifications

The following minimum preemployment screening qualifications should be established for private security personnel:

1. Minimum age of 18;
2. High school diploma or equivalent written examination;
3. Written examination to determine the ability to understand and perform duties assigned;
4. No record of conviction, as stated in Standard 1.7;
5. Minimum physical standards:
   a. Armed personnel—vision correctible to 20/20 (Snellen) in each eye and capable of hearing ordinary conversation at a distance of 10 feet with each ear without benefit of hearing aid;
   b. Others—no physical defects that would hinder job performance.

Commentary

In order to improve the effectiveness of private security personnel, minimum preemployment screening qualifications should be established. At present, criteria for employment vary among employers, if they exist at all. This standard proposes a set of criteria that can be used by all private security employers in their preemployment screening.

The qualifications suggested are minimum. Certain employers may wish to establish stricter criteria, depending on the nature of the assignment. Also, the qualifications are directed to operational personnel and generally would be inappropriate for supervisors, managers, and other specialized personnel whose duties would require more advanced knowledge and/or experience.

Age Requirements

A minimum age of 18 is recommended for all personnel. Public law enforcement agencies have constantly been hampered in recruitment by the lack of opportunity to employ sworn personnel immediately upon completion of high school. Likewise, the private security industry should not restrict itself from obtaining qualified personnel by setting unrealistic minimum or maximum ages. Many individuals are capable of performing as efficiently at age 18 as at age 21. The military services, for example, have effectively used personnel in security positions under the age of 21 for many years.

Because the establishment of career paths is an important need in the industry, age requirements need to be low enough to attract qualified applicants before they are committed to other careers. It is likely that an individual reaching age 21 would have already identified career aspirations, and a job in private security would, at best, be only a secondary interest. As mentioned previously in Goal 1.1, personnel will function more effectively when they are performing the job they want to do.

Educational Requirements

The *RAND Report* (Vol. 1) stated that, in response to a survey questionnaire, two-thirds of the regulatory agencies indicated that minimum educational requirements should be mandatory for private security personnel. Of the two-thirds favoring minimum educational requirements, one-third indicated that private security personnel should be high school graduates. Others thought education beyond high school would be a more appropriate requirement for some categories. For example, two recommended college education for investigators; two proposed polygraph-school graduation for lie-detection examiners; one believed that supervisors should have some college training. Significantly, one-third of the survey respondents thought no minimum educational requirements should be established.

For the purpose of this standard, educational requirements are classified in two main categories: (1) basic educational qualifications and (2) ability to understand and perform duties assigned. The basic educational qualifications can be met by a high school diploma or an equivalent written examination designed to measure basic educational aptitudes. The employer should be careful, however, to utilize only those tests that have been proven valid and reliable.

The second educational requirement—the ability to understand and perform duties assigned—is determined through a written examination. Here, again, the employer should use only validated tests. Furthermore, there should be a close cause-effect relationship between the tests and the job description in accordance with the following Equal Opportunity Employment Commission guideline on employment testing procedures:

> The Commission accordingly interprets "professionally developed ability test" to mean a test which fairly measures the knowledge or skills required by the particular job or class of jobs which the applicant seeks, or which fairly affords the employer a chance to measure the applicant's ability to perform a particular job or class of jobs. The fact that a test was prepared by an individual or organization claiming expertise in test preparation does not, without more, justify its use within the meaning of Title VII (Civil Rights Act of 1964).

The two categories of educational requirements are not mutually inclusive or exclusive. For example, a high school graduate might have psychological characteristics that would indicate this person should be armed. Conversely, a person who did not graduate from high school but passes the equivalent written examination might be found to be psychologically qualified to carry a weapon. A high school diploma, in and of itself, should not necessarily be a prerequisite for armed personnel, but regulatory agencies, for administrative reasons, may set such a requirement.

The National Advisory Committee on Criminal Justice Standards and Goals (NAC) did not agree with the Task Force's position that a high school diploma or equivalent written examination should be a minimum preemployment screening qualification for all private security personnel. Although agreeing that this requirement was appropriate for armed guards and certain security activities, the NAC believed that a written examination to determine if an individual had the ability to understand and perform the duties involved was adequate for other security assignments. The NAC believed that individuals who were competent to perform these other security assignments would be denied employment in the field if the high school education level requirement was a minimum standard. However, it is the opinion of the Private Security Task Force that the basic knowledge engendered by a high school diploma (or equivalent written examination) is important for emergency situations that may arise. The written ability examination may not test for those skills outside the private security employee's job description, and he may, therefore, not be able to handle the emergency situation. Also, in the furtherance of the development of a professional private security industry, high-school-level education is considered necessary in the judgment of the Task Force.

Conviction Records

Conviction records, except for certain minor offenses, should preclude private security employment. Standard 1.7 discusses this topic fully and points out the responsibilities assumed by private security personnel to the public and to the role of crime prevention. For the public to have confidence in private security personnel, employers should select persons of high moral integrity. In order to facilitate implementation of this standard, this report calls for the cooperation of government agencies in supplying pertinent conviction records.

Physical Requirements

Physical requirements should not be unnecessarily restrictive. In most cases, specific physical qualifications, such as height and weight, would be inappropriate. The results of a study released by the International Association of Chiefs of Police and the Police Foundation, and published in [the] Dec. 1, 1975, issue of *Crime Control Digest*, confirm that height requirements, for example, have little relation to performance and tend to unnecessarily reduce the available pool of qualified applicants:

> The authors . . . say that they found no data, either from their survey of five police departments or from their search of literature on the subject, that show that the height of a police officer does affect performance. . . .
>
> . . . Height requirements can vastly reduce the pool of applicants who have personal qualities needed by police departments.
>
> For example, 56 percent of young adult males and 99 percent of young adult females would be excluded from employment by a minimum height requirement of 5 feet 9 inches.

Although the authors of this study were hampered in their research by the lack of a large comparative population, the results point the way to a selection system without height requirements.

However, private security employers should not totally disregard physical standards or take them lightly. One employer cited in the *RAND Report* (Vol. 1) said, "Some standards are a joke. While we require a physical exam for employment, if the man can take three steps he passes the physical." In general, physical requirements should be determined by the nature of the job the applicant would be performing. Any physical defect that would interfere with ability to perform assigned duties would disqualify the applicant.

Differentiation should be made [between] physical qualifications for armed personnel and others. Obviously, good eyesight and hearing are vital to anyone who carries a weapon; therefore, specific vision and hearing qualifications should be established for armed private security personnel in consideration of protecting both themselves and the public.

Standard 2.5
Preassignment and Basic Training

Any person employed as an investigator or detective, guard or watchman, armored car personnel or armed courier, alarm system installer or servicer, or alarm respondent, including those presently employed and part-time personnel, should successfully:

1. Complete a minimum of 8 hours formal preassignment training;

2. Complete a basic training course of a minimum of 32 hours within 3 months of assignment. A maximum of 16 hours can be supervised on-the-job training.

Commentary

Other standards have highlighted the lack of training in the private security industry. This lack has inspired much criticism, most of it directed specifically at the failure of the industry to properly and adequately prepare its operational-level personnel. *The Other Police,* a report on the Ohio private security industry, contains a section entitled "Training: Infrequent, Incomplete, and Misdirected." It points out that fewer than 25 percent of Ohio's guards hold training certificates from the Ohio Peace Officer Training Council and that training throughout the State is decreasing instead of increasing.

Lack of private security training also tends to generate friction with public law enforcement agencies. For example, law enforcement officers, working in the same community with private security guards, investigators, and so forth, often look down on their abilities and question their judgments, because private security personnel are untrained. The public law enforcement has made tremendous progress in the past decade in both adequacy of training and quality of courses, but the private security industry has barely taken a step in this direction.

A survey of members of the American Society for Industrial Security (ASIS) indicated a present range of 4 to 80 hours of training for newly hired personnel. Table 2.2, from the *RAND Report* (Vol. II), further illustrates the wide range and general inadequacy of initial training in a sample of 11 private security companies.

Other findings from the *RAND Report* (Vol. II) indicate that a large percentage of private security guards do not know their legal powers to detain, arrest, search, or use force. Frequently, in fact, they lack understanding of the basic policies and procedures of their functions. The following comment from a former guard, who was beaten during a robbery, vividly illustrates the need for additional training:

> For $1.60 per hour I wouldn't stick my neck out again. Anybody who does is crazy. I stand around looking cute in my uniform. Don't let anybody tell you a guard doesn't need training. If I'd had it I might had known what the hell was going on.

Private security professionals do recognize the importance of training. The previously mentioned ASIS survey revealed that 76 percent of the respondents believed training standards were "very important" 15 percent, "somewhat important"; and 1 percent, "not important." Yet, until specific standards are required, private security training is not likely to improve.

Preassignment Training

This standard recommends that training requirements be initiated for all operational private security personnel. A RAND survey of private security personnel in California revealed that 65 percent of the respondents had received no training prior to beginning work. Because the instruction received at this stage familiarizes the employee with the responsibilities of the job and establishes certain basic skills and concepts, it is recommended that every private security employee successfully complete 8 hours of preassignment training before commencing work.

Due to the complexity of functions performed by private security personnel, the final determination of subject content for preassignment training will need to be made by employers and regulatory agencies; however, the following topical outline is recommended as a general guide. It is based on a model originally prepared by the Private Security Advisory Council, included in their *Model Private Security Licensing and Regulatory Statute,* and designed for guards. Obviously, some additions in content were necessary to expand it to meet the broader spectrum of personnel included in this standard.

Private Security 8-Hour Preassignment Training Course

Section I—Orientation: 2 hours that include the following topics:

- What is security?
- Public relations.
- Deportment.
- Appearance.
- Maintenance and safeguarding of uniform and/or equipment.
- Notetaking/Reporting.
- Role of public law enforcement.

Section II—Legal Powers and Limitations: 2 hours that include the following topics:

- Prevention versus apprehension.
- Use of force.
- Search and seizure.
- Arrest powers.

Section III—Handling Emergencies: 2 hours that should include appropriate topics pertinent to the job functions to be performed by the employee:

- Crimes in progress.
- Procedures for bomb threats.

- Procedures during fires, explosions, floods, riots, and so forth.
- Responding to alarms.

Section IV—General Duties: 2 hours that should include the appropriate topics pertinent to the job functions to be performed by the employee:

- Fire prevention and control.
- Inspections.
- Interviewing techniques.
- Patrol.
- Safeguarding valuable property.
- Safety.
- Surveillance.

The following model preassignment training programs are intended to explain how the program could be implemented for guards or watchmen or alarm respondents. Again, specific recommendations are not established because of the complexity of training needs, but the outline may prove helpful as a general guideline. The hour designation used in all training standards is a 50-minute block of instruction that is standard for training and education curriculums.

Model Preassignment Training Program for a Guard or Watchman

Section I—Orientation (2 hours)	Minutes
• What is security?	15
• Public relations	15
• Deportment	15
• Appearance	10
• Maintenance and safeguarding of uniforms and/or equipment	20
• Notetaking/Reporting	15
• Role of public law enforcement	10

Section II—Legal Powers and Limitations (2 hours)

• Prevention versus apprehension	40
• Use of force	25
• Search of seizure	15
• Arrest powers	20

Section III—Handling Emergencies (2 hours)

• Procedures for bomb threats	40
• Procedures during fires, explosions, floods, riots, and so forth	60

Section IV—General Duties (2 hours)

• Patrol	40
• Fire prevention and control	30
• Safety	30

Table 2.2. Current Private Security Guard Training Programs

Program	Initial Prework Training								Initial On-the-Job Training				Total Initial Training (hours)
	Talking with Supervisors (hours)	Read Manual	View Films/Slides (hours)	Class (hours)	Test	Firearms Range	Trained on Previous Job	Total (hours)	By Supervisor (hours)	By Fellow Employee (hours)	Written Post Orders	Total (hours)	
Company A: Small Contract Guard Firm	½ to 1	None	None	None	None	N/A	None	½ to 1	8 to 16	None	Yes	8 to 16	8½ to 17
Company B: Small Contract Guard Firm	1 to 2	Yes	None	None	Yes	Yes	None	2½ to 3½	8 to 16	None	Yes	8 to 16	10½ to 19½
Company C: Medium Contract Guard Firm	1 to 3	Yes	1½	None	Yes	Yes	None	5 to 7	8 to 16	None	Yes	8 to 16	13 to 23
Company D: Large Contract Guard Firm (full and part-time)	1 to 2	Yes	2	None	Yes	Yes	None	6½ to 7½	1 to 8	None	Yes	1 to 8	7½ to 15½
Company E: Large Contract Premium Guard Firm	1 to 2	Yes	2	40 to 80	Yes	Yes	None	46½ to 87½	1 to 8	None	Yes	1 to 8	47½ to 95½
Company F: Large Contract Guard Firm													
a. Regular	None	Yes	1	9	None	Yes	None	12	1 to 8	None	Yes	1 to 8	13 to 20
b. Temporary	3 to 4	None	1	None	None	None	None	4 to 5	½	None	None	½	4½ to 5½

Company G: Large Contract Guard Firm													
a. Regular	None	Yes	None	10	Yes	Yes	None	11	½ to 1	None	Yes	½ to 1	10½ to 11
b. Temporary	None	None	None	8	None	None	None	8	½	None	None	½	8½
Company H: Small Contract Patrol Guard Firm	1 to 2	None	None	None	None	Yes	None	3 to 4	16	None	Yes	16	19 to 20
Company I: Inhouse Guards (Bank)	2 to 4	Yes	None	None	None	Yes	Occasionally	5 to 7	80 to 120	None	Yes	80 to 120	85 to 127
Company J: Inhouse Guards (Research)	1 to 4	Yes	None	None	None	N/A	None	3 to 6	None	160	Yes	160	163 to 166
Company K: Inhouse Guards (Manufacturing)	½ to 1	Yes	None	None	None	N/A	Mandatory	½ to 2	None	24	Yes	24	25½ to 26

Source: Kakalik, James S., and Sorrel Wildhorn. *The Private Police Industry: Its Nature and Extent*. Vol. II, R-870/DOJ. Washington, D.C.: Government Printing Office, 1972, p.33.

Model Preassignment Training Program for an Alarm Respondent

Section I—Orientation (2 hours)	Minutes
• What is security?	15
• Public relations	10
• Deportment	10
• Appearance	10
• Maintenance and safeguarding of uniforms and/or equipment	30
• Notetaking/Reporting	15
• Role of public law enforcement	10

Section II—Legal Powers and Limitations (2 hours)	
• Prevention versus apprehension	25
• Use of force	25
• Search and seizure	30
• Arrest powers	20

Section III—Handling Emergencies (2 hours)	
• Crime in progress	20
• Responding to alarms	80

Section IV—General Duties (2 hours)	
• Interviewing techniques	40
• Patrol	30
• Safeguarding valuable property	30

Model Preassignment Training Program for an Armored Car Guard[1]

Section I—Orientation (2 hours)	Minutes
• Protective transportation:	50
History of armored car industry	
Basic elements of service	
Interface with the financial community	
• The company:	
History of employer	15
Organizational structure	15
Wages and benefits	20
Driver/guard	
Messenger/guard	
Custodian/guard	

Section II—Legal Powers and Limitations (2 hours)	
• Parameters of operation	
We are not policemen or stationary guards	10
Theory of bailment	10
Use of selective force in defensive role	25
Weapons philosophy	25

Physical force and its operational application	20
Restraints in dissemination of confidential information	10

Section III—Handling Emergencies (2 hours)

- Emergency situations (an overview)

Defining the threat	30
Robbery	
On the sidewalk	
In customer's premises	
In the truck	
Political terrorists versus conventional criminal	70
Extortion	
Abduction	
Ambush	
Bomb threats	

Section IV—General Duties (2 hours)

• Fire procedures	25
• Traffic accidents	25
• Rules and regulations	40
Uniforms	
Equipment (familiarization)	
Armored truck	
Handtruck	
Seals and bags	
Terminals	
Vaults	
Security areas	
• Deportment	10

In implementing the suggested preassignment training programs, the following factors should be noted:

1. All topics in Sections I and II should be covered in some portion of the 2 hours assigned.

2. Only pertinent topics in Sections III and IV need to be included in the 2 hours assigned.

3. Supervised, on-the-job training cannot be used to meet preassignment training.

4. Lectures, films, programmed learning, and other training methods can be used.

Basic Training

Upon successful completion of preassignment training, the employee should be allowed to begin work, but training should not stop at this point. Additional training is needed to provide the skills, knowledge, and judgment necessary for efficient, effective job performance. Although the importance of this training cannot be overemphasized, it is recognized that the high cost of training may place a heavy economic burden on some employers. Therefore, a realistic minimum of 32 hours of basic training is recommended in addition to preassignment training. This training should be completed over a 3-month time period and may include a maximum of 16 hours on-the-job training.

Although many may believe that the 32-hour training standard is totally inadequate, it is a progressive step in terms of the amount of training presently provided. Admittedly, it is far short of the 400 hours recommended in 1973 for sworn police officers by the National Advisory Commission on Criminal Justice Standards and Goals. It should be understood, however, that Federal, State, and local tax dollars support training for public law enforcement officers, but only limited monetary resources are available to provide training for private security personnel. Ultimately, a large portion of the cost would have to be borne by the consumer. Although, in some instances, employees are required to pay the cost of their own training, this practice is discouraged unless such training is personally sought by the individual to prepare himself for private security employment. The 32-hour minimum basic requirement is believed to be economically feasible for implementation by all; those employers financially capable of providing additional training should surpass the 32-hour minimum.

Basic training requirements, as stated in this standard, should apply to both presently employed and part-time personnel. Because of the prevalent lack of training throughout the private security industry, many present employees are not adequately prepared for the responsibilities of their positions. Thus, they should be required to have the same training as newly hired personnel if uniform quality of performance is to be achieved. Part-time employees also assume the same responsibilities and need the same amount of training.

By allowing 16 hours of the basic training to be completed on the job, employers can maximize the training effect. However, it is very important that close supervision is provided for employers to meet the intent of the standard. With appropriate supervision, an employee can effectively relate classroom instruction to the specific job performed. In this manner, training can take on added significance and reality.

Responsibility for implementation of private security basic training would rest with employers and State regulatory agencies. As with preassignment training, these persons ultimately would have to determine the actual subjects presented in basic training. However, to provide general guidance in determining curriculums, the following topical outline for a 32-hour basic course of training is offered:

Private Security 32-hour Basic Training Course

Section I—Prevention/Protection

- Patrolling.
- Checking for hazards
- Personnel control.
- Identification systems.

- Access control.
- Fire control systems.
- Types of alarms.
- Law enforcement/Private security relationships.

Section II—Enforcement

- Surveillance.
- Techniques of searching.
- Crime scene searching.
- Handling juveniles.
- Handling mentally disturbed persons.
- Parking and traffic.
- Enforcing employee work rules/regulations.
- Observation/Description.
- Preservation of evidence.
- Criminal/Civil law.
- Interviewing techniques.

Section III—General emergency services

- First aid.
- Defensive tactics.
- Fire fighting.
- Communications.
- Crowd control.
- Crimes in progress.

Section IV—Special problems

- Escort.
- Vandalism.
- Arson.
- Burglary.
- Robbery.
- Theft.
- Drugs/Alcohol.
- Shoplifting.
- Sabotage.
- Espionage.
- Terrorism.

To allow flexibility for individual situations and yet provide reasonable controls, the following items should be considered:

1. A minimum of 4 classroom hours should be provided in each of the sections.

2. A maximum of 16 hours supervised, on-the-job training should be permissible.

The following models explain how the basic training course can be implemented:

Model 1. Maximum classroom hours

Section	Minimum	Maximum
	Classroom hours	
• Prevention/Detection	4	16
• Enforcement	4	16
• General/Emergency Services	4	16
• Special problems	4	16

Discussion: The maximum of hours in each section can be modified in any way that is appropriate to the training needs; however, 4 classroom hours should be provided in each section. For example, an alarm response runner could follow these courses:

Section	Classroom hours
• Prevention/Detection	20 or 16
• Enforcement	4 or 5
• General/Emergency services	4 or 5
• Special problems	4 or 6

(May use any combination provided a minimum of 4 classroom hours are in each section and the total hours are 32.)

Model 2. Minimum classroom hours

Section	Classroom hours
• Prevention/Detection	4
• Enforcement	4
• General/Emergency services	4
• Special problems	4

(Should include 16 hours of supervised on-the-job training.)

Discussion: In many cases needs can best be met by training the employee in the job setting after providing basic knowledge and skills. This model provides the necessary latitude for these situations.

Model 32-hour Basic Training Course for Armored Car Guards[2]

Section I—Prevention/Detection

(Operating procedures)—6 hours	Minutes
• Crew operations	100
In the terminal	
On the street	
On customer's premises	
• Armored truck and equipment drills	50
• Packaging	25
• Receipting system	50
• Reporting and forms preparation	25
• Police liaison	50

Section II—Enforcement (Robbery and loss)—4 hours

- Case studies of attacks on men and equipment   50
- Role playing   150

Section III—General/Emergency Services
           (Emergency response)—6 hours   **Minutes**

- Trauma treatment (10-minute medicine)   100
    - Gunshot
    - Explosion
    - Burns
    - Vehicle accidents
    - CPR training
- Basic firefighting techniques   25
- Basic self-defense   75
- Bomb threats   50
    - Bomb recognition
    - Vehicle inspection
    - Tactical reaction to a bomb
    - Bomb call threat to terminal
    - Customer premises threat
    - Suspicious device located
        - On vehicle
        - In the terminal
        - In customer's premises
- Use of communications   50

Section IV—Special problems (Emergency drivers)—4 hours   **Minutes**

- Defensive driving   40
- Philosophy of offensive driving   30
    - Counterambush
    - Urban
    - Rural
- Night driving   30
- Hands-on driver training   100

(Should include at least 12 hours of supervised on-the-job training to include examination and course evaluation.) (Note: A number of industry representatives indicated that more than 12 hours of supervised on-the-job training would be provided to meet employees' needs.)

Discussion: Because the vast majority of armored car guards are armed (and to meet the firearms training of Standard 2.6), the Training Committee of the National Armored Car Association included the following outline as part of the basic training program:

Firearms Training

Company and industry policy on use of weapons
Legal limitations
Firearms safety

Care and cleaning
Basic revolver training
    Combat firing
    Use of gunports
    Use of shotgun
    Qualification and certification

The previous models provide the extremes of the standard. The 32 hours of training could be implemented in a variety of ways, with the following factors in mind:

1. The total basic training program encompasses 32 hours.
2. The minimum classroom hours are 16.
3. The maximum supervised on-the-job training is also 16.
4. The ratio between the minimum classroom hours and the maximum supervised, on-the-job training can vary (e.g., 20 classroom hours and 12 on-the-job training hours).

Several final points involving this training standard are offered for purposes of clarity:

1. The issue of an exemption from the requirements of this standard—a "grandfather" clause—for all private security personnel was considered and rejected because the training standard is a basic minimum and all personnel should receive it.

2. Formal or classroom training, both for preassignment and basic, can be lectures, films, slides, programmed instruction, and the use of other training media.

3. Supervised, on-the-job training means that personnel receive close observation and supervision. Merely being assigned to a job cannot be called on-the-job training.

4. The 3-month period to complete training is included to allow employers the flexibility to group personnel into training sessions that best meet the employers' and employees' needs, and also to minimize the economic losses caused by training persons who leave after a short period of time.

5. At least 1 hour for examinations should be included in the training curriculum and should be taken as a reduction in the supervised, on-the-job training hours. Depending on the delivery system, it may be advisable to have a testing block of time for each section.

6. Part-time personnel means all personnel who work less than full-time and includes personnel listed temporary, half-time, and so forth.

7. Some may view the 8-hour preassignment training as totally inadequate preparation before starting employment. More preassignment training, as appropriate is encouraged. Many subjects in the basic course could be included in an expanded preassignment course.

As stated earlier, many security professionals would believe that the training recommended is minimal and that additional specialized training would be needed, depending on the skills, knowledge, and judgment required for certain assignments. For example, private investigators and detectives may require more training than this standard specifies. The specific amount of time and course content would have to be determined on an individual basis. The following list is presented to illustrate the types of specific subjects that could be included in the additional training:

- Background investigation.
- Civil court procedures.
- Civil damage suits.
- Criminal court procedures.
- Collection and preservation of evidence.
- Crime prevention.
- Custody and control of property.
- Fingerprints.
- Followup investigations.
- Identification of persons.
- Industrial investigations.
- Insurance investigations.
- Interviews.
- Investigation and security as a professional vocation.
- Investigator's notebook.
- Mock crime scene.
- Modus operandi.
- Motion and still cameras.
- Obtaining information from witnesses.
- Plaintiff investigations.
- Preemployment investigations.
- Preliminary investigations.
- Preventive security.
- Principles of investigation.
- Purpose of private investigation.
- Report writing.
- Retail store investigation.
- Rules of evidence.
- Search and seizure.
- Sources of information.
- Surveillance and stakeout.
- Taking statements.
- Testifying in court.
- Undercover assignments.

Although many of these topics may seem more important to public law enforcement investigators, they are also relevant to private investigators. For example, many cases developed by private investigators end up in civil court while others are filed in criminal court. Thus, the training of private investigators should properly prepare them for this eventuality.

Guards or watchmen, couriers, alarm system installers or repairers, and alarm respondents may also require additional training, and similar, expanded subject outlines can be developed to provide the needed training. The use of investigators and detectives as one example should not be construed as an indication that they are the only categories of private security personnel who might need specialized training.

Selected References

1.   Brennan, Dennis T. *The Other Police.* Cleveland: Governmental Research Institute, 1975.

2.   Criminal Justice Institute: "88-Hour General Security Program." Detroit: Criminal Justice Institute.

3.   Eversull, Kenneth S. "Training the Uniformed Officers," *Security World,* May 1967.

4.   Ford, Robert E. (supervising ed.). *TIPS: A Continuous Program of Training and Information for Private Security.* Santa Cruz, Calif.: Davis Publishing Company, Inc., 1975.

5.   Kakalik, James S., and Sorrel Wildhorn. *The Private Police Industry: Its Nature and Extent,* Vol. II, R-870/DOJ. Washington, D.C.: Government Printing Office, 1972.

6.   Kelly, James. Address before the Private Security Advisory Council, Chicago, Ill., July 11, 1975.

7.   National Advisory Commission on Criminal Justice Standards and Goals. *Police,* Washington, D.C.: Government Printing Office, 1973.

8.   National Council on Crime and Delinquency. "Minimum Standards for the Training of Private Security Guards." Hackensack, N.J.: National Council on Crime and Delinquency, May 1973.

9.   Norell and Acqualino. "Scarecrows in Blue," *The Washingtonian,* August 1971.

10.   O'Hara, Charles E. *Fundamentals of Criminal Investigation.* 3d ed. Springfield, Ill.: Charles C. Thomas Publishers, 1973.

11.   Post, Richard S. "Application of Functional Job Analysis to the Development of Curriculum Guidelines for Protective Services Field." Ph.D dissertation. Madison: University of Wisconsin, 1974.

12.   Private Police Training Institute. "The Course Outline." Louisville, Ky.: Jefferson Community College, 1975.

13.   Private Security Advisory Council. *Model Private Security Licensing and Regulatory Statute.* Washington, D.C.: Law Enforcement Assistance Administration, 1975.

14.   Private Security Task Force. "American Society for Industrial Security (ASIS) Survey Results." (See Appendix I to this report.)

15.   "Survey of Security Instruction Time." *Security World,* February 1972.

16.   Vanderbosch, Charles G. *Criminal Investigation,* Gaithersburg, Md.: International Association of Chiefs of Police, 1968.

17.   Wilson, O.W. *Police Administration.* 2d ed. New York: McGraw Hill, Inc., 1963.

Notes

1.   This model preassignment training program was prepared by the Training Committee of the National Armored Car Association at the request of the Private Security Task Force.

2.   Prepared from model 32-hour basic training course presented to the Task Force by the Training Committee of the National Armored Car Association.

Standard 2.6
Arms Training

All armed private security personnel, including those presently employed and part-time personnel, should:

1. Be required to successfully complete a 24-hour firearms course that includes legal and policy requirements—or submit evidence of competence and proficiency—prior to assignment to a job that requires a firearm;

2. Be required to requalify at least once every 12 months with the firearm(s) they carry while performing private security duties (the requalification phase should cover legal and policy requirements).

Commentary

Armed personnel are defined as persons, uniformed or nonuniformed, who carry or use at any time any form of firearm. The serious consequences, for both employers and employees, when untrained personnel are assigned to jobs that require firearms are obvious. These consequences can be generally outlined as:

1) Self-injury because of mishandling of the weapon;
2) Injury to others, often innocent bystanders, because of lack of skill when firing the weapon; and
3) Criminal and/or civil suits against both employers and employees resulting from the above actions.

A 1974 study by the Institute for Local Self Government revealed that 45 percent of licensed California private security agency heads admitted to providing no formal preassignment instruction in firearms use, and 40 percent indicated a lack of weapons retraining. Even more revealing and disturbing, 55 percent of the employees surveyed said they sometimes carry firearms, but only 8 percent had received firearms training in their present jobs.

The *RAND Report* (Vol. II) indicated that 49 percent of private security personnel carried firearms, but only 19 percent had received any firearms training in their present jobs. The following statement from the *Philadelphia Magazine* pointedly reveals one employee's feelings:

> One guard who shot two people within two weeks in Philadelphia complained that the detective agencies were "taking young jitterbugs off the street, putting guns in their hands and giving them no training. The companies are cleaning up, man, and they ought to spend some of that money to train us."

Statistics and reports, such as the above, emphasize the vital necessity of adequate training for all personal who are to carry firearms in their private security duties, even if they are instructed never to use them. Employers cannot ignore this need or attempt to evade it, as was done in the following example: An article in the January 1973 issue of *Police Weapons Center Bulletin* reported that a Virginia firm was manufacturing fake replicas standard police revolvers and marketing them to security agencies for issuance to guards. According to the article, 30 private security agencies had purchased these replicas to equip their guards, thus eliminating the problem of issuing real firearms to untrained or semitrained personnel. The consequences of this action could be tragic. No firearms should ever be issued to private security personnel, unless the weapons are authentic and employees are well trained in their use and legal implications.

The intent of this standard is that employees should not be allowed to carry firearms while performing private security duties unless they can demonstrate competency and proficiency in their use. In attempting to construct an appropriate training course for firearms instruction, many existing courses were reviewed. The recommended course that follows is designed for persons armed with revolvers and may require modification for other weapons or for adaptation to local situations. Dick Mercurio, training coordinator, Southwestern Illinois Law Enforcement Commission, indicated that persons were trained in 1974 and 1975 with about a 90 percent successful completion rate by generally following this classroom outline. In general, the recommended course includes 6 hours of classroom and 18 hours of range firing.

Classroom

Topic I Legal and policy restraints—3 hours
1. Rights of private security personnel to carry weapons and powers of arrest
2. Statutory references
3. Policy restraints

Topic II Firearms safety and care and cleaning of the revolver—2 hours
1. Nomenclature and operation of the weapon
2. Performance of cartridge
3. Safety practices on duty and at home
4. Range rules
5. Care and cleaning of the weapon

Topic III Successful completion of written examination—1 hour
1. At least 20 questions on the above topics with a minimum passing score of 70 percent
2. Should be designed so that persons with other and/or prior experience can demonstrate competence in the subject areas.

Range[1]

Topic I Principles of markmanship—2 hours
1. Shooting stance
2. Gripping and cocking the revolver
3. Sighting
4. Trigger control
5. Breathing control
6. Speeding loading and unloading techniques

Topic II Single action course—8 hours
- Distance: 25 yards
- Target: silhouette
- Rounds fired for qualification: 30
- Minimum passing score: 18 hits (60 percent)
- Stages of the course:
  1. Slow fire—consists of 10 shots fired in a total time of 5 minutes.
  2. Time fare consists of two strings of 5 shots each. Each string is fired in a time limit of 20 seconds.
  3. Rapid fire—consists of two strings of 5 shots each. Each string is fired in a time limit of 10 seconds.
- Courses fired:
  1. Slow fire practice—30 rounds
  2. Time fire practice—6 strings—30 rounds
  3. Rapid fire practice—6 strings—30 rounds
  4. Practice course—30 rounds
  5. Record course—30 rounds

Topic III Double action course—8 hours
- Distance: as outlined below
- Target: silhouette
- Rounds fired for qualification: 72
- Minimum passing score: 43 hits (60 percent)
- Stage of the course: 7 yard line—Crouch position
  a. First phase:
     (1) load; draw and fire 1 and holster on the whistle command (6)
     (2) load; draw and fire 2 and holster on the whistle command (6)
     (3) repeat (1) and (2), using weak hand (12)
  b. Second phase:
     (1) strong hand—time 30 seconds—load; draw on the whistle, fire 6; reload and fire 6 more (12)
     (2) weak hand—time 30 seconds—load; draw on the whistle, fire 6; reload and fire 6 more (12)
- Courses fired: The above courses will be fired 4 times in the following sequence:
  1. A practice course (72)
  2. Skip loading with 3 rounds each string (24)
  3. Preliminary record course (72)
  4. Firing for record (72)

The purpose of range training is to ensure that private security personnel meet minimum proficiency requirements. If, for example, a student qualifies during the preliminary or practice rounds, it may be appropriate to remove him from the range course and give the instructor more time with students who are having difficulties. However, no person should be considered proficient, and assigned to a job that requires a firearm, unless he meets the minimum qualifications outlined.

Although not specifically stated in the standard, all instructors should be qualified through the National Rifle Association or other comparable qualifications programs.

In summary, the following requirements should be stressed for personnel carrying firearms:

1. Competence in the classroom subjects (minimum score of 70 percent) and proficiency with the weapon (minimum score of 60 percent) should be met before assigning any personnel to jobs that require firearms.
2. Personnel should be trained in the use of any weapon they carry.
3. They should meet the weapon proficiency requirements at least once every 12 months.

One study, *Private Security Survey and Ordinance for St. Petersburg, Florida,* recommended a more stringent requirement for point three—retraining courses to be held at 6-month intervals.

Employers also should consider preparation of a firearms policy form, including safety rules, policies regarding discharge of weapons, and other pertinent matters. Employees would be required to sign the form every 3 or 4 months, indicating they understand the policies. Their supervisors also would be required to sign the form. This system has been used for a number of years in the military services and has been an effective reminder of firearms policy.

No amount of required training can guarantee that weapons abuses will be eliminated or that accidents will cease to occur. However, a firearms training program, as outlined, can reduce the incidence of these types of problems. The necessity of training is apparent; the risks are too real without it. The private security industry should immediately provide training for all of its armed personnel.

Selected References

1. Chapman, Samuel G., and Thompson S. Crockett. "Gunsight Dilemma: Police Firearms Policy," *Police,* March-April 1963.

2. Institute for Local Self Government. *Private Security and the Public Interest.* Berkeley, Calif.: Institute for Local Self Government, 1974.

3. International Association of Chiefs of Police. "A Questionable Practice: Security Officers 'Armed' with Fake Weapons," *PWC Bulletin,* January 1973.

4. Kakalik, James S., and Sorrel Wildhorn. *The Private Police Industry: Its Nature and Extent,* Vol. II, R—870/DOJ. Washington, D.C.: Government Printing Office, 1971.

5. Mallowe, Mike. "Willie Lee Weston Is Armed and Dangerous." *Philadelphia Magazine,* August 1975.

6. Martensen, Kai R. "Private Security Survey and Ordinance for St. Petersburg, Florida." Sunnyvale, Calif.: Public Systems Incorporated, 1975.

7. Silvarman, Allen B.I. "Firearms Training," *Security Distributing and Marketing,* December 1974.

8. Strobl, Walter M. "Private Guards: Arm Them or Not," *Security Management,* January 1973.

Notes

1. The training hours for the range may seem excessive. However, it must be remembered that many of the personnel may have had no previous firearms training. Other factors that cause delays, such as the number of shooting positions available in relation to the number of students, should also be considered. The outline for the range course was supplied by Dick Mercurio, training coordinator, Southwestern Illinois Law Enforcement Commission.

Standard 11.2
Registration Qualifications

Every applicant seeking registration to perform a specific security function in an unarmed capacity should meet the following minimum qualifications:
1. **Be at least 18 years of age;**
2. **Be physically and mentally competent and capable of performing the specific job function being registered for;**
3. **Be morally responsible in the judgment of the regulatory board; and,**
4. **Have successfully completed the training requirements set forth in Standard 2.5**

Commentary

The 1967 *Task Force Report: The Police* of the President's Commission on Law Enforcement and Administration of Justice stated that "policing a community is personal service of the highest order, requiring sterling qualities in the individual who performs it . . . . Few professions are so peculiarly charged with individual responsibility." Although the quote is directed toward law enforcement personnel, it is equally applicable to private security personnel, who likewise often must make instantaneous decisions affecting lives and property.

As pointed out in the preceding standard, the nature of the role of the private security industry demands that steps be taken to upgrade the quality of its personnel. Research has indicated that far too many security personnel, charged with protection of life and property, are either incompetent or of questionable character. Yet, existing personnel selection requirements and procedures do not screen out the unfit. If costly and dangerous losses both to business and society are to be prevented, measures for improvement need to be devised.

Chapter 1 of this report makes a number of recommendations for improving the quality of private security personnel. These recommendations reflect reasonable standards that should be established. However, despite the validity of the recommendations, it is recognized that certain actions may never be instituted unless mandated by law. Therefore, in order to improve the quality of security personnel, it was felt that certain minimum qualifications should be established for registration.

Recognizing the desire to attract high school graduates who might make a career in the private security field, a minimum age requirement of 18 is suggested, thus enabling businesses to compete for qualified young people. It is believed that personnel who do not possess the necessary maturity so often associated with age would not meet other requirements. No attempt is made, however, to impose a maximum age restriction. Any individual who can meet the physical and mental qualifications established by the regulatory board should be allowed to perform security functions, regardless of age.

Physical qualifications are not specifically enumerated, because each particular job function requiring registration calls for different physical qualifications. For example, performing the duties of a guard may require a higher level of hearing and better eyesight than are necessary for an alarm servicer. Similarly, certain physical deformities or limitations may adversely affect performance as an alarm respondent but have no appreciable effect upon performance as an investigator.

The area of physical qualifications should be carefully studied by the private security regulatory board. These qualifications should become part of their rules and regulations after careful consideration of the relationship between specific duties to be performed by the registrant and any physical problems. Provisions should be made to consider questions of physical competence on an individual applicant basis.

The need for private security personnel to have emotional stability and sound judgment is apparent because of their important roles in maintaining order and protecting lives and property. Whether a person is guarding a remote rock quarry, patrolling a residential area, or investigating business losses, a certain level of mental competence is required. This does not infer that a specific level of educational accomplishment alone would qualify the individual; some people with high school diplomas possess neither commonsense nor emotional stability. Persons whose background investigations indicate they possess sound judgment and emotional stability should be allowed to register as security personnel, regardless of their level of formal education.

Measuring or determining mental competence is not easy, particularly when such determinations must be made for thousands of applicants in the initial stages of registration. Two recommended methods that perhaps can be gradually worked into the registration process are psychological tests and interviews by trained professionals. The present limitations of these methods are recognized, but their validity and usefulness may be increased through continued research. Private security regulatory boards, therefore, should study these methods and keep abreast of research so that the best available means of measuring mental competence can be determined and applied.

The need for morally responsible security personnel cannot be argued, but questions over what, in fact, constitutes being morally responsible are likely. One solution for adding preciseness to the term would be to require that no person who has been convicted of a felony or misdemeanor that reflects upon ability to perform security work should be allowed to register. However, in many cases, the regulatory board may find that an individual has a long list of criminal charges that have never resulted in a conviction but the nature and number of charges may indicate that the person is not morally responsible.

Finally, this standard incorporates the specific training recommendations set forth in Standard 2.5. As was pointed out in Chapter 2, training can significantly improve the competence of security personnel to aid in crime prevention and control. Training is one of the most common areas in the private security industry needing the most improvement. However, unless requirements are mandated by law, the majority of private security personnel may never receive the necessary training. The benefits of training to employers, private security workers, consumers of security services, and the public are too great to be left to the option of employers or individual workers.

It would, of course, be preferable if all security personnel met stringent, professional requirements. However, this report recommends that the initial government-mandated qualifications should be minimum. It is impossible to determine the number of people who would have to register with the private security regulatory boards. It is also impossible to accurately assess the impact of strict qualifications upon the industry. If the requirements are too high and cannot be met by those applying for registration, a serious shortage of available manpower could occur, adversely affecting the industry and those who seek to use it for protection. Thus, the requirements set forth in this standard are minimal but designed as an initial step for eliminating undesirable applicants. The regulatory board should constantly evaluate the requirements. If a particular requirement is too restrictive and is keeping competent and ethical persons out of the field, that requirement should be eliminated. Likewise, if serious problems are occurring that could be corrected by a different or ore stringent requirement, it should be added. Although constant evaluation requires maintenance of records and careful analysis, such efforts are necessary in order to balance the interests of the private security industry and society.

Selected References

1. Brennan, Dennis T. *The Other Police.* Cleveland, Ohio: Governmental Research Institute, 1975.

2. Harrigan, James F., Mary Holbrook Sundance, and Mark L. Webb. "Private Police in California: A Legislative Proposal," *Golden Gate Law Review.*

3. Institute for Local Self Government. *Private Security and the Public Interest.* Berkeley, Calif.: Institute for Local Self Government, 1974.

4. Kakalik, James S., and Sorrell Wildhorn. *Private Police in the Untied States: Findings and Recommendations,* Vol. I, R—869/DOJ. Washington, D.C.: Government Printing Office, 1972.

5. National Advisory Commission on Criminal Justice Standards and Goals. *Report on Police.* Washington, D.C.: Government Printing Office, 1973.

6. Oglesby, Thomas W. "The Use of Emotional Screening in the Selection of Police Applicants," *Police,* January-February 1958.

7. President's Commission on Law Enforcement and Administration of Justice. *Task Force Report: The Police,* Washington, D.C.: Government Printing Office, 1967.

Standard 11.3
Qualifications for Armed Security Personnel

Every applicant who seeks registration to perform a specific security function in an armed capacity should meet the following minimum qualifications:

1. Be at least 18 years of age;

2. Have a high school diploma or pass an equivalent written examination;

3. Be mentally competent and capable of performing in an armed capacity;

4. Be morally responsible in the judgment of the regulatory board;

5. Have no felony convictions involving the use of a weapon;

6. Have no felony or misdemeanor convictions that reflect the applicant's ability to perform a security function in an armed capacity.

7. Have no physical defects that would hinder job performance; and,

8. Have successfully completed the training requirements for armed personnel set forth in Standards 2.5 and 2.6.

Commentary

Some of the most serious problems in the private security industry are caused by the use of weapons. Throughout this report, various tragic examples have been cited in which injury or death resulted from weapons abuse. Other private security studies have cited similar incidents. Although no statistics are available to determine the frequency of these incidents, it remains unquestioned that the carrying of a firearm includes the potential for serious and dangerous consequences.

Armed security personnel take on an awesome responsibility. Split-second decisions with lethal weapons can result in death or serious injury, and the lives of armed security workers are constantly endangered. Walter M. Strobl stated, in "Private Guards: Arm Them or Not," "the very fact that a weapon is visible will cause the criminal to assume a more violent attitude that could trigger the most violent actions."

Many responsible individuals within the private security industry have long argued against arming security personnel. Proprietary security executives have encouraged executives within their organizations to abandon the use of weapons, and contract organizations have discouraged consumers from requesting armed personnel. One large contract company actually offers incentives to sales personnel who set up contracts that do not require armed personnel; this action should be commended and encouraged.

It is sad [but] true reflection on our society that some situations require the arming of certain security personnel. It would be foolish in situations in which lives are under constant threat to forbid the use of firearms. But is not unwise to place firm restrictions on the use of firearms and equally firm requirements on those who are allowed to carry them. For this reason, higher qualifications are established for those who seek registration as armed security personnel than for those who would be unarmed.

A minimum age requirement of 21 years for persons desiring to be registered as armed personnel was first considered. However, it is believed that there is little correlation between maturity, good judgment, and age. An applicant who can meet all of the other requirements should be allowed registration, regardless of age. Therefore, this report recommends that a minimum age requirement of 18 years should be established for registration of armed personnel.

In the area of educational requirements, a higher level should be required for armed registrants than for other security personnel. The basic education qualifications can be met by a high school diploma or by an equivalent written examination designed to measure basic educational aptitudes.

The qualification for mental competence can enable the board to determine if the applicant is able to understand and perform security functions in an armed capacity. A written examination designed to measure the knowledge and skills required or the psychological makeup of the applicant should be used. This qualification is given along with the education requirement, because it is recognized that such formal education or equivalent does not automatically indicate a person is psychologically capable of carrying a weapon.

Although almost totally ignored by both existing State regulatory boards by private security employers, psychological testing to screen out the obvious cases of emotionally unstable or unsuitable persons should be an important and integral portion of the competency requirement. This step could prevent psychopaths or other serious mentally ill persons from being certified as armed guards.

It is difficult to list the specific acts that would indicate that an individual was not morally responsible to carry a weapon. Sometimes a person may meet the listed qualifications, but a review of his records may indicate a very questionable background. A long list of criminal charges or a series of jobs that ended in firing would perhaps be incidents to watch for. Because of the requirement for a hearing before denial, this requirement is not believed to be too general. Any applicant denied registration on this ground would have an opportunity to be heard and to show if the decision was arbitrary and capricious.

Any person who has been convicted of a felony involving the use of a weapon should not be registered in an armed capacity. No exception should be made, regardless of extenuating circumstances, passage of time, or indications of rehabilitation. The responsibility of carrying a firearm is too grave to take the chance that a person previously misusing a gun would not do so again.

Although no flexibility is recommended for felony convictions involving weapons, convictions for other offenses should be carefully studied before denying registration. It is in the public interest to assist the rehabilitation of convicted offenders by removing restrictions upon their ability to obtain employment. But it also must be recognized that the ex-offender is being registered to perform a security function in an armed capacity. Therefore, if an applicant has a conviction record, the regulatory board should carefully consider whether such convictions reflect upon the applicant's ability to perform a security function in an armed capacity. In making its determination, the regulatory board should consider the following:

1. The specific security function the applicant is registering to perform;
2. The nature and seriousness of the crime;
3. The date of the crime;
4. The age of the applicant when the crime was committed;
5. Whether the crime was an isolated or repeated incident;
6. The social conditions that may have contributed to the crime; and
7. Any evidence of rehabilitation, including good conduct in prison or in the community, counseling or psychiatric treatment received, acquisition of additional or vocational schooling, successful participation in correctional work-release programs, or the recommendation of persons who have, or have had, the applicant under their supervision.

The next qualification concerns physical requirements. Such requirements should not be unduly restrictive and should not include height and weight specifications or other requirements that have little relation to performance in an armed capacity. Physical standards, however, cannot be totally disregarded. Obviously, good eyesight and hearing are vital to anyone who carries a weapon. In order to protect the individual and the public, specific vision and hearing requirements should be carefully considered and delineated by the regulatory board.

Finally, this standard incorporates the specific training recommendations set forth in Standards 2.5 and 2.6. As pointed out in Chapter 2, training can greatly improve the competence of security personnel to aid in crime prevention and control but needs perhaps the most improvement of any private security area. However, unless requirements are mandated by law, the majority of private security personnel may never receive such training. The benefits gained through training to employers, private security workers, consumers, and the public are too great to be left to the option of employers or individual workers. Competence and proficiency in the use of a firearm should be demonstrated by those who seek to be registered as armed security personnel. This can best be shown by successful completion of the required arms training recommended in Standards 2.5 and 2.6.

In summary, any individual allowed to carry a weapon needs to be able to make decisions that require mature, calculated, and sound judgment. The armed security worker should also possess the physical and emotional makeup to act with split-second timing, if necessary, and be thoroughly trained in the use and legal implications of the weapon to be carried. Considering the life-or-death potential involved, every effort must be made to prevent any but the most qualified and capable individuals from performing in an armed capacity. Although there is no magic panacea to ensure that a life will not be taken accidentally or unnecessarily, the risks involved demand strict qualifications for registration of armed personnel.

Selected References

1. Brennan, Dennis T. *The Other Police,* Cleveland, Ohio: Governmental Research Institute, 1975.

2. Harrigan, James F., Mary Holbrook Sundance, and Mark L. Webb. "Private Police in California: A Legislative Proposal," *Golden Gate Law Review.*

3. Institute for Local Self Government. *Private Security and the Public Interest.* Berkeley, Calif.: Institute for Local Self Government, 1974.

4. Kakalik, James S., and Sorrel Wildhorn. *Private Police in the United States: Findings and Recommendations,* Vol. 1, R-869/DOJ. Washington, D.C.: Government Printing Office, 1972.

5. New Jersey State, P.S. 1968, c. 282 (C.2A: 168A).

6. Strobl, Walter M. "Private Guards: Arm Them or Not?" *Security Management,* January, 1973.

Appendix I
A Commentary and Checklists for Security Surveys

Security Surveys Checklists

At the start, physical security surveys were developed for defense industrial plants and military installations. It was recognized early by civilian police personnel that the survey technique could be applied to areas, buildings or activities of all types to identify the conditions of property or the interaction of people most conducive to criminal activity. Some police and security personnel have tried to maintain a distinction between the physical security survey and the crime prevention survey. In actuality, both types of surveys have the same goals: the identification of risks and the recommendation that those risks be eliminated or minimized through the employment of security measures. As noted in Chapters 4 through 9, physical barriers, lights, alarms, guards and security awareness programs for all employees can materially reduce the risk to lives and loss of property or proprietary information.

Initially, security surveys were conducted by experienced criminal and intelligence investigative personnel. Their job was to inspect various facilities and recommend installation of some of the basic protective devices. Shortly the precursor of the Defense Department established some minimal standards for fences, lighting, alarms and guards. Because security measures had to meet those standards, long lists of the requirements were prepared in advance of the inspections. Thereby the inspectors' jobs were made easier, despite the need to prepare a narrative report of the inspection. This involved a lot of writing, and few inspectors enjoyed the tedium. In time, checklists evolved from those long lists of standards and some security survey reports were accepted with little narrative information added.

Over time, the basic security survey checklist was found to have some drawbacks. It did provide a general plan to inspect a facility of several buildings or a separate activity. It also provided lists of general questions concerning fences, lighting and guards, as well as other aspects of security. But as unique facilities with unusual security problems required surveys, the original checklists were found lacking. Specialized checklists had to be devised to meet the new requirements, hence, the development of checklists for retail, bank and EDP operations.

Many checklists contain the warning: "This checklist is merely a guide and may not cover all the areas needed for every specific survey." It did not take long to find out that a checklist devised for one specific building, activity or facility might not adequately address the security problems in the next building, activity or facility. Only the fast food chains or retail stores that are built in one style and require strict adherence to standard operational policies might be suitably inspected by a standard checklist. Still, all checklists have room for additional remarks when warranted.

Qualifications of the Surveyor

Modern-day security survey checklists have not eliminated the need for a well-trained and experienced surveyor. During the early days of security surveying, the criminal or intelligence investigator generally had extensive field experience, as well as the benefit of military service schools that specialized in security. With the establishment of the National Crime Prevention Institute at the University of Louisville in the early 1970s, civilian-oriented crime prevention courses and instruction in security surveys were offered to enrolled police students. Since then, security surveys have been taught as a semester-long course in colleges or by three- to five-day-long courses offered by private organizations such as the American Management Association and the American Society for Industrial Security. Recent references to the qualifications of surveyors do not reflect any change over the years. Surveyors are still recommended to be well-trained and experienced.

A well-trained and experienced surveyor cannot be calculated by the number of training courses attended, the college credits accumulated or the number of years of employment by a police or security department. A well-trained and experienced surveyor is the person who takes to the job site the knowledge and understanding that crimes are committed by all kinds of people—young and old, male and female. These people come from all walks of life: congress members, judges, police officers, ministers, mechanics and laborers. Some people have illegally entered facilities or premises using helicopters, trucks, ladders, overhanging tree limbs and false identification. Crimes ranging from murder, theft, industrial espionage and vandalism have been committed inside those premises, and, when caught by the authorities, those criminals more often than not denied the acts and threatened a legal suit for any violation of their legal and civil rights. A surveyor needs to know these things and how to cope with them satisfactorily. One should not limit oneself to thinking *like* a criminal to prevent criminal activity; one should think better than that criminal in order to prevent the crime.

Texts (such as this one) and survey checklists reflect the research and experience of many surveyors and authors. These are excellent starting points for a surveyor, but one must be ever mindful of the caveat explained earlier: "This checklist is merely a guide and may not cover all the areas needed for every specific survey." An open and inquisitive mind will help the surveyor fill in the gaps left in this text and in standard checklists. A surveyor who can perform these tasks with confidence is well-trained and experienced.

Conducting the Survey

Chapter 5 clearly explains the administrative procedures for a security survey. Upon completing the tasks outlined in the section titled *Preliminary Activities*, a surveyor should have a grasp of the size and location of the facility, the number of persons who may be encountered and the scope of the daily operations. From this preliminary study tentative checklists can be assembled. Yet it must be remembered that many more items may have to be added to that tentative checklist.

After an orientation tour of the facility, and all subordinate supervisors have been advised of the intent of the survey, the real work begins. A basic or general type survey checklist, such as the one included in this appendix, can be used while the surveyor visits and observes every physical location of the facility. Preferably, the survey is started from the entry area outside, until every part of the facility has been inspected. The checklist can be expanded when needed.

Most surveyors will develop an ability to estimate sizes, heights and numbers of objects with some accuracy and use these for their reports. That is not a good idea. A survey report needs accuracy in every respect. Therefore, a surveyor should be familiar with and carry tape measures, chalk, paper for sketches, and a camera.

Some surveyors walk through buildings and point and ask, "Is that door locked?" Given an affirmative answer, the door is not checked. Only if it is checked can it be known for certain that it was in fact locked. Never take for granted what appears to be obvious. And never accept for a fact any description or explanation by an employee or supervisor. They will often intentionally lie or mislead the surveyor because they want their section to look good on the report or because they are covering up a problem.

The first visit of the facility should be during daylight hours to better see the physical plant and learn what is normal. Some facilities burn outdoor lights 24 hours a day; otherwise, a night visit is necessary to see if all the lights work. Some gates are opened only for shift changes. Sometimes rail access gates are never closed or are guarded only at night; sometimes they are used as shortcuts by employees. Such valuable information can be learned during the daytime.

As mentioned earlier, all doors, gates, bins or other objects that are purportedly locked should be physically checked. If there is a padlock on the hasp, is it locked? If the padlock is hanging on an opened hasp, is the padlock locked so that it cannot be replaced temporarily with a look-alike by a thief? If the window is reported as always locked, are there signs that it had been opened recently? Are the bars over the windows secure, or are they so rusty they would fall off if the surveyor pulled on them? If an exterior light bulb is loosened, how long will it be inoperative? Questions that come to the surveyor's mind during the survey should at least double the items on any checklist.

The nighttime survey of a facility encompasses the same physical areas in an effort to determine whether there are security weaknesses that occur only at night or are not obvious during the day. If the facility is nonoperational at night, are there guards or janitorial personnel on the premises? Do off-duty employees or vendors return at night? Is equipment or property stolen or used by these visitors? Do guard personnel entertain friends while on duty? Are all security policies enforced? Again, any imaginative surveyor could double the checklist during a nighttime inspection.

Coordinating Interviews

In order to engender support for this and future surveys and the overall security program, the discrepancies or suggestions should be reviewed with the appropriately responsible supervisor before the formal report is submitted. There must be an emphasis that the survey is not a punitive inspection; rather, it is a joint effort to prevent losses and promote profitability. Often the lower-level supervisors can be given credit for their input and cooperation; this may promote further individual support necessary for the security awareness efforts after the surveyor leaves the facility.

The Follow-up Survey

Another important reason to maintain a businesslike, yet friendly, relationship with the facility personnel is that those people will have to take the corrective actions if the discrepancies are to be remedied. If they are not remedied, the surveyor's efforts are wasted. One method to determine if the deficiencies are corrected is to perform a follow-up survey. This survey is normally undertaken 30, 60 or 90 days after the initial survey is reported. Only those areas with reported deficiencies are checked, but sometimes new concerns predicate the expansion of the follow-up survey to include newly developed problem areas. The report of the follow-up survey generally includes only the list of discrepancies and a description of the remedial action undertaken. There have been occasions when several follow-up surveys were requested by management before corrective steps were taken to rectify the discrepancies. This again demonstrates the need to develop a cooperative relationship with the supervisors affected by the survey. Without their support, no security program will succeed.

Frequency of Survey

As stated in Chapter 11, there is no magic number or time frame to conduct security surveys. New or changed facilities or activities dictate a survey. So would continual losses, damages or injuries. Often security surveys will not solve the existent underlying problems that cause the losses, damages or injuries. At such times the surveyor must suggest that a security or safety awareness program would be more effective to stem the increase of unwanted incidents. During normal surveys there will be a lot of personal contact with supervisors and employees. It does not take long to distinguish between a healthy competitive spirit and a lingering animosity. People in both groups talk about what they have on their minds. Low pay, swing shifts, partiality of supervisors and poorly explained rules frequently are topics mentioned by employees caught stealing or damaging merchandise or equipment. There is no final number of surveys that will solve those problems, but a management attuned to the problems can reduce the inherent problems by an educational program. Any such program that will reduce losses, damages or injuries is truly an effective security program.

Security Survey Checklists

Included in this appendix are two sample security checklists. Most of the items in the checklists have been handed down from surveyor to author to surveyor. Use these items freely, but do not limit a survey to these few specific items. Even a surveyor with limited training and experience should be able to double each list while on the job.

BASIC SECURITY SURVEY

Preparing agency: _____ Name and address of facility surveyed: _____

Date of survey: _____ Date of report: _____ Date of previous report: _____

Name and title of person responsible for facility: _____

Name and title of Security Supervisor: _____

No. of security personnel: _____ No. of employees: _____

No. of acres: _____ Total sq. ft. of building space: _____

No. of bldgs: _____ No. of rooms: _____

No. of floors in tallest bldg. _____

No. of miles of roadway: _____ No. of visitor parking spaces: _____

No. of registered vehicles: _____ No. of vendor parking spaces: _____

Total no. of parking spaces: _____

A brief history and description of the business carried on at the facility:

Name of person making survey (typed): _____

Signature of person making survey: _____

Name of person making report (typed): _____

Signature of person making report: _____

Part I: Facility Environment

	Yes	No	Remarks

1. Do employees feel secure at this location?
2. What is the crime rate?
3. Can local police observe approaches to the facility?
4. Do other buildings and structures present security hazards?
5. Does landscaping or shrubbery present a security hazard?
6. Do trees, poles or fences offer easy access to the roof?

Part II: Perimeter

7. Is facility surrounded by a fence or other barrier?
8. Are fences properly constructed with an outrigger top guard?
9. Height of fence?
10. Describe fence construction.
11. Is selvage twisted at top and bottom of fence?
12. Is bottom of fence within two inches of solid ground?
13. Is the fence other than chain link?
14. If perimeter barrier is constructed of stone or other masonry, what is its height?
15. If a wall, is it protected at the top by a proper guard of wire or broken glass?
16. Are perimeter barriers increased in height at junctions with buildings and other critical points?
17. Are barriers inspected for defects? If so, by whom and how often?
18. Are openings (culverts, manholes) which are 96 sq. in. or larger protected by mesh or wire?
19. Is mesh no greater than 2 sq. in.?
20. How many gates and entrances are in the perimeter?

Yes   No   Remarks

21. Are all perimeter entrances secured with locking devices?
22. Are all entrances closed and locked when not in use?
23. Are perimeter openings inspected by guards for security?
24. Are warning signs posted at all entrances?
25. Are "No Trespassing" signs posted to be observed for at least 50 yards?
26. Are clear zones maintained on both sides of perimeter area?
27. Is parking allowed against or close to perimeter barrier?
28. Do guards patrol perimeter area?
29. Are perimeter barriers protected by intrusion alarm devices?

Part III: Exterior Lighting

30. Does facility use municipal lighting? Is it dependable?
31. What type of lighting is used?
32. Are night lights activated automatically?
33. What is the plan for replacing burned out lights?
34. Is there adequate lighting around buildings, company vehicles and cargo?
35. Are customer and employee parking lots lighted sufficiently?
36. Does the lighting provide adequate illumination over perimeter and entrances?
37. Is there an auxiliary source of power for lighting?
38. What is plan for standby or emergency lighting?
39. Does the emergency lighting activate automatically when needed?

Part IV: Doors

40. Do all doors lock from both sides except for the main entrance door?
41. Are all unlocked doors properly protected?
42. Are the doors, locks and hardware in good repair?
43. Are the exterior doors strong?
44. What type of lock is used on doors?
45. Are electrically-operated overhead doors locked when not in use?
46. Are overhead doors operated by rollers on tracks sufficiently strong?
47. Are unnecessary doors bricked or permanently sealed?

Yes   No   Remarks

Part V: Windows

48. What type of glass is used in the windows?
49. How are windows located less than 18 ft. from the ground protected?
50. Are the windows more than 14 ft. from trees, poles, etc.?
51. Is valuable merchandise visible through the windows?
52. If windows are connected with an alarm system, what type?
53. Are unnecessary windows bricked and sealed shut permanently?

Part VI: Keying System

54. Is there a key control officer?
55. Are all locks and keys supervised and controlled by the key control officer?
56. Are personnel required to produce their keys periodically?
57. Is a dependable person responsible for the master keys?
58. Are key holders allowed to duplicate keys?
59. Are keys marked, "Do not duplicate"?
60. Are keys issued to anyone other than installation personnel?
61. Is the removal of keys from the premises prohibited?
62. Are files kept on the buildings and entrances for which keys are issued?
63. Are files kept on the number and identification of keys issued?
64. Are files kept on the location and number of master keys?
65. Are files kept on the location and number of duplicate keys?
66. Are files kept on the location and number of keys held in reserve?
67. Are files and keys kept in a locked, fireproof container?
68. Is the fireproof container kept in an area of high security?
69. Are losses and thefts of keys promptly investigated by the key control officer?
70. Must requests for reproduction or duplication of keys be approved by the key control officer?

Yes   No   Remarks

71. Are locks changed when keys are lost or stolen?
72. Are locks rotated within the facility at least annually?

Part VII: Storage Areas Outside Building

73. Are dangerous materials or chemicals stored outside the building area?
74. Is the area protected by a fence?
75. Are trespassing signs posted?
76. Are the areas adequate for the materials being stored?
77. Are these areas locked and secured?
78. Are these areas illuminated?
79. Are these areas patrolled?

Part VIII: Employee Lockers

80. Are lockers provided to all employees?
81. What type of lock is used on lockers?
82. Does the company have a key to enter employee lockers?
83. Does the company have written consent from the employee to open his locker at any time?
84. Are the lockers located away from removable merchandise?
85. Are regular and unscheduled inspections made of the lockers?
86. What is the company policy if stolen merchandise is found in a locker?
87. Do employees have access to each others' lockers?

Part IX: Outside Parking for Employees or Customers

88. Is parking in a designated area outside the perimeter?
89. Are parking areas patrolled?
90. Are parking areas well-lighted?
91. Is parking allowed near a loading dock?
92. Is there any barrier between loading docks and parking area?
93. Where are company vehicles parked? Are they in keeping with good security practices?

Part X: Fire Protection

94. Has a fire department ever surveyed this facility?
95. Were there any recommendations?
96. Were these recommendations followed?
97. Does the facility comply with fire regulations and ordinances?

	Yes	No	Remarks

98. Are fire doors protected with panic bars and door alarms for emergency use?
99. Does the facility have a fire safety program?
100. Have employees been adequately trained and drilled on the fire procedures?
101. Do employees know where fire equipment is located?
102. Are fire extinguisher locations distinctly marked?
103. Is the fire department number posted by all telephones?
104. Is there a sprinkler system?
105. Is the sprinkler system inspected regularly?
106. What is the average response time for the fire department to arrive at the facility?
107. Is there adequate water pressure at the facility?
108. Are signs posted for procedures to follow in case of fire?
109. Do employees know what to do in case of fire?

Part XI: Guard Force

110. Is there a security or guard force?
111. Is it adequate for the security and protection needed?
112. Is the force reviewed periodically to ascertain its effectiveness?
113. Can the guards use the communications equipment properly?
114. Do the guards meet minimum qualification standards?
115. Are the guards on duty armed? Describe weapons.
116. Are the weapons inspected periodically?
117. Are guards required to complete basic courses in firearms?
118. Is there in-service training on security and firearms?
119. Does each guard carry a flashlight?
120. Do the activities of the guards follow established policy?
121. Does each guard write a daily report?

Part XII: Personnel Identification and Control

122. Is an identification card or badge used?
123. Is a picture of the employee on the badge?
124. Is the picture updated?
125. Is there a Standard Operating Procedure for the identification system?
126. Are personnel knowledgeable about the system?
127. Is special identification required for high-security areas?

	Yes	No	Remarks

128. Are visitors issued a visitor's pass or badge?
129. Can this badge be used only in a designated area?
130. Is everyone required to wear an ID badge at all times in the facility?
131. Do guards at entrances and exits compare the badge photo to the bearer?
132. Are badges recorded and controlled by an accountability procedure?
133. Are replacement badges identifiable as such?
134. Are temporary badges used?
135. Are rosters of lost badges posted at guard control points?
136. Are badges distinct in appearance for different areas?
137. Do procedures ensure the return of ID badges upon termination of employment or transfer?
138. Is ID system under the supervision and control of security officers?
139. Is there a visitor escort policy?
140. Are visitor arrivals recorded?
141. Must a visitor's ID badge be displayed at all times?
142. Are visitors allowed to move about the facility unattended?
143. Must visitors turn in ID passes when leaving the facility?
144. Is visitor departure time recorded?
145. What is the procedure if a visitor fails to turn in an ID pass?
146. Are permanent records of visitors maintained?
147. Are restriction notices displayed prominently at appropriate entrances?
148. Is there inspection of all packages and materials carried in and out of the facility?

Part XIII: Sensors and Switches

149. Are there sensors and switch devices?
150. Where are they located?
151. Are the security devices adequate for the degree of security required?
152. Is there an operation of a photographic or CCTV identification camera in security-sensitive areas?
153. Are security devices adequately protected against attacks?
154. Are these security devices inspected regularly to insure working condition?
155. Are the security devices connected to a silent alarm?

	Yes	No	Remarks

156. Are local alarms loud enough to alert a civic-minded person in the area?
157. Would a police force nearby respond to a sounding alarm?
158. Who is responsible for the security devices at the facility?
159. Is there an auxiliary power source for the alarm system?
160. Are all wires for the alarm system underground so they are tamper-resistant?
161. Are the alarm systems designed, and are locations recorded, so repairs can be made rapidly in an emergency?
162. Is there someone available at all times to make repairs to the alarm system?
163. Is there someone available at all times to make repairs to the communications system?
164. Note other deficiencies or irregularities:
165. Note security measures implemented but not listed above:
166. Recommendations:

SECURITY SURVEY OF MOTEL/HOTEL

This specialized checklist is designed to supplement the Basic Security Survey Checklist.

Name and address of facility: _____

Facility owned by: _____

Facility officially coordinating survey: _____

Date of survey: _____ Date of report: _____ Previous survey: _____

Name and organization of surveyor: _____

	Yes	No	Remarks

1. Are entrances to non-public areas marked "Employees only"?
2. Are ID badges issued to employees?
3. Are entrances from outside monitored and access controlled?
4. Is a package check system used?
5. Are salespeople and vendors screened by management before being allowed entrance?
6. Are goods delivered to the loading platform and/or premises properly received?
7. Do supervisors inspect trash removal procedures?
8. Do all emergency exits provide a clear path of egress?
9. Is a system used to control stock of alcoholic beverages?
10. Are bars stocked with a predetermined quantity of each item?
11. Is the quantity of each item at the bar regularly counted?
12. Are bar receipts and cash checked for accuracy and honesty?
13. Are alcoholic beverages stored separately from other supplies?
14. Is the main alcoholic beverage storeroom a high-security area?
15. Are bars always attended or secured by hardware?
16. Are hotel liquor bottles marked in some way to prevent "bar padding" by bartenders?
17. Is there dual control for taking liquor inventory?
18. Are sales slips or records provided for each drink served?
19. Are sponsors of parties warned to keep account of liquor consumption to prevent "padding" by dishonest employees?
20. Are bar employees trained in applicable laws governing alcoholic beverages?
21. Are patrons who are obviously drunk denied additional liquor sales?
22. Are age limit regulations concerning the sale of alcohol strictly adhered to? Are appropriate signs posted?
23. Have meat and produce purchasing specifications been established?
24. Are incoming meat and produce orders inspected for weight and freshness?
25. Are goods from storerooms and kitchens dispersed only upon signature by an authorized person?

	Yes	No	Remarks

26. Do kitchen employees eat food on the spot?
27. Do supervisors inspect areas where food could be hidden for a planned theft?
28. Is a cashier responsible for the pricing and totaling of checks and handling all money?
29. Is surplus food incorporated in future dishes to cut down on waste in preparation?
30. Is garbage controlled to prevent theft?
31. Are all laws affecting restaurant operations strictly adhered to?
32. Are claims of illness by customers thoroughly investigated?
33. Are credit cards checked against "hot sheets"?
34. Are measures used to protect the cash flow of the hotel?
35. Is the hotel's safe combination changed regularly and access restricted?
36. Are cash and change funds adequately secured and are they checked at unannounced intervals?
37. Are vending machines cleared of their cash on a routine basis and checked by the head cashier?
38. Is the money transported to the bank in a secure container, and are different routes and time schedules applied?
39. Are preventive measures taken to deal with robberies?
40. Are employees instructed how to act during an armed robbery?
41. Does the hotel check suspected stolen credit cards?
42. Is there a policy for cashing checks?
43. Are cashiers of the hotel checked randomly for accuracy and honesty in cash transactions?
44. Are cashiers bonded?
45. Are cashiers trained to check for counterfeit bills, forged checks and bogus credit cards?
46. Does the hotel provide a theft-resistant, fireproof vault or some type of cabinet for protection of guests' "valuable items"?
47. Do customers check personal belongings with management?
48. Is the hotel staff trained in the preventive measures of fraud against the hotel?
49. Are pass keys issued to maids checked in and out daily?
50. Are maids told to be alert for possible thieves?
51. Do maids leave the doors to rooms open when they are being cleaned?

| | Yes | No | Remarks |

52. Is an inspection made of a room as soon as it is vacated?
53. Are secure areas provided for convention displays shipped ahead of time?
54. Are rooms inspected for personal belongings after meetings and banquets?
55. Are there certain procedures used for guests who are thought to be "skippers"?
56. Do maids keep utility and storage closets locked?
57. Is linen stored in a secure location?
58. Is linen marked with adequate identification?
59. Is it possible to determine what part of the linen cycle is losing the greatest amount of goods?
60. Are parking garages patrolled?
61. Is the parking lot enclosed by a fence to discourage trespassers?
62. Are damages to guests' cars carefully investigated?
63. Is the hotel responsible for the contents of guests' cars?
64. Is recovered, lost, abandoned and unclaimed property accounted for and properly secured according to policy?
65. Is there a written fire prevention policy?
66. Are all fire exits marked clearly?
67. Do all employees know what to do in case of fire?
68. Is there a disaster plan?
69. Have the employees been trained in how to handle bomb threats?
70. Does the hotel security director have a VIP protection plan?
71. Is there a written plan for strikes, civil unrest or any other type of disturbances?
72. Do the employees and security officers know how to detect drug use, loan sharking, illegal gambling and prostitution on the premises?
73. Are management employees instructed in how to deal with criminal activity?
74. Are all laws pertaining to the business clearly understood by the employees? Are references readily available?

Index

481

Problem solving, principle of security and, viii
Professional associations, 29. *See also* specific associations
Professional Certification Board (PCB), 391, 397
Professional development and training, 42-43. *See also* Education; Training
Professionalism, 29-30. *See also* Education
codes of ethics and, 367-368, 368-369
commentary on, 369-370
Professional Security Television Network training modules, 117-121
Project Blue Lights, 386-387
Proprietary central control system, 313
Proprietary guard services, 24, 25, 53-54. *See also* Security personnel
vs. contract security services, 93-94
Protection system, practical tests for, 310
Protective lighting systems. *See* Security lighting
Protective signaling devices, for fire detection, 184
Pruit-Ingoe housing project, 23
Public and private utilities, specialized security in, 78
Public housing
security in, 83
and "Social Design Theory," 23
Public law enforcement. *See also* Policing
private security and, 23, 24, 49, 94-95
privatization, security, and, 28-29
ratings of private security by, 374-375
shift to private security and, 375-376
Public law enforcement records, security personnel and, 103
Public police officers
compared to private security personnel, 94-95
legal comparison to private police, 357-359
moonlighting as private security, 372-374
Public security, contrasted with private security, 23, 24
Public services, for emergency planning assistance, 203-204
Pueblo IV period, security and crime prevention in, 11-12
Pueblo kiva architectural styles, 12
Push-button combination locks, 292

Quad multiplexing, 329
Quality, private security growth and, 363
Questioning, 356

Race, in security employment, 106
Radio telemetry, 315
Railroads
security forces of, 21
specialized security in, 64
RAND Corporation, 95, 364
Rate-of-rise heat detector, 323
Reaction chain, in combustion process, 172-173
Reasonable risk theory, 359, 360

Recertification, of CPP designation, 396-397
Recommendations
alternative policing arrangements, 377
alternative policing modes, 379
police authority determination, 379
police involvement in community planning, 377
security expenditure tax credits, 378
special police officer status for private security, 378
transfer of selected police services to private security, 376-377
Recording locking devices, 287
Recruitment, of personnel, 98-107
Registration. *See* Licensing and registration
Regulation. *See* Certified Protection Professional (CPP) program; Government regulation(s); Licensing and registration
Reiss, Albert J., Jr., 373
Replacement figure costs, 151
Resources. *See* Services/resources
Retail industry
individual retail establishment security, 77
shopping centers and mall security, 76
specialized security in, 76-77
Revocation, of CPP certification, 397
Rim lock, 299
Risk assessments, 146-148. *See also* Security survey
computers and, 146
cost-benefit analysis for, 162-164
fraud and, 146-147
links, 410
loss probability and, 149-155
purpose of, 148, 149
terrorism, 423-426
workplace violence and, 147
Risk identification procedures, 427-434
background, 427
compliance and assessment, 429
existing procedures, 427-428
recuperation, 429-430
safeguards, 430-434
Risk management, 145-166
Risks, reduction and elimination of, vii
River Police Office, 15
Robbery, 216, 229-230
Robbery alert system, 324
Roof, access to, 258
Rowan, Charles, 16-17
Rudolph, Eric Robert, 79-80

Sabotage, 243-244
Sacramento Valley High-Tech Crime Task Force, 387
Safe Manufacturers National Association (SMNA), 337
fire-resistant safe specifications of, 337-338